D0710702

Unwanted Sex

364.153
Sch81

Unwanted Sex

The Culture of Intimidation
and the Failure of Law

STEPHEN J. SCHULHOFER

HARVARD UNIVERSITY PRESS
Cambridge, Massachusetts
London, England   1998

WITHDRAWI

LIBRARY ST. MARY'S COLLEGE

Copyright © 1998 by the President and Fellows of Harvard College
All rights reserved
Printed in the United States of America

Library of Congress Cataloging-in-Publication Data
Schulhofer, Stephen J.
  Unwanted sex : the culture of intimidation and the failure of law
Stephen J. Schulhofer.
    p.   cm.
  Includes bibliographical references and index.
  ISBN 0-674-57648-9 (alk. paper)
    1. Sex crimes—United States. 2. Sexual harassment—Law and
legislation—United States. 3. Sex and law—United States. 4. Law
reform—United States. I. Title.
KF9325.S38   1998
345.73'0253—dc21   98-18020

For Laurie

Contents

Preface

After decades of intense scrutiny and repeated attempts at ambitious reform, our laws against rape and sexual harassment still fail to protect women from sexual overreaching and abuse. What went wrong?

In more than twenty years of teaching criminal law, and more than ten years of speaking and writing about sexual violence, I have talked with countless victims of sexual abuse. They are often shocked by the stinting, inadequate protections that our legal system affords against sexual misconduct. Yet I have also talked with many people, women as well as men, who think that our society already goes to absurd extremes in attempting to regulate sexual interaction. They believe that "radical feminists" greatly exaggerate the problem of rape and the need for stronger legal remedies. Fifteen years ago, at a time when the issue of rape was rarely mentioned in traditional law school classes, I helped pioneer the effort to make rape an important topic of discussion in the first-year criminal law course. I have seen students jarred out of their preconceptions, made aware for the first time of harms they never dreamed existed. I have also seen attempts at discussion frozen by tension and suppressed rage; I have seen classes explode with anger and antagonism. The demand for change and the resistance to change are equally emphatic and uncompromising. Underlying the intensive public discussion of President Clinton's alleged sexual behavior was fundamental disagreement about whether such conduct, if it occurred, was or should be illegal.

Unwanted sex pervades the landscape of workplace interactions, relationships with doctors and lawyers, and contacts with strangers, acquaintances, and even our dating partners. Physically violent rape is its most obvious instance, but not its most common form. Sex can be compelled by overt brutality, by physical intimidation, by the coercive effects of status, power, or authority, and by the manipulative abuse of trust. Sexual misconduct is considered rape only when a man deploys physical force—and often not even then. Yet consent is far from voluntary when it is given in response to extortionate threats or the persistent sexual demands of a woman's doctor, lawyer, or psychiatrist. Sex can be coerced in a multitude of ways that the law tolerates and sometimes tacitly encourages.

For many, law's limited role in regulating sexual interaction seems all but inevitable. Choices are almost never *fully* voluntary, after all. People seldom notice that our laws and our social practices fail to acknowledge a right that should be among our most basic entitlements—the right to choose whether and when to be sexually intimate with another person. This right, the right to sexual autonomy, is simply missing from the list of essential rights that our society grants us as free and independent persons.

In the pages that follow, I undertake to show how our laws and our social practices devalue what should be every person's unambiguous right: the right to choose—or refuse—sexual contact and to do so freely, without undue pressure or constraint. And I undertake to show how an adequate system of law must place sexual autonomy at the forefront of concern and afford it comprehensive protection, in the same way that we protect property, labor, informational privacy, the right to vote, and every other right that is central to the life of a free person.

It is not obvious, of course, exactly what a right to sexual autonomy should include. What should be the boundaries of permissible conduct when positions of authority, economic power, differences of status, or abuses of trust might conceivably influence a person's consent to sex? Respect for autonomy requires protecting our freedom to refuse sexual contact, but it also requires protecting our freedom to seek emotional intimacy and sexual fulfillment with willing partners. Stringent safeguards that fully protect sexual autonomy for one person can easily destroy it for another.

Existing laws resolve this dilemma by placing virtually no restriction on assertive male sexuality, so long as it steers clear of physical violence. They leave all of us, and women especially, unprotected against coercive sexual abuses that any decent society should consider morally wrong and legally intolerable. My hope is to show, through a close examination of threats, coercive "offers," and abuses of power, trust, and professional authority, that we can do better, that sexual autonomy can be and must be protected and supported by law.

My effort to understand the dilemmas of sexual autonomy and the failures of law has taken an unusually long time, even by academic standards. Many of the ideas developed here were first presented as a Fortunoff Lecture at New York University in February 1989. My approach developed and my diagnosis changed as a result of comments and criticisms I received in the course of numerous subsequent workshops and public lectures, including a presentation to the Association of American Law Schools in January 1993; the Katz Lecture at the University of Chicago in November 1993; a Distinguished Speakers lecture at McGeorge Law School in November 1994; presentations to the American Political Science Association in September 1994, the American Philosophical Association in April 1995, and New York University Law School in February 1997; and faculty workshops at the University of Chicago, the University of San Diego Law School, and the McGeorge Law School.

Over the same period I tested these ideas in a number of academic articles. One of them, in the journal *Law and Philosophy*, was awarded the 1995 Fred Berger Prize of the American Philosophical Association. I am grateful to the Berger family for the opportunity that this award provided to defend my conception of sexual autonomy before an audience of sophisticated philosophers who helped me see how to sharpen the ideas and explain them to teachers and students in a variety of academic disciplines.

Many colleagues and friends generously shared their thoughts and criticisms as this project took shape. I am especially indebted to those who gave me detailed comments on the manuscript: Albert Alschuler, Mary Becker, Mary Coombs, Richard Craswell, Deborah Denno, Susan Estrich, Lynne Henderson, Sanford Kadish, Jane Larson, Catharine MacKinnon, Martha Nussbaum, Gary Palm, Richard Posner, Carol Steiker, and Alan Wertheimer. I was lucky to have Mary Coombs, Leslie Francis, Dorothy Roberts, and Patricia Smith as forceful but constructive commentators at colloquia where early versions of this book were presented. Thanks are due as well to Larry Alexander at the University of San Diego School of Law, Graham Hughes at New York University, Geoffrey Stone at the University of Chicago, and Michael Vitiello at the McGeorge Law School for arranging conferences and lectures at their respective schools.

To one colleague, I owe a special debt. Martha Nussbaum convinced me that this book was worth doing, joined with me in teaching a seminar in which many of the chapters were refined, and gave me comments on every page of the manuscript. Her insight and her commitment to justice contributed enormously to the final result.

The proposals I develop here benefited from discussions over the years with students at the University of Pennsylvania, the University of California (Berkeley), and the University of Chicago. I am particularly grateful to the Chicago students in law, philosophy, and other disciplines who joined with Professor Nussbaum and me for an extraordinarily productive seminar in Sexual Autonomy and the Law during the 1996–97 academic year.

I want to thank a number of others whose aid was essential. Stephen Andrews, David Gossett, Michael Maimin, Renee Newman, and Kari Sanderson were enthusiastic and dedicated research assistants. The Russell J. Parsons Faculty Research Fund and the Sonnenschein Fund at the University of Chicago supported my research. Bill Schwesig at the D'Angelo Law Library and Ann Hawthorne, my manuscript editor at Harvard University Press, provided invaluable help. My secretary, Brenda Huffman, deserves special thanks for many years of unflagging efficiency and good humor. Joyce Seltzer of Harvard University Press played an especially important role, helping me define the direction this book should take and offering incisive criticism at every point along the way.

One person deserves thanks that I can never adequately express. My wife, Laurie, not only provided all the essential forms of moral support but took a close look at each detail of my argument, subjecting every step to careful (and often critical) scrutiny. She has been an intellectual partner at each stage of this project. To her this book is gratefully dedicated.

Chicago
April 1998

Unwanted Sex

1

Unchecked Abuses

A young Illinois woman stopped to rest while biking along an isolated reservoir near the college town of Carbondale. A stranger approached and struck up a conversation. After chatting with him for a few minutes, she got on her bicycle and started to leave. At that point the man, Joel Warren, put his hand on her shoulder. When she said, "No, I have to go now," he replied, "This will only take a minute. My girlfriend doesn't meet my needs." He added, "I don't want to hurt you."

Perhaps Warren only meant "We'll both enjoy this." But to the woman his comment sounded ominous, a hint of what he might do if she resisted him. In any event, she had little time to consider nuances. Warren quickly lifted her off the ground and carried her into the woods. He was six feet two inches tall and weighed 185 pounds. With no one else in sight, the young woman, who was only five feet two and weighed 100 pounds, did not attempt to scream or fight back, actions that she feared might prompt him to start choking or beating her. Once Warren had her hidden from view, he pulled off her pants, pushed up her shirt to expose her breasts, and subjected her to several acts of oral sex.

Police eventually identified Warren, prosecutors charged him with sexual assault, and the jury found him guilty. Yet an Illinois court set aside the conviction, saying that "the record is devoid of any attendant-circumstances which suggest that complainant was forced to submit."[1]

Despite three decades of intensive public discussion and numerous statutory reforms, the problem of rape has not been "solved." The reasons are many. Sometimes the laws in the statute books are highly protective but aren't effectively enforced. Whatever the law may say, jurors often assume that it is neither abnormal nor harmful for a man to make aggressive physical advances to a silent, passive, or openly reluctant woman, literally to sweep her off her feet, pull off her clothes, and penetrate her, all without any explicit indication of her consent. Some jurors assume that women who submit to these advances really want the sexual contact, that they could easily resist if they don't, or that it would be unfair to punish a man who, after all, was only doing what (so they may think) nature intended.

But attitudes like these are no longer universal. Our sexual culture has changed. Prosecutors sometimes file charges and juries sometimes convict in cases that would have been laughed out of court in the 1960s or 1970s. Yet the law itself continues to pose obstacles, blocking enforcement and denying remedies even when juries are prepared to condemn a defendant's conduct as outrageous. With its many gaps and limits, law even tends to validate and reinforce many of the traditional attitudes—the strands within our culture that persist in seeing aggressive male sexuality as a biological given that poses no problems. Unsatisfactory standards are especially evident in the criminal law, but civil and administrative remedies share many of the same failings.

Criminal law's most obvious weak spot is its continuing vagueness, a surprise after all the effort devoted to reform. Penal law standards remain extraordinarily murky, especially for determining when a man's behavior amounts to prohibited force and when a woman's conduct signals her consent. And where criminal law is murky, the benefit of the doubt usually goes to the defendant, in theory and often in practice. But criminal law rules are sometimes quite clear, especially when they *exclude* certain kinds of abuse from the reach of penal law.

In the fall of 1988 a young Montana woman wrote an anguished letter to her local school board. She claimed that two years earlier, during her senior year in high school, the school's principal repeatedly forced her to submit to sexual intercourse by threatening to block her graduation. After an investigation by the school board and the county prosecutor, the principal was charged with two acts of "sexual intercourse without consent," a felony under Montana law.

Like many cases of rape, indecent assault, and sexual harassment, the Montana case bristled with credibility questions. But the Montana Supreme Court decided that the victim's story, even if true, could not support criminal charges. In Montana, as in most states, a sexual assault charge normally requires proof that the abuser used physical force or threatened the victim with physical injury. Submission to avoid other kinds of harm is not enough to meet the statutory requirement of intercourse "without consent." The court itself was appalled by the narrow scope of the statute. The judges dismissed the case "with a good deal of reluctance," noting their "strong condemnation of the alleged acts," and adding, "If we could rewrite the statutes to [punish] the alleged acts . . . we would willingly do so."[2]

In a situation like the one in Montana, the victim has a hard choice to make. An exceptionally self-possessed young woman might just tell her principal to get lost. But if she submits to the man's sexual demands, then—as far as the criminal law is concerned—she has consented.

Rape laws have moved far since the days when women were required to resist "to the utmost." Today, "reasonable" resistance is supposed to be sufficient. In the more progressive states, no resistance is required at all—provided that the assailant used force or threatened to inflict bodily injury. But in nearly all states intimidation short of physical threats is still treated as if it were mere "persuasion." When it succeeds, courts will usually say that the victim "consented."

We have all heard of cases in which police, judges, or juries refuse to believe that a woman's "no" really meant no. But the problems run deeper: even when jurors are convinced that a woman was unwilling, unwillingness is not enough. In the face of clearly expressed objections, intercourse still is not considered rape or any other form of felonious assault, unless the assailant used physical force or threatened bodily injury.

That stinting approach to legal safeguards once pervaded criminal law as a whole. In the sixteenth century, the common law of theft protected an owner's property only when a wrongdoer physically removed it from the owner's possession, against the owner's will and by force (*vi et armis*—with force and arms).[3] Shippers and servants who made off with property entrusted to them and scoundrels who obtained possession under false pretenses could not be prosecuted, and the law of theft didn't protect intangible interests or immovable property (real estate) at all. As commerce and the nature of valuables became more complex, the law evolved, slowly at first, to fill the intolerable gaps, though many of them survived into the early twentieth century. Today the law of theft protects property owners comprehensively. It guards against embezzlement by employees and dispossession by fraud, and it protects intangible items of value such as debts, contract rights, trade secrets, and, most recently, computer software. It punishes virtually all interference with property rights without the owner's genuine consent.

Yet there has been no comparable evolution and modernization of the law of sexual assault. In nearly all states, rape laws continue to require proof of physical force. And the law's conception of what counts as physical force remains extremely demanding. The physical acts of lifting a woman up, pushing a woman onto a bed, and accomplishing sexual penetration usually aren't enough. The "force" must be something beyond the acts involved in intercourse, something that physically "compels" the woman to submit. The Illinois case involved a risk of severe physical injury, but the court didn't think that Warren had made a threat. In the Montana case, the principal allegedly made an explicit threat, but the threat was still insufficient because the injury that the student faced for refusing him was not a physical one.

Because nearly all states require proof of physical force in prosecutions for rape and sexual assault, many serious abuses are classified as "nonviolent," and penal sanctions are assumed to be inappropriate. The abuses are not really nonviolent, of course. It is more accurate to say that they don't involve what the law regards as the *required kind* of force. The force that they do involve is seen as normal and therefore permissible.

When men use only the "right kind" of force, prosecutors seldom bother to file charges. But sometimes these sorts of cases are brought to court, often because of an aggravating element such as the youth of the victim. When prosecutors bring these cases, judges usually take the occasion to remind them that the demanding force requirement will be strictly enforced.

In a Mississippi case, a fourteen-year-old girl I will call Sally was visiting her married sister Elizabeth, who had recently separated from her husband, Dennis McQueen. One day Dennis stopped by Elizabeth's house and asked to take their two-year-old baby for a ride in his truck. Elizabeth did not want to leave Dennis alone with the baby, so she asked Sally to go along. When they returned, Sally was shaking and crying. She told her sister that Dennis had pulled off onto a deserted road and told her to get out of the truck. He told her to take off her clothes, lie down on the front seat, and put her legs up on his shoulders. Sally explained that she was scared of him because he had been drinking and was afraid he was going to hurt her. She said she complied, crying throughout, as Dennis penetrated her and quickly had intercourse.

Because Mississippi sets its age of consent for intercourse at fourteen,[4] Dennis McQueen was not charged with statutory rape. He was prosecuted for forcible rape, and the jury found him guilty. But the Mississippi Supreme Court set aside the conviction because McQueen "did not threaten to injure [Sally], did not forcibly remove her from the truck, did not remove her clothes, and did not forcibly make her lie down in the truck."[5]

When the victim is only fourteen, most states would be able to charge a man like McQueen with statutory rape. But when the young woman is eighteen—or in many states only sixteen—statutory rape charges are no longer possible; the man is likely to escape any criminal sanction. Once a woman passes the statutory age of consent, the law of sexual assault requires proof of force in a direct, physical sense. In contrast to the modern law of theft, our sex offense laws make no attempt to protect us comprehensively, from all forms of unwanted interference. The law seeks only to assure the absence of force. It does not require the presence of genuine consent.

The narrow scope of contemporary criminal law becomes especially significant when a woman confronts sexual pressure from a man who holds professional power over her. Women face recurrent sexual demands from teachers, job supervisors, psychotherapists, doctors, and lawyers who misuse their authority to compel sexual submission. The best available estimates suggest that each year roughly one million working women are pressured to have sex with their job supervisors, and thousands (probably hundreds of thousands) of college women face unwanted sexual demands from their professors. Thousands more women submit each year to unwanted sex with their psychotherapists and physicians.[6] Yet rape law offers no help in these situations because the tactics the men use, though sometimes flagrantly coercive, are not physically violent. And civil suits, along with administrative penalties, often prove ineffective as well. Men who abuse their status or professional authority to coerce sexual compliance often face no significant sanctions.

Karen (not her real name), the mother of three children, sought legal help to escape a troubled marriage. She hired a lawyer and paid him a $2,500 retainer. Later, distraught and insecure, she went to see him to discuss her case. He locked his office door, unzipped his pants, and asked her for oral sex. Convinced that he would drop her case and abandon her if she refused, Karen complied, and on two later occasions she submitted to his demands for intercourse. After several months she could no longer cope with the lawyer's sexual demands. She fired him and sued for malpractice. But in a 1990 decision, an Illinois court said that she had no claim, even though the lawyer had exploited her vulnerability and used his professional position to coerce her consent. The court ruled that lawyers can be held accountable for malpractice only when their misconduct has an adverse effect on their client's *legal* problem. Emotional harm from coerced submission to repugnant sexual demands was, the court said, "insufficient"; the woman had no remedy because she "did not claim that her legal position in the divorce proceedings was harmed."[7]

In many states, strict force requirements apply even when the assailant is a prison guard who holds almost life-or-death power over the woman who supposedly "consents" to his demands. In 1996 more than a dozen guards at Dwight Correctional Center in Illinois were investigated for having sex with female prisoners. The prisoners reported that guards never directly threatened them: "They will not say nothing, but you know what will happen."[8] The women believe that they must satisfy the guards' sexual demands in order to remain housed in one of the honors cottages, and they fear that guards will place contraband in their personal effects or discipline them for other reasons if they do not cooperate. When sexual activity is discovered, the guards are typically reassigned to another prison, while the inmates—the victims—lose their good behavior credits because they violated prison rules. The guards' misconduct violated no criminal law because the inmates' acquiescence was treated as valid "consent."[9] In Tennessee, a teenage girl who was subjected to sexual groping (but not intercourse) by her guard at a juvenile detention center said she was reluctant to complain because his actions were "part of everyday life."[10]

"Nonviolent" abuse occurs among social equals as well. Criminal law standards are especially important in that context because other safeguards, such as rules of professional ethics, usually do not apply; criminal sanctions are often the only source of protection. Yet when social equals are not physical equals, as the Illinois bike rider and countless other women know, intimidation can take forms that existing law largely ignores.

Drinking situations add another dimension to the problem. A widely reported 1996 trial involved an upstate New York woman who went to a restaurant with her date. Both were drinking heavily. The woman passed out in the bathroom. Her date, waiting for her to join him outside, fell asleep in his pickup truck. Meanwhile, four men carried the woman from the bathroom to a booth, where they undressed her. All four then allegedly raped her, left her in the booth, and returned to their beer and sandwiches.

The four men admitted the acts of intercourse, pleaded guilty to minor misdemeanor charges, and received sentences limited to fines of $840 each. But after a political uproar over the leniency of the sentences, prosecutors managed to get the guilty pleas set aside and brought the first of the defendants to trial on felony rape charges. At trial the man's lawyer argued that "if the woman had consumed enough alcohol to be helpless, as she testified, then she could not be sure that she had not consented to sex." He didn't say of course that the men should be sure that she *had* consented. Genuine willingness on the part of the woman simply isn't required. The jury acquitted.[11]

A notorious case in 1991 at St. John's College in New York involved a twenty-two-year-old junior, a black woman from a sheltered Caribbean Catholic background. Sandra, as I will call her, was being driven home by Michael, a friend from the college riflery team. Michael stopped at his home, ostensibly to get gas money, and asked her to come in to meet his roommates.[12] Once there, he offered her a drink from a pitcher of vodka and orange juice that was on hand, already mixed. Though Sandra initially declined, explaining that a rum drink had once made her sick, Michael insisted, saying "It's only vodka. It can't do anything to you." Sandra drank one cup and, at Michael's insistence, two more in quick succession.

Sandra quickly became sick, started to shake, and was unable to stand up. As she slid to the couch, Michael allegedly stripped off her shirt, forced his penis into her mouth, and performed a number of acts of intercourse and fellatio. Three of his roommates, all members of the lacrosse team, appeared and allegedly took turns performing acts of sodomy and fellatio while Sandra passed repeatedly in and out of consciousness. At one point she screamed, but one of the roommates slapped her and yelled, "You can't scream in here. This is a residential neighborhood!" When it was all over, the men tossed Sandra's limp body into the back seat of a car, drove her to a campus fraternity house, and unceremoniously dumped her there.

After Sandra reported the incident, Michael pleaded guilty to sexual assault charges and agreed to testify for the prosecution at the trial of the three others. Another roommate also testified and corroborated Sandra's account. A toxicologist testified that Sandra's symptoms indicated she had consumed the equivalent of seven or eight shots of eighty proof alcohol, suggesting that the three cups she had been served contained an exceptionally strong drink. None of the three defendants testified, but their attorney argued that she "knew she was getting drunk but continued to consume the alcohol to cast off her inhibitions." He also suggested that if she could remember so many of the details, then she was not too drunk to consent. As one commentator on the case noted, the defense managed to place her in a no-win situation: either she was sober enough to have resisted, or so drunk that her testimony lacked credibility.[13] The argument carried the day. The three defendants, all young white athletes from "good" families, were acquitted. Along with jury attitudes affected by race, economic class, and social background, the law itself made a difference. Even when a woman is heavily intoxicated and unable to stand, criminal law comes into play only if a man uses a certain kind of physical force. Actual consent isn't necessary.

In a 1991 case at Stanford University, the facts were less extreme but probably more common. A seventeen-year-old freshman I will call Anne described spending several hours visiting Robert, a twenty-three-year-old varsity athlete, in his dorm room.[14] At Robert's suggestion they played a card game called "drink blackjack": after each hand, the losing player had to down a glass of schnapps. Over a period of about two hours, Anne drank some beer and eight glasses of schnapps. She soon had a headache and felt sick to her stomach. She lay down on the bed.

At that point Robert lay down beside her, they kissed, and Robert began to undress her. Anne reported that when she realized Robert

intended to go further than just
stop. Several times she protested
boyfriend." Robert replied reassuring holding her, she told him to
have to know," and saying, "If you wan... can't do this. I have a
But Anne never indicated she did "want... er, "It's O.K., he doesn't
saying several times that she couldn't do wh... K. I won't hurt you."
did not stop. When he penetrated her, she said... ntinued to object,
then withdrew, but a minute or so later, ignoring y... wanted. Robert
penetrated her again.

Despite Anne's clear protests, Robert's vastly greater ... er protest, he
(he was six feet seven inches tall), and her weakened cond... strength
nia prosecutors decided they did not have enough evidence... alifor-
a charge of forcible rape. California law also permits a rap... port
when the victim "is prevented from resisting by any intoxicating...ge
substance . . . administered by . . . the accused."[15] But there were dou...
about whether Anne was so drunk that she was completely prevented
from resisting. The California law was too narrow in another respect as
well. Like most American statutes on the subject, the California provision applies only when the victim is completely unconscious or when the
alcohol is "administered" by the accused. Because Anne accepted the
drinks and knew they contained alcohol, the law probably would not
consider Robert responsible for her condition. Like the men in the New
York bar, Robert was permitted to exploit his victim's drunken condition
because he had not personally forced it on her.[16]

Anne's case and countless others underscore the limited focus and
unsatisfactory boundaries of existing laws against sexual abuse. Criminal law standards are especially narrow. They protect women's sexual
freedom from physical violence—but not from much else. Despite three
decades of supposedly dramatic change in cultural attitudes and legal
standards, criminal law still fails to guarantee a woman's right to determine for herself when she will become sexually intimate with another
person. It still refuses to outlaw coercion and abuses of trust that prevent
a woman from deciding freely whether to choose or refuse a sexual
relationship. And when she does refuse, the law still fails to ensure that
her clearly expressed preferences will be honored and enforced. So far
as the criminal law is concerned, American women simply do not have
such a right.

...se impressions in this respect. Resis-
have been restricted or abolished. But
early and insistently, the man can still roll
clothes, and penetrate her, all without com-
les in these cases are not conflicting versions of
questions, and the notorious difficulties of sorting
he said . . . she said . . ." The man can simply admit
or less with impunity. His conduct, even today, remains
because he has not used what the law calls force, that is,
in addition to the force that is intrinsic to intercourse.[17]
shot is that resistance requirements remain in effect even
he law says they have been abolished. The woman's right to
integrity and her right to control her sexual choices just do not
—until she begins to scream or fight back physically.

Criminal law easil
tance requirements
when a woman sa
on top of her, r
mitting rape. Tl
the truth, cr
out the fac
to the fac
perfectl
physi
he
wl

The Myth of Radical Change

These large gaps in American law will seem surprising to anyone whose impressions are formed by recent media coverage of the antirape movement and its supposedly far-reaching success in achieving legal change. Opponents of rape reform have managed to convince a wide audience that standards of permissible conduct are now dictated by "hypersensitive" young women and by "radical" feminists committed to a highly restrictive, Victorian conception of sexual propriety. Radical feminists, they argue, have enjoyed unparalleled success in promoting their agenda and now impose their prudish standards of sexual restraint on all Americans through campus behavior codes and overbroad statutes that pliant lawmakers, cowed by feminist demands for political correctness, have been obliged to enact.[18]

The reality is far different. The claim that legal rules, campus behavior codes, and company policies enshrine radically overprotective, puritanical rules of conduct is a myth. It is a particularly unfortunate myth because it obscures the serious risks women continue to face and blocks informed discussion of reforms that are still urgently needed.

What have recent reforms accomplished? When a woman says "no" insistently and attempts any degree of physical struggle, courts today, far more than in the past, are likely to see the assailant's conduct as rape.

When a man's language carries a threat of bodily injury, the woman's failure to resist no longer precludes a conviction.

Yet once we move beyond situations of potentially severe physical violence, the limited reach of recent reforms becomes apparent. In most states, verbal resistance—saying "no"—still isn't sufficient to bring criminal law safeguards into play. This is so for two reasons. The first is the continuing hold of the old idea that women who say "no" sometimes mean yes. A readiness to find consent in sexual matters still permeates our culture. Even in the late 1990s, the great majority of states have no law requiring courts (or sexual predators) to accept a verbal refusal at face value.

Yet factual disputes about what "no" really means are not the only problem, because there is a large legal obstacle as well. Today many judges and jurors are prepared to accept a woman's "no" as a sign of genuine unwillingness. But in the eyes of the law, a woman's unwillingness does not suffice to turn a sexual predator into a rapist, because physical force is required as well. The criminal law's continuing fixation on force means that a woman's right to determine the boundaries of her own sexual interactions is, at best, only partially protected. The law guards against the risk of violent injury to life or limb. But sexual autonomy—the right to self-determination in matters of sexual life—is not directly guaranteed.

Sexual harassment suits provide an alternative remedy for women who are coerced by tactics that stop short of physical force. It would be natural to assume that these laws fill the gap left by criminal law's strict force requirement, because sexual harassment laws are so often portrayed as exceedingly restrictive. The vocal critics of these laws imply that they impose draconian sanctions on any man who dares use off-color language or the slightest hint of sexual interest in the presence of an exceptionally sensitive woman. In fact, sexual harassment laws do nothing of the kind. On the contrary, these laws remain limited in their coverage and effectiveness.

With few exceptions, sexual harassment laws, both state and federal, extend protection only to employees and students. They are no help at all when a medical patient is pressured for sex by her doctor or when a client in a divorce proceeding is coerced by a lawyer who threatens to stop working on her case if she won't meet his sexual demands.

Even in the workplace, sexual harassment laws are only partially effective. The laws apply if a supervisor or professor is stupid enough to tell a woman that he will hurt her career unless she submits to him. But sexual harassment laws often ignore the pressures that lurk beneath the surface of sexual demands from a professor or job supervisor. And even when an explicit threat can be proved, sexual harassment remedies are limited. The law permits civil damage suits against universities and firms, and such suits are often well publicized. What is less well known is that even when clear abuses are committed, the offender himself isn't personally liable for damages; sexual harassment remedies apply only against the university or business firm as an entity.[19]

In Oregon the supervisor at a U.S. Postal Service facility called one of his subordinates into the copy room and demanded oral sex. The woman refused at first, but she eventually complied because she feared she would be fired. Over the next several months the supervisor repeatedly summoned her to his office, discussed her work, and then demanded sex in a way that left no doubt that her performance evaluations would depend on her willingness to meet his sexual demands.[20] The woman hesitated to report the situation, convinced that her supervisor would retaliate against her. She became anxious, lost weight, and tried to commit suicide. Finally she reported the problem, sued, and recovered a small damage award from the Postal Service. Meanwhile her boss held his job. Years later he was still employed at the same facility. He faced no personal liability for damages, and of course he had violated no criminal law because he had never threatened the woman with physical force.

Should Women Be Stronger?

Must we accept the Tennessee teenager's sad view that these kinds of abuses are all just "part of everyday life"? Should we insist that a woman who dislikes these forms of sexual attention must simply assert herself a bit more? Critics of the rape reform movement don't see that as too much to ask. Some even ridicule demands for stronger laws as efforts to gain "special protection" for women. They portray women who enter a man's dorm room or drink with him in private as very foolish individuals, who shouldn't be surprised if things get out of hand. Men, after all, don't ask the law to protect them from their own weakness and poor judgment.

Or do they? Suppose that John, an eighteen-year-old student, gets falling-down drunk at a fraternity party. While he staggers upstairs to find a bed to collapse into, Bill, another student, reaches into John's pocket and takes his wallet, over John's slurred and feebly murmured protests. Is John a very foolish young man? Of course. But do we treat him as "consenting" to Bill's actions? Would we tell him to "stop whining" or to just "get over it" if he filed a complaint for theft? Of course not.

Suppose that a homeowner leaves his bedroom window open on a hot night. In the early morning a stranger climbs through the window and steals the television. Is the stranger's urge for the easy buck an inevitable human instinct? Probably. Was the homeowner foolish to leave his window open? Perhaps. But do we say that the homeowner has only himself to blame or that he really "consented"? Not for a minute.

We live in a world in which the law vigorously protects all of us against force, stealth, abuse of authority, and deception that impair our control over our property. We live in a world that never for a moment entertains the idea that a victim's gullibility or "contributory negligence" lessens the criminal responsibility of a person who takes advantage of the situation by intimidation, extortion, or abuse of trust. Yet when women seek comparable protection for their bodily security and sexual integrity, they are disparaged as pleading for special privileges or wallowing in victimhood.

The law's narrow scope leaves women vulnerable to male sexual aggressors, but its flaws are more general. The law systematically fails to protect the interest that both women *and men* have in their bodily security and in their ability to choose freely whether to be sexually intimate with another person. Outside prisons the danger of sexual abuse is seldom a major concern for men. But the law's sexual double standard—its stinting protection for sexual autonomy compared to other interests—is not just a problem that women have with predatory men. Men too are the victims.

Like women, men suffer from overt violence, tacit threats, intimidation, and abuse of authority by parents, teachers, employers, prison guards, psychiatrists, and the like. The aggressors are often other men, not necessarily gay men, and sometimes the aggressors are women. Like the abuse of women, the victimization of men persists in a twilight world of confusion and self-blame, intense social taboos, systematic underreporting, and massive failures of enforcement.[21] A related but rarely discussed problem is the sexual abuse of women by other women, including their lesbian partners.[22]

There is no reason to believe that men outside the prison setting are victimized anywhere nearly as often as women are. But sexual abuse is not just a women's problem. And the demand for protection of sexual autonomy is emphatically not a demand for extraordinary remedies or special privileges. It is simply a demand to end the special, *dis*favored treatment of women's bodily integrity and of sexuality itself. Society's refusal to provide comprehensive protection for sexual autonomy—for women and men—is puzzling and, for countless Americans, especially women, hard to accept.

Yet it is not so easy to define, clearly and specifically, what an appropriate system of protection for sexual autonomy should look like. It is not so easy to set the boundaries for permissible conduct when positions of authority, alcohol, threats, promises, or abuses of trust have some effect on a sexual interaction.

A prison guard's power clearly prevents an inmate from choosing freely whether to accept or refuse a sexual proposal, but do we say the same about a college professor and a nineteen-year-old student in his course? If so, do we also say the same about a corporate vice-president and a junior executive working in another division? There are problems in such relationships, to be sure. But if sexual interaction is ruled legally out of bounds every time one of the parties has any possible source of power over the other, our opportunities to find companionship and sexual intimacy will shrink drastically. To create a legal barrier to every relationship not formed on the purely neutral ground of the singles bar or the church social would be pathetic and absurd.

A woman too drunk to stand up should not be expected to resist physically or to protest explicitly—even if she downed all the drinks of her own accord and knew exactly what was in them. But do we say the same about any woman who has had two or three beers, or too many drinks to drive a car safely? Should we conclude that a woman's consent is invalid if she said "yes" because she was feeling relaxed and uninhibited after having a glass of wine? The law's willingness to find consent in cases of severe alcohol impairment should be considered intolerable, but a standard that suggests rape anytime alcohol plays a part in sexual consent would be intolerable as well.

Respect for sexual autonomy requires protecting sexual privacy against abuse and overreaching. But—equally important—it also requires that the law protect our freedom to seek emotional intimacy and sexual fulfillment with willing partners. Despite decades of discussion and years of ambitious feminist reforms, adequate protection of sexuality remains elusive, in part because freedom from unwanted sex and freedom to seek mutually desired sex sometimes seem to be in tension. A workable notion of sexual autonomy appears to require compromises and "balancing," the kind of chore that lawyers and academics often regard as a technical problem of "line-drawing." But the problem is neither simple nor unimportant. What is at stake is nothing less than women's bodily security and every person's right to control the boundaries of his or her own sexual experience.

Existing criminal law resolves the dilemmas of sexual autonomy by making almost no effort to control abuses that are not physically violent. This "solution" indirectly places an imprimatur of social permission on virtually all pressures and inducements that can be considered nonviolent. It leaves women unprotected against forms of pressure that any society should consider morally improper and legally intolerable. What may be even worse, the existing approach distorts social conceptions of legitimate behavior and raises the threshold for the kind of physical violence that the law is willing to recognize as "abnormal" force. As became starkly clear for the Illinois woman who was accosted while bike riding, current standards are so strict that they shelter many truly intimidating and physically dangerous abuses that the law in theory claims to forbid.

Interference with autonomy in matters of sexual life should be considered unacceptable—and illegal—whether that interference takes the form of threats of physical injury, threats to inflict other kinds of harm, abuse of trust, exploitation of intoxication and physical helplessness (as in the St. John's case), or exploitation of authority and economic power. We can insist on this point—and give it clear, understandable content—without resorting to impossibly vague standards, without demeaning women's capacities for self-assertion, and certainly without blocking the opportunities that both women and men properly value for the pursuit of emotional intimacy and sexual fulfillment.

Delayed by many hundreds of years, effective safeguards for our sexual autonomy have begun to emerge in the reforms of the past two decades, but the solutions remain halting and incomplete. Protection against violence, important though it is, cannot be the only concern. The underlying problem is to provide comprehensive protection for our right to determine the boundaries of our own sexual lives. Neither the recent legal reforms nor our evolving social standards yet afford decent protection for our bodies and our sexual choices.

2

Disappointing Reforms

In both criminal and civil law, safeguards for our right to sexual self-determination remain incomplete despite decades of effort and countless legal reforms. The legislative changes inspired by the feminist antirape movement accomplished very little. What went wrong?

Part of the explanation lies in the intensely personal—and intensely controversial—character of sexual behavior. What do men seek from casual sex or from long-term relationships outside marriage, and are these sexual encounters "immoral"? When do women want to have casual sex, and is there a different standard for judging whether a sexual encounter is inappropriate for a woman or harmful to her? Americans have probably never given uniform answers to these questions. But differences of opinion have widened and intensified enormously over the past three decades. The attitudes we bring to thinking about questions of sexual consent are strongly held but often incompatible with the views of our neighbors and friends, especially if they are members of the opposite sex.

When people so often disagree about what "consent" or "force" is, the rape law of statutes and court decisions often appears irrelevant or meaningless. Social attitudes are tenacious, and they can easily nullify the theories and doctrines found in the law books. The story of failed reforms is in part a story about the overriding importance of culture, about the seeming irrelevance of law.

Yet we cannot ignore the legal details. The details are themselves a window into our sexual culture. The details also have a life of their own. The intricacies of legal doctrine stand between the concrete facts of an outrageous abuse and the formal conclusion that a crime has or has not occurred. The details not only reflect a certain culture but also interact with that culture. They reinforce certain understandings, delay the recognition of others, and free predators whose conduct the courts condemn as despicable—but not illegal. The law's technicalities, just because they are technicalities, merit close attention. They play a central role in molding society's understanding of what sexual abuse is.

In the eighteenth century, Blackstone defined rape as "carnal knowledge of a woman forcibly and against her will."[1] Until the 1950s, American statutes almost uniformly preserved Blackstone's definition, with minor verbal differences. Rape included only a few instances of intercourse that wasn't compelled by force, notably consensual intercourse with a minor and intercourse with a woman who was unconscious or asleep. Conversely, because of the notorious "marital exemption," rape did not include a man's conduct in compelling intercourse with his wife, even if he did use physical force. Between husband and wife, the law's conception of consent remained the one that the British Chief Justice Lord Hale had set forth in the seventeenth century: "by their matrimonial consent and contract, the wife hath given up herself in this kind unto her husband, which she cannot retract."[2]

When the restrictive definitions were met and rape was committed, the crime was typically punished by long prison terms or (in many states) by the death penalty.[3] Rape was not the only severely punished offense, but it was singled out for a special set of safeguards for the defendant. Courts were obsessed with the idea that a woman might fabricate an accusation of rape, either because she feared the stigma of having consented to intercourse or because she was pregnant and needed an acceptable explanation for her condition. Judges also worried that a woman might falsely accuse a man for reasons of revenge or blackmail. Lord Hale again set the tone. Courts repeatedly cited his pronouncement, in 1680, that rape "is an accusation easily to be made and hard to be proved, and harder to be defended by the party accused, tho never so innocent."[4]

To guard against false accusations, courts imposed strict rules of proof that were unique to rape cases. One requirement barred prosecution unless the victim had filed her complaint promptly after the incident. Another rule barred conviction unless independent witnesses or physical evidence corroborated the victim's testimony.[5] In language echoing Lord Hale's, juries in rape cases were routinely warned that they must examine the victim's testimony with special care because a rape charge was "easily made and, once made, difficult to defend against, even if the person accused is innocent."[6] To make sure that women complaining of rape had really been unwilling, courts required them to show physical resistance, usually expressed as "earnest resistance" or even resistance "to the utmost."[7]

With the important exception of cases in which a white woman accused a black man of rape, the resistance requirement was tenaciously enforced. There were heartbreaking facts in a nineteenth-century Wisconsin case. A man named Whittaker accosted a Milwaukee woman and forcefully held her down. She testified, "He had my hands tight and my feet tight, and I couldn't move from my place even." When she screamed for help, he threatened to use his revolver. Still, she tried once again to cry out. She testified, "I couldn't do any more, I got so tired out. I tried to save me so much as I could, but I couldn't save myself, and he held me, and . . . I couldn't help myself any more . . . I worked so much as I could, and I gave up."

This was more than enough for the Milwaukee jury, which found Whittaker guilty of rape. But the Wisconsin Supreme Court reversed his conviction. Said the court, "This is not a case where the prosecutrix was overcome by threats of personal violence." Whittaker's threat to use his gun was merely "conditional upon her attempting again to cry out." As the Wisconsin judges saw it, "The testimony does not show that the threat of personal violence overpowered her will, or . . . that she was incapable of voluntary action." Consent, in the court's view, need not imply actual desire. On the contrary, "submission . . . , *no matter how reluctantly yielded,* removes from the act an essential element of the crime of rape." The court concluded that the victim's resistance "ought to have continued to the last." Because she "gave up," she had, in their view, consented.[8]

In the early twentieth century, courts intensified their insistence that women resist "to the utmost." The requirement became impossibly difficult to satisfy and dangerous to any victim who tried. In 1906, reversing another rape conviction, the Wisconsin Supreme Court wrote that a victim must make "the most vehement exercise of every physical means or faculty within the woman's power." Modern science was invoked to buttress the rule: "A woman," the court said, "is equipped to interpose most effective obstacles by means of hands and limbs and pelvic muscles. Indeed, medical writers insist that these obstacles are practically insuperable in the absence of more than the usual relative disproportion of age and strength between man and woman."9 The court assumed, in other words, that no matter how strenuously a woman had protested, her assailant's success in achieving penetration showed that she must have been willing.

The story was endlessly repeated. Reversing a 1947 conviction, the Nebraska Supreme Court said that "submission" would count as consent "no matter how reluctantly yielded." Said the court, "carnal knowledge, with the voluntary consent of the woman, no matter how tardily given or how much force had hitherto been imposed, is not rape." For the Nebraska court, like so many others, "consent" meant something far short of willingness or sexual desire. Only if a woman resisted physically and "to the utmost" could a man be expected to realize that his actions were against her will. "She must persist in such resistance," said the court, "as long as she has the power to do so until the offense is consummated."10

The Flawed "Model" Code

In the 1950s the American Law Institute, a prestigious body of judges, lawyers, and legal scholars, began an ambitious project to examine the whole of American criminal law. The institute's goal was to draft a proposal for replacing the disorganized and archaic statutes of the time with a coherent, modern code. When they turned their attention to rape, the reformers were alarmed by the low rate of conviction in clear cases of serious abuse. The reformers—all of them men[11]—attributed this problem to three defects in the law: the resistance requirement, the undue preoccupation with victim consent, and the inclusion of too many diverse kinds of misbehavior within a single felony that carried extremely severe punishments.

In their proposal for a "Model Penal Code," the reformers suggested changes that reflected this accurate but limited diagnosis. Most of their recommendations made no break with traditional assumptions. The code preserved the rules requiring a prompt complaint, corroboration of the victim's testimony, and special cautionary instructions to the jury.[12] The reformers not only preserved the "marital exemption" but extended it: The code barred prosecution in cases of compelled inter-course when the assailant and victim were "living together as man and wife," regardless of whether the couple was formally married. Interest-ingly, the code placed substance over legal form by extending the marital exemption to unmarried couples who were living together, but it placed form over substance by preserving the exemption for most legally mar-ried couples who were living apart.[13] The consistent thread in both situations was that fear of false accusations and appreciation for a man's sexual needs prevailed over his partner's claim to determine for herself whether to permit sexual intimacy.

To make rape prosecutions more effective, the reformers proposed three major steps—abolishing the resistance requirement, eliminating all mention of victim consent from the definition of the offense, and dividing rape into several offenses with distinct penalty levels. Even in these promising proposals, however, modern concerns about underen-forcement were mixed with starkly traditional assumptions about women's passive role in sexual encounters and inability to be forthright about their sexual desires. Those attitudes shaped the reform proposals, which, in turn, continue to shape rape law today.

The reformers' proposal to divide rape into two separate offenses reveals the limited reach of their ambitions. In order to get convicted of the more serious offense—the only crime called "rape" in the code—a sexual predator practically had to kill his victim. The offense of rape was reserved for defendants who had inflicted or threatened "serious bodily injury," "extreme pain" (ordinary pain wasn't enough), or "imminent death."[14] A man who threatened to kill a protesting woman the next morning would not be guilty of rape, because he had not threatened to carry out his threat immediately.

The crime called "rape" in the code, though limited to extremely violent misconduct, was still too broad to satisfy the Law Institute draftsmen. They proposed subdividing the offense they called rape into two degrees. Life-threatening sexual abuse was treated as a first-degree felony (with a potential for a life sentence) only if the parties were strangers or if the perpetrator actually inflicted serious bodily harm. Rape involving acquaintances—life-threatening rape—was down-graded to a second-degree felony (with a maximum sentence of only ten years' imprisonment) any time the defendant did not inflict serious bodily harm. The assumption was that if the woman knew her attacker, the attack was inherently less serious, or that juries and prosecutors would see the matter that way.

The sentencing proposals, though puzzling by today's standards, reflected two legitimate concerns. One was to facilitate convictions by ruling out the severe sanctions that sometimes prompted juries to acquit even when guilt was clear. The other concern was the Law Institute's deep revulsion against the race bias then evident in many southern states, where courts imposed extremely severe sanctions—including the death penalty—on blacks accused of raping white women.

To deal with conduct that was not imminently life-threatening, the Model Penal Code proposed creating a less serious felony to be called "gross sexual imposition." This offense (with a maximum sentence of five years' imprisonment) would reach aggressors who threatened less serious or less immediate physical injury. The code's new offense would also extend the criminal prohibition beyond the common law of rape, to reach threats to inflict some nonphysical harms. Under the code, nonphysical threats, such as a threat to destroy a woman's business or to expose a shameful secret, were made criminal, but only when the threat would prevent resistance by what the code called (without further definition) the "woman of ordinary resolution."[15] The code extended the common law of rape, but it left men free to make any sort of threat that judges or juries might think the "woman of ordinary resolution" should resist.

The model code's third recommendation was to eliminate from the definition of the offense all mention of the victim's consent. Ideally, the law should have been moving toward *greater* emphasis on consent, not less, and the reformers themselves acknowledged that the central mission of rape law was to protect "freedom of choice" and "meaningful consent."[16] Nonetheless, they wanted to sidestep the question of the victim's consent and to focus instead on the man's conduct; they made it a crime for him to "compel her to submit" by force or threat.[17] One reason for this move away from consent was surely progressive and well intended. The reformers saw the concept of consent as an invitation to put the victim on trial and to divert attention from the defendant's misconduct. Focusing the jury's attention on the behavior of the man would, they hoped, minimize those risks.

Unfortunately, there was a darker side to the decision to avoid the issue of consent. The reformers pushed consent to the sidelines, not just to help prosecutors tactically at trial but also because the reformers themselves were not sure what "consent" might really mean. Their reports on the draft code were saturated with the assumption that women who say "no" might not mean it. Their commentaries disparaged consent as a "deceptively simple notion" and warned: "Often the woman's attitude may be deeply ambivalent." The reformers stressed that a woman may have "a barrage of conflicting emotions at the time of the assault" and that "inquiry into the victim's state of mind . . . often will not yield a clear answer."[18] Women were thought to be unable to express their sexual desires directly; beset by "conflicting emotions," women, in this view, might not know what they themselves actually wanted.

To cope with this supposed ambiguity of consent, the commentaries to the code proclaimed that criminal law must draw "a line between forcible rape on the one hand and reluctant submission on the other,"[19] as if reluctant submission were not a serious injury in itself. As a result, the reformers ultimately gave little weight to their own insight that "meaningful consent" was the law's main concern. In the end the code set up an undefined but stringent requirement—*forcible compulsion*—as the only reliable indication that the woman's claims of nonconsent were genuine. Autonomy, though supposedly central, was shunted aside, as it had been before.

The Law Institute's work proved heavily influential. During the 1960s, legislatures throughout the United States extensively revised their criminal laws. The Model Penal Code was often used as a point of departure. But the code's modest recommendations for rape reform were diluted in the legislative process. At most, states adopted only isolated parts of the institute's cautiously progressive agenda. They often followed the code's technical suggestions about the grading of offenses, but they seldom accepted language that had the effect of extending liability. Traditional concerns about the risk of false accusation continued to operate, as did the traditional assumption that "some aggression is an expected part of the male role in sexual encounters."[20] With these perspectives still ascendant, there was little evidence of concern for strengthening women's freedom to make their own sexual choices.

In the reforms of the 1960s, all states retained the marital exemption and the special rules requiring prompt complaint, corroboration, and a cautionary instruction to the jury. Legislatures virtually ignored the model code's proposal to eliminate the resistance requirement. Revised statutes often divided rape into degrees of seriousness and reserved the most severe penalties for brutal, life-threatening assaults. But no state enacted the code's recommendation for a lesser offense covering threats to inflict some sorts of nonphysical injuries. Instead, states following the Model Penal Code approach usually defined rape as intercourse by "forcible compulsion."[21]

The end result was that the law's fixation on physically violent misconduct was not relaxed; it was reinforced. The New York statute adopted in 1965 was typical in requiring proof of extreme violence. Rape, as the statute defined it, was committed only when a sexually aggressive man used "physical force that overcomes earnest resistance" or when he made a threat of "immediate death or serious physical injury."[22] A woman who succumbed to threats of lesser injuries was treated as consenting, so the man's conduct was not criminal at all.

These stringent requirements produced disturbing results in case after case. In one, the victim said she submitted to intercourse, without resisting or crying out, because the defendant had threatened her with a box cutter. She testified that afterward she managed to get the weapon away from him, but submitted to intercourse a second time because the defendant pulled her hair, choked her, and told her that he could kill her. The jury found her testimony compelling and convicted him of rape. Yet in 1973 a New York appellate court set aside the conviction. Rape, the court insisted, "is not committed unless the woman opposes the man to the utmost limit of her power. The resistance must be genuine and active. It is difficult to conclude that the complainant here waged a valiant struggle to uphold her honor."[23]

Other states, in one way or another, emphasized the same central idea. Aside from the rare case involving an unconscious victim or statutory rape prosecutions in which the victim was an underage minor, rape convictions were possible only when the defendant deployed extreme physical violence. There was one important exception: the stringent force requirement was usually ignored when a black defendant was accused of raping a white woman. In that situation courts apparently assumed that the man's sexual overtures were inherently terrifying or that there was no conceivable possibility that the woman might want to consent. But interracial rapes were a small minority of the total, only 6 percent in one study.[24] In all other contexts, women were protected only from physical violence. Unwanted sexual imposition was not in itself a crime—or even an aberration.

Criticism of rape law intensified in the 1970s. Susan Griffin and Susan Brownmiller, two of the early feminist writers on rape, renewed complaints about the difficulty of winning convictions, but they also raised broader themes.[25] They stressed the ordeal that rape victims faced at the hands of the justice system itself, and they focused attention on stereotypes about "good" and "bad" women that led men (and other women) to doubt the rape victim's credibility. Prosecutors and police often assumed that a woman was fabricating her rape accusation or blamed her for provoking the incident by her supposedly suggestive clothing or behavior. At trial the victim could expect to face extensive, humiliating cross-examination. Defense attorneys routinely used the rape victim's prior sexual experiences to suggest that she was a "loose" (and therefore untrustworthy) woman or that she probably had been willing to consent because she was no longer a virgin.

Other writers and advocates, Catharine MacKinnon most prominent among them, extended the critique. Brownmiller, MacKinnon, and other feminists following their lead argued that the law of rape did not in fact protect women at all. On the contrary, rape law, through its expectations of proper female behavior and its refusal to condemn many sorts of force, actually enhanced male opportunities for sexual aggression, increased women's dependence on a male protector, and reinforced the dominant position and social power of men as a class.[26]

The worst failures of rape law were hidden from public view. Police skepticism and insensitivity discouraged many victims from filing complaints. And when victims did complain, police and prosecutors often dismissed their complaints without pressing charges. If a woman had worn a short skirt or tight sweater, had been drinking, had gone voluntarily to a man's apartment, or had accepted a ride in his car, police usually assumed that she had really consented or had only got what she deserved.[27]

When police could be convinced that a rape had occurred, a further barrier was posed by the need for independent evidence corroborating the offense—a requirement imposed for no other crime. In a 1974 case in Washington, D.C., a twelve-year-old girl testified that while she was visiting at a friend's apartment, two of the men there grabbed her by the legs and dragged her to a bedroom. They closed the door, blocked it with a dresser, and threw her on the bed, where each of them penetrated her while the other held her down. Afterward the girl ran into the street, found a police officer, and reported the incident. One of the men, Wiley, was brought to trial, with prosecutors relying for corroboration on the testimony of the two police officers at the scene. They had observed the victim's distress and disheveled clothing when she ran from the apartment without a coat, on a cold March day, to report the crime.

Wiley was convicted of rape. His appeal went to the U.S. Court of Appeals for the District of Columbia Circuit, at the time one of the nation's most progressive courts. His attempt to invoke the corroboration rule as a shield was heard by a three-judge panel that included Judges John Minor Wisdom and David Bazelon, perhaps two of the most liberal judges ever to sit on the federal bench. Yet the court gave little weight to the corroboration rule's discriminatory impact on women. Wisdom and Bazelon insisted that the case was incomplete without live medical testimony from the doctor who examined the girl after the incident, to back up her testimony that intercourse had occurred. (The doctor had been present in court on three previous trial dates but was away on vacation on the fourth date, when the case was finally tried.) Wiley's conviction was set aside.[28] Judge Bazelon wrote a long, agonized opinion struggling with feminist concerns but ultimately opting to preserve the status quo. For judges of that era, "liberal" meant above all maximizing safeguards for the defendant and strengthening the rules that protected black defendants from false accusations and excessive punishment in interracial cases; it did not mean giving priority to women's demands for equal treatment and effective protection from rape.

In New York, the situation for women was especially bad. Decisions throughout the 1950s and 1960s persistently tightened the corroboration requirement.[29] Prosecutors were often able to convince juries in the cases they brought to trial. But the appellate courts, reversing convictions in case after case, insisted that it was not enough for witnesses to support the victim's credibility and confirm the essence of her story. Instead, the courts held, independent evidence must corroborate "every material fact essential to constitute the crime."[30]

New York prosecutors tried to avoid the harsh effects of this rule by dropping rape indictments and settling for conviction on lesser charges. But the New York courts treated that strategy as a shameful evasion of the law. They ruled that corroboration requirements had to be met even in prosecutions for less serious sex offenses such as attempted rape or corrupting the morals of a minor.

The stringent New York rule produced distressing and even illogical results. Medical corroboration of intercourse obviously could not be required when a victim claimed that the rape attempt was foiled before penetration. But if the victim said penetration had occurred, the New York courts then insisted upon corroboration of that claim, regardless of whether the defendant was charged with completed rape or only the attempt. In the absence of medical evidence, a rape defendant could still be convicted of a sex crime, but only if the victim testified that penetration had *not* occurred. If she said she had been penetrated, then the defendant could not be convicted of any crime at all! New York's corroboration rule became so strict that in a typical year in the early 1970s, thousands of rape complaints were filed, but prosecutors obtained convictions in only eighteen cases.[31] For other felonies, conviction rates were typically ten to twenty times higher.[32]

In the relatively few cases that made it to court, the procedures at trial became another source of injustice. Susan Griffin focused attention on the victim's courtroom ordeal in her pathbreaking 1971 article for *Ramparts,* one of the first articles to bring rape to the center of feminist concern.[33] Griffin described a rape trial held in San Francisco a few months before. Prosecutors charged that a thirty-six-year-old jeweler, along with three friends, forced a twenty-three-year-old woman, at gunpoint, to enter a car and drove her to his apartment. Once there, prosecutors alleged, the four men raped her and then held her overnight, subjecting her to further sexual assaults. The woman testified that the men freed her in the morning, with a warning that she would be killed if she spoke to anyone about the incident. Several other women testified that the jeweler had lured them to his apartment on various pretexts and then forced them to have sex.

The young San Francisco woman spent a harrowing day on the stand under cross-examination. In an effort to portray the entire episode as consensual, the defense attorney peppered her with insinuating questions. He demanded to know if she had ever worked as a "cocktail waitress." (In fact she had done so once or twice.) He asked whether she had left one job in the financial district because she was discovered having sex on a couch in the office, and he asked whether she had once had an affair with a married man. (The victim heatedly denied both accusations.) Finally, he asked, "Isn't it true that your two children have a sex game in which one gets on top of the other and they _____ " At which the victim exploded, "That's a lie. They are wonderful children." The damage, however, was done. The jury initially deadlocked ten to two for acquittal, and after the jurors asked to have the woman's testimony read back to them, they returned with a verdict acquitting the defendant of the rape and kidnapping charges. For some jurors, even today, questionable occupations, "loose" morals, and unconventional "family values" imply that a woman is likely to consent to sex, even with a complete stranger who accosts her at gunpoint. And the law of the 1970s permitted the San Francisco defense attorney to make full use of those preconceptions.

Law professor Vivian Berger showed in a 1977 article that similar distortions of the trial process were widespread. Berger noted that case reports were filled with examples of hapless victims subjected to abusive and demeaning cross-examination. Defense attorneys routinely asked victims whether they used birth control or attended bars unescorted, and victims were required to enumerate their prior sexual experiences.[34] Judges allowed such tactics on the assumption that a woman who had had sex with her boyfriend might have consented to sex with a stranger as well. Juries often agreed or, perhaps, acquitted on the theory that a sexually experienced woman deserved whatever she got.

When juries could be persuaded to convict, the law's strict requirement of resistance presented another obstacle. Cases that managed to survive stringent screening by police, prosecutors, trial judges, and juries were often reversed by higher courts on appeal. In a 1972 Illinois case, Janice (not her real name) met Bain on a blind date arranged by her friend Linda. After spending some time at Linda's house, Bain left to drive one of his friends home, and Janice joined them for the ride. Janice testified that Bain dropped off his friend, returned by a back way, and then stopped on a lonely country road. She said that she asked to be taken back and reached for the door, but Bain pulled her away from the door, pushed her down on the seat, and hit her in the mouth with his fist. He then pulled off her pants and had intercourse.

With clear evidence of physical force, corroborated by police officers who observed the cuts and bruises inside Janice's mouth, Bain was convicted of rape. But the Illinois appellate court saw a gap in the evidence, because Janice "did not kick, scream, hit or scratch." The court did not think that fear could possibly account for Janice's failure to resist, because she admitted sitting close to Bain in the car before the incident and admitted kissing him twice when they were at Linda's. Concluding that "it is readily apparent that the girl made no serious physical effort to resist," the Illinois court set aside Bain's conviction.[35] From the court's perspective, Janice was the one in control, the one to be held accountable. She had encouraged the encounter by kissing Bain and by offering only perfunctory resistance instead of a "serious physical effort." Bain's direct use of force was not decisive because physical aggressiveness was considered a perfectly normal part of the male role in sexual interactions.

Feminist Reforms Take Hold

Prompted by shocking examples such as these, antirape activists pressed for extensive change in statutes and standards of judicial interpretation. In Michigan a grass-roots women's network grew into an intensive lobbying effort that culminated in the 1975 enactment of the first important feminist reform statute.[36] The National Organization for Women formed a National Task Force on Rape that coordinated efforts for legislative reform nationwide.[37] The political climate was—at least on the surface—receptive to women's demands to end discrimination. At the same time an influential movement for crime control and victims' rights was generating widespread momentum for new statutes to help crime victims in general.[38] In this atmosphere, antirape activists found state legislatures throughout the country willing to consider ambitious reform packages.

Many items on the feminist "wish list" were quickly enacted into law. Like the American Law Institute two decades earlier, feminist reformers focused much of their effort on trying to facilitate conviction in the outrageous cases that existing criminal law supposedly covered already. Change in the rules of evidence was a major priority. The corroboration requirement and special cautionary instructions to the jury came under concerted attack, and in the course of the 1970s virtually every state repealed these discriminatory rules. Similarly, by 1980 nearly every state had enacted some type of "rape-shield" law to restrict efforts to cross-examine the victim about her prior sexual relationships.[39]

In many states antirape activists gave much of their attention to symbolic issues. They worked to write new rape laws using gender-neutral language, so that sexual penetration of male victims would be covered. In many states they sought to replace the traditional term "rape" with captions referring to "sexual assault" or "sexual battery," in hopes of stressing the violent character of the offense.[40]

Though evidentiary and symbolic issues were in the forefront of reform efforts in the 1970s, reformers also pushed to expand the range of misconduct actually covered by rape law. Two problems absorbed most of their attention: the resistance requirement and the marital exemption. Complete repeal of both doctrines was a priority for reformers, but they achieved only partial success.

Most states retained (and still retain) some form of spousal rape exemption. In Michigan, where reformers had the benefit of strong support from the media and from the state's political establishment, legislators balked at repeal of the marital exemption, claiming that such a step would encourage blackmail by disaffected spouses in divorce proceedings. Reformers eventually accepted defeat on this point in order to win passage of the rest of their bill.[41] In 1977 Oregon became the first state to abolish the marital exemption, and a few states followed suit.[42] Many others narrowed the exemption by permitting rape prosecutions when the spouses were legally separated or living apart at the time of the rape incident.[43]

A number of states, including Michigan, Ohio, Pennsylvania, and New Jersey, repealed the resistance rule. Yet this remained a minority position. The great majority of states retained (and still retain) some form of resistance requirement, but the requirement was softened considerably.[44] During the 1970s, by either statute or judicial decision, nearly all states began to abandon the old insistence on resistance "to the utmost." In effect, "reasonable" resistance became sufficient.

These victories on the resistance issue were important but incomplete. As one court put it, "The rule of . . . 'resistance to the utmost' has been repudiated or relaxed, but not to the extent of doing away with the need of showing some resistance or showing facts which fairly indicate some good reason for not resisting."[45] Another court stressed that although the victim need not resist "to the utmost," there must be a "genuine *physical* effort on the part of the complainant to discourage and to prevent her assailant from accomplishing his intended purpose."[46] This remains the prevailing view: Most courts still insist on some evidence of physical resistance. Verbal protests alone are not enough, unless there are threats and fear sufficient to make resistance seem futile.

Statutory definitions of force and consent were another major concern, but here reformers divided sharply over tactics and strategy. All the reformers understood that a man's failure to obtain genuine consent was the essence of the offense. But reformers worried that statutes making consent a formal issue at trial would focus attention on the dress, behavior, and prior sexual experiences of the victim and might encourage defense attorneys to argue, even in cases involving physical violence, that the victim had encouraged the man's attentions. Like the Model Penal Code draftsmen two decades earlier, nearly all the feminist reformers of the 1970s concluded that the best course was to eliminate from the statutes all references to the victim's consent and to focus instead on the conduct of the assailant. They sought to define the offense by describing the male behavior they wanted to prohibit.

This meant renewing the emphasis on "forcible compulsion" as the gist of the offense. Many of the new statutes elaborately defined "force" or "forcible compulsion" and created separate degrees of the crime for causing severe injury or using a deadly weapon.[47] But however defined, force remained the central concept in these statutes, and it was almost always described in terms suggesting physical violence.

The Michigan statute was the most ambitious and detailed of these efforts. It never mentioned "consent." Instead, it made sexual intercourse a felony (called "criminal sexual conduct" rather than "rape") whenever a person "uses force or coercion to accomplish the sexual penetration."[48] "Force" was defined as including cases in which the defendant "overcomes the victim" by applying or threatening physical violence. But the reformers also understood the need to limit defense arguments about whether the victim's will was really "overcome." As a result, their statute specified that a defendant would automatically be guilty of criminal sexual conduct whenever he engaged in intercourse while armed with a weapon or while committing any other felony. The reformers' goal was to draw attention away from what the victim might have done and to make certain types of coercive conduct criminal in themselves. Even the ambitious Michigan statute, however, did little to stretch the concepts of force and coercion beyond situations of violent or potentially violent misconduct.

Not all the reformers accepted the strategy of stressing force rather than consent. A few of the new statutes took the opposite tack, making nonconsent the central element of the offense. Statutes enacted in several states defined rape simply as "sexual intercourse without consent." But the seemingly broad reach of these provisions was deceptive. Elsewhere in their statutes, nearly all these states specified that evidence of physical force was required to prove the absence of true "consent."

The case of the Montana high school principal illustrates the net effect of this convoluted approach. A seventeen-year-old senior claimed that he forced her to have sex with him, by threatening to prevent her from graduating. The principal was charged with violating the state's rape statute, which makes it a felony to have "sexual intercourse without consent with a person of the opposite sex."[49] On its face the statute seems to focus attention just where it should be—on the question of genuine consent. But another provision of Montana law reintroduces the requirement of force, using terms that echo the stringent Model Penal Code approach of the 1950s. That provision defines "without consent" to mean that the victim was "compelled to submit by force or by threat of imminent death, bodily injury, or kidnapping."[50] Because the principal had not threatened to inflict any physical injury, the threats he allegedly did make were insufficient; the young woman's allegations, even if true, could not support criminal charges.[51]

The upshot was that even when reform statutes seemed to protect women from sex without their consent, force almost always reentered the picture as an essential requirement for conviction. Only two states—Wisconsin and Washington—enacted statutes that punished nonconsensual intercourse without requiring proof of force.[52]

Meager Gains

Despite their failure to challenge the law's preoccupation with physical force, the reforms of the 1970s did make major changes. They abolished the corroboration requirement in virtually every state. They imposed "rape-shield" limits on defense efforts to humiliate the victim during cross-examination. They softened (and in some states eliminated) both the resistance requirement and the marital rape exemption. And they improved statutory terminology and penalty provisions.

The shift in legal doctrine was extensive, but it had surprisingly little practical effect. Cases throughout the 1980s made clear that the gains were slender. Rusk met a young woman named Pat at a Baltimore singles bar, where one of Pat's friends seemed to know him by name. Rusk and Pat chatted cordially and shared similar concerns. Both were separated from their spouses, and each had a child. When Pat told Rusk she had to leave, he persuaded her to give him a ride home. Arriving in front of his apartment at 1:00 A.M., she refused his invitation to come in. But Rusk insisted, took her car keys, and said, "Now, will you come up?" At that point, unfamiliar with the neighborhood and feeling scared, she followed him to his apartment.

After talking for a few minutes, Pat asked if she could leave, but Rusk, who still held her car keys, said he wanted her to stay, pulled her by the arms to the bed, and started to undress her. At his request she removed the rest of her clothing and his pants, but then she begged him to let her leave, telling him, "You can get a lot of other girls down there, for what you want." When Rusk said no, she became "really scared" and asked him, "If I do what you want, will you let me go without killing me?" (Rusk didn't respond to that question, and Pat's court testimony didn't show whether she was sure he had heard it.) Pat started to cry, and, as she testified, "he put his hands on my throat, and started lightly to choke me." Finally she said, "If I do what you want, will you let me go?" When Rusk said yes, she submitted, performing an act of fellatio and then vaginal intercourse. After that, Rusk let her leave. Pat immediately looked for a police car, and at 3:15 A.M. she reported the incident.

Rusk was convicted of rape, which Maryland defined as intercourse by "force or threat of force." But an appellate court, reflecting the traditional view, reversed the conviction. It found the evidence insufficient because Rusk didn't use force and "she was [not] prevented from resisting by threats to her safety."

In a 1981 decision, Maryland's highest court reinstated Rusk's conviction. The court accepted the jury's view that Rusk intended to immobilize Pat and that she feared he would kill her unless she submitted. Yet this eminently sensible conclusion was supported by a bare four-to-three majority of the court, and to justify its result the court was impelled to place "particular focus on the actual force applied by Rusk to Pat's neck." What, one may wonder, would have been the result if this one factual detail had been missing? As it was, the three dissenters chided the court for distorting the force element: "The law regards rape as a crime of violence. The majority today attenuates this proposition."[53]

A North Carolina case showed that minor factual nuances could still prevent conviction even in a case of clear abuse. Alston and his girlfriend Carol (not her real name) lived together for six months in a troubled relationship. Carol testified that he often struck her when she refused to give him money or do what he wanted. She said she often had sex with him just to accommodate him, remaining entirely passive while he undressed her and had intercourse. Eventually Carol became fed up with the relationship. One day, after he hit her again, she moved out and went to live with her mother.

A month later, Alston accosted Carol on the street, blocked her path, and demanded to know where she was living. When she refused to answer, he grabbed her arm and said she was coming with him. Carol agreed to walk with him if he released her, and they walked around briefly and talked about their relationship, which Carol told him was over. Carol testified that Alston threatened to "fix" her face to show her he was "not playing" and said he had a "right" to have intercourse with her again. At his insistence, she followed him to the house of one of his friends, but when Alston asked her if she was "ready," Carol made clear she did not want to have sex. She said that Alston then pulled her up from a chair, undressed her, pushed her legs apart, and penetrated her, while Carol remained passive and cried.

Alston was convicted of rape, but in 1984 the North Carolina Supreme Court set aside the conviction. The court conceded that there was "unequivocal" evidence of Carol's refusal to consent. Nonetheless, the court said, the prosecution had failed to prove *force:* Carol hadn't resisted physically, and Alston hadn't specifically threatened her at the moment of intercourse. Alston's threats earlier in the day, the court said, were "unrelated to the act of sexual intercourse." The court acknowledged that Carol's "general fear of the defendant may have been justified by his conduct on prior occasions." But a "general fear," the court held, was not sufficient.[54] As law professor Susan Estrich noted, the court in effect defined force from the perspective of two schoolboys arguing in a playground.[55] There was no fistfight in the *Alston* case, so the court was unable to see any use of "force."

The Michigan reformers had made an ambitious effort to avoid these kinds of traps on the issues of force and consent. The Michigan statute specified that a defendant was guilty of criminal sexual conduct in the first degree (a felony subject to life imprisonment) whenever he engaged in intercourse while armed with a weapon or while committing any other felony. Reformers expected these provisions "to create a conclusive presumption that sexual acts cannot be entered into by choice when the actor has a knife or gun."[56] But the Michigan courts saw the matter quite differently.

In one of the early cases under the statute, a young woman testified that Hearn abducted her from her motel room at gunpoint, forced her to drive away with him, and then raped her. Police found her in his car, crying hysterically. Hearn claimed that the victim had been hitchhiking. He said that he had offered her a ride and that she had voluntarily agreed to have intercourse with him.

Prosecutors argued that since Hearn was armed with a gun, the statute made it unnecessary to consider his defense of consent. The jury found him guilty, and he was sentenced to life imprisonment. But the Michigan court of appeals reversed the conviction. Though the statute said nothing about a consent defense, the court held that the jury should have been allowed to consider Hearn's claim of consent. Whether or not he had a gun in his car, the court reasoned, the legislature could not have meant to preclude him from proving consent as a defense to the accusation.[57]

Of course, Hearn's story may sound like an implausible tale, and a jury might well decide not to believe him. But it is easy to see why the court thought it was essential to decide whether Hearn's story really was phony. The legislature could not have intended to imprison a defendant for life, in a case of truly consensual intercourse, just because he had a gun in his car at the time. Though the *Hearn* decision was a frustrating defeat for reformers, the court's basic point was nonetheless correct: consent may be an elusive concept, but when the alleged victim is an adult woman not suffering from mental incapacity, her consent surely cannot be made irrelevant.

With the same logic, but somewhat less common sense, the Michigan courts also read a consent defense into the state's "other felony" provision. The Michigan statute specified that a defendant commits criminal sexual conduct whenever he engages in intercourse while committing any other felony. Reformers expected that this provision, like the one that applies to defendants who are "armed with a weapon," would "preclude the defense of consent."[58] But in a case involving a defendant who allegedly kidnapped and then raped his victim, the Michigan court of appeals held that consent remained a defense, adding, "We are not persuaded that consensual sexual intercourse is necessarily impossible in the course of a kidnapping."[59]

In the end, the prior law's requirements of force and nonconsent remained firmly in place. Despite the elaborate wording and detailed gradations of Michigan's new statute, the jury still has to consider the issues of force and consent, just as it did before. Consent can easily become a stumbling block for rape prosecutors, but reformers cannot enact it out of existence, as the Michigan reformers attempted to do.

Holes in the new approaches to force and consent were not the only sources of disappointment. Other gaps in the law persisted as well. The effort to protect married women from rape by their husbands remained stalled, as few legislatures were willing to repeal the traditional marital rape exemption.[60] In several states, courts stepped into the gap and rejected the exemption as outmoded or even unconstitutional.[61] But most states permitted prosecution of husbands only in narrowly restricted circumstances (if at all).

A 1984 Virginia case showed the beginnings of progress on this issue. A man forcibly raped his wife eleven months after she moved out of their common home. The Virginia Supreme Court upheld his conviction for rape. The court ruled that he could not invoke the marital exemption, because his wife had made clear that she regarded the marriage as over.[62]

A few months later the court confronted a roughly similar case. Kizer and his wife separated, and he filed suit to obtain custody of their child. For six months they had no sexual relations, and the wife insisted that he notify her in advance when he was coming to see their child, so that she could arrange to be elsewhere when he arrived. They discussed seeing an attorney to obtain a formal separation, but the wife told Kizer she did not want to do so "right now." Nonetheless they continued to live apart, and the wife avoided having contact with him. One night Kizer went to his wife's apartment. After she refused to admit him, he kicked in the door and carried his wife to the bedroom. She managed to break away and rushed to the window, screaming for help. Undeterred, Kizer ripped off her clothing and forcibly penetrated her, while she screamed, scratched, kicked, and pulled his hair.

Kizer was convicted of rape. But this time the Virginia Supreme Court let the husband claim the marital exemption and overturned his conviction. Because Kizer's wife had once said she wanted to make the marriage "work" and because she had hesitated to file for divorce, the court treated her conduct as "vacillating" and said that her behavior was too "equivocal, ambivalent and ambiguous" to show that she considered the marriage to be over.[63] Legally, Kizer's brutal attack did not qualify as rape.

A Pennsylvania case spotlighted another striking gap in the law. A fourteen-year-old girl I will call Debby committed a theft and was sent to a juvenile detention home. Mlinarich agreed to assume custody for her, and she was placed in his care as her foster parent. Mlinarich made sexual advances, and Debby eventually acquiesced and had sex with him, but only after Mlinarich threatened to send her back to the detention home unless she complied with his demands. Mlinarich was convicted of corrupting the morals of a minor (a misdemeanor) and rape. But in 1985 a Pennsylvania appellate court set aside the rape conviction. The court concluded that Mlinarich's conduct, though "reprehensible," did not meet the rape law's requirement of "forcible compulsion," because that requirement had "historically been understood . . . to mean physical force or violence."[64]

Cases such as *Rusk, Alston, Kizer,* and *Mlinarich* are not just isolated examples. Many others like them fill the case reports. And broader studies of the way cases were processed in the lower courts and police precincts paint a similar picture. When convictions could be obtained, the appellate courts of the 1980s were somewhat less likely to overturn them. But in the wider universe of rape complaints and rape prosecutions, the reforms of the 1970s had little effect.

One positive result was that police and prosecutors began to treat rape victims more sensitively. And rape-shield laws, despite their loopholes, succeeded in reducing the harassment and humiliation of rape victims at trial.

Unfortunately, when researchers looked closely at individual states and cities, they found that there were few concrete improvements in the actual outcome of rape cases. In California and Washington, studies found that new statutes produced no significant change in reporting by victims, in prosecutors' charging practices, or in conviction rates. The Washington study isolated the factors that determined whether a prosecutor who received a victim's complaint would be willing to file charges. The decisive factors included the evidence of force, the existence of corroboration, the nature of any prior contacts between the victim and the suspect, and the race of the parties.[65] Washington had extensively revised its rules of evidence and its definition of rape. Yet prosecutors felt that exactly the same factors were still necessary to win convictions.

A comprehensive study of six jurisdictions—Georgia, Illinois, Michigan, Pennsylvania, Texas, and Washington, D.C.—confirmed these points. The study found that only Michigan had any improvement in the reporting of rapes, and none of the jurisdictions had an increase in its conviction rates.[66] Most disappointing was the finding that in these places, as in Washington State, reforms had little effect on the way officials evaluated cases. In all six jurisdictions, police, prosecutors, and judges still considered a victim's resistance important, whether or not the new statute had eliminated resistance as a formal requirement.[67] In Michigan, charges were somewhat more likely to be filed in cases of acquaintance rape, but contrary to expectations, the acquaintance-rape cases, once in the system, were taken no more seriously than they had been before: dismissal rates, conviction rates, and sentencing severity were comparable to what they had been prior to reform. The researchers concluded that the impact of reform, in all six jurisdictions, was "minimal."[68]

The meager results of the 1970s effort remind us that law, and especially criminal law, never functions independently of the culture in which it is set. Our sexual culture was changing in the 1970s, but it was not changing as fast as the statutes and the aspirations of their feminist sponsors. It should not have come as a surprise that social attitudes of an earlier era persisted and continued to shape the law in action. One Michigan law enforcement official dismissed the attempt to expand the coverage of rape laws in that state as "messing with the folkways."[69]

For many advocates of reform, the disappointments of the 1970s effort signal that social attitudes are thoroughly controlling. Many feminists, even those trained in law, discount the importance of legal doctrine and direct much of their reform effort toward the battle for cultural change.[70] Yet law itself influences society's view of what sexual abuse is, and the relationships between law and culture are complex. Social attitudes sometimes control legal outcomes, but those attitudes are shaped in turn by legal rules. The place to look for the impact of legal reform, therefore, is not only in cases decided right after a new statute takes effect, but in the attitudes and enforcement patterns that develop years later, as new legal standards gradually come to be taken for granted. The evaluation studies, which typically compared the years immediately following a law's enactment with the years immediately before, give us little picture of this process and no reason to dismiss the long-term potential of legal reform in general.[71] Where the statutes of the 1970s did change legal standards, the impact of the new rules, though hard to measure, is just beginning to be felt.

But the reforms of the 1970s also proved disappointing for reasons rooted in the language of the reform statutes themselves. Despite their many important changes, the 1970s reforms remained tied to the traditional conception of rape as a crime of physical violence. Force was the decisive concept in most of the reformed statutes, but it was seldom defined, and when it was, the terms used implied some form of potentially violent misconduct. The Michigan reform statute, the most ambitious of the period, never mentioned "consent" and did little to stretch the connotations of force beyond those of physical violence. Far from breaking the association of rape with aberrational violence, nearly all the 1970s reforms served to reinforce that perspective. Autonomy—a woman's right to choose the boundaries of her own sexual life—was relegated to the background, as it had been so many times before.

Two states—Washington and Wisconsin—diverged from this pattern by enacting statutes punishing any act of intercourse without "freely given" consent.[72] Unlike the other reforms of the 1970s, these statutes attempted a major shift in focus, to a concern with protecting sexual self-determination, not just physical safety. These more ambitious statutes also had little immediate impact.[73] But neither Washington nor Wisconsin defined the kinds of pressure or coercion that would prevent "freely given" consent. With all other states continuing to insist on proof of physical force, the Washington and Wisconsin reforms probably needed more content and more clarity to get their distinctive message across. In the end, for a complex mix of reasons, none of the legal reforms of the 1970s produced significant improvements for women.

Overrated Changes in the 1980s and 1990s

The past two decades have seen a deluge of writing about rape and other sexual abuses. Feminist critics insist that rape laws—and the culture they reflect—continue to shelter the abusive overreaching of predatory, sexually aggressive men. And feminist demands for change have generated many new laws and court decisions that seem responsive to these concerns. Campus behavior codes have heightened students' awareness of date-rape issues, and courts have interpreted federal law to prohibit sexual harassment in education and in the workplace. Courts now cite feminist critiques with approval, and they regularly announce decisions that seem to extend legal prohibitions and reduce barriers to conviction.

The Violence Against Women Act, passed by Congress in 1994, is a high-visibility example of these trends. The Act adopts a host of provisions to help deter rape and sexual harassment, including funding for rape education in schools and colleges, and grants to improve lighting in parks and subway stations. Among the new measures is a much-touted provision permitting women who are the victims of a sex crime to sue the offender for damages under federal civil rights laws.

Yet there is much less here than meets the eye. Sexual harassment law has heightened awareness of abuses in the workplace, and there are other scattered examples of significant progress. But the seemingly important new statutes and court decisions in fact have quite limited reach.

Civil damage remedies for sexual harassment laws are a prime example. Critics of the rape reform movement often claim that sexual harassment laws go to absurd lengths to protect certain kinds of women, who are portrayed as hypersensitive prudes, cringing at the first raw word or the mildest expression of sexual interest. This picture is based less on actual court decisions than on the most extreme claims attempted in a few especially imaginative lawsuits. It radically misrepresents actual legal standards, which normally require the worker to prove that she indicated clearly and in advance that the sexual comments or propositions were unwelcome.

Even when this hard-to-meet federal standard has been violated, there are enormously important gaps in the available remedies. One major gap in protection results from a legal detail that is almost invariably overlooked. Federal law holds public officials liable for extreme forms of sexual harassment, but in the case of private individuals, federal antidiscrimination law provides a remedy only against *institutions*—the school, university, or business firm as an entity. The institutions are not always liable for the offending actions of their employees, and even when they are, the employee himself—the offending teacher or supervisor—is not liable personally.[74] The sexually predatory teacher or supervisor may (or may not) face a risk of job-related sanctions such as suspension, reassignment, or dismissal. But in any event, the sexual predator usually faces no other punishment for his abusive conduct—so long as he steers clear of coercing sexual compliance by threats of *physical* force.

As one result of these porous civil remedies, working women continue to face high levels of sexual harassment. The federal government, which has conducted comprehensive surveys of its 1.7 million civilian workers since 1980, has found almost no change in either the frequency or seriousness of unwanted sexual attention. In 1980, 42 percent of women in the federal workforce reported that they experienced sexual harassment over the preceding two-year period. The figure remained at 42 percent in a 1987 survey and rose to 44 percent in 1994. The most serious form of harassment, pressure for sexual favors, was reported by 9 percent of women in the 1980 and 1987 surveys and dropped somewhat, to 7 percent, in the 1994 survey. The U.S. Merit Systems Protection Board, the government's personnel agency for civilian workers, concluded in a 1995 report: "The fact that the incidence of unwanted sexual attention has not decreased since the last Government-wide survey is naturally a cause for concern. Despite very widespread training and information efforts that have successfully raised workforce sensitivity to the issues surrounding sexual harassment, the persistence of this amount of unwanted sexual attention in the Federal workplace suggests that the Government's programs to eradicate the problem need some serious reexamination."[75]

There was much celebration among feminists and their supporters when Congress passed the 1994 Violence Against Women Act, which gives women the right to sue their abusers for damages under federal civil rights laws. There was anguished hand-wringing as well. An op-ed piece in the *Wall Street Journal* called the Act an example of "old-fashioned paternalism" and said it would "give an official seal of approval to a radical ideology that sees American women as victims of systematic gender terrorism."[76] Stephanie Gutmann wrote in the *National Review* that the Act was "sexual politics with a vengeance." Patching together quotes from various feminist sources, Gutmann suggested that the Act had gone to what she considered an absurd extreme by "codif[ying] the true nature of rape" as "any sexual intercourse without mutual desire." Gutmann predicted that the Act would shift time and energy "away from prosecuting real offenders for real crimes" toward "endless surreal courtroom struggles."[77]

What most opponents and even many supporters of the new remedy overlooked was its extremely narrow terms. The federal suit can be filed only when the woman has been the victim of a criminal offense that is classified as a felony in the state where the conduct occurs.[78] The result is business as usual: in most instances teachers and supervisors who engage in sexual harassment still face no personal risk of civil or criminal liability.

The Montana high school case illustrates the point. If the school's principal forced one of the seniors to have sex with him by threatening to prevent her from graduating, his act constituted an egregious violation of federal sexual harassment law. The school district presumably could be held liable for damages. But since the principal did not threaten physical force and his seventeen-year-old victim had passed Montana's sixteen-year age of consent, the principal himself faced no liability under federal antidiscrimination law. And he could not be sued under the Violence Against Women Act, because he did not commit forcible rape, statutory rape, or any other crime under Montana law.

Campus behavior codes are another well-worn target of those who believe that rape reforms exceed all sensible bounds and impose absurdly strict regulations. Katie Roiphe's widely discussed book, *The Morning After*, asserted: "According to common definitions of date rape, even verbal coercion or manipulation constitutes rape." Roiphe derided feminists for "promoting the view of women as weak-willed, alabaster bodies, whose virtue must be protected from the cunning encroachments of the outside world." She ridiculed institutions for deploying sanctions to protect "the cowering woman, knocked on her back by the barest feather of peer pressure."[79]

Roiphe's picture is a caricature, of course. The truth is that college codes are usually cautious, vague, ineffective, or all three. And even the strictest college disciplinary codes have had limited impact, in part because colleges operate under great pressure to maintain confidentiality and to avoid inflicting severe sanctions.[80] In any event, antireform critics who imagine a society governed by the protective rules of campus life forget that these rules have limited effect because the great majority of women are not in college.[81] Most women, even the majority of younger women, must manage their sexual interactions (wanted and unwanted) with no protection from the college codes.

Recent reforms in criminal law are easily overestimated as well. Despite the many new statutes and court decisions that respond to feminist concerns, the basic framework of the law of rape—the framework that emerged from the reforms of the 1970s—has proved amazingly durable. Though the sheer volume of new legal materials naturally creates an impression of significant change, in fact there has been no new wave of reform for at least two decades. A brief review is necessary to give a clear picture of what the recent developments have—and have *not*—accomplished.

Most states have at long last reformed their law of marital rape. No state retains the spousal exemption in its original, unqualified form, and fifteen states have abolished the exemption completely. Yet the great majority of the states still retain an exemption for marital rape under some circumstances.[82] In Virginia a 1986 statute overruled the egregious

Kizer decision, in which the court set aside the conviction of a husband who had brutally raped his estranged wife after breaking down the door of her apartment. The new Virginia law permits prosecution for marital rape whether or not the spouses are living apart.[83] But many other states bar prosecution for rape when spouses are living together, no matter how severe the injuries inflicted, and in some of these states, prosecution continues to be barred even for spouses living apart, until one of them obtains a formal decree of legal separation.[84]

In virtually all states, rape and sexual assault laws remain limited to situations of actual or potential physical violence. One state court—in New Jersey—has in effect abandoned the force requirement altogether, and in Pennsylvania, though rape still requires proof of force, the courts no longer insist that "force" must always be physical.[85] But these innovative approaches to sexual assault remain exceptional. Nearly everywhere else, the physical force requirement is still applied strictly.

This is not to say that nineteenth-century conceptions of consent remain completely unchanged. When a man throws a woman to the floor, pins her down, and tears off her clothes, courts today, unlike many in the past, are usually willing to uphold a conviction for rape.[86] Courts seldom insist on physical resistance when a woman has been threatened with a weapon or a punch in the face. Such improvements should not be overlooked, and they are sometimes touted as significant breakthroughs. But judicial decisions relaxing the force requirement remain exceedingly cautious.

Many states, for example, relax the rigorous requirement of explicit physical force when the victim is a young girl sexually abused by her own father.[87] In one New York case, involving a nine-year-old girl, the court said that a father's superior size, age, and authority can be sufficient to meet the requirement of force.[88] But not always! In a later case, in 1990, the New York appellate court reversed a father's conviction for the rape of his daughter. The court's opinion did not bother to detail the facts and gave no indication of the girl's age (except that she was under seventeen). It simply said that "there was no proof that the difference in size between defendant and his daughter created an implied threat of force." The victim had also testified that the defendant threatened her the day after the incident, but the court dismissed this point too, stating that "threats made after the sexual act do not constitute forcible compulsion."[89]

Fathers who exploit their authority and physical strength to abuse their children do not necessarily escape all punishment, because their conduct still qualifies as incest and statutory rape, both crimes that carry potentially severe sanctions. But decisions that define rape restrictively apply even in settings where subsidiary charges like incest and statutory rape are unavailable. When courts find that a father's authority over his child is insufficient coercion for forcible rape, even when the victim is a young girl, the result sends a message that makes convictions doubly difficult to win when the victim is an adult. These signals affect more than just the handful of cases that reach the appellate courts. They have exponential impact on the initial screening process, warning prosecutors, in cases lacking clear evidence of physical force, to settle for lesser charges or to drop complaints altogether.

Ohio's experience shows just what this stringent interpretation of the force requirement means in practice. A 1994 case involved a girl who was only thirteen years old. Laura (not her real name) met Waites at a 4-H gathering, where Waites told Laura and her mother that he was a doctor. When he learned that Laura had a learning disability, Waites offered to test her. On that pretext, he took Laura to his home on several occasions. During these visits, Waites would order Laura to disrobe for a physical examination, and he then subjected her to sexual fondling and, in one instance, fellatio and intercourse. Laura's sister and two other members of Laura's 4-H Club, all between the ages of twelve and fifteen, had similar experiences with "Doctor" Waites.

At Waites's trial the prosecution relied heavily on Ohio cases holding that a father can be convicted of raping his minor child when the force he uses is "subtle and psychological."[90] Waites was convicted on numerous counts of rape, corruption of a minor, and related charges. Because the victims were all under Ohio's sixteen-year age of consent, Waites's convictions for corruption of minors (an offense which carries a normal maximum sentence of eighteen months' imprisonment)[91] held up on appeal. But the Ohio court of appeals set aside his convictions for rape and all the other charges based on his alleged use of "force." The court said that Ohio's flexible test for force did not apply because Waites was not the girls' father. "Obviously," the court wrote, "appellant's conduct was deceitful and reprehensible; however, unlike [a situation involving] a parent, there was no implicit threat of punishment for not complying."[92] The court's 1994 decision stays remarkably close to the traditional doctrines of forty years earlier. Criminal law safeguards remain limited almost exclusively to protecting women from force, and "force" still means direct physical violence, something more than the "ordinary" physical aggressiveness that is considered a normal aspect of the male sexual role.

Disappointing results such as these have convinced large numbers of antirape activists of the need for new and far more ambitious reforms. Feminist writers supply wide-ranging criticisms of existing law and a steady stream of ideas for reshaping the culture that supports aggressive, predatory male sexuality. But questions of tactics and even of basic goals evoke sharp disagreement. Which legal reforms hold any hope of breaking the tenacious hold of traditional concepts of force and consent? Which practical steps, if any, will ever change the thinking and behavior of the many individuals—police, prosecutors, judges, and jurors—who determine the legal system's day-to-day output? Antirape activists agree on the inadequacy of the status quo, but when it comes to designing specific steps to move forward, there are few concrete proposals and little consensus.

Outside the circle of committed feminists, the disagreements are even more basic. Controversy persists over the boundaries of decent behavior and the need for society to enforce norms of decent behavior by law. The search for solutions is a search not only for workable legal tools but also for an understanding of the character and potential abuses of sexuality itself.

3

Fear and Desire

Writes feminist scholar Elizabeth Stanko: "To be a woman—in most societies, in most eras—is to experience physical and/or sexual terrorism at the hands of men . . . We are wary of going out at night, even in our own neighborhoods. We are warned . . . not to trust strangers. But . . . [m]any men familiar to us also terrorize our everyday lives in our homes, our schools, our workplaces."[1]

Says Joe, a nineteen-year-old college freshman: "If I'm on a date and a girl's dressing sexy and acting sexy, why doesn't she want to have sex? . . . The women who say they feel humiliated when a guy whistles at them: deep down, they really like it, it's boosting their egos."[2]

April, a young woman raped by a recent acquaintance: "The penetration was very violent. [He pushed me onto the floor, slammed me headfirst into a corner, and we struggled until he raped me.] When it was all over, he asked me if I usually fight so much during sex. I don't think it ever occurred to him that he had raped me."[3]

Sam, an eighteen-year-old college freshman: "I used a little bit of force once where I overpowered a woman. She didn't mind it after it was over. If she'd started crying or something I would've stopped."[4]

Legal scholar Lynne Henderson: "I was asleep in my bed, when I awoke to find a man on top of me . . . His fist hit my face repeatedly . . . I left my body but I didn't . . . Three weeks after the assault, and only one week after the cast was taken off my nose, [the man I was dating] said irritably, 'Why are you still so angry?'"[5]

Joe again: "There has to be some point in every rape where the woman relaxes and enjoys it. I'm not saying that ladies *want* to be raped *because* they enjoy it, but there has to be some point where they enjoy it, because it's enjoyable. Sex is enjoyable."[6]

Law professor Robin West: "Women are taught early in life . . . to look for protection against dangerous men from relatively safe men . . . to be accompanied by a man, through marriage, in life, and in the home, is the 'best way' to avoid more dangerous and damaging forms of sexual assault . . . the sex in such a relationship is damaging to the woman; it diminishes her sense of self, her sense of autonomy, her sense of sovereignty over her body."[7]

Stan, a single man in his mid-thirties: "Women knew when I was attracted to them . . . I definitely felt played with, used, manipulated, like women were testing their power over me. I hated it with a passion! . . . I wanted to slam someone's head up against a wall."[8]

Mike, a thirty-year-old writer: "The available alternatives are to be strong, aggressive, and inconsiderate and do well with women, or to be weak, considerate, and a eunuch. It's almost as if to be powerful, you have to be insensitive. You're forced to be aggressive even though you don't want to be."[9]

Is there any hope of finding common ground? Men and women talk past each other, often finding each other's views incomprehensible or outrageous. Each can claim allies from the opposite sex, but differences of opinion between men and women are especially sharp. Some see novelty and adventure where others see danger and a risk of death. Some see sexual desire where others see reluctance, emotional alienation, unwillingness, or fear. One person's idea of sexual pleasure is another person's nightmare. For some, fear and desire are intertwined.

When citizens hold widely divergent views, law often declines to intervene. Criminal sanctions are normally reserved for conduct that deviates sharply from accepted social norms, demonstrating serious moral fault and inflicting grievous injury on others. Rape law reforms have proceeded cautiously, in part because there is no clear social consensus about when it is fair to condemn a man for making aggressive sexual advances. And when law does take a stand, it usually sidesteps the social disagreements. The law requires "consent," it prohibits "force," and it affords protection when a woman's fears of physical harm are "reasonable." But the law says little or nothing to resolve the persistent and intense disputes about what "consent," "force," and "reasonable" fears are.

Many believe that there is no alternative. The law relies on requirements of reasonableness all the time. Despite their inherent imprecision, reasonableness requirements usually are good ways to reflect community expectations about proper behavior when factual nuances are important. But sexual dynamics pose unique problems that drain a reasonableness standard of much of its content. Part of the reason that the law of sexual abuse works poorly is the wide range—and politically controversial character—of the disagreements about "facts" that the law makes decisive.

Fear and intimidation are important examples. Physically assertive conduct that seems alluring to one woman may seem terrifying to another. Darkness and isolation feel intimidating to many women but not to all. And these differences among women are minor in comparison to the contrasts between the perceptions of women and those of men.

Nearly everyone feels nervous sometimes when walking alone after dark, and men often think that women's fears are not "special," because men too are afraid of being robbed or assaulted. But the gap between the attitudes of the sexes is enormous. When men and women in the twenty-six largest American cities were asked whether they felt safe in their own neighborhoods at night, 68 percent of the men but only 39 percent of the women said that they felt reasonably safe. Only 12 percent of the men but 33 percent of the women said they felt "very unsafe."[10]

Differing levels of fear produce sharp contrasts in behavior. Some are predictable. One study found that 68 percent of women but only 5 percent of men say that they won't go to bars or clubs alone after dark. Other differences are more surprising: 47 percent of women but only 8 percent of men say that they never go downtown alone after dark, 25 percent of women but only 3 percent of men never walk alone in their own neighborhoods after dark, and 75 percent of women but only 32 percent of men refuse to go to movies alone after dark. More than 80 percent of women report that they sometimes drive rather than walk because of fear of being harmed and sometimes go somewhere with a friend just for protection; most men report that they "never" take these kinds of precautions.[11]

It is not surprising that women on the whole feel more vulnerable in certain situations than men do. Everyone faces the risk of robbery, but outside of prisons, men seldom face the additional risk of sexual assault.

Unfortunately, men often fail to see why women feel threatened or vulnerable in situations that are not threatening to men. As Robin West notes, "the claim that women's lives are ruled by fear is heard by these men as wildly implausible. They see no evidence in their own lives to support it."[12]

Many men assume that sexual overtures—such as whistling, touching, commenting on a woman's body, or standing unusually close—are flattering to a woman or just "part of life." They cannot understand why a woman receiving such "compliments" should fear an impending physical attack. Often they have no clue that women are upset by such behavior, or they dismiss fearful reactions by some women as simply paranoid. Yet, as West writes, "Street hassling is not trivial . . . It makes [us] feel sexually ridiculous, exposed, dirty, vulgar, vulnerable and afraid."[13] And the problem of clashing perceptions extends well beyond men's and women's differing reactions to "wolf whistles" and sexual comments. Men often assume that many of the ways in which they use actual force—lifting a woman off her feet or pulling at her clothes—are flattering expressions of their passion. But many women interpret the same actions as preludes to a violent assault.

A woman who is a target of these physical advances often experiences conflicting emotions. Elizabeth Stanko notes that women are taught to regard many common forms of male behavior—the male professor's sexual advance toward a student, the "wolf whistle" on the street, or the man's brushing up against a female secretary's body in the Xerox room—as "natural expressions of maleness." Many women assume that they should regard these kinds of conduct as nonthreatening or even flattering. Nonetheless, Stanko notes, "Often women themselves are confused—sometimes defining male behaviour as typical, other times as aberrant—but nonetheless feel[ing] threatened by displays of either . . . Confusing though they may be, women's experiences point to a potential for violence in many of women's ordinary encounters with men."[14]

One result of these perceptions is a "gender gap," with men tending to differ from women in the kinds of things they fear, and in their assessments of when another person's fears are "reasonable." It is probably futile to try to determine whether Stanko is "right" to feel as she does, or whether the contrasting perceptions of Camille Paglia are more valid. Interestingly, Paglia herself seems to agree that women face pervasive danger; for Paglia, however, the dangers are not simply frightening but "sexy" and fun: "The minute you go out with a man, the minute you go to a bar, there is a risk . . . part of the sizzle of sex comes from the danger of sex . . . I think it's a very exciting kind of sex. But you have to realize you are risking injury and not just rape but *death* . . . I'm encouraging women: *accept* the adventure of sex, *accept* the danger!"[15]

Paglia's iconoclastic views seem plausible to some, simply wacky to many others. Either way, the very existence of strongly held but sharply contrasting beliefs, even among women, makes clear that few problems in rape enforcement can be solved by relying on judgments about reasonableness. It is simply not possible, in the present state of American sexual relationships, to have an objective standard of "reasonable" conduct.[16]

Legal standards that prohibit men from using "force" or exploiting a woman's "reasonable" fears tend to minimize these clashes of social perception. They imply that any differences of opinion are simply the result of disagreements about the statistical probability of harm. Yet the underlying disputes are not just empirical but social and political, rooted in sharply clashing perceptions of how sexuality should be experienced and expressed.

For many, the controversial character of the disputes only reinforces the reasons for law not to choose sides. But law cannot avoid taking sides by opting for vague or abstract standards like "force" and "reasonableness." Vague standards tend to keep difficult, contentious issues hidden, but the issues are inevitably resolved, one way or the other, every day. What vague standards do is to leave contested issues to be settled in an unforeseeable, ad hoc manner by whichever police officers, prosecutors, or jurors decide whether to file charges or impose sanctions in a particular case. And this ad hoc approach has a built-in tilt, especially in criminal law enforcement. When standards are debatable and expectations have not been communicated in advance, the law ordinarily resolves doubts—and it should resolve doubts—in favor of the accused.

The upshot is that the prevailing legal approach to issues of force and intimidation is not a neutral or costless solution. Rather, the prevailing approach represents a particular way of taking sides, one that gives primacy to male claims for sexual freedom and protection from criminal conviction without fair warning. Those who believe that this is the right approach (or the least bad alternative) can fairly be asked to defend it on its merits, with full recognition of its impact on women who feel the coercive effects of aggressive male sexuality.

Coercion and Desire

Clashing perceptions of coercion don't result solely from differing views about physical danger. Women sometimes submit to sexual encounters because of subtle mixtures of physical intimidation, unstated threats, psychological demands, and the pressures of male status and authority. Yet on this problem the law, especially criminal law, does not equivocate or refuse to take sides. The man's behavior is considered criminal only when he threatens to inflict *physical* injury. Other types of pressure are seen as perfectly consistent with valid "consent." Yet for many women, consent that results from nonviolent pressure is anything but freely chosen, healthy, or legitimate.

Feminist critics of existing legal and social standards insist that "force" includes not only physical violence but other forms of power. "For women to be truly free and autonomous," argue psychologists Charlene Muehlenhard and Jennifer Schrag, "we must be free of all forms of coercion." Unacceptable coercion, they insist, can be economic, as when women "have to choose between either submitting to unwanted sexual advances or losing their jobs," and when "economic need [pressures] women into marriage [or] to remain in unhappy marriages." Free choice, they argue, can also be defeated by "status coercion," as when women submit to sex to maintain a relationship with a man of high social standing. And they likewise condemn "verbal sexual coercion," cases in which women submit to unwanted sex because "they had been overwhelmed by a man's continual arguments and pressure" or because of emotional appeals—"threatening to end the relationship [or] telling a woman that her refusal to have sex was changing the way [he] felt about her."[17]

As Muehlenhard and Schrag make clear, nonviolent coercion covers a wide territory. We all face pressures and constraints on our choices every day. If any disparity of economic or social power is sufficient to

establish coercion, then unacceptable force is pervasive in sexual relationships and in all human affairs. Truly voluntary consent, as Muehlenhard and Schrag conceive it, exists for none of us in this lifetime. If we
take the step from defining force as physical violence to a view that
includes all other forms of power and pressure, if casual sex and even
marriage are considered involuntary when induced by a partner's financial status or social prestige, how much room is left for sexual relationships that are legally or morally acceptable?

Many intimate relationships are founded on mutuality of attraction
between social equals. But the claim that coercion results from any
difference in status or power has the jarring effect of suggesting that all
other sexual relationships are morally tainted. And the implications do
not stop there. For feminists who see our society as thoroughly dominated by the overt power and subtle cultural controls of "patriarchy," a
woman is *never* the social equal of a man. The argument that inequality
of any sort involves coercion leads in short order to the conclusion that
virtually all heterosexual sex is coercive.

Many widely known feminists openly embrace this radical conclusion. Catharine MacKinnon argues throughout her work that men's
domination of social life pervasively constrains women's choices and
conditions them to acquiesce in male advances. Describing a world in
which "desirability to men is supposed a woman's form of power"
MacKinnon writes that this "so-called power presupposes more fundamental social powerlessness." The law of statutory rape is, for MacKinnon, a telling illustration of the point:

> The age line under which girls are presumed disabled from con-
> senting to sex, whatever they say, rationalizes a condition of sexual
> coercion which women never outgrow. One day they cannot say
> yes, and the next day they cannot say no. The law . . . by formally
> prohibiting all [underage] sex as rape, makes consent irrelevant on
> the basis of an assumption of powerlessness. This defines those
> above the age line as powerful, whether they actually have power
> to consent or not.[18]

The law's implicit assumption—that adult women have the power to
refuse sex—is, for MacKinnon, fundamentally flawed:

women are socialized to passive receptivity; may have or perceive
no alternative to acquiescence; may prefer it to the escalated risk
of injury and the humiliation of a lost fight; submit to survive.
Also, force and desire are not mutually exclusive under male su-
premacy. So long as dominance is eroticized, they never will be . .
. When sex is violent, women may have lost control over what is
done to them, but absence of force does not ensure the presence
of that control . . . If sex is normally something men do to women,
the issue is less whether there was force than whether consent is a
meaningful concept.[19]

In effect, MacKinnon suggests, the search for a line separating permissible from abusive encounters is naive. "Rape," she writes, "is
defined as distinct from intercourse, while for women it is difficult to
distinguish the two under conditions of male dominance."[20]

In this leading strand of feminist thought, consent can seem coerced
even when a woman *initiates* a sexual encounter, believing that she
desires emotional intimacy and gratification with her male partner. In a
famous essay, poet Adrienne Rich argues that "women's choice of
women as passionate comrades, life partners, co-workers, lovers, tribe,
has been crushed, invalidated, forced into hiding and disguise," with the
result that contemporary society has created a "compulsory heterosexual orientation for women."[21] For Andrea Dworkin, heterosexual intercourse always "occurs in a context of a power relation that is pervasive
and incontrovertible." She writes:

men have social, economic, political, and physical power over
women. Some men do not have all those kinds of power over
all women; but all men have some kinds of power over all women;
and most men have controlling power over what they call *their*
women . . . The power is predetermined by gender, by being male
. . . This may be because intercourse itself is immune to reform
. . . Intercourse remains a means or the means of physiologically
making a woman inferior.[22]

The claim that social conditions distort women's sexual preferences
and inherently coerce their consent to sex has a truly radical sound. Yet
the Dworkin-MacKinnon-Rich claims have roots in mainstream philo-

sophical concerns that predate modern feminism by more than a century. John Stuart Mill, writing in 1869, put the problem in terms strikingly similar to MacKinnon's:

> All men, except the most brutish, desire to have, in the woman most nearly connected with them, not a forced slave but a willing one . . . and they [turn] the whole force of education to effect their purpose. All women are brought up from the very earliest years in the belief that their ideal of character is the very opposite to that of men . . . All the moralities tell them that it is the duty of women, [and] their nature, to live for others; to make complete abnegation of themselves . . .
>
> When we put together three things—first, the natural attraction between opposite sexes; secondly, the wife's entire dependence on the husband, every privilege or pleasure she has being either his gift, or depending on his will; and lastly, that . . . all objects of social ambition can in general be sought or obtained by her only through him, it would be a miracle if the object of being attractive to men had not become the polar star of feminine education and formation of character. And, this great means of influence over the minds of women having been acquired, an instinct of selfishness made men avail themselves of it to the utmost as a means of holding women in subjection, by representing to them meekness, submissiveness, and resignation of all individual will into the hands of a man, as an essential part of sexual attractiveness.[23]

Perspectives like these still ring true for many women today, as the wide impact of MacKinnon's work attests. And even those who consider her claims of present-day coercion exaggerated must acknowledge her basic point: culture, education, and social pressures unquestionably influence our values, our priorities, and the kinds of things we want.[24] And external forces can make us reluctantly forgo what we want; in this respect economic, social, and psychological power bears important similarities to physical duress.

The large problem in the work of MacKinnon, Dworkin, and Rich is not that their views about the importance of social power are false. Rather, the problem is that these views draw no distinctions, accept no boundaries, and thus seem not to acknowledge the possibility of genuinely acceptable forms of sexual intimacy between men and women. When Mill wrote, women's subordination to men was an un-qualified fact of formal legal and political disabilities, absence of the vote, the outright denial of higher education, and insuperable barriers to entry into middle-class occupations and the professions. In ques-tioning whether the preferences and sexual desires women held under these conditions were truly their own, Mill could speak with no ex-aggeration of "the wife's entire dependency on the husband, every privilege or pleasure she has being either his gift, or depending on his will."[25]

Vestiges of those conditions remain with us, but the world has changed. We can no longer be so certain that women's desires and choices are inauthentic. We cannot simply dismiss as "false conscious-ness" the perceptions of women themselves.[26] And for many women, sweeping attacks on the possibility of uncoerced sex between men and women in today's world are greatly overdrawn; they misdescribe far too much of women's own experiences. Lynne Henderson, a leading femi-nist scholar and committed rape reformer, finds "MacKinnon's denigra-tion of women's ability to tell the difference between sex and rape" oversimplified and implausible.[27]

MacKinnon's far-reaching claims about cultural pressure have opened many eyes to the multiple constraints on women's freedom to make independent sexual choices. At the same time, by collapsing the distinctions *between* kinds of social pressure, feminism of this sort doesn't advance the effort to draw workable legal lines. Sometimes this strand of feminism even seems to impede the legal reform effort, because it tends to obliterate differences between the kinds of pressure that society will inevitably tolerate and the kinds that it might plausibly forbid.

In their work on sexual coercion, writers such as Dworkin, Mac-Kinnon, and Rich focus not on legal reform but rather on a broader moral critique of sexual interaction. But even in those more general terms, their theories combine insight with confusion. Far-reaching claims about cultural constraint make it more difficult to see morally important *differences* between various sorts of coercion. A woman who submits to unwanted sex in order to avoid losing her job normally undergoes a degrading and psychologically injurious experience. In its emotional as well as its sensual and erotic content, the encounter will feel altogether different from ones she would have in an intimate relationship that she initiates and pursues because of a strong sexual attraction. The differences are profound, even when the sexual attraction arises in part because of her confidence that the man is committed to caring for her financially and emotionally. A feminism that de-emphasizes these sorts of differences springs from legitimate concerns, but it doesn't help—and may even impede—necessary efforts to understand the effects of sexual behavior and to make appropriate social judgments.

This strand of feminism also tends to obscure the moral responsibility of individuals. Sometimes it makes sense to hold a man accountable for conditions he played no part in creating. A man is responsible for having sex "without consent" when he knowingly has intercourse with an underage girl, even though he is not the cause of her incapacity. But it is far from clear that we should criticize a man who maintains a lasting relationship with a woman whose emotional bond to him is, as he knows, founded partly on his commitment to providing a stable, financially secure home for the two of them and their children. Much less is it plausible to criticize a man for marrying a woman whose heterosexual orientation is the result of cultural influence. By minimizing and sometimes disparaging distinctions that are morally crucial, the most far-reaching feminist claims sometimes conceal as much as they clarify.

Radicalism of this sort is well intentioned but stultifying. The refusal of some leading theorists to draw moral distinctions among the many forms of pressure women face maintains a certain purism for these feminist projects, but it vastly oversimplifies the psychology of sexual desire.[28] And it oversimplifies the give-and-take of social power in a complex, imperfect, but not uniformly oppressive society. What is worse, the impatience with efforts to reposition legal boundaries offers sympathy but little hope for the many women who experience abuses that existing law does not effectively prevent or even attempt to reach.

These broad conceptions of coercion nonetheless raise serious concerns that need to be confronted, not disparaged or dismissed. Yet, outside the circles of feminist theory, sympathetic criticism is rare. Instead, the Dworkin-MacKinnon-Rich perspective has been widely ridiculed, misrepresented, and misunderstood. One result has been a potent cultural backlash. Katie Roiphe spoke for many women when she wrote: "The idea that women can't withstand verbal or emotional pressure infantilizes them . . . We should not nurture this woman on her back, her will so mutable, so easily shaped . . . Whether or not we feel pressured, regardless of our level of self-esteem, the responsibility for our actions is still our own."[29]

Roiphe's critique struck a responsive chord precisely because feminist claims about nonviolent coercion sometimes seem wildly overbroad. In view of MacKinnon's attack on the age-of-consent boundary for statutory rape and her claim that male-dominated society creates "a condition of sexual coercion which women never outgrow,"[30] the charge that feminist claims sometimes appear to "infantilize" women is not entirely invented. Yet Roiphe's insistence that women "take responsibility" easily leads to trivializing not only emotional and cultural pressure but all the other kinds of nonviolent coercion that women confront.

In the angry reaction that Roiphe's writing epitomizes, the minimal safeguards of existing law, tarred by association, begin to seem *over*protective and "infantilizing," while egregious gaps in protection against sexual abuse simply disappear from view. Roiphe juxtaposes quotations from the most sweeping feminist definitions of rape with her own loose comments on the reach of current law, as if the legal and radical feminist standards were identical. To explain existing criminal law requirements, Roiphe quotes a disappointed defense attorney who complained, after losing a rape appeal, that under current legal standards, "You not only have to bring a condom on a date, you have to bring a consent form as well."[31] In this picture of the world, feminist claims that rape law needs to be stricter are easily made to appear ludicrous, if not paranoid.

This dismissive reaction to feminist concerns likewise infects the details of day-to-day decisions in the local courthouses and police precincts where rape law's actual content is determined. Insistence that women "take responsibility" slides quickly into blaming the victim who did not—and exonerating the man who took advantage of an intimidating situation. The strongest and most far-reaching feminist claims often succeed in raising consciousness, energizing women, and promoting more vigorous enforcement. But at the same time, opponents of reform exploit these claims to fuel backlash attitudes that undermine enforcement.

In the face of these radical disagreements about what coercion is, law has taken the narrowest view. Acquiescence and "reluctant submission"[32] are equated with sexual desire and valid consent, unless submission was compelled by threats of violence. With isolated exceptions, the law ignores the power relationships and cultural forces that influence the shape of sexual desire, and it largely ignores all the other forms of nonviolent coercion—even those that impel women to submit reluctantly to psychologically damaging encounters that they themselves know they don't want. What is needed is what few protagonists in the cultural battles supply—a way to identify the kinds of sexual pressure that should be left unregulated and the kinds that can justifiably be outlawed or restrained by law.

Knowing Consent When We See It

Intercourse often "happens" after voluntary hugging, kissing, and sexual touching, without coercive threats but also without either of the parties ever saying, "Yes, let's agree to have sex now." In one of the most frequent scenarios, the woman remains silent and relatively passive; she may even push the man's hands away several times or say "No, don't." The law requires "consent," but it doesn't say what consent is.

For many, the often-heard feminist view—that "no" means NO!—now seems obvious and uninteresting. In fact it is neither. By repeating the mantra that "no means no," antirape activists have sensitized many men and made some progress in changing assumptions about how women express interest in sex. But beneath the surface, in the messy, emotionally ambiguous real world of dating, petting, and sexual exploration, "no" *doesn't* always mean no. Just as individuals differ sharply in their perceptions of physical danger and the "reasonableness" of a woman's fears, individuals make sharply differing assumptions about when a woman's conduct signals her consent.

The most obvious problem is that "no" doesn't mean no to a great many men. When a man says he thought "no" really meant yes, he may simply be lying. If not, he may be dense, self-deluded, or driven by wishful thinking. These are the men to whom the emphatic warning—"no means no"—is addressed. It's high time that these men "get it."

But there is much more to the question of what men should hear when a woman says "no." Many women have become comfortable taking the initiative in dating situations and are now willing to express sexual interest directly. Yet it remains true, even in the 1990s, that men are ordinarily expected to make the first (and most subsequent) moves.[33] When men take the initiative, many women still respond by giving oblique or contradictory signals. Men know this and interpret a woman's "no" accordingly. At Indiana University a male undergradu-ate, who apparently considered himself enlightened, announced proudly to his sociology class that he had a "three-no rule." He thought he was being sensitive and modern because he was willing to desist after a date's third protest, but he saw nothing wrong with disregarding her "no" the first two times.[34]

Attitudes like these do not form in a vacuum. They are influenced not only by what men see on television or hear from one another in the locker room, but also by the mixed signals they sometimes get from women they date. Recent studies find that even in the 1990s, most women indicate sexual interest by using subtle and extremely indirect cues.[35] Many say that they express their desire for sex by offering the man a glass of wine or suggesting that they dance. Many will indicate sexual interest verbally, but only *indirectly:* by having a good conversation but keeping the conversation focused on nonsexual topics. In one survey, less than 20 percent of the women were willing to indicate sexual interest by talking about a sexual or romantic subject or by mentioning their desire for sex directly (as in "I'd love to stay with you tonight").[36] Almost 30 percent of the women said they would do *nothing* to indicate their sexual interest and would rely entirely on male initiative or just the "natural" course of events.

In a 1994 survey at the University of Michigan, women acknow-ledged that the "most effective" way to signal sexual interest was to talk directly about sex, guide her partner's hands to her genital area, or start undressing. Yet the women seldom used these methods. Instead, what they actually did, when they wanted to have sex, was to dress well, laugh easily, act interested in what the man said, or sit close to him. Apparently, the Michigan researchers noted, direct communication is "much more costly for women than for men," because even today women still must "go to great pains to avoid being labeled promiscuous." And because men are expected to take the initiative, women who desire sex wait for men to make the advance: "women often need to do nothing to promote a sexual encounter. Simply existing in time and space and being naked under their clothes is often enough to trigger approach attempts by men."[37]

Despite recent changes in the dynamics of sexual courtship, two basic ground rules remain much the same as they were in the 1950s, especially when a couple has not previously had sex together. In all matters physical, the man normally takes the initiative. And when the woman wants intercourse, she normally does not say so explicitly.

The ground rules do not require women who want intercourse to respond to a man's initiative by saying "no." Women who are hoping for their date to make the move need not pretend to reject it when it happens. And men presumably should be able to distinguish between women who respond warmly to a sexual initiative and those who say "no." But the ground rules assume that men should be persistent in the face of a woman's passivity or reluctance.

The dynamic of male persistence gets reinforced by a culture that still considers it sexy for a reluctant woman to be overborne by a virile, aggressive man. As Cornell's Andrea Parrott notes, "Men overriding women's protests to win their adoration—even after raping them—is a recurring theme in movies and television."[38] Stories of male persistence overcoming female passivity and reluctance are presented as erotic, not only in male-oriented pornography but also in the Harlequin romances (popularly known as "bodice-rippers") that are widely read by a largely female audience.[39]

Messages of this sort shape the attitudes of both men and women. In one rape case, the victim's claims were corroborated by hospital records detailing her physical injuries. Nonetheless, a *female* juror wasn't persuaded; in her view, "Abrasion of the vagina still doesn't mean rape—she might want that force."[40] In many segments of society, women as well as men consider it normal for a man to make persistent sexual advances despite a woman's attempts to rebuff him. Novels and films reflect and reinforce these attitudes by favorable portrayals of men who ignore and overcome a woman's objections to sexual inter-action.[41]

Complaints that cultural messages legitimate male dominance and aggression are such a staple of feminist antirape literature that skeptics may be tempted to dismiss them as the tired refrain of a few narrow ideologues. But the basic point is simple and should not be considered the least bit controversial. As the empirical studies repeatedly show, some aggression remains an expected part of the male role in sexual encounters.[42]

One result of these cultural messages is a gender gap in sexual communication. As Robin Weiner explains:

> Men and women frequently misinterpret the intent of various dating behaviors and erotic play . . . A woman may believe she has communicated her unwillingness to have sex—and other women would agree, thus making it a "reasonable" female expression. Her male partner might still believe she is willing—and other men would agree with his interpretation, thus making it a "reasonable" male interpretation. The woman, who believes that she has con-veyed her lack of consent, may interpret the man's persistence as an indication that he does not care if she objects and plans to have sex despite her lack of consent. She may then feel frightened by the man's persistence, and may submit against her will.[43]

The best available study of American sexual attitudes provides chill-ing evidence confirming the problem. The survey, conducted in 1992, found that 22 percent of American women felt they had been forced to have sex, almost always by a husband, boyfriend, or close acquaintance, yet only 3 percent of American men said they had ever forced a woman to have sex. After discounting the possibility that the men or women had lied, or that a few men were responsible for forcing many different women, the researchers concluded that most of the men simply did not realize that their sexual partners were unwilling. The researchers noted: "There seems to be not just a gender gap but a gender chasm in perceptions of when sex was forced."[44]

In the struggle to protect women from frightening and abusive male behavior, the "gender chasm" in sexual communication creates a huge pitfall. In the face of two plausible interpretations of what a woman really meant in a sexual encounter, did she or did she not consent? Depending on one's perspective, the scenario Weiner describes could be considered rape, or it could be considered just an ordinary, permissible sexual courtship.

It might seem too obvious for discussion that consent means consent in the mind of the person who is supposed to be giving it—in this case, the woman. But in a criminal case, the court must decide whether the defendant is at fault. That question—at least as typically posed—returns attention to the *man*'s perspective. The issue for the jury becomes: Are they persuaded, beyond a reasonable doubt, that the man knew the woman hadn't consented? The question that should be control-ling—what did the woman herself mean?—gets transformed into a question about what *he thought* she meant.

The law has one tool it can use to control the self-absorbed individual who doesn't stop to consider the wishes of others. The law can (and sometimes does) impose liability—even criminal liability—when the individual's beliefs are unreasonable. But perceptions of consent are much like perceptions of physical danger: social attitudes remain so divergent that a "reasonableness" standard answers few questions.

The core of the problem in assessing consent is not the exceptionally insensitive man who thinks a woman's "no" really means she is burning with desire for him. What makes the gender gap troublesome is that widely shared assumptions often make it "reasonable" for him to think this. A reasonableness standard gives no content to the requirement of consent and simply allows all the difficult, culturally contentious issues to be resolved case by case, behind closed doors, by police, prosecutors, and juries.

An alternative approach would be to focus on the meaning of "no" to the person who is supposedly giving consent—the woman herself. Here, however, we bump up against some inconvenient facts about sexual communication.

What do women themselves mean by "no"? Antirape activists often assume that the problems of determining "consent" start and end with the radical difference between the ways that men and women under-stand language. For Weiner, MacKinnon, and many others, a woman who says "no" means "Stop!! Now!!" But men are not the only ones who believe that "no" can mean yes. Women sometimes share that vocabulary themselves. The gender gap—though it undoubtedly exists—is far from clear-cut and uniform.

Some antirape activists are tempted to overlook this detail, but effective reform depends on facing it squarely. Feminism has not abolished social taboos and personal ambivalence. Even in the liberated and crudely explicit world of the 1990s, societal pressure and individual psychology continue to complicate the expression of sexual desire. Many women still say "no" when they want to express a more complex feeling—or the opposite intention entirely. Recent studies consistently find that 35–40 percent of women sometimes say "no" when in fact they were willing.[45]

What the future may hold in this regard is anyone's guess. The trend toward more open expression and the decline of the "double standard" are strong. But it is very safe to assume that inhibition, shyness, and indirection in sexual communication will not disappear from human relationships anytime soon. The uncomfortable truth, especially uncomfortable for those who are committed to rape reform, is that the "no means no" claim isn't uniformly true—*even for women.*

The reasons are revealing. Surveys find that fear of appearing promiscuous, the supposedly outmoded "double standard," still motivates women to say "no" when they mean yes. More surprising is the importance of what researchers Charlene Muehlenhard and Lisa Hollabaugh label "manipulative" reasons. Forty-eight percent of the women in their study said that wanting to be more in control was an important reason for saying "no" when they meant yes. Twenty-three percent said an important reason was some form of "game playing," such as wanting the man "to beg," wanting him "to talk me into it," wanting "to get him more sexually aroused by making him wait," and—most disturbingly—"wanting him to be more physically aggressive." All told, 87 percent of the women who said "no" but meant yes gave "manipulative" reasons for doing so. Many of them viewed male-female relationships as "adversarial," agreed that it was "acceptable for men to use physical force in male-female relationships," or said that "women enjoy it when men use force in sexual relationships."[46]

Because "no" doesn't always mean no, even for women, we have to add several more items to our list of inconvenient facts. One is that a man who takes seriously the woman's perspective can *sometimes,* in *some* settings, interpret "no" as "keep going," or "try harder," or even "get physical." A man who always translates "no" to mean yes will usually be wrong. But sometimes, in some settings, his mistake will be understandable, even from the perspective of his date and other women like her. And sometimes, in some settings, his attempt to read her intentions will be exactly right.

That point leads to still another inconvenient truth: mistakes—including reasonable mistakes—are not impossible or even rare. Sexual communication is so often indirect and contradictory that it is a wonder mistakes do not occur more often. What seems certain is that miscommunication about sexual desires is entirely commonplace. If we consider actual behavior of real people in our world as it stands, mistakes about consent, including mistakes about the meaning of "no," are undoubtedly frequent. And *sometimes*, in *some* settings, those mistakes will be "reasonable," even from the perspective of many women.

Several feminist scholars and antirape activists acknowledge this uncomfortable fact. Social psychologist Antonia Abbey notes that in light of some women's continuing practice of saying "no" when they hope to have intercourse, "It is easy to see how a man who has previously turned a 'no' into a 'yes' might force sexual intercourse on a date who says 'no' and means it."[47] Muehlenhard and Hollabaugh conclude their study by stressing that the patterns they observed "encourage men to ignore women's refusals. If a man encounters a woman who says no and he ignores her protests and finds that she is indeed willing to engage in sex, his belief that women's refusals are not to be taken seriously will be strengthened."[48]

Some supporters of rape reform prefer to set aside these empirical findings. They probably fear that evidence of this sort will only reinforce society's willingness to tolerate male behavior that poses enormous risks for women. But sexual ambivalence and miscommunication, though they undoubtedly exist, do not automatically justify permissive legal standards. They need not dictate impunity for men who ignore a woman's verbal protests. On the contrary, it is precisely because of these stubborn facts that legal requirements such as "consent" and "reasonableness" solve so few of the difficulties.

Interestingly, many antirape activists and their harshest critics are united in disparaging legal solutions to the consent problem. Camille

Paglia has gained wide attention by challenging antirape reformers to face up to the messy facts of confused and conflicted sexual exploration. She writes as if ambivalence, miscommunication, and the undercurrents of force in some consensual sex must lead inexorably to a hands-off attitude for law. She posits that "we can never fully legislate the human psyche," and insists that "in the absence of physical violence, sexual conduct cannot and must not be legislated from above."[49]

But it's an odd idea—that messy facts, misunderstanding, danger, and psychic injury in recurrent human interactions are a reason to do nothing. On the contrary. It is just because of these messy facts that there is a need for clarification and for law, a need that requirements of "consent" and "reasonableness" scarcely address.

The messy facts of a no-means-yes culture spell danger for women. One sex researcher, writing primarily for a male audience, makes the problem clear. His subject is not rape or the feelings of women, but rather the anxieties that *men* have in handling the complexities of sexual communication:

> The problem for the man is how to differentiate between sincere rejections and requests on the one hand, and those that are ambivalent or merely facades on the other hand. Since the task is difficult and since the risks [to his self-esteem and sense of virility] in backing off when the rejection is not real are so grave, many men simply give up trying to make the distinction and forge ahead regardless of what the woman says.[50]

Men who "simply give up trying to make the distinction" are not close to being reasonable, of course. But when we assume that the interpretation of a woman's real preferences depends on verbal nuances, body language, and similar subtleties, the trial system will rarely be able to tell the difference between the man who tried in good faith and the man who didn't. In practice, both will be acquitted. In all likelihood, neither will even be charged. Neither one will have much reason to change his behavior. And most important, women will be left to face a situation in which the man can and will "forge ahead regardless of what [she] says." Ambiguity and the messy facts of sexual communication create a powerful need for standards that can channel dangerous behavior and reduce risks. Yet ambiguity, messy facts, and the lack of social consensus have until now served primarily as reasons for law, especially criminal law, *not* to take sides.

Society's greater willingness to protect property rights reflects, in part, this concern for consensus. When property is taken or exchanged, social judgments about the rights and wrongs of the transaction are much less diverse, and they seldom split sharply along gender lines. Yet in the era when criminal law was first extended to reach nonviolent interference with property rights, people held widely divergent views about law's proper role in property matters. And people do differ, even today, in their judgments about acceptable behavior in property transactions. There are especially strong disagreements about the extent to which society should protect interests in "intellectual property," such as trade secrets or computer software. The law nonetheless takes sides in these disputes and sets enforceable standards—including the criminal law standards brought home to us at the beginning of every rented video-tape. Social disagreement cannot by itself explain society's insistence on limiting protection in most sexual encounters to cases of direct physical coercion.

Sexual encounters differ from property transactions in another way that should make sexuality an especially important subject of legal concern. Sexual behavior evokes more intense controversy, but it also puts at risk a much more sensitive, physically and psychologically precious interest—our bodily independence and our right to control our own exposure to sexual intimacy.

In determining "consent," as in making judgments about force, fear, intimidation, and "reasonableness," law's vague, abstract standards are especially troubling in this respect. Law has not simply opted for a neutral solution to these socially contested issues. In each instance, law has chosen sides. The law gives priority to the interest (the predominantly male interest) in seeking sexual gratification through advances backed by physical strength and social power. And the law gives priority to protecting sexually assertive individuals (predominantly men) from the risk of conviction without clear warning in advance. At the same time the law denies protection to women, whose sexual independence is so often at risk, and leaves them to fend off sexual pressure as best they can, with self-help their only remedy.

Many people believe that these are legitimate solutions to hard social problems. But they are not the only possible solutions, and they need to be explained and defended. Political and cultural disagreements cannot by themselves justify recourse, by default, to vague formulas and limited, least-common-denominator standards. On the contrary, the deep differences of opinion in assessing sexual behavior are among the primary reasons why existing law often works so poorly. Far from justifying the status quo, the sharp clash of viewpoints on sexuality and the wide splits between the perceptions of men and women are a source of danger. They are an important reason to search for better ways to protect women's sexual independence and *every* person's right to control the boundaries of his or her own sexual life.

4

The Search for Solutions

Despite their many disputes over theory and tactics, critics of existing rape law largely agree in tracing its inadequacies to its overly narrow conception of force. Protection of autonomy—a woman's right to control her own sexual choices—is not ignored. It remains the ultimate goal and a frequent rhetorical theme.[1] Yet few reformers attempt to make autonomy or consent a formal legal requirement.[2]

One reason is practical. Many antirape activists see tactical risks in focusing on autonomy and consent. They worry that evidence about the victim's personal life might become relevant and that extensive cross-examination of the victim might have to be permitted if legal proof focuses on her state of mind rather than on the defendant's behavior. There is a more basic point as well, a concern that autonomy simply has no meaning independent of some notion of coercion. Through all the reform struggles of the past, reformers and their critics alike shared the assumption that autonomy means—and can only mean—freedom from force or duress.

As a result, most contemporary reformers stress autonomy only in their rhetoric; they avoid making autonomous choice a formal requirement. Instead, the leading proposals for change urge two distinct but complementary reforms. The first is to insist that "no means no." The second aims to bridge the gaps in existing legal protection by expanding traditional notions of force, coercion, or duress. Both approaches have led the reform effort to unexpected dead ends.

"No" Is Never Enough

The argument that a woman's "no" should always establish her unwillingness remains intensely controversial, especially in the context of dating relationships that include voluntary necking, petting, and other sorts of sexual exploration and foreplay. But even if the "no always means no" argument were accepted—a step that most states still refuse to take—that change by itself would accomplish very little. Winning legal recognition for the principle that "no means no" would make it much easier for women to show that they were unwilling. But unwillingness alone is never enough.

The rule on this point astonishes most nonlawyers, but it is nonetheless basic to the offense of rape as it is currently defined. Even when the absence of consent is clear and undisputed, rape is committed (under existing law) only when the defendant has used "force."

A recent Pennsylvania case made this difference between rape and "mere unwillingness" especially clear. Linda (not her real name) was a nineteen-year-old sophomore at Pennsylvania's East Stroudsburg State, a college well supplied with modern date-rape awareness programs and seminars on such subjects as "Does 'no' sometimes mean 'yes'?" After classes one afternoon, Linda drank a martini (to "loosen up a little bit") and then went to meet her boyfriend, with whom she had quarreled the previous evening. While waiting for him at his dorm, she entered the room of an acquaintance, Robert Berkowitz, and sat on the floor for a while chatting and mentioning some of her problems with her boyfriend. After a few minutes, Robert moved to the floor, sat beside her, and began kissing and fondling her. Linda said, "No, I gotta go, let me go," but Robert disregarded her protests, got up, and locked the door so that no one from outside could enter. (The lock did not prevent someone inside from leaving, however.)

At this point, Robert pushed Linda onto the bed, lay on top of her, removed her undergarments, and penetrated her. Linda continued protesting, saying "no" throughout the encounter, a point that Robert acknowledged in his own account of the events. (He said that she was continually "whispering . . . no's" in a manner he interpreted as "amorously . . . passionately" moaning.) When it was over, Robert said, "Wow, I guess we just got carried away." Linda immediately replied, "No, we didn't get carried away, you got carried away." She quickly dressed, grabbed her books, raced downstairs to meet her boyfriend, and burst into tears.

Rape? The Pennsylvania statute states explicitly that "the victim need not resist," and Linda had repeatedly protested. The jury believed her and convicted Robert Berkowitz of rape. Nonetheless, in 1994 the Pennsylvania Supreme Court reversed the rape conviction.[3] The court agreed that Linda's verbal protests proved her lack of consent; it did not pretend that her "no" really meant "yes." Yet the court held that there was no rape, because, in its view, Robert had not deployed *force*. After a local outcry over the *Berkowitz* decision, the Pennsylvania legislature amended its statute to create a lesser degree of sexual assault for any case of intercourse without consent. But Pennsylvania's new statute puts that state very much in the minority. Most states still follow the approach that the Pennsylvania judges applied in their 1994 decision. Under that approach, courts can decide that "no" really meant "no" and still conclude that a woman in a situation like Linda's was not raped.

We have all heard of cases in which police, judges, or juries refuse to believe that a woman's "no" really meant genuine unwillingness. But the problems run deeper: Even when jurors are convinced that a woman's "no" signaled unwillingness, unwillingness is not enough. In nearly all American jurisdictions, intercourse is not a crime, even in the face of a woman's clearly expressed objections, unless the assailant threatened to use "force." And the force must be something beyond the acts involved in intercourse, something that "compels" the woman to submit. The claim that "no means no" does nothing to break this boundary—legal protection remains limited to cases of physically violent misconduct.

Pennsylvania's statutory solution, creating a separate felony for cases of intercourse without consent, fills an important part of the gap. Indeed, at first glance, the Pennsylvania solution appears to eliminate the problem entirely, by making proof of force unnecessary.[4] But the conundrums of the force requirement are not so easily avoided. The Pennsylvania solution works well when the woman verbalizes her opposition by saying "no" unequivocally and persistently. A man who penetrates her under such circumstances clearly commits a crime. But the loopholes and technicalities of existing law often prove most troublesome when the woman's "no" is *not* clear and persistent.

In the notorious St. John's College case, several lacrosse players were charged with gang raping a young woman after luring her to their apartment and plying her with strong drinks. The men were acquitted even though she became so heavily intoxicated that she could not stand up, fight back, or speak coherently.[5] In the *Rusk* case, a Maryland woman submitted to a man who took her car keys and refused to let her leave until she "consented" to sex.[6] Time and again, abusive sexual encounters escape sanctions under existing law when an unwilling woman reluctantly acquiesces in a man's sexual demands. In cases like these, problems immediately reemerge, even under Pennsylvania's ambitious statutory solution, because the woman's "no" was not clear and persistent.

One reason for this additional complexity is that the law refuses to assume that unwillingness, once expressed, is permanently controlling. The principle that "no means no" works well when we are able to picture a sexual encounter as a static snapshot: At the moment of intercourse, the woman is saying "no" and the man is proceeding to penetrate her. There *are* cases like that; the *Berkowitz* episode is an example. But the dynamics of sexual interaction are often more complex. When a woman says "no," and the man keeps trying, as Berkowitz did, she may at some point disrobe, lie back, or do what he asks her to do. Or, if the man continues to pressure, cajole, or attempt to arouse her, she may give in and explicitly say "okay" or even "yes."

Have these women consented, or are they submitting under duress? Are the men behaving decently when they try again, or are they refusing to hear and honor the women's preferences? Would the men be violating a rule that "no means no"? Our volatile sexual culture gives no uniform answers.

One approach could be to insist that genuine respect for women requires men to recognize that a "no" is not only literal but final. The man who "refuses to take no for an answer" is simply ignoring a woman's expressed preferences.

Susan Estrich offers a suggestive argument for this approach, with a provocative comparison between sexual advances and police questioning of criminal suspects in custody. In police interrogation, a suspect's consent to talk about the crime is considered involuntary if he says "no" at first but changes his mind because police cajolery or questioning persuaded him to speak. Under the famous *Miranda* rules, once an arrested suspect expresses the desire to remain silent, that desire must be respected.[7] In this regard, Estrich notes, women get less respect than criminal suspects do: "a suspect's 'no' must mean no, and questioning must be terminated," but in sexual interactions a woman's "no" never has to be accepted as final.[8] Following this train of thought, we could consider applying a "Miranda" approach in rape cases: a woman's consent would be invalid if her "no" was followed by cajolery, psychological ploys, or continued demands that led her to acquiesce.

This "Miranda" approach would have the advantage of replacing inconclusive debates about coercion with a clear-cut, automatic rule. But in many kinds of sexual interactions, a rule treating a woman's "no" as invariably final would prove overbroad and implausible. Three variations can suggest some of the complexities. First, suppose that a college instructor tries to initiate a sexual relationship with a graduate student who comes to his office for advice on her paper. She rejects his advances, but she later acquiesces after he tells her he may not approve her application for a fellowship. Many would feel comfortable saying that the student's initial "no" should be taken as final.

But consider a second case. Another instructor tries to initiate a relationship with a student who comes to his office. She too rejects the instructor's advances. His response is not to threaten her but to tell her in detail about his personal life, his recent separation from a steady girlfriend, and his attraction to her. She then agrees to go to his apartment for dinner, and that evening she has sex with him there. It seems plausible to view the first student's initial rejection as her real preference and to consider it controlling. But it seems much less convincing to insist that the second student's "no" should be treated as irrevocable. Some might still say that the second student's consent to sex was in some way defective. But this view rests primarily on the potential pressure inherent in the instructor's supervisory role, and not on any inherent finality in the student's initial "no."

A bright-line, automatic rule becomes even less plausible when we move to the complexities of dating relationships. As a third variation, suppose that a woman says "no" to her lover before dinner and then changes her mind after several hours of relaxation and intimate conversation. Assuming that her lover's goal all along was to have sex that evening and that he used romantic atmosphere and conversation to further this purpose, would his behavior count as a "psychological ploy"? If so, would the woman's consent to sex have to be considered invalid? That is exactly the result that the *Miranda* rules require for suspects in police custody, but it cannot be the right result for all cases of changing intentions during sexual interaction. Women on dates with chosen companions don't automatically lose their ability to act as free agents, in the way that arrested suspects in police custody do.

The importance of the criminal-suspect analogy is the insight that a man who refuses to take "no" for an answer may resort to cajolery or pressure to make his date change her mind. But a "no means no" rule does not help us sort out whether the things he does in response to her initial "no" are legitimate or abusive. To separate appropriate emotional interaction from abusive pressure, we need substantive standards of permissible conduct. The prohibition on resorting to physical violence is one standard of this sort—at present the only standard. An expanded concept of force might do the job, but then we are thrown back to the problem of trying to specify what that expanded concept should include. By itself, the "no means no" rule does not enable us to complete the essential step.

In sum, a flat rule that "no always means no" would give much more protection for women in many cases, but it cannot carry us very far toward filling the gaps in the existing law of rape. A "no means no" rule doesn't clarify the standards of behavior that apply *after* the woman says "no." And a "no means no" rule doesn't tell us how to treat a woman's expressed intentions when she initially said "no" but was not saying "no" at the moment of intercourse. Those problems return us, once again, to the elusive question of what should count as legally sufficient force. Winning legal recognition for the principle that "no means no" will not solve this puzzle.

Rape-law reformers have an answer. They hope to overcome the remaining problems by extending the definition of "force" from physical violence to other kinds of coercion. Their hope is to start with accepted notions of force and expand them by a process of extrapolation and analogy.

From Explicit to Implicit Force

The first obstacle is the common practice of limiting rape prosecutions to cases involving an *explicit* threat to use force. Many courts do not recognize a man's indirectly intimidating conduct or the frightening character of a situation as sufficient, even when the circumstances leave the victim in fear of immediate harm. Instead, these courts insist on proof that the defendant explicitly threatened to inflict physical injury. Again, the *Rusk* case is a telling example. The nuances of the encounter were crucial. Eddie Rusk met Pat at a singles bar, persuaded her to give him a ride home, and then took her car keys when they arrived in front of his apartment at 1:00 A.M. Unfamiliar with the neighborhood and feeling scared, Pat followed Eddie to his apartment. Once there, she begged him to let her leave, and when he refused, she became frightened. She testified that when she started to cry, "he put his hands on my throat, and started lightly to choke me." Finally, she said, "If I do what you want, will you let me go?" Eddie said yes, and Pat submitted.

Maryland's highest court was able to uphold Eddie Rusk's rape conviction, but only by stressing "the actual force applied by Rusk to Pat's neck." The other frightening circumstances—her isolation, in the middle of the night, in a strange neighborhood, by a man who took her car keys and refused to let her leave—these circumstances did not, even taken together, add up to a reasonable fear of bodily harm.

When courts insist on proof of explicit threats, details like Rusk's "light" choking become decisive for legal results. Courts hesitate to treat indirect intimidation as a form of force, even when the man is a complete stranger. The case of the woman who was accosted on an Illinois bike path underscores the point. She had stopped to take a break, but when she attempted to leave, a man who was almost twice her size lifted her off the ground, carried her into the woods, and then performed several sex acts. Because the woman did not attempt to scream or fight back, an appellate court set aside the man's conviction for sexual assault. Only if he had threatened physical violence explicitly would the court have excused her failure to resist.

Courts could easily uphold the convictions in such cases, simply by recognizing that threats can be equally powerful and intimidating when they are implicit, arising from the circumstances. Even in the 1940s, a California court recognized that a woman surrounded by "four big men" would fear injury and need not resist, even though "they did not tell her they were going to do anything to her if she refused."[9] But courts are reluctant to accept a woman's fears as sufficient when just one very big man, even a complete stranger, lifts her up or orders her to undress.

A California case from the late 1980s shows the beginnings of a more sensible approach. Marsha M. went to the home of a neighbor, Joaquin Barnes, whom she had known for several years. She smoked some marijuana with him and then tried to leave. She went out of the house and asked him to open the front gate. Barnes initially refused and expressed anger that she wanted to leave so soon. He said he would open the gate, but first, on a pretext, he got her to return inside. There he acted angry again and flexed his muscles in a threatening manner. Next Barnes turned suddenly affectionate. Fearing that he was "psychotic," Marsha feigned compliance to avoid injury and cooperated in an act of intercourse.

Though the jury found Barnes guilty of rape, an intermediate California court set aside his conviction because he hadn't explicitly threatened to inflict physical harm. In a 1986 decision, the California Supreme Court reinstated the conviction. The court found that Barnes's conduct carried an implicit threat sufficient to meet the state's requirement of "force or fear of immediate and unlawful bodily injury."[10] This approach, recognizing both implicit and explicit threats as forms of force, is now widely accepted, at least in theory.[11] With an implicit-threat standard, well-intentioned courts should have much less trouble reaching sensible results in cases like *Rusk*.

But shifting the legal analysis to focus on implicit threats doesn't solve the problems; it only restates them. Courts still must identify some conduct that amounts to an unstated threat. If the implicit-threat standard requires evidence tied to the defendant's behavior at the time of the incident, physical and verbal details (flexing of the biceps, actual choking) will remain crucially important. In a case like *Alston*, in which no express threats were made at the moment of intercourse,[12] a claim that there was force will remain vague and debatable.

The problem here is that even when implicit threats can count as force, the standard remains artificial because it focuses narrowly, in snapshot fashion, on specific comments and gestures at the time of a rape incident. The legal analysis proceeds without considering the broader context, such as the abusive prior relationship in the *Alston* case or the complete absence of any prior relationship in the case of the Illinois woman who was accosted while bicycling.

To escape the artificially narrow focus on the man's behavior at a specific moment, courts could consider the entire context, including the setting of the incident, the possibilities for running away or calling for help, the prior relationship between the parties, their relative size and strength, and so on.[13] On this basis, the four big men clearly exerted force when they surrounded a complete stranger and told her to submit. In the Illinois case, a single very big man clearly exerted force when he carried off an isolated woman who was virtually half his size.

Intimidation sometimes arises from the man's specific acts, past or present. Barnes articulated no threat, but he flexed his muscles in a threatening way. Rusk took a woman's car keys, heightening the insecurity she already felt just from being alone, late at night, in a strange neighborhood. But intimidation can also arise spontaneously from a situation, as when four big men are alone with a woman, whether or not they use menacing words or flex their biceps.

This broader, more contextual approach is clearly attractive, but it poses a large problem. By shifting the force requirement from a man's threatening actions to his *capacity* to inflict harm, this approach makes the line between voluntary encounters and coercive sex hard to locate. If disparity of size, strength, and fighting ability is sufficient to establish force, then rape is implicit in nearly every heterosexual relationship.

No court will permit a standard like this to extend to the limits of its logic, of course. The more serious concern is that, in practice, a principle of this sort will seldom be used at all. So long as the contextual approach fails to separate, in a roughly predictable way, what is legitimate from what is abusive, courts will bend over backward to ensure that men are not convicted of a serious offense unless they have "fair warning" that their conduct was criminal. Prosecutors, juries, and appellate courts will have no clear guidance and, much worse, no strong imperative to act. *Under*enforcement will be the all-too-foreseeable result.

A Maryland case illustrates the kind of "line-drawing" problem that sabotages efforts to treat implicit threats as a form of force. A twenty-five-year-old man met an eighteen-year-old sales clerk and told her he was a modeling agent. On the pretext of interviewing her for a modeling assignment, he met her after work and drove her to his "studio," where he disrobed her (over her protests), pushed her down on the bed, and had intercourse. The young woman testified that she submitted out of fear, because she was alone with "no one to help her if she resisted," and because he was "much larger than she was." The court reversed the defendant's rape conviction, holding that "in the complete absence of any threatening words or actions by [the defendant], these two factors, as a matter of law, are simply not enough to . . . be the equivalent of force."[14]

A court willing to abandon the search for "implicit force" could have chosen several other ways to handle a case like this one. The court could have counted the defendant's acts of pushing the woman down and penetrating her as force in itself. It might have said that force wasn't necessary at all, and that her verbal protests were sufficient, period. Or it might simply have accepted the jury's conclusion without insisting on factual specifics. But short of these more radical steps, courts applying an "implicit force" approach need evidence of some force beyond the physical act of intercourse. They can recognize that force takes indirect forms, including a man's inherent advantage in size and strength, or intimidating background circumstances such as an isolated setting. But in order to ensure that men are convicted of rape only when they have fair warning and deserve criminal punishment, courts need some way to decide *when* it is appropriate to hold the man responsible for the fears that these situational factors can arouse.

Was She Reasonable?

Courts that currently accept the implicit-threat and inherent-capacity-to-harm standards, such as the "four big men" test, keep those approaches within bounds by invoking a "reasonableness" limitation. An implicit threat or an intimidating capacity to inflict harm will count as "force"—and the woman will not have to fight back physically—but only when her fears of injury are considered "reasonable."

The reasonable-fear requirement seems a plausible limitation. Courts understandably will consider it unfair to convict a man of rape when a woman who cooperates in a sexual act has done so because of an unreasonable fear. Yet a reasonableness standard immediately destroys most of the gains that the more flexible implicit-threat standard was supposed to achieve.

A Wyoming case shows an extreme example of the "reasonable fear" limitation at work. Gonzales met the victim in a bar. She refused his request for a ride home, but when she got into her car, he got in on the other side. At first she refused again, but she became scared and began driving. After she had driven for a while, Gonzales asked her to turn down a side road and then asked her to stop so he could "go to the bathroom." He got out of the car, taking her keys from the ignition so that she could not drive off and leave him. When he returned, he told her he was going to rape her. The woman tried to talk him out of it, but Gonzales got mad, put his fist in her face, and said, "I'm going to do it. You can have it one way or the other." After this threat, the woman submitted without further protest.

The trial judge convicted Gonzales of rape, but in 1973 the Wyoming Supreme Court reversed the conviction. The court said that the victim was required to resist physically unless she had a reasonable fear of bodily injury, and the court concluded that "the evidence of the nature and sufficiency of the threat to justify nonresistance is far from overwhelming in this case."[15] It's hard to ignore the obvious conclusion that the *Gonzales* decision is just flatly wrong, possibly even outrageous. But to say that the Wyoming court should have reached the opposite result, to say it should have held that the woman's fears *were* reasonable, does nothing to change the basic legal framework or to guarantee better results in future cases.

The reasonableness standard here is the Achilles heel of effective enforcement. Reasonableness standards are common in law, and often they work tolerably well, especially in areas of behavior such as highway driving, where norms of conduct are widely shared and moderately well understood. When norms are more controversial and stakes are high, as in the use of deadly force in self-defense, a general standard of reasonableness is seldom sufficient; the law uses elaborate rules to specify the kinds of threats that are serious enough to justify a lethal response, the circumstances that require the threatened person to retreat rather than shoot in defense, and so on.[16]

In the case of sexual encounters, perceptions of danger differ widely, especially between men and women, and appropriate norms of behavior are intensely disputed. Our culture is at best ambivalent about whether a bit of physical aggression is attractive or unacceptable in male sexual initiatives. In these conditions, a reasonableness standard doesn't just keep the implicit-threat approach within common-sense bounds. Instead, a reasonableness standard radically undercuts the effort to make traditional requirements of explicit force more realistic. A reasonableness standard does little to challenge our culture's widespread willingness to condone men's physically assertive sexual advances. And it blocks recognition of the reasons why that willingness—and the behavior it encourages—pose dangers for women.

As a result, the reasonableness standard leaves legal requirements almost as narrow or unpredictable as they were before. Without some limitation, courts feel, reforms that stretch force requirements from explicit to implicit threats and from actual conduct to inherent capabilities would have intolerable scope—they would render virtually all heterosexual sex coercive and therefore criminal. But with a limitation to "reasonable" fears, the move to include implicit threats and inherent capacities as forms of force will ultimately achieve very little.

From Violence to Power

Reforms centered on implicit-threat and inherent-capacity ideas like the "four big men" test are inadequate in another way, because they stretch the force requirement in only one direction. They relax the requirement that the threat be explicit, but they preserve the notion that the threat—whether implicit or explicit—must involve some risk of *physical* harm. With this limitation, many of the most troubling sexual abuses will continue to escape legal control, even when predatory men make their threats explicit.

We have seen numerous examples. In Pennsylvania, a foster parent made sexual advances to a fourteen-year-old girl who had been placed in his care. When he threatened to send her back to the detention home unless she complied with his demands, she acquiesced and had sex with him. Yet the appellate court set aside his rape conviction, saying that the rape law's requirement of "forcible compulsion" meant "physical force or violence."[17] In Ohio, a man took a thirteen-year-old girl to his home on the pretext that he was a doctor. He told her to disrobe and subjected her to sexual fondling, fellatio, and intercourse. The appellate court held that he hadn't used force and set aside his rape conviction. Because he was not the girl's parent, the court said, she faced "no implicit threat of [physical] punishment for not complying."[18]

These illustrations are only the tip of a large iceberg. The need to prove that a man threatened *physical* injury complicates every case in which psychological pressure and physical intimidation are subtly intertwined. An ambiguous mixture of orders, nonphysical threats, and fears of physical harm permeates cases like those involving the Pennsylvania foster parent, the pseudodoctor from Ohio, and the female prison inmates who "consent" to have sex with their guards. In *Rusk,* the case of the Maryland man who took a woman's car keys in a strange neighborhood, the defendant himself posed a threat, at the same time that he limited the woman's freedom of movement and exposed her to danger from others. Yet in countless cases like these, a rape conviction can stand only if prosecutors can show that the risks of physical injury were clear and specific. And rape convictions are precluded in situations that involve only the manipulative misconduct and coercive-but-nonviolent threats of teachers, job supervisors, lawyers, doctors, and psychiatrists.

The natural step to overcome this obstacle is to extend the concept of force from physical violence to other forms of power. In the case of the Pennsylvania foster parent, a dissenting judge sought to uphold the rape conviction by pointing to the broad language of common dictionary definitions of "force." He argued that force should be understood as including acts that "constrain or compel by physical, moral, or intellectual means or by the exigencies of the circumstances."[19] This move to expand the notion of force from violence to other kinds of power is echoed in the work of numerous rape-law reformers and feminist scholars in law, philosophy, and other disciplines. It may now represent the dominant strand in feminist thought about rape. It combines revealing insights about law and radical criticism of contemporary culture with ambitious but ultimately unmanageable prescriptions for reform.

5

Feminist Conceptions/Judicial Innovations

Economic pressure, emotional demands, nonviolent threats, and the coercive leverage of social status and professional authority are all—in the eyes of the law—permissible means to achieve submission to sexual demands. Only when a person threatens physical harm does the law of rape come into play. Civil law prohibitions and professional regulations seldom go much further. To address this problem, many feminist critics of rape law argue that the law's concept of force should be extended from physical violence to other forms of power. Several state courts have recently adopted similar solutions. Yet the leading feminist proposals and the judicial innovations that reflect their influence do surprisingly little to protect women against coercive sexual abuse.

A 1976 article in the *University of Chicago Law Review* illustrates one common feminist approach. The article argues that "a woman's decision to submit to physical force may be less agonizing than her decision to have intercourse with a person who holds economic or emotional power over her." Noting "the reality of mental injury and the power of economic duress," the article concludes that a man who obtains intercourse by threats of nonphysical harm should be subject to criminal punishment. "The freedom of sexual choice which is to be protected by rape law can be as effectively negated by nonphysical as by physical coercion."[1]

As a proposal for workable reform of the law of rape, this suggestion suffers from one major flaw. Some degree of "economic or emotional power" is present in most, possibly all, social interactions. If a difference in economic status or emotional need is sufficient to establish force, then illegal coercion is present in virtually all sexual relationships. This conception of force offers no way to distinguish acceptable from unacceptable pressures, and it may even imply that virtually all heterosexual intercourse bears significant similarities to rape.

Many prominent feminists express related views, arguing that gender inequality produces important continuities between commonplace forms of intercourse and forcible rape. Catharine MacKinnon, most notably, argues that "rape is defined as distinct from intercourse, while for women it is difficult to distinguish the two under conditions of male dominance."[2] There are grains of both truth and exaggeration in this view. But whether this perspective is valid or not, the stress on continuities between intercourse and rape does not offer reformers a concrete way to change the definitions of rape or the day-to-day practices of legal institutions.

MacKinnon acknowledges the importance of legal line-drawing, and she offers one specific suggestion for doctrinal reform of criminal law. "Rape," she writes, "should be defined as sex by compulsion, of which physical force is one form. Lack of consent is redundant and should not be a separate element of the crime."[3]

This approach aims to offer a more protective standard than "force" or "coercion," but it is hard to be sure that it does. In fact the recommendation to ignore consent and to focus on compulsion (not limited to physical force) forms the linchpin of the Model Penal Code proposal, an approach that has done little to tighten the legal standard or to change the law's enforcement in practice. MacKinnon herself does not attempt a definition of "compulsion." Yet her other essays emphasize the broad ramifications of male dominance. They portray "sexuality as a social sphere of male power to which forced sex is paradigmatic" and argue that life in male-dominated society creates "a condition of sexual coercion which women never outgrow."[4] These premises suggest that compulsion is ever-present for women in society as MacKinnon sees it. What MacKinnon properly calls the "elusive" search for a line between legitimate sex and rape could remain elusive, under her approach to defining the offense.

Line-drawing is essential. But how can we distinguish the kinds of sexual relationships that law should permit from the abusive encounters that should be subject to criminal punishment? Recent feminist thought answers this question in two ways—both of them unsatisfactory. Scholars such as Columbia University law professor Vivian Berger, a leading proponent of shield laws to protect rape victims from hostile cross-examination, insist that rape laws should retain their focus on threats to inflict physical injury.[5] This is a coherent, well-bounded approach, but it offers little hope of preventing any but the most flagrant sexual abuses.

Most moderate feminists prefer to protect against nonviolent coercion, without casting doubt on all heterosexual relationships. They want to start from the premise that there is good, decent, acceptable sex, even in a society still marked by sex discrimination and elements of male power. They therefore accept that a woman's preferences and her own beliefs about what she wants are genuine. Or, if her preferences are not thoroughly genuine in some ultimate sense, these preferences are all that law can plausibly work with. Moderate feminists are therefore willing to treat a woman's consent to sex as valid, provided that the consent has been given for what they consider legitimate reasons.

These moderate reformers still need some way to separate legitimate from illegitimate sex. Most of them try to make that crucial distinction by relying on some conception of force, coercion, or duress. Susan Estrich suggests one possibility, drawing on the standards used to assess the validity of consent in an exchange of property. She argues that force and coercion should include "extortionate threats" and "misrepresentations of material fact."[6] This seems a promising way to start thinking about the validity of consent. Unfortunately, Estrich does not develop her notion of either extortion or misrepresentation. Because her concept of coercion (and therefore of rape) might extend even to a person who obtains consent to sex by insincerely professing love for his or her date, many committed feminists are dubious about Estrich's analysis.[7] If it carries some implicit limits, her approach is plausible but vague. If it has no built-in limits, the proposal is clear but, for many, far too broad.

Feminist philosopher Lois Pineau offers a more ambitious theory. To separate legitimate from illegitimate sexual encounters, she begins by considering the motivations that lie at the heart of uncoerced sexuality. She posits that sexual intercourse should be a "communicative" experience, in which each person has "the obligation to promote the sexual ends of one's partner." For Pineau,

> persons engaged in communicative sexuality will be concerned with more than achieving coitus. They will be sensitive to the responses of their partners. They will, like good conversationalists, be intuitive, sympathetic, and charitable. Intuition will help them

to interpret their partner's responses; sympathy will enable them to share what their partner is feeling; charity will enable them to care. Communicative sexual partners will not overwhelm each other with the barrage of their own desires. They will treat negative, bored, or angry responses as a sign that the erotic ground needs to be either cleared or abandoned. Their concern with fostering the desire of the other must involve an ongoing state of alertness in interpreting her responses.[8]

Starting from this conception of a legitimate, mutually satisfying interaction, Pineau suggests that when the circumstances do not point to a "communicative" experience, no unconstrained woman would agree to it. If the woman did agree, Pineau argues, her participation should be treated as the result of illegal pressure rather than voluntary consent: "it is not reasonable for women to consent to aggressive non-communicative sex . . . Hence acquiescence under such conditions should not count as consent."[9]

Legal scholar Martha Chamallas takes a similar approach but allows a broader range of motives to count as acceptable. Chamallas treats procreation, emotional intimacy, and physical pleasure as genuine, untainted reasons to want sex. Any other inducements, she argues, would mark the sexual encounter as abusive and render the woman's consent invalid.[10]

The vision of sexual relationships that these scholars posit is unquestionably attractive to many people. But as a model for legally enforceable standards, these approaches do not easily translate into workable rules. Because Pineau and Chamallas make so much depend on the woman's motivations, many—including many feminists—worry about the kind of evidence that would be needed to establish the victim's underlying intentions, not to mention the risk of unfairness to men who misunderstood their partner's real reasons for consenting.[11] And the Chamallas-Pineau approaches could encourage searching cross-examination of the rape complainant to probe aspects of her private life and sexual history that might be inconsistent with her claimed motivations.

But technical problems of this sort are the least of the difficulties. The concern for fair warning, for example, could be met by limiting criminal liability to cases in which the defendant knew that the woman's desires were not "communicative." The more basic problem is that many women do not accept Pineau's or Chamallas' vision of ideal sexuality as right for themselves. Pineau, for example, would treat consent as unreasonable, and therefore legally ineffective, when it was motivated by desire to conceive a child or to experience noncommunicative physical pleasure—the "zipless fuck" immortalized in Erica Jong's *Fear of Flying*. Chamallas accepts these as legitimate reasons to consent to sex, but seems to reject many others, including curiosity, financial gain, a desire to impress peers, and an interest in adventure or rebellion.

Many consider these "unreasonable" or psychologically damaging reasons to consent to sex. Those who do should certainly continue fighting the kinds of cultural messages that lead women to make these choices. But the problem in legal reform is to determine whether society should formally prohibit a woman from acting on the preferences she has, however risky or unwise they may be. Any woman who wants only communicative sexual experiences should, of course, have a well-enforced right to withhold her consent in "noncommunicative" encounters. Existing law, which often fails to honor that right, is clearly in need of repair in this respect. But the Pineau approach would also require punishing a woman's male partner when the woman wanted to have sex and gave express consent, if she did so for reasons that Pineau considers "unreasonable."

A basic guidepost of regulation in a free society is that it is ordinarily harmful (and illegitimate) for law to interfere with an adult's decisions about her own welfare, even when it would have been "better," in someone else's opinion, for her to have made a different choice. A free society is best understood as one committed to promoting, not hindering, autonomy—the ordinary citizen's right to determine the shape of her own life, by deciding for herself what goals might be valuable. Law prohibits some voluntary transactions because they injure third parties (bribery, for example), and it must protect against threats that interfere with a person's ability to decide for herself what she prefers. But legal controls normally have little plausibility—and even less hope of effectiveness—when they go further and disregard uncoerced personal choices that pose no risk of harm to others.

Only rarely does the law seek to punish the uncoerced choices of mature adults whose actions cause no immediate harm to third parties.

Laws against prostitution are one example. Antiprostitution laws are seldom vigorously enforced, and they remain controversial, especially for feminists who believe that law should respect women's ability to judge their best interests for themselves. Antiprostitution laws might nonetheless be defensible if the practices they prohibit involve coercion, lack of capacity to make competent decisions (on the part of teenaged prostitutes, for example), or a substantial risk of harm to third parties. Beyond these concerns, antiprostitution laws rest on shaky ground, and it seems implausible to suggest extending them to prohibit uncoerced, noncommercial sexual relationships that both participants want to pursue.

Once we accept preferences as they stand, we must acknowledge that some women sometimes enjoy the "zipless fuck," the "masterful seduction" by a strong, silent stranger, as portrayed in the popular Harlequin romances,[12] or other sexual experiences that differ from the "communicative" ideal. Robin West writes that the "expropriation" of a woman's sexuality in a relationship of male dominance and female submission "is sexually desirable, exciting and pleasurable—in fantasy for many; in reality for some."[13] Women (like men) sometimes initiate sexual relationships to further goals that are independent of deep communication or even physical pleasure—goals such as social status, peer approval, personal self-esteem, or financial security. Such choices often deserve criticism, on grounds of morality, psychological well-being, and other values. But to raise these concerns (as I would) is not to say that the choices, once freely made, should be considered illegal. As law professor Catharine Wells notes,

> women's sexual interests cannot be defined in any one construct. There are, in fact, many women who share a "masterful seduction" view of sex and romance. There are women who support themselves by prostitution or by marriage to wealthy men. There are lesbians who enjoy patterns of domination and subordination that are commonly found in "male" pornography. In short, millions of women do not seek—and may not want—the kind of communicative sexual relationships that Pineau describes.[14]

Ironically, in seeking to expand conceptions of coercion in order to protect unfettered choice, approaches like those of Chamallas and

Pineau deny competent adult women the right to make important choices in defining their sexual lives. In effect, these approaches *negate* women's sexual autonomy. This sort of solution is neither practically workable nor politically realistic. And more basically, it should not command support even in theory. The goal law should pursue is just the reverse—to protect and enhance autonomy, not to restrict it.

Creative Judicial Interpretation

In two states, progressive judges have sought to bridge the many gaps in existing rape law by unusual innovations in legal doctrine. Like the feminist approaches, the judicial innovations—one in Pennsylvania and a contrasting approach in New Jersey—do not focus directly on sexual autonomy. Rather, they start with the concept of force and stretch it to cover related but nonviolent abuses.

Pennsylvania's rape statute requires proof of "forcible compulsion."[15] For many years the Pennsylvania courts insisted that forcible compulsion meant a threat of *physical* violence. Pennsylvania courts overturned rape convictions in cases like that of the foster parent who compelled a fourteen-year-old to submit to sex by threatening to send her back to a detention home.[16] They reversed the rape conviction of a father who got his seventeen-year-old daughter to submit to his sexual demands by claiming that she had a religious obligation to comply and by threatening to humiliate her in public.[17]

A 1986 case put Pennsylvania's requirement of physical force to the test. An eight-year-old girl was playing near her home when Rhodes, a twenty-year-old neighbor, led her to an abandoned building, told her to lie down on the floor, and told her to pull her legs up. He then lay on top of her and penetrated her, both vaginally and rectally. The victim arrived home crying and frightened, with her clothing dirty, her underwear bloody, her vaginal area red, and her rectum torn and bleeding. Rhodes was convicted of statutory rape (which carried a ten-year maximum sentence) and forcible rape (which carried a twenty-year maximum). But an appellate court set aside the conviction for forcible rape. Said the court: "[There is] not one iota of evidence that sexual intercourse was accomplished by forcible compulsion or by threat of forcible compulsion . . . Although we do not minimize the heinous nature of appellant's act, it seems clear that the act of [intercourse] was criminal because of the provisions . . . defining statutory rape and not because it was a forcible rape."[18]

The Pennsylvania Supreme Court rejected this approach and reinstated the conviction for forcible rape. The problem, however, was the lack of any evidence that the defendant had specifically threatened to hurt the little girl physically if she refused to comply with his demands. To avoid this difficulty, the court held that the statutory requirement of forcible compulsion "includes not only physical force or violence but also moral, psychological or intellectual force used to compel a person to engage in sexual intercourse against a person's will."[19]

This test makes a clear break with prevailing law's strict insistence on proof of physical threats. Yet, attractive as the new approach seems, its reach is very broad. As stated, it could convert a sexual relationship into rape if the woman's consent were prompted by a man's emotional appeals for intimacy, by his expression of feelings of hurt and rejection, by his indicating an intention to start dating another woman, or even by his offer of a luxurious Caribbean vacation. The Pennsylvania court, obviously concerned about the potential impact of its holding, tucked into a footnote an important limitation:

> forcible compulsion . . . requires much more than simply convincing an initially reluctant consenting adult to engage in sexual intercourse by moral, psychological or intellectual persuasion . . . [The statute] requires actual forcible compulsion or the threat thereof which is used to compel the victim to engage in sexual intercourse against that person's will such that the act of sexual intercourse cannot be regarded as consensual.[20]

The court's convoluted caveat resurrects most of the traditional—and highly troublesome—limits that its holding had promised to erase. Though the court at first seems to treat nonviolent pressures as sufficient, its footnote draws an unexplained distinction between moral, psychological, or intellectual *persuasion*—which remains permissible—and moral, psychological, or intellectual *force*. The court stresses that the man's actions must amount to "actual forcible compulsion," and it then insists that even forcible compulsion is not necessarily enough; the force must *compel* the victim to submit, *against her will,* so that her act *cannot be regarded as consensual.*

However vague, the *Rhodes* test at least gives prosecutors a much-needed opening to show that a man's nonphysical threats were overwhelming and coercive. But it does little more than that. It does nothing to indicate what kinds of inducements are permissible, what kinds of conduct are prohibited, and what kinds of situational pressures will invalidate consent. It leaves in place all the slippery, subjective judgments that enable police, prosecutors, judges, and juries to conclude that pressure is not really "compelling," that a woman's decision to submit is voluntary rather than "against her will," and that her choice can be "regarded as consensual."

If vague but progressive standards are the best we can do, many reformers would gladly choose them in place of the inadequate protections usually afforded. But when earlier, far-more-specific reforms produced so little change in criminal justice practices, there is little reason to think that the amorphous Pennsylvania approach can improve official responses to sexual abuse.

Experience to date bears out these expectations. Pennsylvania courts have cited the broad *Rhodes* test in almost 300 cases, but virtually all of them involve either traditional forms of physical force or abuse of a child victim by an adult in a position of authority. Philadelphia sex crimes prosecutor Mimi Rose confirms that, apart from situations involving physical threats, the *Rhodes* test for force is used mostly in cases against teachers and parents.[21] In Harrisburg, chief deputy prosecutor Debbie Curillo explains that thanks to *Rhodes,* "Forcible compulsion for children may be found from a guardian, parent or neighbor . . . whereas with an adult woman we [still] need a gun, knife, or a severe threat."[22] In more than a decade since it adopted its more flexible standard, Pennsylvania has reported only one "forcible" rape conviction that was not based on physical force in the traditional sense.[23] And because the *Rhodes* standard gives no guide to determining which "courtship behaviors" or "seduction strategies" cross the line of illegality, its value in shaping conduct or "sending a message" about socially expected behavior is minimal. In rape law, flexibility almost inevitably means *under*enforcement and *non*compliance.

If it were ever seriously enforced, the Pennsylvania approach would pose the opposite problem—a significant risk of convictions without fair warning. One implicit assurance of fair warning is the common sense of the jury. Conviction is hardly likely unless the man deploys pressures that are perceived as extreme. Yet Pennsylvania's most significant attempt to invoke the theory of "psychological force" shows that the risks are not simply imaginary.

Becky M. and David Meadows were friends and companions. David was twenty-three years old; Becky, a deaf-mute with a partial ability to speak, was fifteen. Becky's sister was the girlfriend of David's brother, and over a three-month period David visited Becky frequently at her parents' house. Gradually coming to feel attached to David, Becky considered him her boyfriend and began teaching him sign language. One day in June, David and Becky met behind a barn on her parents' property and engaged in consensual "petting." Interrupted by Becky's sister, they walked away to a nearby field. There Becky kissed David and stretched out on the ground. David lay down beside her and had intercourse with her. He claimed that the intercourse was voluntary, that Becky expressed no protest of any sort. But Becky told a school nurse that she had been forced, and at David's trial for rape she testified that while he was pulling down her zipper, she said aloud, "No," and "Off."

David was prosecuted under the Pennsylvania statute making it rape to engage in sexual intercourse "by forcible compulsion." After hearing the testimony, the jury started deliberating but then returned to the courtroom and asked the judge to define "forcible compulsion." The jury also asked, "Can Becky consent to a point and then say no? . . . can she consent 95 percent and just prior to intercourse say: No, no. Off, off. Is this forcible compulsion?" In response, the judge reminded them that "forcible compulsion" can include psychological, moral, and intellectual force. He then explained: "It is up to you as the jury . . . to determine whether you have forcible compulsion of the various types . . . look at all of the circumstances that were occurring that day . . . and ask yourself: Is it physical force; is it moral; is it intellectual; is it psychological? And I can give to you no more guidance than that." With this clarification, the jury convicted, and David Meadows was sentenced to five years' imprisonment, the mandatory minimum term for rape under Pennsylvania law.[24]

The record of the trial implies that Becky probably said "no" and that David probably realized she was unwilling. On that view of the facts, there is little reason to question the fairness of the conviction.[25] But the trial judge, using the broad *Rhodes* test, allowed the jury to sidestep what should have been the crucial question—whether Becky ever expressed consent. The jurors might have thought that Becky acquiesced *without* saying "no." Or they might have concluded that she gave David express permission, but only because of the psychological pressure he had exerted. The appellate court concluded that the conviction was proper even under this view of the facts, with Becky's consent obtained by *psychological* force:

> the victim was psychologically vulnerable to the Defendant . . . [She] is a deaf mute, fifteen years of age and the Defendant is twenty-three years of age. In addition the victim had an adolescent crush on the Defendant and the Defendant was aware of her feelings for him. Furthermore, the sexual intercourse took place in a secluded field. The circumstances of this case show that psychological coercion existed and . . . such coercion is sufficient to meet the requirement of forcible compulsion.[26]

This way of justifying the conviction has unsettling implications and potentially far-reaching effects. The fact that the incident occurred in a secluded field scarcely limits the result, since sexual encounters typically occur in just such locations, and since Becky went there entirely of her own accord. The young woman's hearing and speech impairments certainly should heighten her boyfriend's responsibility to be sure he had her consent. But there is no apparent reason why her deaf-mute condition should be relevant to the question whether her consent—if given—was psychologically "coerced," since, by all indications, Becky's mental capabilities were normal. If taken at face value, the court's approach permits a jury to find "forcible compulsion," and hence to convict for the first-degree felony of rape, any time a young woman participates in a sexual encounter with a somewhat older boyfriend to whom she is "psychologically vulnerable" because of "an adolescent crush."

If this is indeed the Pennsylvania standard, it is wrongheaded in the extreme. Anyone who has ever had the experience of being head-over-heels in love can confirm the feeling of "helplessness" that a powerful infatuation can unleash. In that sense, the Pennsylvania court's approach, like the radical feminist critique of male dominance, does have a genuine kernel of truth. But to view the choices we make in that condition as "coerced" by the strength of our own emotions is to empty the concepts of free choice and coercion of all intelligible meaning. Barring major mental disorder, a lover's "irresistible impulse" for sexual intimacy with her beloved in no way deprives her of free will or of responsibility for her decisions.

The problem here is the same one that bedevils all current rape laws and all efforts at reform—the problem of identifying the boundary between autonomy and compulsion, between free choice and coerced consent. On one reading, the Pennsylvania approach simply obliterates that boundary and criminalizes all sexual choices influenced by any form of intellectual or emotional pressure. Obviously the court did not intend, and almost none of us would want to accept, such an unworkable and socially destructive result. The more plausible reading is that Pennsylvania law distinguishes between psychological *persuasion* (which is legally acceptable) and psychological *force* (which is not). But the Pennsylvania test provides no basis for locating the boundary between the two. It not only fails to distinguish between two difficult philosophical concepts, but, of more practical concern, it suggests no line of demarcation between a legally permitted consensual encounter and a first-degree felony subject to severe punishment.

An essentially empty formula of this sort poses obvious risks of unfairness to defendants. At the same time, it offers little promise of better protection for potential victims, because it sets no intelligible standard of expected behavior and sends no clear message to men. Nor does it offer any understandable benchmark to the criminal justice officials who must translate legal aspirations into enforcement decisions on the ground. As the judge told the jurors at David Meadows' trial, the only rule of thumb is to "look at all of the circumstances . . . [The law gives] no more guidance than that." Not surprisingly, no other state has adopted this accordionlike definition of force.

New Jersey has taken a technically different but equally far-reaching approach. In New Jersey a person is guilty of sexual assault if he commits an act of sexual penetration using "physical force or coercion." The precise meaning of the statutory requirement of "physical force" became crucial in a 1992 case involving a fifteen-year-old victim I will call Carol and a seventeen-year-old juvenile defendant, identified only as M. T. S., a boy I will call Mark.[27]

Mark was temporarily residing at Carol's home with the permission of her mother. He slept downstairs on a couch; Carol had her own room on the second floor. Carol and Mark offered radically conflicting descriptions of their relationship. Carol said Mark frequently attempted to kiss her and once tried to put his hands inside her pants, but that she rejected all his advances. According to Mark, he and Carol were frequently "kissing and necking" and discussed having sexual intercourse. He said Carol repeatedly encouraged him to "make a surprise visit up in her room."

Carol testified that one night she awoke and saw Mark standing in her doorway. She said she walked past him to use the bathroom, then returned to bed and fell asleep. She reawakened with Mark on top of her, her shorts and underpants removed. She said "his penis was into [her] vagina." As soon as Carol realized what had happened, she slapped his face and "told him to get off [her]." Mark complied immediately; according to Carol, "he jumped right off of [her]." After Mark left the room, Carol fell asleep crying. The next morning she told her mother about the incident and said they would have to get Mark out of the house.

Mark told a much different version of the encounter. He said that after he entered Carol's bedroom, the two began "kissing and all," eventually moving to the bed. Once they were in bed, he said, they undressed each other, continued to kiss, and then proceeded to engage in sexual intercourse. According to Mark, he "did it [thrust] three times," and then the fourth time, Carol said "Stop, get off," and he "hopped off right away." When he asked Carol what was wrong, she replied with a backhand to his face. He asked her again what was wrong, and she replied, "How can you take advantage of me." Mark said he got dressed and told Carol to calm down, but she began to cry. Before leaving the room, he told her, "I'm leaving . . . I'm going with my real girlfriend . . . stay out of my life [and] don't tell anybody about this . . . it would just screw everything up." He then walked downstairs and went to sleep.

In a juvenile delinquency proceeding against Mark, the judge didn't completely accept either teenager's story. The judge concluded that

Carol had not been sleeping at the time of the encounter and that she had consented to kissing and heavy petting. But he also found that Carol did not consent to the act of sexual penetration. On that basis the judge ruled that Mark was guilty of sexual assault.

Two rounds of appeals followed. Initially, a New Jersey appellate court set aside the conviction because Mark had not used "physical force": he didn't push Carol down, prevent her from leaving, or threaten to injure her. On a further appeal, the New Jersey Supreme Court rejected this reasoning and reinstated the conviction. The highest court held that the statutory requirement was met because the act of penetration itself involved physical force.

The *M. T. S.* prosecution presents several complicated issues. The ambiguous facts and conflicting testimony are not unusual, of course. Once the trial judge determined that penetration occurred without Carol's consent, it is natural to conclude that Mark was in the wrong. Nonetheless, the "physical force" requirement in New Jersey law posed a serious obstacle to conviction. Recognizing the obvious physical character of penetration appears to be a straightforward, commonsense response to this problem. But since the statute requires proof of both penetration *and* "physical force," it seems intended to add something extra, a requirement of some force *beyond* that inherent in intercourse. And unless an extra element of some sort is required, the court's reading of the statute produces absurd results: The requirements for a felony conviction—penetration and physical force—would be met by the physical thrusting involved in every act of mutually desired intercourse.

In rape, as distinguished from consensual sex, the penetration often results in tearing of tissue, bleeding, or severe abrasions. Yet many rape victims escape these kinds of harm, and no physical injury was present in the *M. T. S.* case itself; by her own account, Carol felt "scared and in shock" but was not otherwise harmed by her experience. Understandably, the New Jersey court did not want to make physical injury essential for conviction. The court's problem, therefore, was to find a way to eliminate the requirement of *extra* force, without criminalizing all physically vigorous intercourse. The solution was to read into the statute a limitation that had not been explicit before, a requirement of *nonconsent*. Said the court: "physical force in excess of that inherent in the act of sexual penetration is not required for such penetration to be unlawful. The definition of 'physical force' is satisfied . . . if the defendant applies any amount of force against another person in the absence of what a reasonable person would believe to be affirmative and freely-given permission."[28]

The net result of the New Jersey approach is that force is largely eliminated as a separate legal requirement. Nonconsent becomes the touchstone of criminal conduct. Somewhat ironically, the outcome brings the tactics of rape reform full circle. New Jersey, like many states, had revised its statutes in the late 1970s to eliminate all reference to victim consent and to focus instead on the forcible character of the defendant's conduct. The hope—soon dashed—was that an emphasis on force rather than on consent would cut through the difficulties of proof and facilitate effective enforcement. With *M. T. S.*, the New Jersey Supreme Court rewrote its statute to take just the opposite approach, emphasizing consent and making proof of force superfluous.

However debatable as statutory interpretation, the New Jersey approach offers several clear benefits for rape reform policy. Prior to *M. T. S.*, in New Jersey as in most states, a man would not be guilty of any serious offense if he avoided physical threats but nonetheless proceeded to penetration while the woman was saying "no, no, no." The new approach eliminates the unwarranted insistence on proof of physical threats. It returns attention to the properly central issue: the woman's consent. Above all it makes clear that a man who engages in sexual intercourse, knowing that he doesn't have the permission of the woman, has indeed committed a crime.[29] Only a few other states—notably Pennsylvania, Utah, Washington, and Wisconsin—have achieved the same result, and all the others needed specific statutory amendments to do so.[30]

Yet the New Jersey approach, equating the required element of force with any physical penetration, suffers from one major limitation. The *M. T. S.* test produces a clear—and appropriate—result for cases in which a man proceeds to intercourse without having a clear indication of consent. Henceforth in New Jersey, as in Pennsylvania, Utah, Washington, and Wisconsin, "no" will mean no. But what protection does criminal law offer to women who do not say "no," who instead acquiesce in a man's demands—for any of a wide variety of reasons?

Under the *M. T. S.* test, the required force is present any time there is penetration in the absence of "affirmative and freely-given permission." Unfortunately, the New Jersey Supreme Court provided no standard to determine *when* consent is "freely given." If broadly read, the requirement of freely given consent would create criminal liability whenever a woman's acquiescence was influenced by emotional demands or social pressure. Like the broadest reading of the Pennsylvania test, this approach would convert a seemingly consensual encounter into criminal assault not only in cases of economic duress or the abuse of institutional authority but whenever the defendant knew—or should have known—that the woman's participation was induced by psychological appeals, by fear that he might start dating another woman, or even by vulnerability resulting from a powerful "crush" on him.

It is safe to assume that the court did not intend these far-reaching results. But in that event, the New Jersey approach, though it starts from a different basis from Pennsylvania's, ends up in precisely the same conceptual and practical muddle. It does nothing to indicate what kinds of inducements are permissible and what kinds of pressures will invalidate consent.

If the answers are left to the good sense of judges and juries, the New Jersey test, again like Pennsylvania's, will do nothing to alter the conflicting, subjective judgments that have traditionally produced extremely cautious administration of the law of rape. Vigorous enforcement would pose a serious risk of convictions without fair warning. But once again, there is little reason to think that vigorous enforcement is at all likely, because the court's vague standard does little or nothing to permit prosecution in cases that fall outside the traditional categories of physical intimidation.[31] Predictably, subsequent New Jersey cases have added no further content to the legal test. Essex County prosecutor Robert Laurino has found the *M. T. S.* test helpful in cases in which a victim never expressed her consent because she was asleep, mentally impaired, or frozen in fear. In other situations, he says, *M. T. S.* makes little practical difference.[32] In Monmouth County, prosecutor Peter Boser notes that after *M. T. S.*, as before, "juries find it hard to believe, in the absence of traditional physical force or demonstrations of it, that there was an absence of consent."[33]

The problem remains, as always, one of identifying the boundary between autonomy and compulsion, between free choice and coerced consent. The innovative New Jersey test, though seemingly straightforward, obscures the problem rather than addressing it. To date, no state has followed New Jersey's lead by equating the required force with the physical act of penetration.

Focusing on "dominance," "force," or degrees of pressure is simply not the way to get at the problem of drawing sexual boundaries and deterring sexual abuse. Although there are similarities between violent threats and other forms of coercion, the analogies do not clarify the underlying problems or help identify the specific features that make some sexual interactions abusive. Formulas tied to notions of force and coercion are therefore bound to remain awkward and incomplete. What is missing from all these patchwork reform efforts is a willingness to focus on sexual autonomy as a basic entitlement worth protecting in its own right. The issue of sexual autonomy must be addressed directly, not as a by-product of the endless and hopelessly confusing definitional debates about the meaning of force.

6

The Missing Entitlement:
Sexual Autonomy

Reform efforts to expand the law's concept of force invariably founder because sexual interactions are influenced by so many different kinds of pressure, coercion, and duress. Institutional and cultural constraints are pervasive and endlessly various, an inescapable feature of social life. For women, the pressures are especially powerful and constraining. Yet reformers' attempts to treat nonviolent constraints as forms of coercion are both too radical and too conservative. They are too radical because they seldom suggest any stopping point. But they are also too conservative because they remain tied to the notion of force; in practice, their impact is blunted by the association of force with physical violence. None of these approaches recognizes (except rhetorically) that the central value to be protected is sexual autonomy itself, the freedom of every person to decide whether and when to engage in sexual relations.

Sexual autonomy, like every other freedom, is necessarily limited by the rights of others. My freedom to swing my arm stops at the tip of your nose. For sexual acts that involve another person, autonomy cannot entail the freedom to have sex whenever and with whomever one wants. Rather, sexual autonomy, like other rights, has two facets. The first is active—the right to decide on the kind of life one wishes to live and the kinds of activities one wishes to pursue, including activities with others who are willing. The other facet of sexual autonomy is the reverse—the right to safeguard and exclude, the freedom to refuse to have sex with any person at any time, for any reason or for no reason at all.[1]

Protection from coercion and protection of autonomy are closely related and, for that reason, sometimes hard to tell apart. Existing rape laws and all the leading reform efforts add to this confusion by blending the two concerns, as if they were simply two sides of the same coin. But the differences between them are crucial. Physical coercion interferes with autonomy, but many interferences with autonomy do not involve physical coercion or any coercion at all.

These distinctions are familiar when interests other than sexuality are at stake. A person may take $100 from me by physical force, or he may take it by coercive but nonphysical threats, for example if he threatens to spread false rumors that will ruin my business. A person may also get control over my property illegally without coercing me at all. He may take my $100 by stealth, when I am not looking, or he may persuade me to give it to him by falsely promising something in return. In these cases, his actions are illegal but not coercive. If our law of theft punished only "coercive" takings, we might try to say that takings by stealth and deception were "in effect" coercive. But we would know that the language was strained, and the law of theft requires no such verbal contortions. It simply punishes takings by force (robbery), by coercive threats (extortion), by stealth (larceny), by breach of trust (embezzlement), and by deception (fraud and false pretenses).[2] All these methods violate my rights because they impair—with no adequate justification—my control over my property.

Much the same can be said for nearly all of our most fundamental interests. The law protects our control over our labor, our vote, our right to receive honest services from professionals, and our privacy, including confidential information about ourselves. Contexts are important, and the details of legal rights vary, but the general point holds: law protects our autonomy in regard to these interests—our freedom to retain them or dispose of them however we may choose. It prohibits interference with meaningful choice by force, by stealth, and, usually, by breach of trust or deception. The law does not strain to say that all these interferences are "coercive"; it simply treats them as impermissible infringements on the liberty and self-determination to which every person is entitled.

Sexual autonomy is treated differently. Few of our other personal rights and liberties, perhaps only our right to life itself, are as important as our right to decide whether and when we will become sexually intimate with another person. The emotional vulnerability and potential physical danger attached to sexual interaction make effective legal safeguards at least as important for sex as they are for the sale of land or the purchase of a used car. Yet sexual autonomy, almost alone among our important personal rights, is not fully protected. The law of rape, as if it were only a law against the "robbery" of sex, remains focused almost exclusively on preventing interference by force. With minor exceptions, other infringements on our right to sexual self-determination aren't covered. In the list of fundamental entitlements the law grants to us as free and independent beings—entitlements to life, to physical safety, to our property, and to our labor—an entitlement to sexual autonomy is somehow left out.

There is nothing intrinsic to sexuality that requires this constricted pattern of protection. Violent threats are just one possible source of a defect in consent, and the law already recognizes a few others in the context of sexual relations. The best-known example is immaturity: the law has long prohibited consensual intercourse with a girl who is below the legally prescribed age of consent. The law likewise punishes acts of intercourse with a woman who is sleeping, unconscious, mentally incompetent, or unaware that a sexual act is being performed—as when a doctor, pretending to examine her with surgical instruments, penetrates her with his penis instead.[3] In these instances we do not say that consent was obtained by force. The man's conduct is illegal because valid consent was never obtained at all.

Traditionally, the law draws no formal distinction between the cases of physical violence and the exceptional cases in which a woman's consent is considered ineffective; all are classified as rape. Yet our terminology keeps force in the forefront. In ordinary language, rape *means* the imposition of intercourse by force. Other accepted definitions include "violent seizure," "carrying away a person by force," and, as a verb, "to seize, take or carry off by force."[4] The various dictionary definitions of rape all center on violent or forcible intercourse and, by extension, other violent misconduct.[5]

The law condemning consensual intercourse with young girls illustrates our verbal confusion. The legal definition of rape has covered this type of sexual abuse since the sixteenth century,[6] and most contemporary statutes continue to classify it as a form of rape. Yet in common parlance, we hedge, calling the offense "statutory rape." This everyday expression is a term of ordinary language, not of law. The term "statutory rape" is not found in the penal codes themselves, and technically it has no legal meaning.[7] By speaking of "statutory" rape, we signal our instinct that consensual sex with a teenager is not *really* rape. It is only *deemed equivalent* to rape by operation of statute. For more than 400 years, the law in English-speaking countries has defined the word "rape" as including consensual intercourse with a minor, but the public's understanding of what the word "rape" means and what a real rape requires—force—has yet to change.

Because force is central to the connotations of "rape," our terminology obscures the importance of sexual autonomy as an interest worth protecting in its own right. Recent efforts to rename "rape" statutes as laws against "sexual assault" do nothing to break this association of the offense with physically violent misconduct, because assault, like rape, is a term implying physical force.

The terminology in turn influences assumptions about the proper scope of rape or assault, for judges, legislators, ordinary citizens, and committed antirape activists alike. Rather than asking whether certain sexual advances unjustifiably impair freedom of choice, we have asked only whether the conduct is so bad that it is equivalent to violent compulsion, whether it is tantamount to rape. Yet intercourse with an apparently willing fifteen-year-old or with a mentally incompetent woman is not prohibited because the man is a potential killer; it is prohibited because the preconditions for meaningful choice are absent. Intercourse with an unconscious woman is prohibited not because the act is considered violent (though it does have violent aspects) but more fundamentally because taking advantage of the woman's incapacity violates, without any conceivable justification, her right to control access to her own body.

Sexual autonomy should not exist so precariously, as a mere by-product of the law's restrictions on the use of force. It is an independent interest, indeed one of the most important interests for any free person. A decent regime for safeguarding fundamental rights should place sexual autonomy at the center of attention and protect it directly, for its own sake, just as we protect physical safety, property, labor, and informational privacy, the core interests of every human being.

And that recognition should shift the focus of debates about the proper reach of law. Attention should no longer focus exclusively on whether a man's behavior is aberrant, egregious, or potentially lethal. Rather, the proper questions for debate are whether each participant in a sexual encounter had a meaningful opportunity to choose, and whether a meaningful choice was in fact made, before sexual penetration occurred. In connection with criminal sanctions, law must also consider whether the defendant can fairly be considered culpable. But culpability cannot be confined to cases of aberrant physical violence; there is ample reason to find criminal responsibility when, for example, a man commits an act of sexual penetration *knowing* that he doesn't have the woman's consent.

Posing the issues in these terms will not by itself resolve all the important issues. The content of meaningful choice and the limits of permissible interference with autonomy must be determined by paying close attention to contexts. We have to consider the dynamics of sexual interaction in different settings and the possible impairment of decision-making capabilities under different circumstances. We have to consider as well the possibility of significant differences between the scope of protection that is appropriate for sexuality and the scope of protection appropriate for other interests that current law protects. But the issue must be framed in terms of sexual autonomy itself, not in terms of a futile search for something we can squeeze under the rubric of "force."

Legal doctrines have begun to move—haltingly—in this direction. But the changes remain incomplete and confused (as new legal developments frequently are). After nearly three decades, beginning with the feminist reforms of the early 1970s, legal doctrines still have not shifted their central concern from force to sexual autonomy.

Changes in patterns of thought and in legal doctrines seldom occur quickly. The narrow, technicality-ridden law of theft, under intense pressure from powerful propertied and commercial interests from the eighteenth century onward, took 150 years to shed its ancient conceptual baggage and assume its modern form.[8] Oliver Wendell Holmes, at the outset of his famous lectures on the common law, stressed how much our categories of thought can block the evolution of needed legal change: "The substance of the law at any given time pretty nearly corresponds . . . with what is then understood to be convenient; but its form and machinery, and the degree to which it is able to work out desired results, depend very much upon its past." And Holmes's lecture notes add at this point: "Imagination of men limited—can only think in terms of the language they have been taught."[9]

By historical standards, the challenge to rape law is still quite recent. But we should not have to wait 150 years to step back and assess the reform effort. Existing laws remain seriously flawed; they do not prevent enough of the misconduct they appear to prohibit, and there remain major gaps in the kinds of abuses that these laws try to reach even in theory. Yet the vagueness and excessive breadth of proposed solutions arouse justifiable controversy and alarm. It seems safe to conclude that continued efforts to elaborate the notion of force will lead only to further dead ends.

It is time to break out of these traps by shifting the terms of the moral and legal debate. As a core interest of every free person, the right to sexual autonomy deserves to stand at the center of attention, protected directly and comprehensively for its own sake.

The question immediately arises whether a criminal offense for violating sexual autonomy should be called "rape," "sexual assault," or something else entirely. Usually the judgment about how to name our offense categories is of little practical interest. In property crimes the labels used are neither uniform nor important.[10] In sexual crimes, however, the labeling decision may be very important. A persistent pitfall of rape reform has been the tenacity of common culture and its influence over the interpretation of ambitious reforms. Rape reformers have paid close attention to labels but have disagreed sharply over the best approach.

Legal scholar Lynne Henderson, who writes as the survivor of a brutal, life-threatening rape, stresses that violent and nonviolent abuse are distinct problems. She warns that "to lose the distinction [between rape and undesired sex] . . . is to trivialize what rape *is* and what it *does* to a woman."[11] In contrast, Susan Estrich, also a rape survivor, insists on the importance of applying the label "rape" to cases in which consent is negated by misrepresentation or nonviolent threats, because this approach will signal that society regards all these offenses as very serious.[12]

There is no sure solution to this problem of symbolism, labeling, and the psychology of legal change. But it seems plausible that a poor fit between legal terminology and ordinary language will tend to impede success in both directions of the legal-cultural dialogue. When courts and legislatures employ unfamiliar word meanings (for example by deciding that "force" can be nonviolent, that acquiescence in economic pressure can be "rape"), they complicate a communication that is already difficult. The risk is nullification at all levels. Prosecutors and jurors may misunderstand the new message (it's not *really* force, not *really* rape). Other citizens may not even hear it.

To avoid such problems, the law of sexual abuse should be organized around two separate offenses. "Rape" should cover cases of intercourse by actual or threatened physical violence. A new offense, "sexual abuse," should cover nonviolent interference with sexual autonomy. It remains necessary, of course, to develop a clear understanding of just what actions constitute an interference with autonomy.

The Contours of Autonomy

Autonomy is a large concept, larger and potentially even more slippery than "force." The word, from *auto*, meaning self, and *nomos*, rule or law, refers to self-governance or self-determination, in a variety of far-reaching senses. Legal and philosophical conceptions of autonomy are not identical. With regard to our property, our labor, and our other vital interests, law protects our autonomy only in certain specific respects. Inevitably, the sort of autonomy that can claim legal protection is far less extensive than the ambitious conception of self-governance that is often advanced as a philosophical aspiration. But before we focus on the features of sexual autonomy that deserve formal protection, it will be helpful to identify the many dimensions of autonomy and the various ways in which autonomy can be impaired.

A person's decision—about a sexual matter or any other—clearly lacks autonomy if the choice is the result of threats or other improper interference. To these external conditions we must add a number of requirements that are internal to the individual. A person can be autonomous only if she has mental competency, an awareness of her options, and sufficient information to be able to choose intelligently between the possibilities that external conditions make available.

Many philosophers insist that autonomy requires even more. For a person to be fully self-governing, they suggest, requires not only that she be free of interference with her choices, but also that she be able to select from a wide array of reasonable alternatives when making any particular decision and when planning the direction of her life in general.[13] Full autonomy also requires that she have extensive information about the available options (and about other pertinent facts), along with freedom from deceptive or other seriously incorrect information.

And still she would not be fully autonomous if the desires she held and the preferences that guided her choices were not truly her own. Because a truly autonomous person would be completely self-governing, even a free and voluntary choice seems to lack full autonomy if the person's desires have been shaped by cultural influences or other forces beyond her control. In such cases it might be plausible to say that the person's preferences lack autonomy, in the sense that she did not freely choose them.

We cannot expect (even in theory) that a person's preferences can be entirely self-generated, because complex preferences, beyond the basic appetites for food, shelter, and sexual release, can hardly form at all in the absence of social influence. And no fully objective method permits us to determine which social influences render a person's preferences inauthentic. Yet it seems reasonable to require that preferences not be deformed by false beliefs, artificially constraining cultural pressures, or the need to minimize psychic stress—a need that leads many people to develop a distaste for jobs and activities that are irrevocably closed to them.[14]

All this is a tall order, but there is more. Because autonomy requires conscious reflection about preferences and a deliberate choice of one's goals, the unreflective, impulsive person is not truly autonomous: she is not really the author of her own life. Some might say she has only herself to blame for this. But society and its laws play a crucial role in making reflection possible. Adequate education, the realistic availability of alternative options, and a culture that supports an adequate degree of personal introspection could thus be added to the prerequisites for considering that citizens, and the choices they make, are truly autonomous.

Must we say, then, that autonomy is absent—that choices are invalid and in effect coerced—whenever any of these ambitious preconditions for autonomy is missing? Or is it all just a question of degree? Some philosophers have tied themselves into knots over these sorts of questions because they have failed to focus on the purpose for which the questions are being asked.[15] Judgments about autonomy always involve questions of degree, but we want to be able to say whether sufficient autonomy is present in a given situation. And this question does permit consistent answers, provided we remember that autonomy may be sufficient for some purposes but not for others.

One perspective, an important one, is purely personal. To the individual who aspires to lead an autonomous life, the philosopher rightly wants to point out that her decisions will not truly be her own, that she should not accept them as valid for herself, in the absence of adequate information and adequate reflection on the importance of her goals. To say this is not necessarily to imply that anyone else is coercing her or that social conditions affecting her decision are unfair (though they might be). And to say to her that an overly hasty decision will lack autonomy certainly does not imply that she shouldn't be bound by her choice once she makes it.

Social conditions sometimes do prevent people from making autonomous choices. A woman may accept work scrubbing floors and cleaning bathrooms only because most other ways to earn a living are closed to her, either by poor education, racial discrimination, or formal legal prohibitions. Here it seems plausible to describe the woman's decision as coerced by forces beyond her control. Yet if we think her decision is not truly voluntary, we seem pushed to conclude that her consent to do the work is invalid. We may feel driven to conclude that her employer is acting immorally or even illegally by participating in the coercive arrangement. But ruling out the woman's opportunity to accept such jobs might make her life even harder than it already is. So there is also some reason to draw the opposite conclusion—that we should respect the choice she makes under tough circumstances, that her consent to the working arrangements is valid after all. It seems then that her decision is *not* really coerced. Yet this conclusion is unsatisfactory too, because we know that unfair social conditions, together with her need to eat, virtually *compelled* her to take the job.

Again, the difficulty of giving consistent answers to questions about autonomy is the result of a failure to be clear about the purposes for which the questions are being asked. To stress the woman's lack of autonomy under unjust social conditions is, of course, to make an important criticism of society and to argue for altering its cultural prejudices, the distribution of its resources, and its laws governing education and eligibility for good jobs. But to say all this would not by itself show that the woman should be able to avoid moral or legal responsibility for an agreement she might make with her employer. Nor would her lack of autonomy, though undeniable, serve by itself to show that the employer should be criticized—or criminally punished—for offering her the job scrubbing floors and for accepting her services.

Sometimes we will criticize—or even punish—the employer. If the wages are low, moral criticism may be called for, and if they are *very* low, below the minimum wage, the employer's behavior could be criminal. But if the employer offers generous wages and treats the woman with decency and respect, the situation requires a more complicated assessment. Under those circumstances, it is still right to say that the woman's consent to work scrubbing floors was coerced by cultural and economic conditions, and that these conditions might require reform. But it is *not* right to say that her employer violated her autonomy or that *he* coerced her consent. His actions, and the resulting relationship between the two, could be legally permissible and perhaps even desirable, though the social conditions are flawed.

The same distinction between individual and social interference with autonomy is crucial to assessing consent in sexual relationships. Social conditions impairing sexual autonomy may require extensive economic, legal, or cultural reform. And sometimes a woman's lack of autonomy justifies a decision to condemn her partner for having sex with her. But the question whether to criticize or punish the man for his behavior is always a different question from the question whether social circumstances deserve criticism and reform. Even when background conditions severely limit a woman's options, it may make sense to honor the choices she makes. Due respect for her autonomy may even require us to do so. And we can condemn the social constraints as unjustified, without being logically compelled to condemn her male partner's behavior as improper. If he treats her with dignity and respect, his conduct may not call for any moral criticism.

The difference between autonomy problems due to background conditions and autonomy problems due to individual behavior must be stressed because this distinction—which is crucial for both law and moral judgment—is blurred or ignored in a large part of academic and popular writing about rape. Both feminist critics of rape law and defenders of the status quo perpetuate the confusion. Feminists rightly stress the distortion of women's preferences and deplore the interferences with autonomy that result from cultural pressure, economic dependency, and women's justified fears of violence from male strangers. Feminists rightly note that under these conditions, women's consent to sex, even when given to a trusted, nonthreatening male friend, may not be the result of a truly free and authentic choice.

But many prominent feminists go further. Andrea Dworkin writes that "intercourse remains a means or the means of physiologically making a woman inferior."[16] Catharine MacKinnon argues that "for women it is difficult to distinguish [rape from intercourse] under conditions of male dominance."[17] Claims of this sort are sometimes understood to suggest that a man's behavior might be viewed as wrongful (as "rape") even when he is a caring partner who is not making any sort of threat. That conclusion is not only a non sequitur, but it lends an air of implausibility and extremism to claims about social coercion that are largely incontrovertible.

Critics of the antirape movement make the opposite mistake. Writers like Camile Paglia, Katie Roiphe, and Christina Hoff Sommers center their discussion of sexual coercion almost entirely on the questions whether a woman should be bound by her consent to sex and whether her partner should face criminal punishment. These writers consider it absurd to imagine that women have no real choices. They insist that it is implausible and unfair to consider a man a rapist when women consent to sex because of cultural signals, verbal persuasion, peer pressure, economic constraints, and the like. Defending the status quo, they stress a concept of autonomy that requires a woman to "take responsibility" for her own actions, an approach these writers present as more authentically "feminist" than the one underlying activist demands for greater protection.

The claim that individual women can fairly be held to their choices and that their male partners should not face sanctions is simply not persuasive in some settings—for example, when a college student submits to unwelcome advances from a teacher who is threatening to block her applications to graduate school. But even when "take responsibility" claims make sense, as they normally do for sexual consent obtained by nonthreatening verbal persuasion, the claim is irrelevant to the further points these writers want to make. Almost in the same breath, these writers conclude that feminists cannot plausibly speak of coercion or impaired autonomy at all. They conclude that there is no reason to worry about the social conditions that impel a woman to submit to sexual demands that she finds thoroughly unwelcome. This second set of conclusions poses altogether different questions.

To keep clearly in focus what autonomy is, and what steps are needed to protect it, we must not confuse these two distinct issues—the wrongfulness of background conditions and the wrongfulness of individual conduct. Sometimes, when freedom of choice is impaired, it makes sense to consider a sexual encounter abusive and illegal, as when a student submits to the professor who threatens to interfere with her career. For other constrained choices—such as an impoverished woman's decision to sleep with a wealthy, older man who doesn't interest her sexually—it might make sense to treat the relationship as morally suspect but legally permissible. If the impoverished woman and the wealthy, older man respect each other and are sexually attracted, their committed relationship could be considered morally desirable, even if the woman might have chosen differently in the absence of unfair economic pressure. Unjust background conditions do not by themselves enable us to judge the moral responsibility of the individuals concerned. To do that, we must consider other features of their relationship.

This microlevel focus on the responsibility of individuals is essential, but it should not be allowed to eclipse the significance of broader questions of social justice and cultural change. Economic dependency powerfully constrains women's options and limits their freedom to choose, or refuse, their sexual partners. For women to achieve full sexual autonomy, it is crucial to attack employment discrimination, economic dependency within marriage, financial distress upon divorce, and a host of other social conditions that constrain options and distort preferences. In focusing attention on the proper scope of criminal sanctions and other remedies for individual misconduct, we must remember that autonomy also can be threatened by broad social and cultural pressures that require different kinds of solutions.

Autonomy as a Legal Entitlement

Once the focus of legal concern shifts from force to sexual autonomy, a much broader range of individual misconduct is called into question.

Fully autonomous choice requires mental capacity, awareness of the available options, adequate information, and freedom from outside interference with the process of choice. When one individual interferes with another person's ability to choose freely in a sexual encounter, legal intervention is appropriate even in the absence of force, just as it is when an individual impairs another person's autonomy in relation to property rights, privacy, and the other entitlements that law already recognizes.

Sometimes it makes sense to hold an individual responsible even when he does not personally interfere with another person's capacity to choose. If a fifteen-year-old girl initiates a sexual encounter with a twenty-year-old man, he violates her autonomy by having sex with her, even though her incapacity is in no sense the result of his own actions. One reason is that sexual conduct involves a physical intrusion. In the absence of consent, that intrusion is in itself a serious wrong.

Sexual autonomy thus has three distinct dimensions. The first two are mental—an internal capacity to make reasonably mature and rational choices, and an external freedom from impermissible pressures and constraints. The third dimension is equally important. The core concept of the person, long protected by the common law, implies a physical boundary, the bodily integrity of the individual. Autonomy, therefore, is not only mental and intellectual, not only the capacity for meaningful, unconstrained choice. It is also physical, the separateness of the corporeal person. Even without making threats that restrict the exercise of free choice, an individual violates a woman's autonomy when he engages in sexual conduct without ensuring that he has her valid consent.

To see just what the protection of autonomy requires, we must look closely at the preconditions for valid choice under different circumstances. We cannot speak in one breath of sexual encounters between a college student and her date, a patient and her doctor, and a prison inmate and her guard. At the same time, laws must be framed with some degree of generality. And satisfactory solutions require us to draw on and fill out general concepts—ideas like consent and coercion that cut across the particularities of different factual settings.

The starting point for any consideration of autonomy is the question whether a person's consent is coerced. A focus on sexual autonomy enables us to distinguish legitimate inducements from threats and from other sorts of pressure (sometimes in the form of "offers") that should be criminally punishable.[18]

Without explicit threats or other improper inducements, freedom of choice can still be affected by the distribution of power in particular settings. Consent can be tainted by constraints that are inherent in relationships between teachers and students, between job supervisors and their subordinates, and between prison guards and inmates. Respect for autonomy normally obliges us not to interfere with voluntary choices and not to criminalize consenting relationships between competent adults. Yet the pressures that pervade some relationships may require legal intervention to protect the weaker party, even in the absence of explicit threats. Criminal law is not always the best tool of regulation, however; civil liability standards and private workplace norms are often better means of protecting sexual autonomy, especially in the absence of illegitimate threats.[19]

Professional relationships pose additional problems for genuine freedom of sexual choice. Like a job supervisor or teacher, the lawyer, doctor, dentist, or psychotherapist can exercise direct power, for example by threatening to withhold services that his client or patient desperately needs. But the professional's actions can also interfere with autonomous choice in more complicated ways. The patient or client who seeks professional help is often vulnerable and exposed; she depends on the professional's commitment to her welfare, in a relationship founded on trust. Her choices are especially susceptible to distortion and manipulation. Sexual relationships between clients or patients and their psychotherapists, doctors, dentists, and lawyers therefore warrant close scrutiny, and legal restrictions are needed even in the absence of explicit threats. But once again, criminal law is not necessarily the best regulatory tool.[20]

The capacity for meaningful choice can also be impaired by deception. We take for granted that criminal law should punish those who obtain property by fraud, but the law places no restrictions—none at all—on the use of fraudulent tactics to obtain consent to sex. Proposals to insist upon the same level of honesty in sexual exchange that we require as a matter of course in property transactions are usually dismissed as impractical or wildly out of touch with reality. Yet good reasons are seldom offered for the law's refusal to protect sexual autonomy from even the most egregious deceptive inducements.[21]

Even if an encounter is completely free of threats, deception, dispari-ties of power, or breach of trust, a sexual act obviously violates auton-omy when one of the parties does not consent. But the question of what counts as an expression of consent is intensely contested: Does "no" always mean no? Is physical resistance necessary to make clear the absence of consent? And can we infer willingness from silence or am-bivalence, from *not* saying "no"? Questions about what should count as consent are central in any sexual interaction, and they become espe-cially controversial in dating situations.[22]

In all these contexts the problems posed are controversial and difficult, but no more so than the issues that law has long been willing to confront, outside the domain of sex, in order to protect freedom of choice and prevent abuses of power. We take for granted, as birthrights, our control over our property, our labor, and our personal privacy. But we also know that these rights have to be defined, nurtured, and sup-ported by law. Sexual autonomy is no less important. Like the other core interests of a free person, sexual autonomy deserves to be respected as a genuine entitlement, fully protected in its own right.

7

Sexual Coercion:

The Problem of Threats and Resistance

In the existing law of rape, it remains perfectly legal for a man to use coercive pressure to compel a woman's consent to sex. Flagrant threats are treated as part of the permissible repertoire of sexual bargaining, provided they steer clear of arousing fear of physical harm. The law seeks, at least in theory, to protect women from serious violence, but until now the law has not been concerned, even in theory, with protecting a woman's right to make a genuinely free choice whether to participate in a sexual encounter.

The narrow focus on violence rather than on sexual autonomy supplies the logic for why the Montana high school principal committed no crime when he allegedly forced a student to submit to sex by threatening to prevent her from graduating. If he had forced her to pay him a few hundred dollars by making the same threat, he would easily be convicted of extortion. But if the young woman gave him sex rather than money, he faced no criminal sanction.[1]

In Pennsylvania, John Biggs repeatedly had sex with his seventeen-year-old daughter. He told her that if she told anyone, he would show people nude pictures of her. If he had forced her to pay him in cash for not showing the pictures, he would be guilty of blackmail, a serious felony in nearly all states. But Biggs could not be convicted of blackmail, because he obtained sex, not money, and he could not be convicted of rape, because, as the appellate court put it, he obtained his daughter's compliance "by threats, not of force, but of humiliation."[2]

In an Ohio case, prosecutors tried to use a broadly worded extortion statute to overcome the usual limits on prosecuting sexual misconduct. Dixie Stone was a medical laboratory instructor at Washington Technical College. In the fall of 1989 she received a series of anonymous letters. The writer asked for information about her body measurements and indicated that he wanted to have sex with her. One letter included a computer-generated picture of a woman performing fellatio, with a caption stating "Dixie Stone the best little hore [*sic*] in town." The writer stated that if she didn't comply with his demands, he would post similar pictures throughout the school. A subsequent letter included a poster with computer-generated pictures of a topless woman, captioned "Dixie Stone The Best Little Hore [*sic*] In The School And She Is Free She's Ready For You." Again, the author threatened to place similar posters throughout the school.

Ms. Stone had the presence of mind to alert the school authorities, and a surveillance of her faculty mailbox succeeded in apprehending the harasser, a man named Paul Stone (who was not related to the victim). Prosecutors charged Paul with extortion, under a statute that made it an aggravated felony to "utter or threaten any calumny against any person . . . with a purpose to obtain any valuable thing or valuable benefit."[3] The jury found Paul guilty of extortion, but in 1992 an Ohio appeals court reversed the conviction. Referring to the language of the extortion statute, the court held that the "phrase 'valuable thing or valuable benefit' must be interpreted to include only things or benefits that have monetary value."[4] As a result, Paul Stone's conduct could not qualify as extortion, even under the broad Ohio statute. His harassing acts were a low-level misdemeanor under Ohio law, but they could not rise to the level of a serious crime, even if Paul had succeeded in coercing Ms. Stone's consent to his sexual demands.

Recognition of sexual autonomy as a fully protected entitlement suggests a different approach to this problem. All coercive behavior, whether violent or nonviolent, seeks to induce sexual intimacy that the coerced individual would not otherwise choose. A person violates another person's autonomy—and therefore should be considered guilty of sexual abuse—whenever he attempts to engage in sexual intercourse with consent that was obtained by coercion.

In an analysis based on sexual autonomy, the critical question is to determine whether actions like Paul Stone's should be considered coercive. Most courts reject this framework because they see social, economic, and psychological pressure as pervasive and unavoidable. Few people would say that a school official should have the right to get sex by threatening to prevent a student from graduating. But if the law makes all nonviolent coercion illegal, must we then condemn as a criminal the college student who threatens to stop dating a girlfriend if she continues to spurn his requests to go "all the way"? A requirement that consent must be completely free, unaffected by any influence whatever, seems extremely broad and uncertain.

Distinguishing coercion from the acceptable influences, incentives, and demands that pervade human interaction can sometimes be difficult, but this problem is hardly unique to sexual encounters. Throughout the domain of social and commercial interchange, "bargaining" is a valued form of behavior, normally beneficial for both parties, but coercion is intolerable. And wherever important interests are at stake, law is normally available to punish conduct that crosses the line from one to the other. Indeed, law must be available to police this line, if freedom of choice is to be preserved and abuse of power prevented.

Standards to identify impermissible coercion therefore need not be created out of whole cloth for purposes of protecting freedom of sexual choice. Such standards are commonplace—and are already developed in detail—in other areas of law, property law in particular. If we begin with notions of valid consent that are routinely accepted when property rights and other important interests are at stake, we can see that the defining characteristics of illegitimate coercion are familiar and for the most part obvious. By drawing on principles already accepted in other areas of law, we can develop a workable and reasonably well-bounded understanding of sexual coercion.

What we cannot do is simply to assume that standards for sexual consent should be identical to the standards that apply in commercial bargaining. Sexual encounters differ from economic transactions in numerous important ways. Yet the notion of treating sex as a commodity to be bargained over and traded like any item of economic exchange has held a curious attraction for lawyers and philosophers who write about rape. The economic model of sexual interaction has been touted not only by Judge Richard Posner, who opposes new safeguards, but also by many committed feminists and others interested in expanding criminal law protections.[5]

These efforts to equate sex with ordinary items of market exchange are in equal parts suggestive and misleading. It is helpful to bear in mind the limits on bargaining that we readily accept for commercial transactions. But the analogy to ordinary commerce cannot be decisive in itself. Concepts of free choice and improper interference depend crucially on context. Sexual encounters have purposes, effects, psychological preconditions, and emotional consequences that differ fundamentally from those of most economic transactions.[6] Many of the differences suggest a need for more caution in regulating sexual behavior. Social norms are far more controversial. And sexual interaction doesn't automatically—even when consensual—take something away from one person and give future control of it to another. Although a sexual encounter can be harmful, it can also give mutual satisfaction; unlike a transfer of property, it doesn't automatically leave one of the parties worse off.[7]

These differences suggest one reason why claims of intimidation and nonconsent give courts more difficulty in cases of sexual encounters than in cases involving property. A man who is six feet tall, weighing 200 pounds, chats for a few minutes with a small, thin woman sitting beside him on a park bench. Suddenly he says, "Hand over your wallet." If she complies, we can feel virtually certain that she did so in fear, not because she wanted to give him a gift. But suppose instead that the man says, "Lift up your dress. I want to have sex with you." If the woman complies, it remains very likely that she did so in fear. But because he was asking for sex rather than for money, there is now some possibility that she complied because she was truly willing, expecting that the encounter would be as pleasurable for herself as for him. Courts have been far too quick to find consent in situations of this kind or to give the benefit of the doubt to men who claim they mistook the woman's fear for awe and sexual interest. But even so, the problems of determining whether the woman consented, and whether the man was at fault for assuming that she did, *are* different when the interaction is sexual. There is a reason, not present in the property case, to hesitate before imposing liability—especially criminal liability.

Yet there are also reasons to impose liability *more* readily in the case of the sexual encounter. The woman who gives her wallet to the man in the park often will be left frightened, shaky, and angry over the loss of her money and credit cards. But if his intimidating actions lead her to comply with a sexual demand, unwillingly and in fear, the experience is likely to be emotionally devastating, leaving scars for life. Bodily privacy and sexual intimacy are especially precious interests, and the psychic injury of unwanted sexual contact is far more serious than the emotional harm that normally accompanies an interference with property rights. The need to ensure that consent is genuine and uncoerced is much stronger in the case of sexual contact. At the same time, determinations of consent can be more difficult, because motivations are so much more complex. The distinctive features of sexual interaction make effective requirements of consent both especially important and especially hard to design. However we resolve the issues, we cannot simply posit that the prerequisites of free choice should be identical for cases involving property and sex.

The simple step of equating legal protection for sexual and nonsexual interests cannot be sufficient for another reason as well. Outside the sexual domain, the interests that law protects are themselves far from uniform, and the concepts of consent that govern for various nonsexual interests are not identical. The standards that define and protect rights to tangible property differ, sometimes sharply, from the standards that apply to the right to preserve confidential information, the right to vote, the right to jury trial, and a variety of other interests. Because there is no single regime of safeguards for the diverse interests that law protects outside the sexual domain, there is no single set of rules that can provide the obvious benchmark for standards of sexual coercion. Nor should there be. No simple procedure can possibly suffice for transferring a complex system of legal protections from one social context to another.

A suitable conception of sexual coercion therefore must grow out of the nature of sexual autonomy itself. The standards of impermissible coercion that protect other important interests are suggestive, but the goal must be to identify the kinds of pressures that should be considered impermissibly coercive in sexual interactions.

To distinguish legitimate influence from impermissible coercion, the best way to begin is to consider whether the inducement being deployed amounts to an offer or a threat. Threats represent a clear-cut interference with autonomy. They are inherently coercive and illegitimate. Offers, along with other kinds of nonthreatening influence, are not automatically permissible, of course. Under special circumstances, offers may have severe coercive effects, or they may be considered illegitimate for other reasons.

An understanding of sexual coercion therefore requires attention to several large issues. We must first decide whether a proposal is an offer or a threat. We must also reexamine the law's traditional assumption that in sexual encounters, threats (even threats of physical force) are not necessarily coercive if a "reasonable" woman could have resisted them. Finally, we must consider whether a nonthreatening influence (an "offer") should be considered impermissible—either because it is coercive or for other reasons. In each case, satisfactory conclusions require attention to the dynamics of sexual interaction and to the kinds of principles used to distinguish permissible from impermissible inducements in other areas of law and life.

A discussion of sexual coercion therefore requires some scope. The distinctions that need to be drawn are sometimes difficult, but they are not simply the stuff of legal or philosophical technicalities. Both offers and threats can induce action, and both kinds of inducements can be powerful, even irresistible. But their power alone cannot be a reason to condemn them. Offers normally enlarge our opportunities and enhance our ability to lead a flourishing life. The capacity to interact in the social world, to make and accept offers with others, is a central feature of autonomy, an essential part of what it means to be a free person. But threats impair autonomy and reduce our freedom. We cannot skip lightly over the difference between the two.

Distinguishing Offers from Threats

A proposal is most obviously a threat when it announces an intention to inflict a serious injury. The classic threat, "Your money or your life," leaves the robbery victim no real choice. When an unemployed executive with few job prospects receives a proposal to work in a low-level sales position, he too may reasonably feel that he has "no real choice" other than to take the job. Yet it would be very odd to describe the job proposal he receives as a threat. "No real choice" therefore cannot be the test for distinguishing offers from threats.[8]

The reason why "Your money or your life" cannot be considered an offer is that the person receiving this proposal has the right to keep both. The same point applies to proposals that contemplate inflicting a non-physical injury. The thug who tells a business owner to pay up or see his store windows broken is making a threat, not an offer, because the owner has the right to keep intact both his money and his windows. The man who proposed to spread false rumors about Dixie Stone, unless she met his sexual demands, was not just making an offer, because she had the right to both her reputation and her freedom of sexual choice.

In contrast, "Pay me five dollars or I won't wash your car" is merely an offer, because the target of the proposal gives up money to get a clean car, something he has no right to obtain without payment. The unemployed executive who receives a job proposal may feel he has no real choice, but the job proposal is an offer because he obviously has no right to receive the salary without doing the work. A surgeon who will perform a life-saving operation, but only for a fee, is in effect saying "Your money or your life." And often the patient will have no real choice but to meet the surgeon's demand. Nonetheless, the proposal is merely an offer, because our system of health care, as it currently stands, gives the patient no right to obtain treatment without charge.

A threat, in other words, is a proposal to make a person worse off than she has a right to be. An offer is a proposal that contemplates making the person better off, in return for her taking the action requested. The determinative idea here, the crucial point of reference, is the set of rights and expectations that the person receiving the proposal is entitled to hold. A proposal that enables a person to improve her situation, relative to that starting point, is an offer. She will be better off if she accepts, and if she refuses, she will be no worse off than she would be if the offer had never been made. But a proposal that will leave her worse off is a threat.

The exact scope of the rights we are entitled to claim may be debatable, of course. Our rights are not preordained, and it is often important to consider whether we should add new ones or reconsider the ones that existing law protects. We cannot avoid making judgments about what the content of our rights should be. What makes a threat coercive and improper is precisely that it proposes to take away from me something that I am rightfully entitled to claim.

By this standard, a school official makes a clear threat if he tells a student he will prevent her from graduating unless she consents to sex. The Ohio man obviously made a threat when he proposed to distribute posters with concocted pictures and defamatory statements about Dixie

Stone. A wide range of behavior currently permitted by the law of rape is unambiguously threatening in just the same way, even though it involves no prospect of physical harm, because the woman who receives the proposal cannot refuse it without finding herself worse off than she is entitled to be.

Sometimes it is more difficult to decide whether an inducement should be considered a threat. What should we say, for example, of the college student who won't continue dating his girlfriend unless she submits to his demand for sexual intercourse? It seems natural to describe his demand as a threat to stop dating her. Yet he might just as plausibly recast his statement as an offer: he proposes to date her in the future, if she is willing to meet his sexual demands. As a purely verbal matter, the choice between the two formulations, between offer and threat, may seem arbitrary. But the underlying concern is to determine whether the young man's proposal will make his girlfriend better or worse off than she is entitled to be. This question is not at all arbitrary; it focuses our attention on the expectations that the two parties should be entitled to have.

To locate the controlling set of expectations, the formal rights of the two parties are one natural place to start. Legally, the woman has no right to compel the man to keep dating her on terms that she alone can decide. The law permits him to stop seeing her for any reason or for no reason. His "threat" to terminate the relationship would not take from her anything that current law entitles her to have, and therefore his proposal has to be considered an offer, not a threat.

The conclusion that the dating proposal is merely an offer might be right, but it seems to oversimplify the situation. If we shift our focus from existing legal rights to the emotional dynamics of the relationship, the issue would have to be discussed in different terms.[9] The woman may feel that the young man should continue dating her without forcing sex before she is ready. She expects their level of sexual involvement to proceed gradually, at a pace she finds comfortable. Psychologically, therefore, her boyfriend's demand feels like a threat. His insistence on sex leaves her with two alternatives—to have intercourse before she feels ready, or to see him break off the relationship. Either option will leave her worse off than she expected to be.

From still another perspective, some might argue that the woman's expectations, though important, should not be decisive. Rather, they might say, the relevant expectations are those it would be reasonable for her to hold, in light of normal assumptions about decent behavior and fair dealing.

We would need to know more about the two students and the history of their relationship in order to make this kind of moral assessment. If the students have just met, and the young man insists on sex as a condition of any further dates, we would probably criticize his goals as superficial, but we could hardly say that he has a moral obligation to continue dating her. If the two students have dated for years and have planned to spend important occasions together in the future, the appropriate expectations are different. The young man's demand to change the trajectory of the relationship might violate a number of implicit commitments. Morally, he should respect his girlfriend's concerns about their level of physical intimacy and honor the expectations that arise from the relationship. If their sexual desires seem incompatible, he might be justified in breaking off the relationship, but only after attempting to work out their differences on a basis of mutual discussion, not unilateral demand. Judged from the perspective of fair dealing—the set of expectations that the young woman is morally entitled to hold—the student's insistence on sexual intercourse probably counts as a threat.

The upshot is that the description of an inducement as either an offer or a threat is not simply a matter of the verbal formula used. Whether a proposal is a threat depends on the parties' expectations and on the perspective from which we determine whether those expectations are reasonable. The robber's proposal "Your money or your life" is an unambiguous threat because from any relevant perspective—moral, legal, or psychological—the person receiving the proposal will be worse off than she is entitled to be. The dating proposal triggers conflicting intuitions because different sets of expectations seem appropriate from different perspectives.

To determine whether a proposal is a threat, we must decide which perspective determines the controlling expectations. Some philosophers struggle over this issue because they assume that the question can have only one right answer—that only one of the perspectives can control.[10] The problem becomes less difficult if we recognize that the correct answer depends on the purpose for which the question is asked.[11] The psychological perspective is the important one if we are trying to determine how a proposal *feels* to the person who receives it. For the woman in the dating situation, the man's insistence on sex probably feels like a threat. But the appropriate perspective must be different when we ask a question of legal responsibility—whether the man should be subject to liability for coercion. For that purpose, neither the moral nor the psychological perspectives can be controlling. Instead, the decisive issue is whether the inducement would take from the woman anything she is legally entitled to have. In the dating situation it would not. Existing law gives the young man the right to stop dating her for any reason at all. Legally, his demand is merely an offer.

This emphasis on the legal perspective, when we set standards of legal responsibility for sexual coercion, might seem unduly narrow or formalistic. Legal rights are not fixed, and if conduct is morally wrong, that fact gives a powerful reason for considering whether the conduct should be made illegal. Yet the relationship between legal and moral duties is not straightforward. Ordinary decency requires us to treat our parents with respect, and even to assist them financially if they need our help, but these are not legal obligations. Lying is almost always a moral wrong, but it is illegal only under special circumstances. In a free society, law leaves room for choice, including—sometimes—the choice to behave badly. Identifying the kind of conduct society should prohibit with rules backed by legal penalties is not just a practical but an intensely moral question in itself.

In the dating situation, we must consider whether the woman *should* have a right to see the relationship continue without acceding to a morally unjustified sexual demand. The answer to that question is reasonably clear. Sexual autonomy includes, as a centrally important feature, the freedom to seek intimacy with persons of our own choosing and to seek sexual fulfillment as a valued goal of an intimate relationship. Sexual autonomy includes, again not just at its fringes but as a centrally important feature, the freedom to decide whether and when to terminate any personal relationship. That freedom extends at least until formal commitments are accepted in marriage or its equivalent. Even after a couple marries, with a solemn commitment to love, honor, and cherish "till death do us part," most states consider it unrealistic and

destructive to require them to remain together if either of them concludes, for any reason, that the relationship is no longer working. Either
party can dissolve the marriage, without fault, after waiting a suitable
period and making equitable financial arrangements. Prior to marriage,
the justifications for freedom to end a long-standing relationship, even
in the face of substantial expectations and reliance, are extremely strong.

As a result, the young man's demand for sex in the dating situation
would not take from his girlfriend any right she is—or should be—entitled to hold. Respect for sexual autonomy, his as well as hers, requires
us to treat the young man's demand as an offer, not a threat.

Although safeguards against coercion would not outlaw all forms of
sexual bargaining, many of the nonviolent pressures permitted under
current law are easily identified as impermissible threats. The Montana
high school principal, for example, clearly made a threat if, as alleged,
he told a young woman he would prevent her from graduating. In the
Maryland case that posed a close question under existing law, Rusk took
a young woman's car keys, in a strange neighborhood, and refused to
return them unless she agreed to come up to his apartment and have
sex with him.[12] The court was willing to treat his conduct as rape only
if the woman had a reasonable fear that he planned to hurt her physically. But whether or not this aggravating fact was present, her consent
to sex was obtained by a threat, because Rusk would not allow her to
leave, as she was clearly entitled to do.

If threats are always coercive, then the consents given by the Montana high school student and the Maryland woman stranded in a
strange neighborhood were obviously coerced and invalid. But intuitions about coercion are sometimes more complex. In sexual situations—and not only in sexual situations—the person threatened may
still have a number of choices. Conceivably, the Montana student might
have been able to complain to a guidance counselor or to her parents.
The Maryland woman might have been able to scream, fight back, use
a telephone to seek help, or just insist on staying fully clothed until Rusk
got tired of waiting and let her leave. Judges and jurors sometimes think
that factual details like these are important. They sometimes wonder
whether the person complaining about a threat was really compelled to
submit to it. Society may take the view that some threats, even clearly
illegal threats, can be and should be resisted, just as Dixie Stone sensibly

chose to do. If the threatened person submits rather than protests, many will conclude that the resulting consent was *un*coerced and therefore should be effective.

That instinct is especially common in the sexual domain. A powerful strand in our culture demands that women targeted by sexual threats should use their capacities for self-protection, that they should "stop whining," stop asking to be treated like children, and stand up for their rights.[13] If they do not, they are seen as consenting and having only themselves to blame for the results. If this viewpoint is valid, then determining that there were wrongful threats against the Montana high school student and the Maryland woman would tell only half the story. We would still have to decide whether their submission was a reasonable response under the circumstances.

Yet many people wonder whether the demand that women resist, in the face of a plainly wrongful threat, is itself a reasonable requirement. The expectations of resourcefulness and resistance imposed on women in sexual interaction often seem to reflect suspect attitudes unique to the domain of gender relations and sexuality. In many other areas of law, a wrongful threat can be sufficient in itself to invalidate consent, and the law imposes no obligation of "resistance." But the law sometimes requires resistance to threats, even in nonsexual settings. To see whether a right to sexual autonomy renders resistance requirements obsolete, we must consider why consent is sometimes considered "voluntary" even when given in response to a wrongful threat.

When Do Threats Coerce?

When someone submits to a demand because of threats, courts sometimes conclude that the submission nonetheless was voluntary. Tidwell, a physician, moved from Tennessee to Georgia in order to join the practice of another doctor, Critz. The two entered into a written agreement that guaranteed Tidwell a share of the profits and specified that the partnership could not be dissolved for three years. Tidwell claimed that a month after the original agreement was signed, Critz threatened to dissolve the partnership unless Tidwell accepted a new agreement that would end his partnership rights and make him an employee on a monthly salary. Tidwell signed the second agreement but then sued to challenge the new terms. In a 1981 case, the court held that Tidwell's consent was not coerced because he could have refused to sign and then sued under the original agreement; the threats were not "sufficient to overcome the mind and will of a person of ordinary firmness."[14]

Cases like this illustrate a common intuition. Courts often treat a choice as coerced only if two conditions are met: The choice must be made in response to a threat (not an offer), *and* the person receiving the threat must have "no reasonable alternative" but to submit.[15] In contract disputes, courts often conclude that a person is not coerced, and is therefore responsible for her choices, unless her other alternatives were inadequate.

The criminal law often takes a similar view. In a 1977 case, Joseph Toscano, a chiropractor, had aided a health insurance scam by filing false medical reports. He agreed to cooperate with the conspirators only after one of them called him and said in a "vicious" voice, "Remember, you just moved into a place that has a very dark entrance . . . You and your wife are going to jump at shadows when you leave that dark entrance." The New Jersey Supreme Court held that Toscano could prevail on his defense of duress, but not just by showing that the phone call amounted to a threat of physical harm. Rather, the court said, Toscano would have to show that "he was coerced [by a] threat to use unlawful force against his person or the person of another, *which a person of reasonable firmness in his situation would have been unable to resist.*"[16] The duress defense cases in criminal law fit squarely into the two-step conception of coercion. A threat is treated as coercive only if it is wrong in itself *and* if the person who submits to it had no reasonable alternative.

In sexual offenses, the law has long followed the same approach. The requirement of resistance in the law of rape echoes the demanding requirement of resistance in the criminal law defense of duress. But we should immediately note the false symmetry of these two resistance requirements. The law imposes the same strict standard in two radically different contexts. The duress defense seeks to block a criminal defendant's responsibility for conduct like Toscano's fraud, which directly harms third parties and society as a whole. When a woman confronts threats demanding her submission to sex, there is quite obviously nothing like the same justification for expecting her to risk serious injury to herself by resisting. In the Victorian view—that any sex outside marriage gravely damages the social fabric—there was a certain perverse logic to rape law's resistance rule. In that view a woman might have been prosecuted for fornication even when she submitted solely because of threats, and her duress defense would succeed only if she could show that she was unable to resist.

This extreme view about society's stake in preventing sex outside marriage, if it was ever plausible, surely does not command wide acceptance today. Perhaps in part for that reason, requirements of resistance "to the utmost" have softened. But rape law still considers threats, even threats of physical injury, insufficient in themselves to trigger criminal liability. Many states continue to require a "reasonable" amount of physical resistance. And where the law on the books has abolished formal resistance requirements, some resistance—physical and otherwise—remains necessary in practice, in order to prove that the defendant's threat would "overcome" the victim's will or "compel" her to submit.[17]

The Model Penal Code's sexual offense provisions preserve and reemphasize the same restrictive idea that wrongful threats are not invariably coercive. On the surface the code claims to abolish traditional requirements of physical resistance. But the old resistance rule reemerges in slightly different words, because the code makes resistance unnecessary only in the face of threats so severe that resistance would be life-threatening and futile—threats of "imminent death, serious bodily injury, extreme pain or kidnapping."[18] Even the old doctrine demanding "utmost resistance" excused resistance in the face of imminent threats of this sort. Resistance was required only in the face of lesser threats, but under the code, lesser threats cannot qualify as rape at all.

To protect women against less extreme threats, the code creates a new crime, "gross sexual imposition." This offense, less serious than rape, is committed whenever a man has intercourse with a woman and "compels her to submit by any threat that would prevent resistance by a woman of ordinary resolution." The code broadens prior law from one direction, by refusing to immunize nonviolent threats. But the old focus on resistance returns, because a threat—violent or nonviolent—is not sufficient in itself to establish a sexual crime. A man's wrongful threat will trigger criminal liability only when it "would prevent resistance by a woman of ordinary resolution" and "compel her to submit."[19]

In sum, despite relaxation of the "utmost resistance" rule, prevailing standards for establishing coercion in the sexual domain continue to mirror the two-pronged requirement imposed in a number of other contexts. The law asks whether a man was justified in deploying a particular threat, but a wrongful threat is not enough to establish coercion. Instead, the law treats sexual threats as illegal only when the person threatened had "no reasonable alternative" to submission.

This approach to coercion, in both sexual and nonsexual situations, presents something of a puzzle. If one person puts himself in the wrong by making an unjustified threat, why should it be a defense that the person he threatened had alternatives to submission? Why are our intuitions, and our laws, sometimes drawn to ask whether the innocent party could have done otherwise? When the person deploying the threat is clearly at fault in creating a dilemma, it seems odd that we sometimes blame the victim for not resisting.

When an obligation to resist makes sense, the reason is usually not that the obligation is inherent in the meaning of "coercion" but only that resistance is required by special social needs in certain situations. The treatment of consent in commercial disputes is an example. Critz's threat to dissolve his partnership was wrongful, in the sense that it apparently was a violation of Tidwell's rights under the first agreement. But disputes about contract rights are common in commercial relationships. Participants frequently perceive a need to renegotiate existing commitments. If Critz's demand for new terms were sufficient to invalidate Tidwell's consent, binding settlement of good-faith disputes would become all but impossible.

In order to enable businesses to resolve disagreements and rely on the resulting compromises, the law sensibly requires disputing parties to make a choice: they must either refuse a demand for new terms or be bound if they consent to it, at least when reasonable alternatives are available. But the law of contracts imposes no such requirement when the wrongful threat is not germane to a legitimate commercial disagreement. If Critz had threatened to break Tidwell's knees or to spread false rumors about his competence as a physician, Tidwell's consent would be considered coerced regardless of his alternatives, on the basis of the threat alone.

Special needs of a different kind explain the resistance requirement in the criminal law defense of duress. Suppose that a mobster threatens to smash Bill's store windows unless he agrees to help smuggle a bomb into a police station. If Bill submits to the threat and plants the bomb, when alternative courses of action were available, there is every reason to say that he was not coerced or, perhaps, that he was not *sufficiently* coerced to absolve him of responsibility for his own illegal conduct. There is every reason to blame—and punish—him. The two-step conception of coercion here reflects the strong obligation justifiably imposed on Bill to avoid inflicting harm on others.

The conclusion that Bill should have resisted in no way excuses the mobster, of course. That qualification makes clear the highly variable, policy-based nature of most intuitions about "coercion." In a duress case, even when we blame the victim and hold him responsible for committing a crime, the person who deployed the unjustified threat remains responsible as well. The mobster normally would be guilty of two crimes—the one he committed by making his threat, and the crime that Bill committed at his direction. The finding that Bill made a "voluntary" choice would not relieve the mobster of liability for his own wrongdoing. Yet the resistance requirement in the existing law of rape is emphatically different. The conclusion that a woman could have resisted an improper threat becomes the basis for excusing the man from all liability for his own unambiguous wrongdoing.

The unique character of the resistance requirement in rape law is underscored by the reach of the criminal offense of extortion. Extortion is the crime of obtaining property by threats. As typically defined, the offense includes threats to inflict bodily injury, to commit any other crime, to accuse anyone of a criminal offense, to expose any damaging secret, and, more generally, to "inflict any other harm which would not benefit the actor."[20] A person commits extortion if he obtains the victim's property by making any of the prohibited threats, whether or not the victim had opportunities to resist.

The target of an extortion attempt almost always has alternatives to meeting the wrongdoer's demands. He may be able to bring suit, complain to the police, or resort to self-help (including physical resistance). Yet if he submits to the threat, he is treated as a victim of extortion. Our intuitions—and our laws—treat the misconduct as coercive and illegal on the basis of the threat alone, even when the victim might have had other options. If Dr. Toscano had paid his caller in cash to avert the threat of injury to his wife, the caller would be guilty of extortion on the basis of the threat alone; the court would have no need to consider whether "a person of reasonable firmness" would have resisted. And if the victim does resist, the person who made the threat is still guilty of extortion; the wrongful threat is coercive and illegal in itself, regardless of the victim's reaction.

The treatment of wrongful threats in the sexual domain is again a striking departure from this pattern. The victim of a sexual threat is expected to resist or avoid the threat if at all possible. If she submits instead, when other options conceivably were available, the courts will treat her submission as a voluntary choice. And the person who made the wrongful threat will escape responsibility for his misconduct.

This effort to assess opportunities for resistance poses an acute problem when the inquiry is directed to sexual interaction. Social judgments about male sexual prerogative and expectations for proper behavior on the part of women are highly variable and intensely contested. (Recall Senator Arlen Spector's famous question to Anita Hill in the hearings on the Supreme Court nomination of Justice Clarence Thomas: "how could you allow this kind of reprehensible conduct to go on right in the headquarters without doing something about it?")[21] Retrospective judgments about "reasonableness" are bound to be subjective and, at best, unpredictable. At worst, they may simply reflect and reproduce the very attitudes that expose women to danger in the first place.

These disadvantages might have to be incurred if there are good reasons to impose a burden of resistance, as there are in commercial disputes and in the criminal law defense of duress. For all its drawbacks, a resistance requirement has some plausibility in the existing law of rape, because the law, as currently conceived, protects women *only* against sexual imposition by force. In that framework courts have asked whether a "reasonable" woman could have escaped the threat, because the man's conduct is considered criminal only when he forcibly compels her to submit. Failure to resist (when resistance was possible) has a bearing on three facts that are crucial to a prosecution under existing law—the victim's unwillingness, the man's use of force rather than persuasion to overcome her unwillingness, and his having a fair chance to realize that she submitted because of force rather than desire. The law shouldn't make resistance a formal prerequisite to conviction, because a man's deliberate use of force is sometimes clear beyond doubt, whether or not the woman resisted. But the desire to weigh evidence of resistance nonetheless reflects concerns about factual proof that are inevitable when the law protects only against physically violent misconduct.

Once we shift the focus of concern from force to autonomy, resistance remains relevant only in limited situations. Resistance will still be important (though it shouldn't be an absolute requirement) when a prosecutor seeks to prove physical force as an aggravating factor. And resistance will still be relevant, in some cases, to determining whether consent was given at all. A couple sits side by side necking on a sofa. While kissing his date, the man presses his body forward, so that the woman is pushed back to a reclining position. He then reaches under her dress to touch her genital area. The woman might or might not be consenting to these sexual contacts. If she says "no," tries to sit up, and pushes his hands away, we are more likely to think she is unwilling than if she does none of these things. Resistance remains relevant when we are not sure whether the woman gave consent.

When threats are deployed, the evidentiary problems are different. It is usually clear that consent (of some sort) was given, and the only question is whether the consent was coerced. In a regime that prohibits not only physical force but *all* unjustified impairments of autonomy, an impermissible threat is, by definition, an improper interference with freedom of choice. There can no longer be a reason to scrutinize the possible avenues of escape or to blame the victim for not pursuing options that might seem adequate in retrospect. A wrongful threat intended to induce sexual compliance is coercive in itself, just as a wrongful threat intended to obtain money is sufficient in itself to constitute the criminal offense of extortion. If a threat is completely trivial ("Comply or I'll drink your soda"), there is no reason to treat it as anything other than a jest; whether the man seeks to obtain money or sexual acquiescence, the threat must be one intended to induce submission. But if one cannot obtain another person's property by threatening "to inflict any harm that would not benefit the actor," there is no reason why one should be able to obtain sexual submission in this way. Such conduct impairs freedom of choice, whether or not it is sufficiently powerful to "compel" submission.

Sexual coercion, therefore, does not depend on elusive assessments of the degree of pressure sufficient to "overbear" a woman's will, and it does not depend on subjective judgments about the degree of fortitude and resistance to be expected from individuals able to "fight back." Sexual coercion is simply any conduct that threatens to violate the victim's *rights*. Conduct that forces a person to choose between her sexual autonomy and any of her other legally protected entitlements—rights to property, to privacy, and to reputation—is by definition improper; it deserves to be treated as a serious criminal offense.

This understanding of sexual coercion suggests a straightforward and much more stringent response to abuses that existing law treats permissively or with only limited remedies. Sexual harassment is an important example. Consider the manager who threatens to block promotion of a female subordinate unless she accedes to his sexual advances. Only recently has the law come to see such demands as a violation of federal civil rights statutes. Even now, federal law applies only to schools and colleges and to employers with more than fifteen employees. If the sexual pressure comes from a doctor or lawyer who threatens to withhold needed services, or from a landlord who threatens to evict a tenant, federal laws against sexual harassment do not apply. Even for employees at work, if the firm is small the manager's threats still do not trigger liability. And even when the firm can be held responsible, the manager himself normally faces no personal liability for damages, because the theory of federal law is that the employer (the firm) has a duty not to discriminate against its employees. Under state law, damage remedies are similarly limited, and in nearly all states criminal law is entirely absent from this field.[22]

Terri Nichols, a deaf-mute employee of the U.S. Postal Service, worked the night shift at a Salem, Oregon, postal facility, under the supervision of Ron Francisco. Francisco, the highest-ranking manager on her shift, made performance evaluations and had the authority to grant employees leave and overtime pay. He was also the only supervisor who was able to communicate with Nichols in sign language. Shortly after she began work, Nichols said, Francisco assigned her to copy some documents, then followed her into the copy room and indicated that he wanted her to perform oral sex. She refused at first but ultimately complied, afraid that she would lose her job.[23]

The routine occurred repeatedly over the next several months. On other occasions, Francisco, prior to preparing Nichols' work evaluation, summoned her to his office to discuss her attendance record and then asked her to perform oral sex. Nichols never sought sexual contact with him, but she continued to comply with his demands. Although he never threatened her explicitly, his discussion of work-related matters and his requests for oral sex occurred in such close proximity that courts later found there was "no doubt" he intended to link job decisions affecting Nichols to her performance of sexual acts.[24]

Nichols became fearful and depressed. She needed the job badly and was afraid that if she reported the situation, Francisco would find a way to retaliate against her. She felt unable to tell her husband, thinking that he would divorce her and take away her two children. She became anxious and irritable. She lost weight, had trouble sleeping, had frequent nightmares, and attempted suicide. In April 1987, six months after the start of Francisco's demands, Nichols' husband filed for divorce, and she applied for a leave of absence to deal with her family problems. Francisco responded by asking her to perform oral sex again. Nichols complied (for the last time), and Francisco then approved her request for leave.

Nichols ultimately reported the matter to the Postal Service, received disability benefits for more than two years, and eventually resumed her employment at another postal facility. She also sued the Postal Service and recovered limited damages—the federal statute at the time restricted her award to back pay for the two-year period she was unable to work, and denied compensation for her medical expenses and emotional distress. Meanwhile Francisco held his job while her complaint was investigated. When another employee made similar charges against him, he was fired, but a civil service appeal led to his reinstatement in April 1988. Six years later he was still employed at the Postal Service's facility in Salem.

Although the Postal Service was found responsible for Francisco's misconduct, he himself was not personally liable for damages. And of course his conduct did not violate any criminal statute. He did not commit rape or any form of sexual assault, because he did not threaten to use physical force. And even in the handful of states that punish some nonviolent threats, his criminal liability still might be debatable because a jury would have to find beyond a reasonable doubt that his misconduct would "prevent resistance by a woman of ordinary resolution."

Yet when a threat like Francisco's is used to interfere with a property right, traditional criminal law standards automatically treat it as extortionate and illegal in itself. The commentaries to the Model Penal Code mention as a classic example of extortion the case of a foreman "who requires the workers to pay him a percentage of their wages on pain of dismissal or other employment discrimination."[25] We already recognize that the foreman has no privilege to obtain personal benefits by bargaining in this fashion. A threat of dismissal violates the worker's right to autonomous control over her wages, and her "consent" to pay a financial kickback is obviously coerced and invalid. Once we acknowledge that the worker's right to autonomous choice includes control over her sexuality as well as her wages, there should be no doubt that she is entitled to legal protection from the manager's threat in both cases. Both civil damage remedies and criminal sanctions are appropriate, regardless of which legally protected interest he targets.

To determine that job consequences *were* linked to sex will sometimes be difficult, of course. When a worker gives money to her boss, it is usually easy to infer that some threat has been brought to bear, because the worker otherwise gets nothing in return. Sexual encounters are similarly one-sided if the worker submits because of a threat. But when we are not sure whether a threat was made, sex—unlike a monetary payment—doesn't by itself suggest a strong likelihood of coercion; the worker *might* have accepted the encounter out of sexual desire rather than fear. And criminal conviction requires that the linkage between the boss's sexual demand and his threat of job consequences be proved beyond a reasonable doubt. But criminal courts make "linkage" determinations all the time in bribery and extortion cases. Politicians can ask for campaign contributions, and they can do favors for their constituents. Yet when circumstances make clear that the two were linked, that there was an implied quid pro quo, the conduct amounts to extortion, a severely punished offense.[26] When proved beyond a reasonable doubt, quid-pro-quo sexual harassment deserves to be treated as a similarly serious crime.[27]

Sexual harassment in education should be analyzed in the same terms. University regulation of student-teacher relationships is still in its infancy, and remedies for sexual coercion are now confined to internal disciplinary measures or, under some circumstances, civil damages.[28] Again, in nearly all states criminal law remains entirely absent from this field. Yet the Model Penal Code commentaries include as an obvious example of criminal extortion the case of "a law professor who obtains property from a student by threatening to give him a failing grade or to influence a prospective employer to hire someone else."[29] On the same principle, a professor who uses the threat of a poor grade or recommendation to induce *sexual* compliance is engaged in extortionate behavior. He should be guilty of sexual abuse—just as he would be guilty of extortion for seeking monetary gain—whether or not the "reasonable" student could have resisted, and whether or not the actual victim did resist. A high school principal who obtains sexual favors by threatening to block a student's graduation should be guilty of a criminal offense for exactly the same reasons.

In some of its other forms, sexual harassment is not always so obviously coercive. Suppose that a manager doesn't threaten to block a deserved promotion but instead demands sexual favors for arranging a promotion that isn't deserved. It is more difficult to say that he threatens to "inflict [a] harm" on the woman who is the target of his demand. His proposal could be classified as an offer rather than a threat. Other women competing for the promotion would be injured, of course. But from their perspective, the woman who got an undeserved advantage might seem to be a participant in the wrongdoing, not the victim of an extortionate threat. Where federal laws against sexual harassment apply, this sort of sexual pressure is now prohibited, but the available remedies are limited, and criminal sanctions for sexual extortion could be considered out of place when the manager links sex to unearned benefits.

The difference between harm and benefit, between threat and offer, is not simply verbal. No worker should have to give up a job to retain control of her sexuality. But if she can either keep her job and refuse the advances, or acquire an undeserved advantage by acceding to them, the manager's offer does not seem to constrain her capacity for choice. If she prefers the second alternative, respect for her autonomy might require that we accept her decision.

The traditional distinction between offers and threats poses a large problem here. When one person holds power over another, an offer to confer a benefit in exchange for sexual favors may disguise an implied threat to interfere and inflict harm if the favors are refused. From this perspective even the seemingly clear case of the Montana school principal could raise factual doubts. If the student was entitled to graduate, and if the principal proposed to interfere, his actions obviously would be a threat. But if the student was in academic difficulty and was not due to graduate, then his proposal could easily be recharacterized. Under the usual approach, focusing on the student's rights, the young woman would merely have a chance to get an unearned benefit: if she submitted to the sexual demand, she would graduate, and if she refused, she would be no worse off than she was entitled to be. From that perspective the principal's alleged actions would amount only to an offer. Yet to make the legality of his conduct turn on the student's academic standing seems very much beside the point.

In these situations, conduct that looks like a mere offer bears many of the hallmarks of coercive abuse. Safeguards against sexual coercion accordingly have limited value if they prohibit only threats. But powerfully attractive offers cannot automatically be condemned as coercive. Effective protection of sexual autonomy requires standards to identify sexual demands that are improper even when they do not constitute threats in the classic sense.

8

Sexual Bargaining:
Legitimate and Illegitimate Offers

In the workplace, in academic settings, in singles bars, and on dates, men use inducements of every conceivable sort to achieve sexual success with women. Decent safeguards for sexual autonomy must afford protection from pressures that are coercive even when they do not amount to threats. A bank manager's proposal to expedite an undeserved promotion for a teller in his department, but only if she submits to his sexual demands, is not a threat. It is an offer, though a morally and legally improper one.

The range of potentially coercive "offers" is daunting. Near one extreme, a poverty-stricken mother of four submits to sexual advances in order to win a desperately needed job. Near the other end of the spectrum, a financially successful fashion model accedes to sexual pressure in order to land a career-enhancing film role or to "catch" a billionaire entrepreneur and marry him. Somewhere in between is the 1988 case of a young doctor in a surgical residency at the University of Puerto Rico; she charged that the physician in charge of her program told her she could operate more often and have her pick of cases if she had an affair with him.[1]

None of these situations involves a traditional sort of threat. But we might still think that some of the women, perhaps all of them, were subjected to a form of coercive pressure. There is little agreement about which of these women, if any, should be considered the victim of a sexual crime. Although sexual harassment in the workplace is now considered unacceptable, the manager who promises special benefits to a subordinate in return for her sexual favors is not generally considered a criminal. And if the subordinate accepts his offer and meets his sexual demands, many people wonder whether she should be seen as a victim, or instead as an opportunist who gained an unfair advantage.

One common instinct is that once we move beyond the realm of direct threats, notions of coercion become too elusive and contestable to support formal legal intervention. On this view, there is no justification for condemning as criminal any of the complex patterns of behavior that make up the give-and-take of courtship, seduction, and sexual bargaining. This view seems plausible only because so few of those who take an interest in the law of rape, whether to attack or to defend it, consider in any detail the limits on permissible offers that our society vigorously enforces in other areas of life. The concept of improper coercion that we take for granted in a wide variety of activities can set perfectly appropriate limits for interactions in the sexual domain as well.

Another strongly held view insists that benefits can never be coercive. If the bank teller can reject her manager's sexual advances or acquire an undeserved advantage by acceding to them, then his offer seems to expand her options rather than constrain them. From this perspective, we might decide to treat the manager's behavior as a harm to other employees or as a violation of his duty to the bank, but we could not reasonably claim that the manager *coerced* her. The difference is important. A manager who violates a duty to his company (for example by taking too long a lunch break or hiring his nephew instead of a better-qualified applicant) commits at most a relatively minor wrong, and certainly not a crime.[2] But if he coerces a woman's submission to unwanted sex, he ordinarily inflicts a major personal injury, and it becomes reasonable to suggest that his conduct should be considered a serious criminal offense. The harmfulness of the manager's behavior and the justification for punishing it depend on whether an offer of this sort really coerces the subordinate or whether it merely infringes on a duty to others.

The fact that a sexual relationship will give the bank teller an undeserved benefit is not the only fact we need in order to be sure that her boss's proposal does not coerce and harm her. We need to know more, for example, about the sequence of the events. The teller might risk psychological harm even if she sought out the sexual relationship in hopes of obtaining a job advantage. But the potential for injury and the sense of intrusion on her freedom of sexual choice can be vastly greater when the supervisor initiates the proposal and forces her to begin seeing her professional role in sexual terms. We also need to know whether the proposal itself is improper. Offers that are entirely legitimate ("Pay me $100, and I will tutor you to help you pass the bar exam") seldom seem coercive, but illegitimate offers ("Pay me $100, and I will give you a higher grade than you deserve") can sometimes carry an implied threat of retaliation if they are refused.

Legitimacy matters, but it can't by itself explain all intuitions about coercion. Illegitimate inducements seem coercive when they can arouse fear ("Sleep with me, and I'll give you a good job rating"). But when illegitimate inducements don't arouse fear ("Sleep with me, and I'll pay you $500") they seem much more like prostitution or bribery than like a nonviolent form of rape. Yet illegitimate inducements can interfere with autonomous choice even when they don't arouse fear: a deceptive inducement (the false promise, "Sleep with me, and I'll marry you") is one possible example. In short, some illegitimate offers can be coercive; some don't coerce, but may interfere with autonomy in other ways; and some don't interfere with autonomy at all. Even in the last case, society may choose to make the inducement illegal, because of its effect on other parties. But the appropriate legal response differs sharply when the inducement impairs the exercise of autonomous choice. The most serious situations are those in which the illegitimate inducement, though framed as an offer, can have powerful coercive effects.

When Offers Coerce

Armstrong, a prosecuting attorney for the city of Monroe, Louisiana, demanded payments from the Wright law firm in return for dropping a drunk-driving case against one of its clients. The firm paid Armstrong $3,000, presumably to secure a benefit that was worth even more to its client. The drunk-driving case was dropped, but federal authorities got wind of the deal and prosecuted Armstrong. The payoff looks at first glance like a classic bribe, with only the city government as the loser. Yet the court held that the firm was not a willing participant in a beneficial arrangement but rather was the victim of a coercive demand. Armstrong was convicted of extortion.[3]

Sheridan, a building inspector, noticed a defect in the elevator that

Stock used in his business. He told Stock he would report the problem to the city buildings department unless Stock paid him fifty dollars. Stock paid up, after first alerting the police, who arrested Sheridan as he left with the money. Sheridan argued that Stock had suffered no "unlawful injury" (as required by the state's extortion statute), because the elevator really was defective, and Sheridan had a duty to report that fact. In effect his proposal left Stock better off than he was entitled to be. The court held that these facts made no difference. Sheridan was convicted of extortion.[4]

Cases like these could be multiplied indefinitely. Wrongful proposals are often treated just like coercive threats, even though they promise undeserved benefits to the victims. The *kind* of wrong committed in these cases is important. The officials obviously are corrupt, and the breach of their duty to the public is a serious wrong in itself. But more than bribe-taking is involved, more than just harm to society's general interest in good government. The citizens making these payments seem to be victims even when they get undeserved benefits in return. And the law reflects this intuition. The official who demands a payment is guilty of extortion, a much more serious offense than bribery. The private citizen is not treated as a co-conspirator or as a beneficiary of the arrangement; the citizen is the victim of a form of theft. Yet these legal rules, and the instincts underlying them, seem to fit poorly with the usual assumption that the offer of a benefit does not make the person receiving it worse off, that it merely enlarges her opportunities.

The intuition that illegitimate proposals can be coercive, even when they provide undeserved benefits, reflects several intertwined concerns. The first point to notice is the iron fist inside the velvet glove. When one person holds power over another, the offer to provide a benefit may mask an intent to inflict harm if the offer is refused. When this concern is present, the illegitimate offer closely approximates a threat in the classic sense.

But extortion cases seldom permit a clear-cut finding of a classic threat. There was no concrete evidence that Armstrong or Sheridan would have retaliated and harmed their victims if the victims had refused to pay. If the Wright law firm had turned Armstrong away, he presumably would have prosecuted, but he would not have violated anyone's rights by doing so. The proposal was considered coercive even though it involved no direct violation of the victims' legal rights. We usually sense that the target of a corrupt offer does risk injury if she turns it down, but the injury is more complex and intangible than in the case of a direct threat.

The character of official power is one important reason. Government agents typically exercise vast discretion, especially in law enforcement. Their discretion makes it difficult to determine the treatment that a citizen would receive in the absence of the corrupt demand. Armstrong might have decided to drop the drunk-driving case even if he had not been paid. Under these circumstances the offer to provide a benefit becomes hard to disentangle from an implied threat to inflict a subtle form of harm—not the deprivation of a formal right but just a decision to proceed more zealously than usual. In France, where certain public employees are forbidden to strike, law enforcement agents have developed a potent negotiating weapon in the form of the "grève du zèle," literally a strike of zeal. Customs inspectors need not stay off the job. They can cause far more havoc by reporting for work and then enforcing to the letter every rule in the book.

Because zealous investigation and oversight is such a common prospect in dealings with public officials (or supervisors of any sort), the citizen who turns down the corrupt offer *can* be left worse off than she is entitled to be. As one court put it, the target of the demand is deprived of "the right to impartial determination of the issue on the merits (i.e. whether to enforce the law . . .)."[5] In effect, the corrupt offer conceals a threat that is not only implicit but indirect, a threat to retaliate simply by meticulously enforcing the rules.

"Offers" can conceal indirect threats even in situations that *require* zealous enforcement, without room for discretion. Sheridan had an obligation to report the elevator defect, but even so, his demand for payment was extortionate. A police officer who demands money for not making an arrest is guilty of extortion even when the failure to arrest would be a clear dereliction of duty.[6] We cannot say that the citizen is deprived of "the right to impartial determination of the issue on the merits" in these situations, because an impartial determination requires enforcement. Anything less leaves the citizen better off. But even when he lacks discretion on the matter at hand, a police officer has countless opportunities to look for other infractions. Any citizen who turns down his "offer" faces the inevitable risk of retaliation in the form of meticulous enforcement.

Corrupt offers can be coercive even when meticulous oversight and zealous enforcement are not realistic concerns. Baptista was executive director of the Redevelopment Authority of New Bedford, Massachusetts. Graham, a consulting engineer, paid Baptista $25,000 in order to get a $250,000 consulting contract from the Authority. The deal was certainly not a threat in the usual sense. Graham stood to gain an enormously lucrative contract, and if he had wanted to keep his hands clean, he could have sought clients elsewhere, with no fear that the Authority could retaliate against him. What he did fear, however, was loss of any chance for a share of the Authority's contracts. Because Graham feared "preclusion from business with the Authority,"[7] Baptista was convicted of extortion.

The result should not be surprising. If Graham did not play ball, some other engineer presumably would do so. A refusal to pay would not risk direct retaliation, in violation of any formal right, but it would leave Graham at a disadvantage in competing for government contracts. In effect, Graham was deprived of the right to compete on fair terms for a share of the business of every prospective client.

Once we note these possibilities, the "offer" begins to look very much like a threat. But the two are not quite the same. The proposal is a classic threat only if the corrupt official signals that those refusing the offer will no longer be treated fairly. Sheridan's elevator inspection proposal is not easy to condemn under that standard, because we cannot be sure that he intended to retaliate in the event of a refusal, or that he said anything to arouse fear that he might do so. We cannot *prove* that he made a threat. When courts deal with demands for monetary payoffs, they see no need to insist on that sort of proof. They make no attempt to separate offers from threats in the way a pure philosophical theory might require. Reflecting commonsense intuitions, the courts understand that the recipient of a corrupt offer is very likely to *feel* coerced—and the person making the offer is very likely to know that he does—because the potential for abuse of power is inherent in the situation. The target of the proposal is likely to fear adverse consequences, and the fears will normally be reasonable, because the corrupt official has chosen to make clear that his decisions need not remain impartial. His offer to help may not be an explicit threat in itself, but it is a potent reminder of his power.

Fear of adverse consequences, however, can't by itself be sufficient to establish coercion. It is commonplace in commercial bargaining for one party to fear that her business will suffer if she doesn't accept an important contract proposal. The other party is often aware of this fear, and he may exploit it to demand top dollar for his services. Suppose that a contractor proposes to repair Stock's elevator for $1,000. Stock thinks that the price is too high, but he may also be afraid to say no. He may fear that if he rejects the proposal, he will be unable to get anyone else to provide competent repairs. But we could hardly say that Stock's fears suffice to make the contractor an extortionist. Even though both the elevator inspector's proposal and the contractor's proposal arouse reasonable fears, only the inspector's proposal is coercive. The difference between them lies not in the degree of pressure they bring to bear but in the illegitimacy of the inspector's offer and in the power he holds over Stock. There are good reasons to leave the contractor free to drive a hard bargain, but the inspector has no conceivable right to solicit side payments from private citizens. And only the inspector has the power to inflict injury, to take from Stock something he is entitled to keep. Stock has no right to be insulated from the danger that a contractor may decide not to deal with him, but he does have the right to be treated impartially by the buildings department. The inspector's "offer" reminds Stock that his rights are at risk; the contractor's offer has no comparable effect.

Pulling these concerns together, we can see that offers become coercive when two conditions are met. To be coercive, an offer must be illegitimate, and it must arouse justifiable fear of injury for anyone who turns it down. The injuries that count as coercive obviously include fear of a direct violation of the recipient's rights. But coercion also arises from more subtle forms of retaliation, such as subjecting the victim to unusually meticulous oversight or enforcement. And illegitimate offers are also coercive when they do not arouse fear of retaliation but merely present the prospect of a competitive disadvantage—the loss of the right to compete on fair terms for a job, a promotion, or a business opportunity.

This concept of impermissible coercion is entirely familiar and uncontroversial in the context of demands for financial payoffs. Extortion, as typically defined, covers demands for money in exchange for not inflicting harm, but it also extends to cases in which the actor is not technically inflicting a harm. It is equally extortion to obtain money by any threat to "take or withhold action as an official,"[8] even when the proposed action does not violate formal rights and even when the action would benefit the person targeted by the demand. The proposal is considered coercive because the official can claim no prerogative to make a proposal of this sort, the proposal is likely to arouse fears of retaliation, and the official usually knows it is likely to arouse those fears. But if the demand is for sex rather than for money, legal standards change dramatically.

Coercive Offers for Sex

Like nonviolent threats, corrupt "offers" are not considered legally coercive or extortionate when sex becomes the currency of exchange. Yet sexual proposals present precisely the same problems as proposals for financial kickbacks, usually in more acute form. Sexual offers often *feel* coercive, usually for the same reasons that prompt feelings of coercion when a person in power demands a monetary payoff. And sexual offers are often illegitimate, plainly beyond the lawful prerogatives of the person making the proposal, in just the same way as corrupt proposals for monetary payoffs.

Once we recognize that our right to autonomy includes control over our sexuality and our bodies as well as our property, it should be clear that sexual demands can be coercive and intolerable even when they are packaged as an "offer" to provide advantages in exchange. A sexual proposal is obviously coercive when it arouses fear of retaliatory acts that violate specific legal rights. But corrupt sexual offers are also coercive when they arouse fear of the more subtle types of retaliation, including exposure to unusually meticulous oversight or the biased exercise of a supervisor's discretion. Likewise, sexual offers are coercive when women who are offered "benefits" cannot refuse them without risk of losing their right to compete on fair terms for a job, a promotion, or a business opportunity. The prospect of these sorts of injury is inevitably somewhat speculative, to be sure. But the mere possibility of an indirect injury has been ample reason, in the case of financial demands, to treat corrupt proposals as coercive when they are made by a person with the power to inflict harm. Sexual autonomy deserves no less protection.

Felton, a Louisiana police officer, drove up to a couple parked in a secluded spot and threatened to arrest both of them (presumably for public indecency) unless the woman would have sex with him. The woman complied. If Felton had demanded money, he would have been guilty of extortion, but in most states he would not be guilty of any crime for demanding to be paid in sex instead.[9] Yet the demand is equally corrupt in both cases, and criminal punishment is equally appropriate, whether the official uses his power to obtain control over one interest or the other. And of course, the proposal is coercive even if Felton is offering his victim a benefit by disregarding an obligation to make the arrest. Because of the broad scope of law enforcement discretion, the person targeted by this sort of demand can reasonably fear retaliation even when the officer, like elevator inspector Sheridan, has an unqualified duty to report the offense.

Government agents are not the only officials with sufficient power to bring coercive pressure to bear. Just as coercion can result from fear of zealous enforcement and abuse of discretion by public officials, sexual coercion can result from fear of meticulous oversight and similar forms of retaliation by private individuals with supervisory power in the workplace or in academic settings.

Margaret Miller was a data processor at a Bank of America office in San Francisco. She claimed that her supervisor told her he could get her a better job if she were sexually "cooperative." When she refused, he had her fired.[10] His proposal, though presented as an offer, was really a threat in the classic sense. He made sure that Miller paid a heavy price for rejecting him. Yet if Miller had acquiesced in her supervisor's demand, she would have no practical way to prove that his proposal was in fact a veiled threat.

Sharon Karibian worked in the fund-raising office of Columbia University. She claimed that her supervisor drew her into a sexual affair, leaving her under the impression that her pay and working conditions depended on her responsiveness to his demands. She said he implied that she would be fired if she stopped sleeping with him. She acquiesced and continued the relationship. After Columbia closed her office and fired her, she sued for sexual harassment. The trial judge dismissed her complaint on the ground that "Karibian had not suffered any economic detriment . . . in fact she had been promoted and received pay raises." But as the court of appeals noted, this approach would make coercion virtually impossible to prove in the very cases in which the victim was unable to resist it: "In the nature of things, evidence of economic *harm* will not be available to support the claim of the employee who *submits* to the supervisor's demands."[11] Like a contractor faced with the demand for a financial kickback, a woman offered an illicit sexual bargain knows that the possibility of retaliation is inherent in the situation even though it seldom becomes visible. Coercive sexual bargains, like corrupt demands for monetary payoffs, will easily escape legal sanctions if punishment is limited to cases involving express threats.

The practical dynamics of retaliation in the workplace make it doubly difficult to distinguish true threats from sexually coercive "offers." Even when a woman resists a sexual proposal and promptly gets fired, the finespun logic of sexual harassment law makes it hard to prove that she was the victim of a threat. If there are flaws in her performance record, her employer can argue that the decision to discharge her did not violate her rights, because she was not entitled to keep the job in the first place. The argument amounts to another variation on the claim that threats can be coercive but that offers to give an unearned benefit are not. The effort to advance this supposed distinction poses a major obstacle to the effectiveness of federal laws against sexual harassment.

Betty Dockter was working as a bartender at the Chicago Bar and Grill. She had only a ninth-grade education and no computer skills, but she was spotted by a customer who found her sexually attractive. After they flirted a bit, he hired her as his administrative assistant in a firm that specialized in selling commodities futures contracts. During her first few weeks on the job, the supervisor repeatedly made sexual overtures to Dockter and in one instance fondled her breast. She rejected all his advances, and a few weeks later the company fired her. Dockter sued for sexual harassment. The company defended on the ground that Dockter was discharged not because she rejected her supervisor's advances but because she was unqualified for the job. The court upheld the company's claims and dismissed the case.[12]

That approach is flawed on two grounds. First, Dockter presumably never viewed the job as an "undeserved" benefit. Since she probably thought she could learn the skills needed for the position, the implicit deal—"Submit to the sexual overtures or get fired"—would feel like a threat, a proposal to take away something that, so far as she knew, she was qualified to keep. But even if the implicit deal was understood as a true offer—"Submit to sexual overtures if you want to keep a job you don't deserve"—the proposal is still coercive, for the same reasons that coercion was present when Baptista demanded money for steering a government contract to Graham. To permit Dockter's employer to fire her, though her lack of skills presumably would have gone unnoticed if she had submitted to her supervisor's demands, is to expose all women in her position to an implicit threat, because the woman who rebuffs the advance can seldom be confident of escaping retaliation.[13] The prospect of meticulous oversight or the biased exercise of the supervisor's discretion is always in the background.

Retaliation is a less plausible danger when an unemployed woman is offered a new job in return for compliance with a personnel manager's sexual demand. She can reject the offer and go on her way, without fear that the manager can impede her search for other jobs. Yet the illegitimate offer still feels coercive, because she cannot turn it down without losing all chance to get the first job on her own merits. Preclusion from the chance to compete on fair terms is the coercive lever that induces submission to most garden-variety demands for financial kickbacks. Sexual proposals raise the problem in an especially acute form. Baptista can put only limited pressure on a businessman like Graham, because Graham can pursue many other clients who will not insist on a financial payoff. But sexual proposals pose a high risk of competitive harm to women.

George Rotary ran a small business he called the Fireside Motel and Coffee Shoppe. He frequently attempted to fondle his waitresses, made suggestive comments, and had a sexual affair with one of them. Waitresses who tolerated his attentions were assigned to the cocktail lounge and the dining room, where tips were generous. When Evelyn Priest rebuffed him, she was assigned to work in the low-tipping coffee shop, and when she continued to make clear that she wouldn't put up with Rotary's sexual overtures, he fired her.[14]

Catherine Broderick graduated from New York University Law School and took a job as a staff attorney with the Securities and Exchange Commission. Assigned to a regional field office in Arlington,

Virginia, she quickly came into conflict with her supervisors. After she rebuffed a few sexual advances, they were not repeated, but she became aware that various supervisors were sexually involved with other women in the small office. One, a secretary, received three promotions, a commendation, and two cash awards over a four-year period. Another secretary received two promotions and an $800 cash award in a single twelve-month period. A third woman, a staff attorney, received three promotions in two years. Broderick, who had made clear she wasn't sexually available, received only one promotion during the entire five-year period she served at the regional office.[15]

Despite much progress in enforcing sexual harassment laws, sexual pressure remains pervasive in the workplace. A 1994 survey by the U.S. Merit Systems Protection Board, the civil service agency for the federal government, found that 13 percent of all women in the federal workforce had experienced unwanted pressure for dates within the past two years and another 7 percent had experienced unwanted pressure for sexual favors, figures that were scarcely changed from those reported in similar surveys in the 1980s.[16] Among the women who faced these sorts of pressure from a supervisor, 45 percent thought they would get job benefits by cooperating (including 36 percent who thought they would get a promotion or good rating), and 60 percent thought they would suffer adverse consequences for refusing (including 45 percent who thought their working conditions would get worse and 47 percent who thought they would be unable to get a promotion or a favorable rating).[17] These sorts of coercion are thought to be at least as frequent in state government and in the private sector.[18] In all likelihood, millions of American woman face the pressure of sexually coercive "offers" in the workplace and in academic and professional relationships.

When exploitation of power for sexual advantage is so common, the competitive impact of refusing to play along is especially great. Yet existing laws against workplace harassment remain largely ineffective in preventing this sort of coercion. Though often vilified for its allegedly excessive breadth and "hypersensitivity," federal law still does not unequivocally forbid this clear-cut form of sexual harassment. In order to prevail in a federal suit for sex discrimination, a woman targeted by a sex-for-benefits "offer" must prove that the offer was "unwelcome," and this requirement has proved notoriously slippery and subjective.[19]

What women can justifiably demand is the right to compete for jobs on fair terms, without consideration of their willingness to be sexually compliant. Our society did not always consider this right important or worthy of legal safeguards, and even now the law remains ambivalent about recognizing and protecting it. But the underlying judgment should not be considered debatable. For the workplace, as for the academic world, women and men should have the right to seek a decent income and professional fulfillment by pursuing the normal activities appropriate to the setting, without being obliged to put their sexual privacy and bodily integrity at risk.[20] A sexual proposal linking a supervisor's job decisions to sex puts this right in jeopardy, even when the proposal is framed as an offer of unearned benefits. An offer of this sort usually will not feel like an opportunity. Because it can easily arouse fear that a person who turns it down will no longer be treated fairly, a proposal of this sort is likely to feel like a threat.

A contractor who pays a financial kickback, because he fears losing his right to compete for new business, is not guilty of bribery. He is a victim of extortion, even if he receives advantages in exchange.[21] For the same reason, a woman who submits to a sexual "offer," out of fear of the consequences of refusing, is not a bribe-giver or a prostitute. She is a victim of sexual coercion, even if she receives privileges in return. And because the person making the offer is violating his duties to his firm, his actions are already considered improper; he can make no claim that his freedom of sexual bargaining should be left unrestricted. He should be guilty of an illegal sexual abuse, just as he would be guilty of extortion if he had obtained a financial payoff by offering the same benefits in return.

We move from extortion to bribery when a citizen gives a cash payoff solely because he hopes to gain special benefits from a public official.[22] The crucial sign marking a transaction as bribery—the "smoking gun"—is usually the citizen's active role in proposing the corrupt exchange. When a contractor *initiates* the proposal, trading cash for special privileges, it is seldom plausible to claim that he acted out of fear.

The same standard normally makes sense for sexual bargains. When a subordinate employee or job applicant initiates the offer to exchange sex for special privileges, and when fear is not her motive, she can no longer claim to be a victim of coercion. Rather, she becomes a culpable participant in a bribery scheme. Again, the "smoking gun" is usually the subordinate's role in suggesting the corrupt exchange. If she could have received fair treatment without proposing a sexual payoff, she can't plausibly complain that she submitted out of fear. For the same reason, an official who accepts sex with her under these circumstances should be guilty of bribe-taking but not of sexual coercion.[23]

Yet fear can make a woman sexually compliant even when a man in power simply waits for her to take the initiative. The entertainment industry's "casting couch" was one notorious example. Many aspiring actresses did not need to have the terms of trade spelled out. They knew that their chances of winning a part depended on their willingness to offer themselves sexually, even when no one ever proposed an explicit bargain. Realistic safeguards against sexual coercion cannot ignore this kind of pressure. But if fear of a competitive disadvantage and similar concerns amount to coercion and invalidate consent—even when no one has offered a corrupt payoff in return—the line between legitimate relationships and coercive misconduct could virtually disappear. Effective safeguards against sexual coercion must afford some means to reach subtle forms of coercion without criminalizing every sexual affair by a man with any sort of financial or professional power.

Financial corruption poses a similar problem. An entrenched political machine ruled Jersey City, New Jersey, in the 1950s and 1960s.[24] Every business holding a contract with the city was expected to pay 10 percent of the contract price to a member of the machine. If city officials knew that a contractor was unwilling to pay, he was excluded from bidding for city contracts. If a contractor didn't pay after being selected, the officials simply held up his payments until the kickback was delivered. As a practical matter, no one could do business with the city without paying the required 10 percent, and virtually every potential contractor knew it. Yet the city's political leaders never made specific demands for the money. They didn't have to. They were convicted of extortion nonetheless. As the courts found, a "thoroughly meshed arrangement" generated a continuing flow of cash. "Demand for payment was built in."[25] Coercion can result not only from an explicit kickback demand but also from custom and expectations.[26]

The implications of this approach for assessing sexual coercion are intriguing—and potentially far-reaching. Practices tacitly linking women's professional advancement to sexual compliance can be found in many segments of the American workplace, as the surveys of the U.S. Merit Systems Protection Board showed. With that pattern of expectations still widespread, some common types of sexual encounters could be considered coercive under traditional criminal law standards. A man who accepts a woman's sexual advances would be "acquiescing in the system." He could be guilty of a form of extortion, just like the leaders of Jersey City's political machine.

But sex can hardly be considered coercive every time a woman initiates an encounter in order to gain some social or financial advantage. As in all extortion cases, the person in a position of power can fairly be held responsible for coercion only when he provides *illegitimate* benefits (or threatens to take away benefits legitimately earned) and when he knows that the victim is afraid of suffering harm—an injury to her legally protected rights—if she does not participate in the corrupt exchange. An exchange of sex for job benefits can't be considered coercive when the subordinate knew she would face no risk of harm if she refused to play along. The subordinate is in effect choosing to pay the manager a bribe, and the sex-for-benefits arrangement is illegitimate but not coercive.

Inducements can sometimes cast doubt on consent even when they aren't coercive. Suppose that a personnel manager promises, in return for sex, to hire an unqualified applicant who knows she has no other chance to get the job. The woman meets his sexual demands, but discovers shortly afterward that he never intended to approve her application. The manager's deceptive conduct obviously violates his responsibilities to his firm, but by ordinary standards it doesn't seem coercive, and the woman might not think she had been coerced—if she had got the job. The lies don't qualify as coercive, in the usual sense, but they might still be seen as undermining the validity of her consent.

The situation is slightly different if a woman on a business trip meets a man who says he is recently divorced and is hoping to find a woman who shares his interests. She sleeps with him, only to discover later that he is married and has no intention of leaving his wife. The inducement he used is not illicit in the same obvious way that the personnel manager's promise was. But his lie nonetheless causes the woman to consent under false pretenses. His actions interfere with her ability to make a fully autonomous choice, even though they are not coercive or illegitimate—apart from the misrepresentation itself.

Noncoercive but Deceptive Inducements

Under current law, deception can make a man's conduct punishable as a sexual offense, but only under unusual, highly limited circumstances. If a doctor tells a patient he needs to insert a medical instrument into her vagina, and then inserts his penis instead, the law treats his conduct as rape.[27] But if the doctor falsely tells his patient that she needs to have intercourse with him in order to improve her health, his conduct is not considered a crime.[28] The law punishes deception about the nature of the act—whether it involves sexual intercourse at all—but the law normally does not punish the use of deceptive *inducements*. So long as the woman realized that she was agreeing to have sex, the reasons why she consented are considered irrelevant. The man's deceptive behavior normally will not be a criminal offense or even a civil wrong. The only exception is a situation recognized in theory but rarely encountered in real life—the man who obtains a woman's consent by impersonating her husband. Other deceptive inducements are not subject to punishment or civil remedies at all.

Lamont Hough knew that a young woman was expecting his twin brother Lenny to come to her apartment late at night. In a 1994 case, prosecutors charged that Lamont went to the woman's apartment at 5:00 A.M., awakened her, and then climbed into bed. While the lights remained out, he allegedly began making sexual advances, and the woman responded, calling him "Lenny." After they had intercourse, he said, "What are you going to tell Lenny?" She then turned on the light and realized that she had just had intercourse with Lamont. A New York court held that Lamont could not be prosecuted for sexual misconduct.[29] Because he had not used force, he couldn't be charged with rape, and the woman's consent was considered sufficient because she knew she was agreeing to an act of intercourse.

A 1985 case involved a California hospital worker who obtained the names and phone numbers of women who had recently come in for medical tests. He called one woman, a recent immigrant from Asia, identified himself as a doctor, and informed her (falsely) that her tests showed she had a potentially fatal disease. The disease, he said, could be cured by a painful surgical procedure that would cost $9,000 and require six weeks of uninsured hospitalization. The only alternative, he explained, would be for her to have sexual intercourse with an anonymous donor who had been injected with a serum that would cure the disease. This procedure, he said, would cost $4,500. When he learned that his victim could pay only $1,000, he agreed to accept that much as a down payment. He met the victim at a hotel, took the $1,000 fee, and then had intercourse with her. The victim agreed only because she thought "she would die unless she consented."[30] But even under these extreme circumstances, the court stood by the traditional rule that fraudulent inducements, no matter how egregious, never render a person's consent to sexual intercourse invalid.

At one time the law imposed severe penalties for a kind of sexual fraud that was particularly common and was considered particularly serious—a man's breach of his promise to marry. A young woman who lost her virginity only to be abandoned by her suitor was likely to have difficulty finding a man willing to marry her. And with few opportunities for her to be self-supporting, she was likely to be a burden on her father for life. As a result, the law long permitted women or their fathers to sue for breach of a promise of marriage, and the offender who dishonored his promise to marry also faced prosecution for the criminal offense of "seduction."[31] But in the 1930s most states abolished civil and criminal penalties for breach of promise and seduction.[32] And apart from the false promise of marriage, the use of other deceptive tactics to induce sexual intimacy is not—and never has been—sufficient for civil or criminal liability.[33]

A variety of factors contributed to abolition of the sanctions for breach of promise and seduction. Much of the public debate about these laws was dominated by claims that lawsuits were being abused as a means for unscrupulous "gold-diggers" to blackmail propertied gentlemen.[34] Put solely in these terms, the argument for abolishing the remedies for breach of promise seems strongly biased in favor of the men: it was far from clear why the harm to male defendants from a false accusation should be of greater concern than the harm to female plaintiffs whose claims were true.

Other concerns were probably more important. The notion of damages for failure to keep the promise seemed to reflect an older, property-oriented view of the purpose of marriage and an outdated conception of the sexual exchange—physical pleasure for the man in return for economic security for the woman. Many of the most prominent opponents of the breach-of-promise remedy were women who today would be described as feminists. They argued forcefully that breach-of-promise suits reinforced stereotypes of women's sexuality and poor judgment, and discouraged economic independence.[35] In addition, the prospect of civil and criminal liability tended to coerce the consummation of unwanted marriages, at a time when society was beginning to appreciate the importance of ensuring that such relationships be mutually chosen.

These objections to a breach-of-promise suit have considerable force when the man's failure to honor his promise results from a good-faith change of heart. But the concerns seem less compelling when the promise to marry was fraudulent from the outset. The man's behavior is far more egregious, and the injury to the woman is not the loss of the economic value of the marriage but the indignity of a sexual experience accepted under false pretenses. Nonetheless, the law reforms of the 1930s generally precluded civil and criminal liability for breach of a promise of marriage, even when the man never had any intention of carrying out his promise. Today, very few states permit liability even in theory, and there are virtually no reports of successful prosecutions.[36]

Yet in contexts other than sexual intimacy, ranging from commercial transactions to medical procedures and surgery, material misrepresentations are considered a serious wrong, subjecting the perpetrator to civil suits and criminal prosecution for theft. The case of the California "doctor" makes the difference between sexual encounters and property transactions especially clear. The court held that the man could be charged with theft—because he had taken $1,000 from his victim under false pretenses. But he did not commit any sexual crime when he used exactly the same false pretenses to obtain her consent to intercourse.

At first glance, the law's willingness to permit egregious deception in sexual encounters seems difficult to understand. A prosecution for a minor misrepresentation ("I love the color of your eyes") would be absurd, but the law of theft addresses just this sort of problem through rules that exclude "puffing" and "seller's talk."[37] And in property transactions a defendant faces criminal or civil sanctions for fraud only when his misrepresentation is *material* and the other party could *justifiably rely* on it.[38] Where these requirements are clearly met, as they were in the case of Lamont Hough and the California "doctor," the deceived woman has suffered serious harm, and there is little reason to tolerate the defendant's misconduct. Many therefore share Susan Estrich's view that a lie used to induce sexual consent should be punished as a serious criminal offense, under the same standards that apply to fraud used to obtain money.[39] Yet many others, including many feminists committed to rape reform, sense that sexual encounters are different. For reasons that are largely instinctive, they resist the property-law analogy in this context, and conclude that liability for fraudulent inducements either should be more limited in the case of sexual encounters or should not be imposed at all.[40]

A variety of concerns, many of them intangible, may lie behind this intuitive reluctance to punish sexual fraud. In property cases, the most significant representations are those that relate to the pecuniary value of the transaction, an issue relatively easy to judge by objective standards.[41] In contrast, the crucial representations in sexual encounters typically relate to emotional attraction and commitment. In that area, it is especially difficult and speculative to decide whether the representations ("I love you"; "I want to spend my life with you") were false and whether the person making them knew at the time that they were false.

These concerns by themselves are not decisive, however. The difficulty of establishing the factual elements of a crime is not an argument against liability when those facts are clearly proved beyond a reasonable doubt. In a 1996 case, a man who lived in Canada (with his wife of twenty years) repeatedly told a New York woman that he was "single, unmarried and available" and that he wanted a "loving relationship which will lead to marriage."[42] After they had sex together in a New York City hotel, the woman learned that he had no intention of leaving his wife. The New York woman's suit was dismissed for the usual reason that fraud in the inducement is never sufficient to invalidate sexual consent. But courts are perfectly competent to decide, in a case like this, whether the defendant knew that his statements were material and false.

Sexual encounters differ from property transactions in other ways that can make legal inquiries into fraud especially complex. The injury that results from sexual deception is in some ways unique. When a woman submits to a sexual demand because of physical force or non-violent coercion (for example, a threat to fire her from her job), she endures sex she knows she doesn't want. That experience is unlikely to give her physical pleasure, and it may cause lasting physical and emotional harm.[43] When her consent is given under false pretenses, in contrast, the psychological experience is different, because the encounter is one that—*at the time*—she believes she wants. She may experience sexual pleasure, and there is no strong reason to think that her feelings at the time of the encounter will differ from those she would have had if the representations had been true.

When the woman discovers the misrepresentations later, she will very likely feel cheated and used. The impact could be devastating, but it might not be. The answer may depend on whether the woman looked to the sexual encounter as an interaction valued primarily for itself, or instead as a cornerstone of a larger and more lasting web of expectations. In any case, the harm will differ from that of sex that a woman knows at the time she doesn't want. And the injury also will differ from the harm caused by misrepresentation in a property case, where the deception (if it is material at all) will typically go to the heart of the value of the transaction. One especially serious and well-documented form of injury can occur when sexual deception is practiced by a physician, psychologist, or lawyer who has given a commitment to care for the woman and has assumed a special position of trust. Deception of this sort often violates rules of professional ethics, and there are strong grounds to make it illegal.[44] For relationships involving acquaintances and romantic partners, there is probably more variation in the impact on victims and less basis for making confident judgments about the need for legal intervention.

Complex ripple effects can make legal intervention debatable even when harm to the victim is clear. Thomas Neal sought a divorce after his wife, Mary, discovered that he was having an extramarital affair. Mary Neal then filed a countersuit seeking damages for "battery," based on Thomas' conduct in having intercourse with her while he was pursuing the secret affair. Her claim was that he had a duty to disclose his infidelity and that she would not have consented to continuing sexual relations if she had known of it. Two lower courts dismissed her case, invoking the usual rule that deception does not invalidate consent when the person consenting understands the nature of the physical act itself.[45] The Idaho Supreme Court, in a 1994 decision, disagreed. The court held that Mary Neal's battery claim could proceed to trial because "fraud or misrepresentation vitiates [her] consent."[46]

The decision appears to be unique, and its implications are far-reaching. Adultery is no longer a criminal offense in most states, and nearly all, including Idaho, have likewise abolished the ancient remedy of suing the third party for damages. The reason is not that adultery is no longer considered wrong. Rather the abolition of criminal and civil suits reflects a recognition that this wrong usually occurs against a background of complex personal dynamics, and that legal sanctions beyond the obvious remedy of divorce are usually out of place and subject to abuse.[47] The Idaho court itself stressed that a suit for divorce is the sole remedy available in that state for a violation of a spouse's duty of "respect, fidelity and support."[48]

The practical problems that led states to abolish damage suits for adultery will immediately reemerge, however, if a state permits deceived spouses to sue (or seek criminal charges) for sexual consent induced by fraud. The Idaho decision largely demolishes the state's system of making divorce the exclusive remedy, because the injured spouse will always have the option of suing for damages—except when the husband ceased having all sexual relations with her as soon as his affair began. That might be exactly what he should do, and there is ample reason to sympathize with the deceived spouse if he does not. Damage suits and criminal prosecutions for sexual fraud would respond to this concern, but the history of criminal and civil sanctions for adultery suggests that litigation may be a poor tool for redressing this kind of personal wrong. And if that is so in the context of marriage, where mutual obligations are strong and where deception is likely to be especially harmful, the case for legal intervention when the parties aren't married could be even weaker. If a married business traveler has an adulterous affair by deceiving a woman he meets in another city, it would seem odd to permit that woman to sue for fraud while denying any damage remedy to his deceived wife.

Another difficulty affecting both marital and nonmarital relationships arises from the elusive nature of "truth" and the complex role of emotional imagination in sexual encounters. What a date or sexual partner says about his feelings of attraction, future plans, or commitment to the relationship may be disbelieved, half believed, or believed but not relied upon. Perhaps more complicated, the parties sometimes may believe and not believe all at the same time. This phenomenon occurs in other contexts as well; witness "seller's talk" in commercial transactions or a politician's promises to reduce taxes and crime, all of which make us "feel good" about buying a product or voting for a candidate. We often want to hear such statements, even though we have conflicting thoughts about whether the speaker expects to be believed and whether we do or do not believe him. This dynamic may be especially common in sexual interaction. And its role there may be especially difficult to isolate, because erotic experience, like storytelling in literature, so often involves fantasy and the "willing suspension of disbelief."[49]

This aspect of sexuality is by no means necessarily a good thing. Some doctors once argued that patients wanted to be reassured (even inaccurately) about the risks of surgery.[50] Many men once thought that women wanted to be coerced into sexual submission. To assume that women generally "want" or "need" to be emotionally misled would be equally inaccurate and offensive. But the distinctions between fantasy and deception, between welcome storytelling and unwelcome lies, may be especially elusive and may contribute to some of the widespread instinct that we should not call upon cumbersome legal machinery in an attempt to enforce a requirement of truthfulness in intimate personal relationships.

Against this background, it may be too soon to reach a judgment about the kinds of misleading comments that should be considered illegal in matters of sexual intimacy. Particularly where feelings, commitments, and relationships with third parties are concerned, there are few solid guides to determining what is material and what is "misrepresentation," as opposed to puffing or "storytelling." Legal evaluation of these questions after the fact can be heavy-handed, and it may be preferable to leave to the individual the decision whether to believe, whether to rely, and whether to assume the risk of deception by trusting the other party.

Certain forms of misrepresentation have less claim to be left unregulated. Misrepresentation of significant health risks is an example. A person who knows he carries the HIV virus or some other sexually transmitted disease can claim no legitimate right to misrepresent his situation or even to remain silent; he should have an affirmative duty to disclose the danger. If he does not, he should be held guilty of a physical assault, as several recent decisions recognize.[51] In this situation, the other person's consent to the sexual act could be considered valid, but she hasn't in any sense consented to HIV exposure. The fraud not only affects the "inducement" to have sex but also conceals the nature of the physical contact she receives. Misrepresentation of this kind should be illegal for the same reason that consent is flawed when a person consents to a medical procedure and suffers a sexual intrusion instead.

An imposter like Lamont Hough can argue that he is only using a fraudulent "inducement." But impersonation is an especially serious form of deception. Although cases of this sort are rare, there is no reason why the law should tolerate them when they arise. A misrepresentation intended to create feelings of isolation or physical jeopardy likewise has no conceivable justification. A person who falsely arouses fear of a fatal disease, as the California "doctor" did, should be subject to prosecution for sexual abuse.[52]

Other concerns about the validity of consent can arise even if an inducement is not deceptive. The trading of sex for status or economic benefit can be morally troublesome and emotionally risky, even when the proposed benefits are delivered as promised. But sometimes the man who makes a sexual offer—the wealthy man who offers to marry a poverty-stricken widow, for example—can plausibly claim a right to act in just that way. And it is not always obvious that the woman receiving his proposal will put her own rights at risk by rebuffing him. When she won't, it's hard to say that the man's offer coerces her. In those situations, her decision to exchange sex for social or economic benefits may be one that law should protect as a part of her autonomy—her right to decide for herself whether to become sexually intimate with another person. The problem is to determine whether an offer of status, money, or professional advancement, in return for sex, should ever be considered legitimate and noncoercive.

Permissible, Noncoercive Inducements

John Walsh (not his real name) was a drifter down on his luck. While hitchhiking, he met Francis Lovely, the manager of a state liquor store in West Lebanon, New Hampshire. Lovely hired him at the store, paid for a room Walsh rented, and later invited Walsh to move into his home. They soon began a sexual relationship. Walsh claimed that when he tried to break it off, Lovely pressured him to submit to numerous acts of homosexual sodomy and oral sex. Lovely, he said, made numerous threats—to kick him out of Lovely's home, to stop paying the rent on his room, and to see that he lost his job. Lovely also reminded him that he had been protecting Walsh from the police. Walsh submitted to Lovely's demands but was unable to stay out of trouble. He was soon enmeshed in a variety of assault, theft, and burglary charges. While under arrest, he told police about his relationship with Lovely, and in 1982 a prosecutor, in an unprecedented move, decided to charge Lovely with sexual assault.[53]

An unusual New Hampshire statute, perhaps the only law of its kind in the nation, makes it a felony to engage in sexual penetration "when the actor coerces the victim by threatening to retaliate against the victim."[54] No other state has attempted to file sexual assault charges based on economic pressure. Even in New Hampshire there is no record, before or since, of any attempt to prosecute when a *woman* was sexually victimized by threats of economic retaliation. But Lovely was charged, and a jury convicted him on twelve counts of aggravated sexual assault. The New Hampshire Supreme Court saw no reason to limit its assault statute to threats of physical violence. Upholding the convictions, the court said that the statute "reach[es] acts that undermine consent through the use of non-violent coercion," and that "threats of economic reprisal" were clearly included.[55]

The court was surely right to grant protection against nonviolent coercion. And Walsh's complaint that Lovely threatened to get him fired makes the claim of coercion especially clear. Criminal convictions for this sort of abuse could send a powerful message, especially if prosecutors were willing to file charges when the victims happened to be women.

The decision nonetheless poses a large problem, because the threat to Walsh's job was not the only economic reprisal that the court took into account. The court treated the threat to stop paying Walsh's rent and the demand that Walsh move out of Lovely's house as illegal reprisals as well. The court allowed the jurors to count these threats as coercive, even if they rejected prosecution claims about the alleged threat to Walsh's job. The court's view implies that Lovely was in effect required to let Walsh continue living in his home, whether or not he and Walsh maintained their sexual relationship. That approach, if the court was serious about it, would surely have far-reaching, not to mention peculiar, results.

Though nonviolent pressure can be enormously coercive, it seems implausible to say that Lovely's unwillingness to house Walsh, once their brief affair ended, was an illegal reprisal in itself. And it would be equally odd to say that Lovely could *not* offer to house Walsh while their relationship prospered. If these intuitions are sound, we cannot automatically condemn every exchange of sex for money, regardless of context. The difficulty is in knowing when, if ever, a person can *legitimately* link sexual intimacy with economic support.

Sexual relationships founded on economic motives seldom seem admirable, and we often regard them as degrading. Yet intuitions about coercion are powerfully affected by the setting in which benefits are offered. The degree of economic need often seems important. The poverty-stricken mother of five who submits to a sexual demand in order to win a desperately needed job is easy to see as a victim of duress. A well-paid supermodel who accedes to sexual pressure in order to land a major film role has choices that the desperate mother and a man such as Walsh lack. However strong the attraction of fame and riches, the model who succumbs to their lure seems free to do otherwise, to find other ways to express her sexuality and to define who she is. Respect for autonomy might imply accepting her choice rather than trying to protect her from it.

This focus on the range of available options and the degree of pressure helps explain why the situations of the desperate mother and the successful model seem so different psychologically. Only the mother seems to have "no real choice." But differences in the degree of pressure are a poor guide to determining which economic inducements should be condemned as illegal. When an unemployed business executive is offered a low-level sales position, but only if he will work ten hours a day at a demanding job, the proposal does not make him a victim of coercion. Even when he has "no real choice" but to accept the job, the offer enhances rather than restricts his autonomy, because he will be better off if he accepts the offer and he will be left no worse off if he rejects it. A legal regime that prohibited those sorts of offers, just because they left the recipient "no real choice," would make it even harder for people in distress to cope with their problems. For the same reason, a proposal to exchange sex for financial support (in marriage, for example) does not necessarily violate a woman's autonomy, even when she is in dire financial straits. A powerful proposal that leaves "no real choice" can still be *non*coercive, if the target of the proposal can refuse it without putting her own rights at risk.

Rights—not the degree of pressure—are the crucial factor in the opposite situation as well. A proposal that puts our rights at risk is coercive even when we have other choices. Financial consultants, construction engineers, and other experienced, sophisticated parties have many options when they seek new business from public or private clients. They can normally find many ways to "resist" a corrupt proposal. Yet the law doesn't expect them to "stop whining" or to rely only on self-help. When they are confronted with illegitimate demands that put their rights at risk, the law unhesitatingly treats them as victims of a serious criminal offense. Sexual choices are entitled to no less protection. An illegitimate sexual proposal should be considered coercive—whether or not the woman who is targeted has other options—if turning it down can leave her worse off.

The ambitious supermodel is a case in point. If she agrees to a film producer's proposal to exchange sex for fame and riches, she was, in a sense, free to do otherwise. She could easily refuse the demand without facing starvation, just as Graham, the engineering contractor, could easily have turned down the Massachusetts official's offer to steer state business his way in return for a kickback. What the woman may prefer, however, is a third option—the chance to compete for the film role on fair terms, without sexual submission. The film producer constrains her decision by foreclosing this choice. He intentionally limits her right to compete on fair terms for every available job.

The same cannot be said when a woman marries a billionaire for his money. Her decision to have sex is still constrained. (Ideally she might prefer the option of wealth and comfort without having to submit to his sexual attention, just as Walsh preferred to live in Lovely's house, without meeting his sexual demands.) But the decisive question is whether she should have the right to receive those economic benefits with no sexual strings attached.

Sex is not a permissible condition of ordinary employment. But sexual fulfillment *is* a legitimate and valued goal of marriage and other ongoing, intimate relationships. The billionaire should not be allowed to use physical force to compel submission to his sexual demands—before or after marriage. But his implicit "threat" ("I won't support you unless we have a sexual relationship") expresses one of the choices he is—and should be—entitled to make in shaping his personal relationships. And his "threat" takes from the woman nothing that she is—or should be—entitled to claim. Her decision to marry or cohabit without emotional attraction might seem unattractive or degrading to her self-esteem—and to his. The personal cost to her might prove very high. But this kind of decision is one that our society properly allows individuals to make for themselves. Her decision would not result from any threat to her rights or any interference with her freedom of choice.

The coercion problem seems different when a man who is attracted to the desperate mother invites her to move into his apartment—on condition that she accept his sexual advances. Unlike the model, the mother faces dire economic pressure that limits her freedom to refuse. The pressure may be even stronger if a man threatens to terminate a current relationship and throw the mother and her children out onto the street unless she meets his sexual needs. The mother may reasonably feel that she has no real choice but to submit to his demands.

As always, however, conclusions about coercion turn not on the degree of pressure but on the legitimacy of the proposal itself. When the producer gives the fashion model a chance to star in a movie, on condition that she sleep with him, the pressure may be slight, but it is clearly illegitimate. When a man offers the desperate woman a chance to have food and a decent home, the pressure is intense, but it might *not* be illegitimate. We have to know whether the man's "threat" to withhold his assistance will violate the mother's rights. If the two parties have married, the woman would be entitled to some degree of financial protection. But when the relationship has been short-lived and without mutual commitments, existing laws would not obligate the man to support her.

If we hope to safeguard sexual autonomy in a realistic way, we cannot ignore the impact of legal rules that leave the desperate mother vulnerable in this way. The problem, then, is to determine whether a man should be allowed to use his economic leverage to compel submission to his sexual demands. An obligation of financial support could certainly be imposed upon him even in the absence of marriage. Domestic relations law has taken a few small steps in this direction,[56] and it is easy to imagine legal rules that would grant even greater protection for economically vulnerable women in long-term relationships that have involved mutual commitments and mutual contributions.

There are limits, however, to how far in this direction the law can sensibly develop, not just because of practical concerns but also because of the values associated with sexual autonomy itself. We no longer wish to live in a world in which premarital sex is strictly forbidden and divorce is practically impossible to obtain. A central component of the autonomy we now claim is the freedom to seek intimacy with persons of our own choosing and to seek sexual satisfaction as a legitimate dimension of an ongoing relationship. Equally important, in the case of relationships short of marriage or its equivalent, is the freedom to move on—to live independently or to seek a new partner—when existing ties become a source of unacceptable emotional and sexual stress.

A legal system that obliged a man to support a former sexual partner, in the absence of the mutual commitments of a long-term relationship, would impose an enormous burden on these components of freedom. We would surely say the same of any rules that obliged an economically vulnerable woman to continue performing household chores that she had willingly provided for her lover in the past—if she decided that she preferred to move out and live with another man instead.

In relationships founded on mutual respect, men and women try to work out difficulties that develop. They try to avoid exploiting each other's economic and emotional vulnerabilities. Efforts to use financial leverage in personal relationships ("Do it tonight or pack your bags") surely deserve criticism under most circumstances. But they should not inevitably violate legal rights. As in the example of the college student who "threatened" to stop dating his girlfriend unless she submitted to sex,[57] proposals that tie financial support to sexual intimacy are sometimes legitimate. For the same reason, Lovely's threat to throw Walsh out of his house and stop paying the rent on Walsh's apartment should be seen as a legitimate exercise of Lovely's autonomy, not an improper intrusion on Walsh's.

The assessment of coercion is roughly similar in a case of outright prostitution. When a man "propositions" a prostitute, he does not impose a sexual condition on activities normally directed to nonsexual goals, such as education or ordinary employment. His proposal does not threaten her rights or interfere in any direct way with her ordinary, nonsexual endeavors. (It may cause indirect psychological injury, especially if it changes her self-concept or her ways of experiencing sexual interaction.) Yet prostitution is typically illegal.

The reasons are complex. The traditional fear—that the ready availability of extramarital sex will threaten the institution of marriage—has largely given way to contemporary concerns about the physical abuse of prostitutes, coercion of unwilling prostitutes, the degradation of a person's conception of sexual intimacy, and the risk of spreading AIDS. Whether these concerns are sufficiently well grounded to justify laws against consensual sex between competent adults remains controversial.[58] Many committed feminists insist that the alleged harms, and their links to consensual prostitution, are too speculative to justify this restriction on freedom of sexual choice. They stress the importance of permitting every woman to decide for herself how to make the best of her circumstances, especially when her other options may in her view be even more dangerous or unsatisfying than life as a prostitute.[59]

Rather than seeking to protect women from their own choices by outlawing prostitution, a society that sought to enhance autonomy should first attempt to assure the availability of jobs not conditioned on sex, and an adequate safety net of welfare and child support for women unable to find work. But a society that values autonomy might still prohibit voluntary commercial sex if it concluded that the harmful indirect effects were sufficiently serious.

Where prostitution remains illegal, as it does in every American state except Nevada, proposals to exchange sex for money are obviously illegitimate. But the man who propositions a prostitute is not necessarily *coercing* her. When a proposal introduces a sexual condition into a normally nonsexual sphere—education, for example—a woman usually cannot reject it without putting at risk her right to compete on fair terms. But in a case of outright prostitution, the woman who receives the illegal offer remains free to turn it down. If she does, she may find herself in a tight financial spot, but it will be no tighter than it was before. The proposal, though illegal, does not interfere with her options, limited though they may be.

In sum, an offer to provide financial benefits in return for sex normally is not coercive if the woman won't put her rights at risk by turning the proposal down. But a supervisor's offer to trade job benefits for sexual favors normally *is* coercive, because the proposal signals his willingness to abuse his power; it almost inevitably arouses fear that he may use his position to inflict harm if his advances are rebuffed.

One of the most troubling scenarios fits neither of these situations. Often a boss or supervisor expresses romantic or sexual interest to a subordinate without saying that her job will be affected by her response. In these common situations, there is power to inflict injury, but there may not be anything overtly improper about the sexual proposal itself. None of the states (and very few private firms) prohibit *all* such proposals, regardless of the circumstances. There is not even any widespread assumption that such sexual advances are unethical. Yet the subordinate may fear retaliation or the loss of her right to compete on fair terms if she rebuffs her boss's advance. Her fears may be virtually identical to those she would experience if the sexual proposition came linked with an offer to get her a plum assignment in return. So there is some reason to consider the boss's sexual advance coercive even when he doesn't explicitly tie it to an illegitimate offer. His power to affect the woman's job is there, and she knows it, whether he mentions it or not.

Yet it is far from clear that proposals of this sort should be treated as unethical or illegal. The pressure on the subordinate may be significant, but if any possibility of retaliation is sufficient to establish coercion, consent to sex must be considered tainted in virtually every situation in which one party has some sort of power over the other. That approach would protect sexual autonomy from one direction, by sheltering the subordinate from sexual advances that put her freedom of choice at risk. But from another direction, that approach would restrict autonomy by barring sexual advances, and perhaps even simple requests for a date, whenever they are initiated by a man who can influence the career of the woman he finds attractive. That might be the right approach, but it would pose a serious obstacle to mutually desired relationships between competent, responsible men and women.

Existing law avoids this difficulty but goes to the opposite extreme, granting psychologists, doctors, lawyers, and teachers almost unlimited freedom to have "consensual" sexual relationships with women whom they hold in their power. That solution is equally unsatisfactory. Effective safeguards for sexual autonomy must identify the situations in which economic power or professional authority unjustifiably impairs the weaker party's freedom of sexual choice. The problem requires close attention to the variety of institutional and professional contexts in which power and sexual attraction (mutual and otherwise) intermingle.

9

Supervisors and Teachers:
The Problem of Power

Any supervisor who offers to exchange job benefits for sex commits a form of extortion that should be considered a clear-cut criminal offense. But sex-for-benefits proposals are seldom spelled out explicitly. Almost invariably, the supervisor's sexual advance and the potential job consequences float alongside one another, with little more than allusion or innuendo to link the two. Sometimes the linkage is extremely crude. In one case, when a woman entered her boss's office to receive her performance evaluation, he unbuckled his belt, unzipped his fly, and said to her, "Okay, I'm going to evaluate your performance."[1] Usually the linkage is more subtle. But subtle or not, once a court is persuaded that a supervisor invited his subordinate to draw the connection—to infer that job decisions would turn on sexual compliance—there should be no reason to hesitate in condemning his conduct.

Matters become more complicated if a manager expresses sexual interest to a subordinate *without* promising any professional benefit. Suppose that Sally and her boss, Bill, are working late together on a project for an important client. When they are ready to leave the office, Bill asks Sally to drive home with him and come up to his apartment for a drink. Bill makes no effort to pretend that he wants to continue discussing their work. His eyes and his smile make clear, in a respectful way, that he finds Sally intelligent and attractive and that he wants a chance to know her personally.

Sally may be just as strongly attracted to Bill as he is to her. She may be delighted by the prospect of having a serious relationship with him. Still, Bill's seemingly innocent act of asking Sally for a date can pose serious problems. He has enormous power to affect her career, whether he mentions it or not. And Sally would know that a decision to turn him down cannot help but color his feelings about her. So Sally might feel under pressure to accept, whether she really wants to or not.

Bill's invitation may hurt Sally in another way, because it signals that he sees her not only in her professional role but potentially in a sexual one. Not everyone would find that message upsetting. Many people are pleased to be told, even in a professional setting, that others find them physically attractive. But for many women, too long accustomed to being treated as sex objects and little else, it can be especially important to know that at work they are seen exclusively as competent professionals. One survey found that when men and women were asked how they would feel if asked by a co-worker to have sex, 67 percent of the men but only 17 percent of the women said they would feel flattered; 15 percent of the men but 63 percent of the women said they would feel insulted.[2] Some suggest that because of women's physical and economic vulnerability, a sexual advance in an unexpected context can arouse anxiety. The woman may even fear that the proposition is a prelude to the use of force.[3]

Yet existing laws do not bar bosses and teachers from making sexual demands on their subordinates. So far as current law is concerned, there is still "no harm in asking," even when the asking is done by a supervisor who completely controls a woman's professional future. Requests for dates, and even direct sexual propositions, are considered perfectly permissible unless they are found to be "unwelcome." And the subordinate bears the responsibility for making "unwelcomeness" clear to her boss. This is no mere technicality, because turning down requests for a date and spurning physical advances are not always considered sufficient to signal that further advances will be unwelcome. One court held that an employee had not communicated that her boss's advances were unwelcome, because "her requests [for him to stop] were not delivered with any sense of urgency, sincerity or force."[4]

The laws against sexual harassment rest on contradictory premises in this respect. The supervisor's power creates the need for safeguards to protect the subordinate from unwelcome advances, but the same power makes it hard for her to *signal* unwelcomeness without fear of retaliation, especially if she must do so "urgently" or "forcefully." Despite the hyperbole that frequently accompanies media accounts of the restrictions imposed under current sexual harassment laws, the constraints on bosses and teachers who seek to initiate a sexual relationship with someone under their supervision remain uncertain and limited.

Beyond the realm of formal legal rules, standards of acceptable behavior in schools, colleges, and the workplace present a similarly mixed and sometimes incongruous picture. Broadly speaking, sexual encounters not induced by physical force or coercive threats are generally treated as private matters and are left unrestricted, even when one of the parties holds enormous power over the other. Yet sensitivity to the abusive potential of institutional power is growing, and many private organizations are beginning to regulate these relationships—sometimes tepidly, sometimes with oppressive strictness, and sometimes with vague, unpredictable standards that can produce the worst of both worlds.

A prominent psychiatrist refers to sex between a man and a woman who have a professional relationship based on power or trust—"specifically when the man is the woman's doctor, psychotherapist, pastor, lawyer, teacher, or workplace mentor"—as "sex in the forbidden zone."[5] The phrase aptly captures the taboos that are beginning to attach to these relationships and the heavy professional price sometimes paid by those who step over the line. But the zone is not really *forbidden,* either by law or by uniform social and professional norms. And it is not clear that it should be. The weaker party's capacity to withhold her consent is obviously at risk in these encounters. But rules that completely bar sexual interaction whenever there is any imbalance of power can endanger autonomy from the opposite direction, by stifling voluntary, freely chosen relationships, many of which can lead to fulfilling, lifelong commitments.

"Antifraternization" policies in the military provide the most extreme example. The American armed forces have always prohibited social contact between officers and enlisted soldiers. The rising number of women in uniform has increased the importance of the traditional policy, and failure to enforce it vigorously has caused major problems at many military installations, as the 1997 trials for the sexual abuse of recruits at the Army's Aberdeen Proving Ground vividly illustrated. But on other military bases, aggressive enforcement of antifraternization rules has caused abuses of its own, destroying careers and restricting freedom to form mutually desired relationships, in situations in which the dangers of coercion and the risks to military discipline are virtually nonexistent.

In 1988 Lieutenant Kathleen Mazure, a Navy dentist stationed at the Air-Ground Combat Center at 29 Palms, California, was prosecuted for fraternization because she had dated a Marine Corps enlisted man. The two were not in the same chain of command, their relationship was conducted entirely off the base, and before the court-martial charges were filed, the two had married. After extensive press coverage and a public outcry, the Marine Corps dropped the criminal charges.[6] None-theless, fraternization rules in the Navy and Air Force apply across chains of command, marriage normally is not a defense, and in all the armed services, interpretation and enforcement are left almost entirely to the broad discretion of the base commander.[7]

If the parties to a fully consensual officer-enlistee relationship can manage to avoid a court-martial, informal pressure and other sanctions remain. Individuals sometimes pay a heavy career price for falling in love. In one Air Force case, two staff sergeants married. The husband subsequently qualified for officer training school and was commissioned as a second lieutenant. Though they were assigned to separate units, she to the Military Airlift Command and he to the Strategic Air Command, the husband's superiors demanded that either he or his wife leave the Air Force. The wife gave up her career.[8]

Problems of this sort will grow as more and more women enter the civilian workforce, the military, and the professions. Standards are ur-gently needed to identify the kinds of sexual liaisons that should be entirely off limits. But it is equally important to avoid overkill. We should not subject freely chosen relationships to an extensive regime of legal regulation and intrusive informal controls. It remains essential to respect the freedom of every competent adult to seek intimacy with a genuinely willing partner. The problem is to determine just when the potential for abuse of power justifies a ban on sexual interaction even in the absence of a coercive offer or threat. Society should not ban sexual encounters that both participants want, unless decisionmaking incompetence, the dangers of retaliation, or potential harms to third parties indicate a high potential for abuse. The problem of designing standards to protect and support autonomy for one person—without at the same time destroying it for another—assumes a distinct form in each of the settings in which power differentials affect the dynamics of sexual interaction.

The very complexity of these concerns is, for many people, strong reason to abstain from regulating consensual relationships between competent adults. Some ridicule such regulations for demeaning or "infantilizing" the women they ostensibly protect. If the affected women *really* do not want the encounter, so the argument goes, they can fairly be expected to say so.[9] Yet this view ignores the concrete ways in which real-world power can undermine freedom of choice and render seemingly consensual encounters involuntary. Abuses of this sort are frequent, serious, and largely unregulated by existing laws. Respect for sexual autonomy requires far more extensive protection than society has so far been willing to afford, including a complete ban on some types of sexual encounters, even when the less powerful participant consents.

Sexual Relationships in the Workplace

Workplace harassment takes many forms, including crude language, open display of sexual posters or reading material, "accidental" body contact, and a wide variety of other acts by supervisors or co-workers that create an offensive working environment. Unwanted demands for sex occur less often than many other forms of harassment, and many of the demands come from peers rather than superiors. A 1994 survey found that over a two-year period, 37 percent of the women working in the federal government experienced unwelcome sexual remarks and 24–29 percent were the victims of suggestive looks or deliberate touching by either supervisors or co-workers. By comparison, over the same period, relatively few women—only 4 percent—were pressured to date their supervisors.[10] Nonetheless, if levels of harassment are comparable (or higher) in private firms, as rough estimates suggest,[11] the survey implies that *more than two million* working women were subjected to unwelcome sexual demands from someone who held their job and their professional future in his power.[12]

Sexual harassment is a far more serious problem for women than for men, and this is especially true of pressure for dates and sexual contact. In the federal survey, only 10 percent of male workers experienced unwanted sexual remarks and only 7–8 percent considered themselves the victims of suggestive looks or deliberate touching. The numbers were even lower for men who were pressured for dates (only 3 percent of working men), and almost all these episodes involved demands by co-workers or even subordinates of the man who received the unwelcome sexual attention. Though the predicament of the male worker pressured to have sex with his boss seems to capture popular imagination and attention (as in Michael Crichton's best-seller *Disclosure*), the problem is statistically infrequent. In the federal survey, over a two-year period, less than one-half of one percent of male workers were pressured to date their supervisor. For women the problem was twelve times more frequent. Nonetheless, even for men, the total number of workers affected could be large, perhaps more than 200,000 men pressured for dates by their bosses at some point during a two-year period.[13]

Even when a subordinate feels able to rebuff her boss's attentions, his advance can cast a cloud over their working relationship. The subordinate may be left feeling physically self-conscious and professionally vulnerable, sensing that she was placed in a sexual role and that her professional boundaries were not respected. She may worry that she will no longer receive desirable assignments, that her work won't be evaluated fairly, that promotions she might have gained will now go to others. Yet her only alternative may be to submit.

Mechelle Vinson applied for a job at the Meritor Savings Bank in Washington, D.C., and was hired to work as a teller-trainee, under the supervision of the branch manager, Sidney Taylor. Vinson claimed that shortly after the end of her probationary period, Taylor invited her out to dinner. During the meal, she said, Taylor suggested that they go to a motel to have sexual relations. Vinson said that she refused at first, but that she eventually agreed, for fear of losing her job.

From that time on, Vinson claimed, Taylor made repeated demands for sex, both during and after business hours. She said she had intercourse with him forty or fifty times over the next several years. Meanwhile, Vinson advanced from teller-trainee to teller, head teller, and eventually to assistant branch manager, all the while remaining under Taylor's supervision. But after four years, Vinson took a sick leave, and when she stayed away from work for two months, the bank fired her for excessive use of sick leave. She then sued the bank, claiming that during her four years on the job, Taylor had subjected her to constant sexual harassment.[14] Vinson never claimed that Taylor threatened to fire her or withhold promotions, and she didn't say that he promised her better job assignments in return for meeting his sexual demands. Her more limited claims nonetheless suggest that a manager's sexual pressure can create a harrowing situation for a woman under his supervision, even when no explicit offers or threats are made.

Sometimes a male employee charges his male supervisor with attempting to pressure him into a same-sex liaison. Stephen Gregory, a producer for a radio talk show, charged in a 1997 lawsuit that on a number of occasions the show's male host grabbed his buttocks or his penis, or kissed him on the cheek. Once, when they were traveling together, Gregory claimed, his boss climbed into his hotel bed and refused to leave, saying, "I just want some affection." Gregory alleged that he avoided these advances, and that his boss retaliated by withholding his pay and eventually firing him. His former boss denied all the allegations, and the charges remain pending.[15]

More complicated configurations also surface. A 1991 case involved facts that could successfully compete with pornographic fiction. Noel Smith, the general manager of a jewelry plating firm in Cranston, Rhode Island, was allegedly having an extramarital affair with his secretary, Carol Marsella. According to the court's findings, Smith told Gary Showalter, one of the firm's employees, that Marsella was sexually attracted to him and that Showalter would have to satisfy Marsella in order for Smith's own relationship with her "to be okay." Smith, the court found, began prodding Showalter to have sex with Marsella, but Showalter resisted the pressure and reminded Smith that he was married. Smith turned angry and told Showalter that if he valued his job, he had better comply. At one point Smith, who knew that Showalter's son had a heart defect that might require open-heart surgery, allegedly threatened Showalter with the loss of his medical benefits. Eventually Showalter submitted to Smith's demands, and on Smith's instructions he participated in numerous sex acts with Marsella alone and as part of a threesome with Smith and Marsella.[16]

Federal law, though increasingly strict in its definition of sexual harassment, does not categorically prohibit managers from asking workers under their supervision for sex. Mechelle Vinson's suit against the Meritor Savings Bank led to a landmark Supreme Court decision that simultaneously validated women's concerns about harassment and ducked the hard questions about sexual attention from supervisors on the job.

When Vinson sued, her boss at the bank, Sidney Taylor, flatly denied all her charges. He said he never had sexual intercourse with her and never even raised the subject. But the trial judge ruled that it didn't matter which of them was telling the truth. Even if Vinson's claims were true, the judge said, she could not claim to be a victim of sexual harassment, because her relationship with Taylor was "voluntary." Taylor did not threaten her job at the bank or her chance for promotions, so the judge held that he did not coerce her.

The U.S. Supreme Court set aside that ruling. Its decision recognized for the first time that sexual harassment in the workplace can violate the federal law (known as "Title VII") that prohibits any employer from "discriminat[ing] against any individual [in compensation or conditions of employment] because of . . . race, color, religion, sex, or national origin."[17] But the Court did not unequivocally uphold Vinson's claim. Instead, the Court recognized two situations in which sexual harassment can amount to unlawful "discrimination."

The first, quid-pro-quo harassment, occurs when an employee must submit to unwelcome sexual contacts in order to retain her job or when her willingness to submit is considered in decisions affecting her employment. Tangible job benefits become the "quid pro quo"—something given in exchange for something else, in this case sexual submission.

The trial judge had thrown out Vinson's case because she had not claimed quid-pro-quo harassment. But the Supreme Court also recognized a second type of liability. The Court ruled that "sexual misconduct constitutes prohibited 'sexual harassment,' whether or not it is directly linked to the grant or denial of an economic *quid pro quo*, where 'such conduct . . . creat[es] an intimidating, hostile, or offensive working environment.'"[18] The Court said that the second sort of misconduct—"hostile environment" harassment—violates the right of every employee to work in an atmosphere free from discriminatory intimidation or ridicule.

Vinson's employer argued that her claim was insufficient, even under the broader "hostile environment" approach, because her alleged encounters with Taylor were "voluntary." The Supreme Court disagreed: "The correct inquiry is whether [Vinson] by her conduct indicated that the alleged sexual advances were unwelcome, not whether her actual participation in sexual intercourse was voluntary." The Court held that the bank would be liable if Vinson proved at trial that her boss's advances were "unwelcome."[19]

The Court took a major step in recognizing that sexual attention from supervisors or co-workers can create intolerable working conditions. After the *Vinson* decision, it is clear that sexual demands can create a "hostile environment," even when the employee never confronts an explicit threat to her job. But the Court refused to rule that sexual demands from a person in authority are inherently coercive or improper. Instead the Court put the burden on the employee to indicate *by her conduct* that the sexual advances are unwelcome. Until she does, the supervisor remains free to ask, even repeatedly. If fear for her job leads the subordinate to acquiesce without protesting, the boss's advances do not count as sexual harassment.

The Court's compromise is clearly an awkward one at best. As in the law of rape, "resistance to the utmost" is an untenable requirement that no modern court would attempt to enforce, but the law still puts the burden on the woman to resist in some fashion.[20] It still refuses to say that a man must have some affirmative indication of her desires in order to claim that she gave genuine consent.

In other ways as well, federal law limits the protection that women can claim in the workplace. There is little doubt that large corporations have tried to improve the working environment for women and to institute grievance procedures for workers subjected to harassment. And some of the recent court decisions have strengthened legal prohibitions. But major barriers to liability for sexual harassment remain. As often happens, the devil is in the details. And the details cast a radically different light on the often-heard complaint that federal law goes much too far in attempting to protect women who are merely prudish or oversensitive.

The first "detail" is that no matter how extreme the harassing behavior may be, the federal statute prohibiting employment discrimination (Title VII) does not hold the perpetrator *personally* liable for his misconduct. If the perpetrator uses physical force, of course, he can be prosecuted for sexual assault and sued for damages under state law. If the perpetrator is a state official who coerces public employees under his control, he can be sued (under a different federal statute) for depriving them of their civil rights.[21] But in private companies, when a manager flagrantly pressures his subordinates for dates or threatens to fire them for not submitting to sexual demands, he can't be prosecuted or sued for damages. The theory of Title VII is that the employer (the firm) has a duty not to discriminate against its employees on the basis of race, religion, or sex, but federal law imposes no duty directly on the supervisor as an individual. As a result, the courts conclude, Congress did not intend to hold the coercive supervisor personally liable.[22]

Another important gap is that Title VII imposes no duty—none whatsoever—on firms that have fewer than fifteen employees. So in small workplaces, the employee who is subjected to blatant pressure for sexual favors can sue *neither* the individual perpetrator nor the firm.

Even when the firm is clearly covered by Title VII, a victim of sexual harassment faces numerous obstacles to bringing a successful suit. Liability is clearest in quid-pro-quo situations, in which a worker submits because her superior makes clear that her job or her advancement will suffer if she refuses.[23] Liability should also be clear under the quid-pro-quo theory when the subordinate rejects a sexual demand and then gets fired or demoted. In that situation, the only additional barrier to liability is *causation:* the employee must show that she was fired or demoted *because* she rebuffed the advance and not for some other reason, such as absenteeism or poor performance. But the causation requirement is in practice a formidable obstacle. Since an employer can almost always find some imperfection in the worker's record, it is usually no simple matter to prove that she was fired in retaliation for rejecting the sexual demand and that any flaws in her record were just a pretext for the decision.

Betty Dockter, the young woman hired by a Chicago commodities broker despite her limited credentials, was fired when she rejected her boss's sexual advances. The court dismissed her harassment suit, finding that she was subject to discharge because her job qualifications were poor.[24] Yet her boss might have overlooked her shortcomings if she had responded favorably to his advances. In cases like Dockter's, courts seem to focus on an entirely artificial question—whether the worker's record would justify some hypothetical fair employer in taking action against her. But people do not work for hypothetical employers, and the decisions that real employers make aren't invariably fair. Competent workers aren't always promoted, and incompetent ones don't always get dismissed. A causation requirement is essential to ensure that sexual harassment laws do not become a guarantee of life tenure for incompetent employees. But the defense should be available only when the employee's failings are so serious that the firm would have fired her *even if* she had submitted to the advances.

This strict approach is inherent in the principle that sexual harassment not only includes threats of reprisal but also extends to offers to give an employee unearned job privileges in exchange for sex. Suppose a supervisor in effect says to an employee, "Your job failings give me the right to fire you, but I won't if you go with me to the motel." His proposal is a clear example of quid-pro-quo harassment, and his firm is unquestionably liable for damages if the employee accepts his "offer" in order to keep her job. The result should be no different if she refuses and then gets fired. A worker has been fired *because of* her refusal—and has therefore suffered quid-pro-quo harassment—whenever she would have escaped the adverse job decision by meeting her supervisor's sexual demands.[25]

There is only a hair's breadth between the supervisor whose sexual proposal is implicitly tied to a favorable job evaluation and the supervisor whose sexual advance isn't linked—or can't be proved to be linked—to decisions he will make affecting the subordinate's career. Yet in the law of Title VII, the second situation presents an entirely different set of issues. Without proof linking the sexual proposal to tangible job benefits, the quid pro quo type of claim fails, and liability for sexual harassment will be recognized only if the worker can show a "hostile environment." And the courts have imposed strict limits on hostile-environment claims, for reasons that are partly practical, partly artificial and conceptual.

When a woman's co-workers and superiors are openly hostile to her, they themselves are not—in the technical eyes of the law—doing anything wrong. Title VII makes sexual harassment unlawful only when it amounts to discrimination *by the firm*. In a quid-pro-quo case, the firm is automatically implicated, because the employee's job status has been linked to sex. But when co-workers or supervisors make crude comments and sexual propositions, they are not performing duties for their company. So most courts conclude that a firm cannot fairly be held responsible for offensive behavior by its employees, unless upper management should have been aware of the situation and was negligent in failing to prevent it.[26] Even when a hostile environment is convincingly proved, the injured employee gets no redress unless she can prove negligence on the part of the company.

One practical problem, constantly in the news, is the potential expense and inconvenience of litigation when disgruntled employees bring phony claims. But unfounded allegations and nuisance suits are an unavoidable danger in any system of laws that restricts an employer's discretion to fire employees at will. Whether a sexual harassment claim is available or not, a disgruntled employee can still claim discrimination on grounds of her sex, race, or religion, and if she is disposed to invent false accusations, she can file a civil suit alleging rape or sexual assault as well. There is little reason to think that one additional ground for litigation will add measurably to the unscrupulous employee's opportunities for filing phony claims. At the same time there is good reason to afford redress to honest employees who suffer genuine abuses that they can prove in court.

A more serious practical problem is the wide range of conduct and speech, by peers as well as by superiors, that might make a work situation feel offensive. A woman may be the target of her co-workers' groping or crude remarks, or she may be made uncomfortable by overhearing sexually explicit conversation that was not directed to her. She may (or may not) be offended by a co-worker's joke, by his proposal to go to a motel at lunch hour, or by a supervisor's request that she join him for dinner. Courts and employers need to protect workers against unacceptable tension on the job without imposing oppressive constraints on ordinary, spontaneous interactions.

In the *Vinson* case, the Supreme Court ruled that harassment would trigger liability under the "hostile environment" approach only when three requirements were met. The employee claiming sexual harassment must show that sexual behavior in the workplace was *unwelcome*, that she *indicated by her conduct* that it was unwelcome, and that it was sufficiently *severe or pervasive* to create an abusive environment.[27]

In considering whether a firm should face sanctions when a manager tells his secretary an off-color joke, or when one bookkeeper tells a female colleague that he likes her new dress, we can quickly see the need to restrict liability by requirements something like those the Court adopted in *Vinson*. Between friends and colleagues who know each other well, a sexual joke or a compliment on a person's appearance can be innocuous or, perhaps more often, a valued break from monotony and routine. But if sexual banter is unwelcome, if the employee makes that clear, and if the banter nonetheless continues in a severe or persistent way, the conduct creates an abusive situation that no worker should be expected to endure.

The requirements adopted in *Vinson* become more questionable when we move from the hypothetical problem of sporadic banter to the more serious sexual pressures that were the real problem in that case. Charles Taylor was not just a co-worker but Mechelle Vinson's boss, and he was not just telling her an off-color joke; he was, Vinson claimed, asking her to go with him to a motel. Yet the Court chose to shelter that kind of sexual advance with the same stringent barriers to liability that apply to casual conversation among peers. In this one-test-fits-all definition of hostile-environment harassment, the special problem posed by the supervisor's power virtually disappears from view. And what disappears with it is the essence of the harm to the employee—not just having to face discomfort at the office, but having to lie naked in a motel bed submitting to sexual intimacy that she did not freely choose.

The Court might have thought that any worker who submits to a sexual demand must be choosing freely to do so, unless she "indicates by her conduct" that the demand was unwelcome.[28] Genuine desire is certainly one possible explanation for a subordinate's failure to signal unwelcomeness. But another, equally plausible, is profound reluctance, coupled with appreciation for the supervisor's power and fear of retaliation for resisting his demands.

The Court's refusal to give any weight to this second possibility is especially difficult to fathom in the context of the *Vinson* case itself. Mechelle Vinson's alleged encounters with her supervisor occurred when sexual harassment laws were in their infancy and when fear of retaliation was the norm. In a survey conducted at almost exactly the same time as the events Vinson alleged in her suit, the U.S. Merit Systems Protection Board found that among women whose supervisors pressured them for dates or sexual favors, 60 percent thought they would suffer adverse consequences for refusing.[29]

The character of the problem is not fundamentally different today. Managers no doubt tend to be more cautious, and lawsuits alleging retaliation are more common. Many women, including some who consider themselves feminists, urge their sisters to be strong and independent, to "take responsibility." They wonder why a woman who does not really want a sexual encounter can't just say so.

There are several concrete reasons. Most forms of quid-pro-quo retaliation remain extremely subtle and hard to prove, the causation requirement poses a further obstacle to an effective damage remedy, and the individual perpetrator of the offense—the supervisor himself—faces neither criminal penalties nor civil damages. We are still a long way from a world in which women can confidently dismiss the danger of retaliation and feel free to signal without fear that their supervisor's advances are unwelcome.

These concerns do not mean that every woman who has sex with her boss is inevitably a victim of abuse. But Title VII is far too weak and loophole-ridden to neutralize the coercive impact of a supervisor's power. And, perhaps equally important, Title VII is fundamentally misdirected. It provides needed protection against discrimination by firms but gives no direct protection for the sexual autonomy of the employee. Federal laws against sexual harassment provide no assurance that a subordinate's consent to sex is the product of a genuinely free choice.

State laws do little to fill this gap. Most states have "fair employment practices" statutes, but many of these simply track Title VII's wording and burdens of proof. A few of the state laws provide more generous damages or cover smaller firms, but in most states the protection afforded is identical to that of Title VII.[30] The major advantage of state law is the possibility of holding the individual perpetrator personally liable. When sexual contact is imposed by physical force, the offender faces criminal prosecution for rape or sexual assault and a civil suit for damages, including punitive damages. But the manager who coerces sexual favors by threatening to injure a subordinate's career commits no criminal offense. And absence of physical force usually precludes civil damage liability as well.[31]

Internal policies at individual firms are an important part of the regulatory picture, offering both more flexibility and more protection from coercion than cumbersome lawsuits can. Personnel managers differ sharply over whether office romances improve employee morale or instead make trouble for the firm. Some companies actually encourage dating among co-workers, while others frown on it, and some have formal policies that prohibit employees from dating one another under certain circumstances.[32]

Wal-Mart at one time banned dating between its workers when one or both were married, and the company would dismiss any employee who committed adultery with a co-worker. In 1993 the company fired Laurel Allen, a customer service representative at its Jamestown, New York, store, and Samuel Johnson, a sporting-goods clerk at the same store, because they had dated while Allen was married—though legally separated from her husband. Allen and Johnson sued under a New York law that prohibits retaliation against an employee for engaging in lawful "recreational activities" outside work hours.[33] After a trial judge ruled that their challenge appeared valid, Wal-Mart abandoned its effort to enforce "family values" and limited its ban to conduct that affects company operations. The revised policy bars only "open displays of affection" and "a romantic involvement between a supervisor and a subordinate."[34]

Many states, adhering to the "employment at will" doctrine, allow companies to fire their workers for any reason other than race, gender, religion, or (in some states) sexual orientation. But in other states, broad antidiscrimination and fair-employment-practice laws impose significant constraints. These statutes restrict corporate efforts to regulate employee dating and sexual interaction, but sexual harassment laws virtually require such efforts, because they oblige companies to ensure that sexual liaisons are free of pressure and to discipline or fire employees who sexually harass other workers.

The intersection between the two sets of laws makes office sex a minefield of potential liability for employers. Companies that fail to discipline suspected harassers have been sued under government rules that require employer action whenever there is a "reasonable belief that harassment has occurred"[35]—whether or not the harasser is actually guilty. On the other hand, companies that do act vigorously often find themselves facing multimillion-dollar damage awards when juries conclude that the suspected harasser was fired without adequate proof of his guilt or without following fair procedures. In one case currently pending, an insurance company fired one of its executives after its investigation supported the complaints of two female employees who said he had made obscene phone calls to their homes. The man sued for wrongful discharge and recovered a $1.8 million damage award based on his claim that the dismissal was premature and the company's investigation inadequate. Meanwhile one of the women sued the company, contending that it hadn't fired the man quickly enough.[36]

Despite the complexities of company intervention, many management experts conclude that the laissez-faire approach to supervisor-subordinate dating is a recipe for disaster. One employment law specialist, Dean Shaner, recommends that firms adopt a written policy banning all "intimate, romantic, or dating relationships" between supervisors and their subordinates.[37] Interestingly, Shaner proposes that when a company learns of a prohibited liaison, it should modify the work relationship by transferring one of the employees. Discharge, he assumes, is unwarranted unless the affair led to preferential treatment or affected company business. Shaner implicitly recognizes that employees are likely to date casually and explore romantic possibilities, in spite of any no-dating rule. In practice a firm probably would not expect them to disclose their involvement or restructure their relationship at work until their liaison became serious.

Protecting Autonomy at Work

Neither the prevailing legal standards nor the various rules adopted by individual firms deal adequately with the dilemmas of sex in the workplace. The relationships usually involve mature, competent adults with some degree of economic and psychological independence. But there are two problems. A worker pressured for sex by her boss isn't completely free to "just say no," because retaliation is an ever-present danger, one that existing law does not effectively deter. And usually she can't "just quit." She may have invested months or years developing skills and personal contacts that can't easily be transferred to another firm. She may lose seniority and benefits by starting over elsewhere. She may have difficulty finding another job at all. And if she does go elsewhere, she may face sexual pressure again; the "just quit" approach may simply transfer the problem to a new setting.

A formal law banning (and perhaps even criminalizing) sex between supervisors and their subordinates would avoid these problems, but at high cost. The supervisor's right to seek intimacy with a potentially willing partner obviously would be curtailed. And the subordinate's autonomy would be curtailed as well, because a no-dating or no-sex rule would put off limits a relationship that she might enthusiastically welcome. The harm of *unwanted* sexual intimacy is extremely serious, but freedom to pursue *mutually desired* relationships is important as well. For most people, the search for personal and sexual fulfillment with a compatible partner is one of life's most important concerns, as important as their jobs, and for some people more important.

The search for intimacy can proceed in other directions even when supervisor-subordinate relationships are ruled out. But a sensible rule against supervisor-subordinate sex would have to include as a "supervisor" not just the worker's immediate superior but also managers further up the chain, and presumably any higher-status employee with power to affect her career. For many workers, the number of fellow employees placed out of bounds, because they stand higher or lower on the corporate ladder, could easily dwarf the number of colleagues who could safely be treated as peers. In practice, a ban on supervisor-subordinate sex could rule out, at many firms, a large portion of the potential relationships.

A ban on most sexual liaisons at work would leave employees the option to date people outside the firm, of course. But the job site is often one of the most sensible places to seek a potential partner. People who work in the same firm typically share common interests and skills. They can form impressions by observing each other's responses in a variety of situations over extended periods. And for all its dangers, the workplace is relatively *safe*. According to sociologist Pepper Schwartz, "There's a certain amount of fear in meeting people we can't locate. In the workplace, there's a sense of safety and familiarity."[38] One report on the dating scene concludes: "Corporate offices have replaced singles bars as a prime mating market and are usurping churches, neighborhoods, social clubs, and family networks as the way couples meet. College is the only other place where we are brought together with so many like-

minded peers. But since more marriages are delayed until after graduation . . colleague relationships are taking the place of coed mating."[39]

Because a legal rule forbidding all supervisor-subordinate relationships would rule out so many potential partners, a formal prohibition is
hard to justify and almost certainly would be impossible to enforce.[40] A
better approach would focus on efforts to enable the less powerful party
to choose freely, rather than trying to protect her from her own choices
by prohibiting sexual encounters altogether. Yet existing legal standards
do not effectively deter coercive pressure. The loopholes in current law
enable firms to escape responsibility for the predatory behavior of their
supervisors, and the actual perpetrators—the supervisors themselves—cannot be held liable at all. To support freedom of choice,
without artificially constraining it, we must seek to minimize the pressures that make it difficult for the subordinate worker to say "no."

An important first step is to break away from current law's reliance
on remedies aimed almost exclusively at corporate entities rather than
at individuals. The prospect of suits by sexual harassment victims has
changed office cultures and put effective compliance programs into
place at many firms. Yet a firm's ability to act vigorously against suspected offenders is limited by the risk of suit from the opposite direction
if the alleged perpetrator of the harassment is disciplined or discharged.
Because companies have complex and conflicting incentives, we cannot
confidently rely on an enforcement strategy that makes firms the exclusive target.

A prerequisite to individual liability, of course, is clear proof that
misconduct occurred. Courts and juries are likely to weigh evidence
carefully when the defendant is an individual rather than the deep
pocket of an abstract business entity. But when wrongdoing is clear,
personal liability is essential—both as a matter of simple justice and as
a way to bring sanctions directly to the source of the problem.

The requirements for imposing personal liability are straightforward.
If a boss indicates that sexual submission will affect an employee's job
or chances for promotion, his conduct has no conceivable justification.
It bears all the features of extortion, and like extortion it should be a
criminal offense. Since it also amounts to quid-pro-quo harassment, the
boss's conduct should subject him to liability for damages in a civil suit
as well.

Even in the absence of threats to a worker's job, unwelcome sexual advances can make the subordinate's work situation tense and uncomfortable. If the behavior is purposely provocative, alarming, or severe, existing criminal laws against harassment and "stalking" already apply.[41] But absent egregious misconduct of that sort, the discomfort resulting from "hostile environment" sexual harassment ordinarily would warrant only civil, not criminal, sanctions.

The most difficult question is whether civil liability should extend beyond existing conceptions of quid-pro-quo and hostile-environment harassment. Even in the absence of a provable quid pro quo, relationships between managers and their subordinates often involve a potential for coercion, especially when the supervisor aggressively presses his sexual demands. Stronger safeguards against retaliation might be sufficient to give the subordinate confidence in her ability to say no without hurting her career. But when there are so many subtle possibilities for retaliation, the subordinate will probably never feel entirely free to reject her boss's sexual advance.

A ban on sexual advances *initiated* by the supervisor could mitigate sexual pressure on the subordinate, without completely forbidding mutually desired relationships. But such a rule would still inhibit desired relationships to a degree, because the supervisor is likely to be a man, and men are still expected to play the more active role in asking for dates and sexual contacts.[42] Pending extensive changes in culture, some entirely voluntary relationships will never get off the ground if managers are barred from making sexual proposals to their subordinates. And any rule that banned relationships initiated by the supervisor while permitting those initiated by the subordinate would produce somewhat artificial results, because it would so often be difficult to know which of the two had really made the first move. A legal ban on romantic and sexual proposals initiated by a job supervisor is a conceivable but cumbersome way to strike a balance between these competing concerns.

A better approach might start from current law's ban on *unwelcome* sexual advances. But courts should give more weight to background circumstances that can help determine when a supervisor's advances were unwelcome. In many of the reported cases, a supervisor confronted his female subordinate with a crude, impersonal sexual proposal. It seldom seems plausible to think that the woman was delighted by the idea or that only reticence prevented her from suggesting such an encounter herself. In cases of that sort, courts should presume that the advance was unwelcome (and therefore impermissible), even when the subordinate has not met existing law's requirement that she indicate by her conduct—before the advance occurred—that she would consider it unwelcome. When dealing with workers under their supervision, managers should not be entitled to assume that anything goes and that there's never harm in asking.

When a supervisor makes advances of a more personal or romantic character, it is much more difficult to be sure that the subordinate would consider her boss's interest objectionable. A single, courteous sexual advance should not presumptively justify a lawsuit. And the subordinate, if she is uninterested, should have little difficulty indicating politely that, for example, she respects her boss but already has a boyfriend. If the boss then renews his sexual proposals, his actions are no longer so benign. Some courts currently refuse to accept a single polite rejection as indicating "unwelcomeness" and insist that the subordinate deliver her rebuff with "force" or "urgency."[43] That approach virtually requires the subordinate to risk bruising her boss's ego and inviting retaliation as the only way to reverse the assumption that she is sexually available to everyone, including those who oversee her work and control her career. A single polite rejection should be sufficient to trigger a strong presumption that any further advances by a job supervisor are unwelcome and impermissible.[44]

Beyond the domain of criminal sanctions and civil damage remedies, individual firms sometimes ban supervisor-subordinate liaisons as a matter of company policy, regardless of which party initiated the encounter. Though some argue that such bans unjustifiably intrude on the private lives of employees, sex between superiors and subordinates poses risks not only for the subordinate but also for the firm. The liaison may distort performance evaluations, lead to other preferential treatment, or create an *appearance* of favoritism that injures the morale of other workers. The difficulties clearly justify a ban on all supervisor-subordinate liaisons, if a company wishes to adopt one. And company restrictions on workplace sex are much less intrusive than formal legal rules, because sanctions can be more flexible and workers uncomfortable with the limits can choose other places to seek work. With input from their employees, firms themselves may be in the best position to decide whether a complete ban on supervisor-subordinate sex is warranted in their individual circumstances.

One important employer—the United States military—prohibits all sexual liaisons (as well as most other close relationships) between personnel of different ranks. The ban on "fraternization" originally applied only to ties between officers and enlisted men, but armed forces regulations have extended the concept to include relationships between two officers or between two enlisted soldiers if the relationship "is prejudicial to good order and discipline."[45] In the Army, the rule against fraternization usually applies only to soldiers in the same chain of command—in effect soldiers in a relationship of supervisor and subordinate.[46] But the Navy and Air Force prohibit liaisons between officers and enlisted personnel when the two parties are in different chains of command and even when they are in different branches of the military service.[47] And unlike bans on dating in private firms, the military's rule against fraternization is a criminal prohibition backed by the possibility of court-martial, with potential sanctions that include dishonorable discharge, loss of service benefits, and imprisonment.[48]

The military's broad ban on fraternization reflects traditions that long predate the presence of women in the armed forces. The original rationale, rooted in a desire to respect differences of social class between officers and enlisted men, gradually shifted to an emphasis on assuring against favoritism on the part of officers who can be called upon to give their subordinates life-endangering combat assignments.[49] In the modern, sexually integrated military, the traditional ban takes on new importance as a way to protect women from sexual pressure. But the modern era also puts the traditional ban under new stresses. Military personnel sacrifice a good deal of their liberty when they join the armed forces, but like everyone else, they are entitled to reasonable opportunities to seek intimacy, romance, sexual satisfaction, and a rewarding family life.

For women and men who pursue military careers, these legitimate aspirations can be stifled when broad bans on "fraternization" place off limits so many of the people they meet and work with. The problems are exacerbated at remote military bases, where potential civilian partners are in short supply. The ban on sexual liaisons has a strong justification when a supervisor-subordinate relationship exists. But the broader bans enforced in the Navy and Air Force have disrupted many lives and destroyed promising careers, even when the sexual relationship carried no danger of coercive pressure and no risk to military order or discipline.[50]

The military's practice of aggressively enforcing its antifraternization rules, even against individuals who are assigned to different chains of command, looks somewhat anomalous when the military, in other respects, sometimes seems insensitive to problems of sexual harassment.[51] Ironically, vigorous prosecutions for fraternization may indirectly support the outlook of commanders who see women in the armed forces as a source of endless trouble. But whatever lies behind them, broad prohibitions and vigorous, inflexible enforcement unjustifiably restrain the sexual autonomy of the many Americans who choose to make a career in the military. There is reason to consider decriminalizing intimate relationships that do not involve potential coercion (such as liaisons not within the same chain of command), and to rely more often on personnel transfers and other flexible administrative responses, rather than on criminal prosecution. When possibilities of coercion and other threats to military order are remote, military personnel deserve, insofar as possible, the same opportunities that civilians have to seek and pursue mutual, fully voluntary intimate relationships.

Teachers and Students

It is one of the oldest of stories. The middle-aged male professor, bored or unhappy in his marriage, feels irresistibly attracted to the bright, attractive young sophomore in his literature class. He falls for her—or goes after her—and before long they are in bed together. Sometimes the affair flourishes, the professor leaves his wife, and the encounter with his student leads to a long and happy marriage. Probably more often, the fling is brief. Teacher and student part, and one of them, often the student, is left with feelings that can range from disappointment or bitterness to emotional devastation.

Despite age differences that are often substantial, there is no reason to think that students are always reluctant participants in these affairs. The student sometimes "admires his mind." A flirtatious student sometimes sets out to seduce her professor, viewing the conquest as a source of status and pride. But teachers who are infatuated or sexually aroused often find that some encouragement helps to get things started. The stratagems they deploy can be flagrantly coercive.

A Yale University undergraduate charged in one case that her professor made an "outright proposition" to give her an "A" in his course if she would meet his sexual demands. When she refused, he gave her a low grade instead.[52] A surgical resident at a teaching hospital in Puerto Rico charged that the doctor who supervised her training told her she could get assigned to perform more interesting operations if she would have an affair with him.[53] At Ball State University in Indiana, a faculty disciplinary committee found that a male professor used the promise of better grades to have sexual encounters with several male students, one of them a seventeen-year-old freshman.[54]

Shauna Parks was a graduate student at South Carolina State University. After she took the examination required for graduation, she was told she had failed. She went to discuss the exam with the department chairman, but he told her, so she charged in a 1995 suit, that she would have to have sex with him in order to graduate. Parks refused but agreed to let him take nude photographs of her. She testified that they agreed to meet later at his house and that she then drove there—with her father concealed in the back seat of her car. When the department chairman met her at the car, she claimed, her father emerged from hiding, and the chairman said, "I give up. You graduate."[55]

Like managers at work, teachers usually avoid such flagrant tactics. But students often face more subtle sexual pressures, even before they reach college. In a 1996 lawsuit, a student at the Rolla Senior High School in Missouri claimed that one of her teachers made sexual advances, and they began having sexual contact, both on and off school premises, in the fall of her junior year, when she was sixteen. Their encounters continued for five months, until her parents learned of the relationship. Two other students signed affidavits stating that they had had sexual contacts with the same teacher, including intercourse on school premises.[56]

At LaPorte High School in Minnesota, a forty-two-year-old female teacher developed a friendship with P. L., one of her sixteen-year-old male students. The two began kissing, hugging, and sexually fondling each other. The contacts usually occurred when they were alone in the teacher's classroom, but the teacher "would also have him sit with her at her desk during class and they would engage in intimate sexual contact hidden only by her desk, while other students were present." She would also ask other teachers to excuse P. L. from their classes so that he could meet with her for "extra help." She wrote him letters suggesting how they could meet for sexual intercourse, but after several months P. L. broke off the relationship. When he sued for damages, the Minnesota Supreme Court held that the school district was not at fault because the teacher's conduct was "unforeseeable."[57] A student who is over the age of consent may have little protection and no prospect of a remedy: the school district will be liable only if its administrators were negligent, and the abusive teacher will normally face no civil liability or criminal punishment unless he or she used physical force.[58]

At Indiana's Southport High School, Janice (not her real name) became friendly with a gym teacher who had been her swim coach for three years. At the beginning of her senior year, when she was seventeen, she agreed to be his assistant during her study hall. In a 1993 lawsuit, she charged that when they were alone in his office, he began kissing her and said he wanted to teach her about sex. A few weeks later, she said, he took her into a bathroom and had intercourse with her. Janice didn't resist him and said that at first she enjoyed their relationship. Though they had little time, usually just fifteen minutes while the teacher's swim class was changing in the locker room, he and Janice allegedly continued to have sex about twice a week, usually in the bathroom or in a room under the bleachers.

As time passed, Janice began to feel disturbed. She said she "found it horrible to sit in her [next] class feeling wet and dirty after sex with [him]." Nonetheless, she felt afraid to tell him "no" and worried that if she reported the situation to her parents or to school officials, she might get in trouble. In January she told him she was uncomfortable with their encounters, but she said she continued to have sex with him throughout the school year and into July, when she finally told him directly that she wanted to stop. Still, at his urging, they allegedly had sex one more time. Later that month she told her boyfriend and her parents about the relationship. The parents informed school officials, who immediately suspended the teacher. He resigned the next day and apparently has not sought to obtain another teaching job. Beyond that, he has not incurred any sanction. A suit against the school district remains pending.[59]

At the college and graduate school levels, sexual interaction between students and teachers becomes more frequent, and much of it is directly or indirectly coercive. Though survey evidence is inevitably imprecise, the best estimates suggest that roughly 10–15 percent of women students are sexually pressured by their faculty supervisors at some point during college or graduate school. One survey found that 15 percent of female undergraduates experienced unwanted sexual advances. In another study, 13 percent of female graduate students had dated a faculty member and 9 percent reported pressure to date or have sex with a faculty member. A study of psychologists found that 17 percent of the women had sexual contact with one of their teachers when they were in graduate school, and 31 percent experienced advances that they rebuffed.[60] If a 10 percent estimate is roughly reliable for the four-year college experience, nearly 250,000 women are pressured to have sex with one or more of their professors every year.[61]

Protections against sexual harassment by teachers closely track the rules applicable to harassment in the workplace. The federal law against discrimination in education ("Title IX") follows the requirements—and limitations—of Title VII. Quid-pro-quo harassment is impermissible, but the victim must be able to prove that the sexual proposal was "unwelcome." And if she rejects the sexual advance, she must prove that any bad grade or other action against her occurred *because of* her refusal, not for valid academic reasons. For a "hostile environment" claim, the victim must prove—as in a Title VII case—that the advances were *unwelcome*, that she *communicated* the unwelcomeness, that the harasser's conduct was *persistent or severe*, and that the college or high school itself was at fault because its administrators were *negligent* in failing to prevent the misconduct.[62]

Even when the school or college can be held liable, Title IX, like Title VII, never imposes personal liability on the individual offender.[63] Other state and federal laws usually do not cover the perpetrator's misconduct either, unless the student is under the age of consent or the teacher resorts to physical force. Since the age of consent for intercourse is often only sixteen (as in Indiana), high school teachers who have sex with their students often commit no crime, and they can usually escape liability for civil damages as well.[64]

Codes of conduct at individual schools and colleges sometimes impose important additional restrictions. In high schools, sexual contact between students and teachers is an obvious impropriety, and violations can lead to immediate dismissal. Policies in colleges and graduate schools are more varied—and more controversial. All colleges and universities prohibit the kind of sexual harassment that would violate Title IX. Some go further, dealing with implicit coercion by prohibiting some teacher-student liaisons even with mutual consent. In 1984 Harvard became the first university to adopt a formal policy addressing consensual relationships, and since then many colleges have followed suit. The policies vary enormously, reflecting the intense disagreement that the issue provokes.[65]

Ohio Northern University and the University of Chicago Law School prohibit any sexual contact between a faculty member and a student, regardless of their academic relationship. A more common approach is to ban faculty-student liaisons only when the faculty member is currently teaching the student or has other responsibility for evaluating her work. Harvard and the University of Iowa follow this approach. Violations can result in serious—but usually unspecified—sanctions. Oberlin College's policy states that liaisons involving inequality of power are a "severe" offense that may result in dismissal.

Many university policies address faculty-student relationships without formally condemning them. The policy at the College of William and Mary states that professors are "advised against" amorous relations with their current students and warns that if they do become involved, the professor must "report the situation promptly and seek advice." The clear implication is that William and Mary does not *prohibit* sexual contact or sexual advances directed to current students. Similarly, the Massachusetts Institute of Technology requires only that when a professor and a current student become sexually involved, the professor must divest himself of his role as the student's supervisor. In effect, MIT aims to mitigate conflict-of-interest problems that might arise after the fact but makes no attempt to neutralize the power imbalance that can make sexual advances uncomfortable for the student from the outset.

Other universities are even more tepid. Stanford's policy is merely advisory, warning that there are "special risks" in faculty-student relationships. Amherst "strongly discourages" such relationships. New York University Law School has a tentatively worded "sense of the faculty" resolution that liaisons between professors and their current students are inadvisable. The University of Minnesota policy states that consensual faculty-student relationships, "while not expressly forbidden, are generally deemed very unwise." And these cautious statements go too far for most university faculties. At the University of Virginia, the University of Washington, and many other institutions, faculties have considered and then voted down policies addressing consensual relationships. The great majority of universities have no policy at all on consensual sex between faculty and students.[66]

The refusal of most universities to regulate consensual relationships reflects a mix of concerns. Many faculty feel that the policies are unenforceable and only create an atmosphere of hypocrisy. Others object in principle to rules designed to protect students from dangerous or undesirable choices. They consider it important for undergraduates to learn to make their own mistakes. The late John Boswell, a history professor at Yale, argued that "our reply [to students who want safeguards] is . . . 'We can't make life simple for you. You must think for yourselves.' Getting across this message has always been the university's ultimate mission."[67] Boswell's point has force when students can choose *freely* whether to enter risky relationships. It does not really apply when coercive pressures *prevent* students from thinking for themselves.

Occasionally, professors defend faculty-student relationships as affirmatively desirable. Many of the arguments are openly self-serving. Joan Blythe, a professor of English at the University of Kentucky, says that administrative restrictions will produce a "desiccated sexuality." At a university, she argues, "the air is alive with sexuality . . . Education is a kind of desire, the desire to learn. You cannot rein it in with the blunt instrument of a policy manual."[68] Jane Gallop, a feminist professor of literature at the University of Wisconsin, believes that a "consensual amorous relation" between teacher and student is inherent in good teaching, and she admits unapologetically: "I sexualize the atmosphere in which I work."[69] William Kerrigan, a professor of English at the University of Massachusetts, argues that he provides a kind of service by responding to the advances of his students:

> there is a kind of student I've come across in my career who was working through something that only a professor could help her with. I'm talking about a female student who . . . has unnaturally prolonged her virginity . . . There have been times when that virginity has been presented to me as something that I . . . can handle—a thing whose preciousness I realize. These relationships, like all relationships . . . are flawed and tragic . . . there often follows disappointment and, on the part of the student, anger. But still, these relationships exist between adults and can be quite beautiful and genuinely transforming.[70]

Defenses of student-faculty sex are usually more cautious. The most frequent argument is that regulation of consensual sex is an unjustified intrusion on private lives, that it's simply "none of the university's business."[71] In one survey of female graduate students, more than half said a ban on consensual sex with their instructor would violate their right to privacy, and 85 percent thought a ban covering all faculty members would be improper.[72] When William and Mary proposed to ban all teacher-student liaisons, Virginia's attorney general ruled the prohibition illegal, as an invasion of privacy, and the college retreated to a loose advisory policy.[73] The privacy objection has some basis when universities prohibit liaisons between professors and students in different departments. But when a student is sexually involved with the professor assigned to evaluate her work, their relationship *is* the university's business. Conflicts of interest are regulated all the time, in universities as elsewhere.

Protecting Autonomy in Teacher-Student Relationships

The question of how to respond to teacher-student liaisons remains deeply contentious. But overall, the available protections are cautious and limited, much more so than they should be. Whether students are in high school, college, or a graduate program, they have—or should have—the right to be educated by their teachers without having to give sexual favors in exchange. Yet existing legal rules and school policies leave indefensible gaps in students' right to protection from sexual pressure.

At the high school level, sexual contacts short of intercourse are usually legal if the student is over thirteen or fourteen years old. And in many states intercourse is legal whenever the student is over sixteen, regardless of the age or status of the other party. In effect these states focus on maturity (age) as the sole measure of capacity to consent, ignoring the problems of power that arise when an adolescent and her sexual partner are not contemporaries. Federal laws against sexual harassment do not apply unless the student has affirmatively indicated that the contacts are unwelcome, and high school students are often too immature or intimidated to think clearly about how they want to react to sexual invitations from a teacher. And even when the student signals unwelcomeness, federal law does not hold the teacher personally liable for his misconduct.

Some states escape these problems because they treat intercourse with an adolescent as statutory rape whenever one of the participants is more than four years older than the other.[74] Another feasible approach is to treat intercourse as statutory rape if one party is under eighteen and the other is a teacher or supervisor. Apart from possible criminal charges, if a teacher initiates sexual contact with a minor, his advances should always be presumed unwelcome, and the teacher should be subject to dismissal, along with personal damage liability for sexual harassment.

In college and graduate school, there is more room for debate about the best approach. But the existing system of protections has several clear deficiencies.

The most obvious problem is that the offending teacher usually faces no personal liability, no matter how egregious his misconduct. The enforcement gap is even more serious in college situations than in the workplace, because college teachers often have tenure. It isn't (and shouldn't be) easy to fire them. Lesser sanctions, such as those commonly imposed by business firms, are unwieldy or inapt; often there is no effective way to demote or reassign an offending professor. And disciplinary sanctions usually require compliance with detailed "due process" procedures, which often include review by a panel of faculty peers.

The colleges themselves are in a tight legal spot. They face liability under federal law if they do not attempt to prevent sexual harassment, but they may incur even greater liability if they try to discharge the harasser and then fail to follow proper procedures. In one case a professor forced to resign after three female students accused him of harassment won a $1.5 million damage judgment against the University of Puget Sound.[75] Because universities face many conflicting incentives and because job sanctions are difficult to impose, it is especially important to ensure that teachers who pressure students for sex can be held personally responsible for their misconduct.

As in the case of a job supervisor, a teacher who indicates that sexual submission will affect his evaluation of a student's work commits an act that has every hallmark of extortion. Like extortion, it should be a criminal offense, as well as a basis for imposing personal liability for damages. And severe forms of unwanted sexual attention can constitute "stalking" or harassment under existing criminal laws.[76] Other forms of "hostile environment" harassment don't involve the kind of harm that is sufficiently serious to warrant criminal penalties, but personal liability for damages is justified whenever a professor initiates unwelcome sexual contact with a current student.

Another candidate for reform is the rule that a student subjected to sexual advances cannot recover damages for harassment unless she *communicated* clearly that the advances were unwelcome. As with subordinates in the workplace, students face innumerable risks of retaliation by the person who evaluates their work. In one study of male faculty members at a large state university, 94 percent agreed that "a subtle yet powerful potential for coercion (by the professor) exists in any consensual sexual relationship between a professor and a [current] student."[77] If anything, academic evaluations are probably more subjective than those in many jobs. So there is an even greater risk that a teacher will feel able to retaliate with impunity. And since his students know this, they can seldom signal unwelcomeness without fear of consequences.

Policies like those at MIT and William and Mary, which try to control conflicts of interest after the fact, are surprisingly insensitive to this problem. At best they may succeed in preventing favoritism when a student accepts a sexual advance. But they treat the advance itself as permissible (again, "no harm in asking") and do nothing to protect against subtle retaliation if a student rebuffs it. They focus solely on the danger of unfair rewards and ignore the enormous problem of unwarranted penalties. Sexual harassment is a concern anytime a professor directs a sexual advance to one of his current students. In the workplace, there is reason to allow space for a supervisor to express sexual or romantic interest to a subordinate, in a polite, respectful way, and his advances can be presumed unwelcome only if they are renewed after the subordinate has rebuffed them. But in teacher-student relationships, the short-term character of the supervisory relationship and the many possibilities for abuse justify a presumption of unwelcomeness even for the professor's initial advance, when the student is currently under his supervision.

When the student actively initiates a sexual encounter, the relationship with her professor can't be considered unwelcome. In that situation, it would be implausible to treat the professor's conduct as a criminal offense. The likelihood of harm to the student is far too speculative, and the reasons to question her capacity for free choice are far too thin. Civil damage liability under sexual harassment laws seems doubtful for similar reasons. As presently conceived, federal laws do not protect students from all harms that can arise in an unwise or even exploitative sexual relationship. Instead, these laws protect students only from *unwelcome* advances, on the ground that unwelcome advances create an uncomfortable learning environment and, in effect, discriminate against the student because of her sex. When the student takes the initiative, it is usually hard to claim that the professor is subjecting her to coercion or discrimination.[78]

But it might still be right for a college to place teacher-student relationships off limits, as many currently do, and to impose severe disciplinary sanctions on professors who violate the policy. The intense controversy over the university's proper role in protecting students from coercion, without interfering in freely chosen relationships, reflects several legitimate disagreements—along with a good deal of unnecessary confusion.

Policies such as Ohio Northern's prohibit liaisons even when the faculty member has no responsibility for evaluating the student's work. Kristine Naragon was a twenty-nine-year-old instructor when she began a lesbian relationship with a freshman at Louisiana State University.

The younger woman was not in any classes that Naragon taught, and there was little chance she ever would be. The student apparently didn't complain about the relationship, but when her parents learned about it, they demanded that LSU intervene. University administrators tried to persuade the two women to separate, but they refused, with Naragon insisting that the relationship was strictly a private matter. When her contract expired, LSU renewed it but removed her from classroom teaching and assigned her to research duties exclusively.

Naragon sued, claiming that the reassignment violated her constitutional rights to privacy and freedom of association. Though there was no possibility that Naragon could use her academic position to pressure the student or give her academic favors, a federal court rejected Naragon's claims. The court accepted LSU's view that "teachers are role models" and that the university had the right to impose sanctions if it felt that intimacy between a teacher and student "undermined the . . . effectiveness of the teacher because of the perception of other students."[79]

Policies of this kind are far too broad and needlessly intrusive. The court wasn't wrong to see that a teacher's effectiveness can be affected by student views about her behavior outside the classroom. But students seem to have unlimited curiosity about their professors' lives, and almost unlimited willingness to pass judgment—moral or stylistic—on what they find out. The range of lawful activities that could conceivably affect student perceptions is impossibly broad. A university might better perform its academic mission by emphasizing that ideas can't be judged by the personality of the teacher espousing them. And a policy banning any student-teacher liaison is much broader than necessary to prevent implicit coercion or conflicts of interest. An across-the-board prohibition imposes major burdens on sexual autonomy by putting a large number of potentially worthwhile relationships off limits.

Liaisons between a professor and a student currently under his supervision involve entirely different considerations. Favoritism—and the appearance of favoritism—are serious risks. The university's interest in maintaining a fair grading system clearly supports intervention whenever a relationship poses a potential conflict of interest. And the conflict-of-interest problem isn't fully solved by rules that require a professor to divest himself of supervisory duties once the relationship gets started.

The professor's objectivity in grading is at risk every time he makes a sexual advance, regardless of whether the student responds positively or rebuffs him.

The refusal of most universities to take a firm stand against the "no harm in asking" approach is difficult to understand, except in terms of faculty self-interest. It is true that such a rule can squelch some mutually desired relationships, because the weaker party, though willing, might hesitate to take the initiative. But the costs of a rule against "just asking" are even more limited in an academic environment than in the work-place. Restrictions on supervisor-subordinate liaisons at work can put a large proportion of an employee's potential relationships off limits, because many other employees may have higher rank or potential supervisory authority, and supervisory relationships are likely to be long-lasting. In academic settings, the line between peers and superiors (students and teachers) is more clearly marked, and few relationships are precluded by a rule against professors' dating their current students, because the restriction expires as soon as the student completes the course. If a professor discovers a genuine attraction for a current student, little will be lost by requiring him to defer any sexual advance until the end of the semester. (An attraction between a graduate student and her adviser is different in this respect, especially if there are no other professors qualified to supervise research in her specialty.)

Universities should provide that it is never appropriate for a professor to initiate a sexual relationship with a current student. Policies that merely "discourage" such conduct have little value because they are difficult or impossible to enforce, especially against tenured professors.[80] The prohibition should be unequivocal.

Whether universities should ban sexual contacts initiated by the student is more debatable. If conflict-of-interest rules make clear that the student can't gain preferential treatment through the liaison, there might be reason to accept her preferences as genuine. And if the professor can no longer supervise her work, there might be little risk of coercion or harm to the academic enterprise. It is usually better to emphasize policies that empower students to choose freely, rather than trying to protect them from their own choices by prohibiting sexual encounters altogether.

Nonetheless, businesses often ban supervisor-subordinate relationships even when the lower-ranking employee invited the relationship, partly to avoid difficult judgments about which party really took the initiative. In an academic setting, there is even stronger justification for a similar rule. Unlike most workers, college students are not yet fully mature or independent, psychologically or financially. In addition, teachers, more than most job supervisors, have a mentoring role that depends on trust, and they usually have some responsibility for the emotional development of the whole person. (Again, graduate students in some fields may be different in these respects.) And a ban on all intimate liaisons between teachers and their current students would stifle few important relationships over the long run, because the student, like the teacher, would be free to act on her attraction as soon as the semester ended.

At the undergraduate level in particular, the best answer to these questions is unlikely to vary from one college to another. Adequate protection of sexual autonomy requires direct personal liability for sexual harassment, together with a flat ban, as a matter of university policy, on any sexual liaison between a professor and his current student.

Prisons

Remote from most people's everyday life and experience, sexual abuse in prisons is an unseen but serious problem. In many states, male inmates face constant risk of violent rape at the hands of fellow prisoners. Abuse of women prisoners by their male guards is also widespread, and in many jurisdictions it appears to be increasing. Yet unlike the rape of male inmates, the abuse of women prisoners often takes forms that are not considered illegal.

Rapidly escalating numbers of women in prison have exacerbated the problem. From 1980 to 1996, a period when the male prison population rose by 295 percent, the number of women in prison grew by 455 percent.[81] Today there are more than 70,000 women in state and federal prisons and another 55,000 serving short sentences or awaiting trial in local jails.[82] The 1980s and 1990s also witnessed growing sensitivity to employment discrimination, and the field of corrections work was not exempt. Vigorous enforcement of antidiscrimination laws opened opportunities for female corrections officers to work in all-male prisons, where control problems are more serious and opportunities for experience and promotion are greater. As female guards moved out of women's prisons and as gender-neutral assignment policies led increasing numbers of male guards to be posted there, more and more women inmates came under the control of male guards. During the same period when the number of female inmates was rising steeply, prison officials' ability to use female officers to guard the women drastically contracted. The results were predictable.

In the District of Columbia, female inmates finally resorted to a class-action lawsuit to challenge the pervasive pattern of rape, sexual assault, and other mistreatment. In a 1994 decision, Federal Judge June Green found that sexual abuse was a recurrent problem at the District's prisons for women. Male guards and other staffers coerced women into sexual submission by overt force, by threats to file disciplinary charges, and by providing inmates with cigarettes, candy, food, and money. Many of the women became pregnant as a result of these relationships.

Judge Green also found that when sexual misconduct occurred, administrative responses were inadequate. Department of Corrections policies contained no clear prohibition of sexual contact between guards and prisoners, and an atmosphere of general acceptance of these relationships prevailed. The procedures in place to prevent sexual abuse were of little value because the Department responded to complaints with "cursory investigations and timid sanctions."[83] When female corrections officers tried to protect inmates from abuse, their male supervisors threatened to retaliate against them.[84]

To remedy the problems, Judge Green required the Department of Corrections to adopt clear policies against sexual harassment and to train personnel accordingly. She also appointed a special monitor to investigate complaints of sexual misconduct. In a 1996 appeal challenging that decision, the U.S. Court of Appeals upheld the judge's factual findings but ruled that most of the remedies she had ordered, including her appointment of a special monitor, were "overly intrusive" and therefore beyond the court's power.[85] The Department of Corrections promulgated a new policy prohibiting "unwelcome" sexual contact, and a District of Columbia statute that took effect in 1995 now makes it a felony for a correctional officer to have any sexual contact with an inmate, even with consent. But enforcement of both regulations remains ineffective, in part because legislation enacted in 1996 limits the authority of federal courts to remedy custodial abuses.[86]

Similar problems are probably common throughout the country. Human Rights Watch, the organization that monitors human rights issues around the world, recently investigated sexual abuse of women prisoners in six American jurisdictions—California, Georgia, Illinois, Michigan, New York, and the District of Columbia. Its report, issued in December 1996, documents pervasive abuses in each of the six prison systems.[87] Forcible rapes and brutal sexual assaults against female prisoners occur in every jurisdiction. More subtle forms of coercion are also common. Inmates submit to sex with their guards just to get such privileges as a few ice cubes or candy bars, a chance to make an extra phone call, or a little time outside their cells after hours. Many of the women have been abused for much of their lives before coming to prison and see nothing unusual in such relationships. One inmate, Susan R., said that she became involved with a male guard primarily out of loneliness: "when a male figure shows you a little attention it made me feel special, worthy of something . . . I wanted the attention."[88] Yet prisoners who initially welcomed these encounters later found they had difficulty extricating themselves from the guards' control. Fear of reprisals tends to keep inmates tied to these relationships.

The prevalence of rape and other physically brutal mistreatment underscores a widespread failure to make a reality of legal standards that are universally accepted in theory. But many of the abuses described in the Human Rights Watch report are not illegal. When a guard asks a prisoner for sex in return for liquor, cigarettes, or extra time outside her cell, his demand—like any corrupt offer—should be considered coercive in its practical effect. But sex obtained in this way is seldom treated as a form of rape, and in many states it is not illegal at all. When a lonely, vulnerable inmate initiates a sexual encounter to get a bit of affection and attention, it is even harder to consider the guard's behavior "coercive," and again, his conduct is not necessarily illegal.

A few states have long-standing prohibitions on sexual contact between prisoners and their guards. As the number of women prisoners has grown, many states have enacted new laws to address the issue. Nonetheless, roughly a third of the states still have no statute making it a crime for a prison guard to have sex with an adult inmate under his control.[89] In Maryland and Virginia, recent efforts to enact such a prohibition were rejected in the legislature.[90]

Several states, in moving to confront the problem, have enacted statutes that are severely flawed. Colorado, Texas, and Wyoming criminalize guard-inmate relationships only when it can be proved that the officer "coerce[d] the victim to submit."[91] Three other states—Arizona, Delaware, and Nevada—permit criminal punishment of *both* the guard and the prisoner.[92] The provision for punishment of the inmate is fatal to hopes for effective enforcement, because it requires the prisoner to pay a steep price for reporting the offense. All told, roughly half the states still have no criminal statute effectively prohibiting sexual contact between guards and their prisoners.[93]

The reason for this resistance to criminalizing sexual contact with inmates is obscure. Some union officials representing corrections officers worry that a statutory ban will encourage prisoners to file false charges. In debates over the prohibition that New York finally enacted in 1996, state assemblyman Michael Balboni objected, "You're handing one of the most litigious populations a powerful tool. You're talking about people who are not particularly believable."[94] But if consensual sex is not prohibited, inmates interested in making false claims can just as easily charge rape.[95] If anything, false charges and ambiguous factual disputes are probably more likely when threats must be proved than when any sex act is automatically illegal. Moving to even shakier ground, Balboni also raised the familiar specter of the helpless male, at the mercy of his own sex drive, victimized by the power of a woman's sexual allure: "I don't want to sound like a Neanderthal, but what about seduction?"[96]

Efforts to safeguard sexual autonomy typically pose a dilemma, pitting the need to avoid *potential* abuses of power against the need to respect the desires of the affected individuals themselves. But most sexual encounters between guards and inmates probably are not voluntary, and even when the inmate's desire for the encounter is genuine at the outset, coercion may enter the picture later if the inmate wants to end the relationship and the guard does not. Though some voluntary relationships undoubtedly exist, the prison setting makes them hard to distinguish from sexual submission motivated primarily by fear. And voluntary relationships are never legitimate in any event. Society has deliberately deprived the inmate of her freedom, including her sexual freedom. Married prisoners are deliberately denied conjugal visits, in part because this deprivation is seen as a legitimate aspect of their punishment. A rule prohibiting sexual contact does not *improperly* restrict the inmate's freedom, even when it blocks a truly desired relationship.

The guard's freedom is also constrained, of course. But if the innocent wife of an imprisoned male offender can lose her right to sexual fulfillment with her spouse during his confinement, as the law on conjugal visits currently permits, the prison guard can hardly claim that *his* legitimate freedom of action is impaired when he loses the right to have sex with a prisoner under his control.

The inmate who willingly has sex with a guard is (in theory) an offender, not a victim of sexual abuse. But voluntary encounters are likely to be a small minority of the total, and any attempt to punish inmate-participants in "voluntary" cases will chill reporting and impede enforcement in the more frequent situations in which the inmate was coerced to submit. Genuine consent could be a mitigating factor in sentencing the guard, but it should never provide a defense for the guard or a reason to prosecute the inmate.

Administrative bans and criminal penalties for guards will mean little, however, if inmate complaints are not taken seriously. Prisoners who complain must be assured of confidentiality and protected from reprisals. Administrators must make serious efforts to prosecute guards who engage in misconduct.[97] Perhaps even more important are steps to reduce the opportunities for abuse. Prisoners should be informed of the limits that guards must respect, male guards should no longer be permitted to serve in women's housing units, and male guards should be accompanied by female guards whenever they are in contact with female prisoners.[98] Vigorous efforts to ban all sexual contact will support the prisoners' right to be free of sexual coercion and in no way impair the legitimate autonomy claims of either the inmates or their guards.

10

Psychiatrists and Psychologists:
The Problem of Trust

When she was twenty years old, confused by an up-and-down relationship with a boyfriend, struggling with the death of her father, poor college grades, and severe depression, Carolyn Bates entered therapy with a psychologist she calls Dr. X.[1] Through many months of weekly therapy sessions, Dr. X was kind, warm, and supportive. Gradually, Bates began to think of Dr. X as a loved and trusted parent, much like the father she missed so much.

Dr. X began pressing Bates to be less dependent on her boyfriend. He urged her to become sexually active with other men, as a way of feeling more independent. He also suggested that her discomfort with having casual sex and her resistance to acknowledging a sexual attraction to him showed her fear of intimacy. He interpreted her hesitancy about sex as indicating an unwillingness to interact emotionally and a possible lesbian orientation.

Nine months into therapy, when Bates came to a session agitated and tearful, Dr. X told her to lie on the floor on her back, ostensibly to relax. The following week Dr. X again told Bates to lie on the floor, and he rubbed her stomach. He repeated the same instructions at her next session, and this time he unzipped her slacks, rolled on top of her, and wordlessly penetrated her. He quickly climaxed, then pulled his pants back on and talked as if nothing had happened. Bates felt confused and ashamed, but she never protested, feeling afraid to challenge Dr. X's judgment about the treatment she needed.

Over the next year, Dr. X had sex with Bates almost once a month. Bates described their contacts as "wordless, compartmentalized encounters, never more than 4 or 5 minutes long, always at the start of the session."[2] Gradually Bates began to realize that Dr. X was exploiting her dependency on him. He knew that her fear of rejection determined her responses to men. Unable to confront Dr. X directly with her feelings of discomfort, Bates cut back the frequency of her sessions, and finally terminated therapy, almost two years after she had begun.

Within two months of ending her sessions with Dr. X, Bates spiraled down into a deep depression, fueled by the combined effect of Dr. X's exploitation and the unresolved problems that had originally led her to seek help. She had violent dreams and became preoccupied with committing suicide. She entered therapy again, this time with a minister, and she gradually told him about her experience with Dr. X. When she learned that Dr. X had abused another woman as well, Bates decided to sue. In the end, three of his victims joined forces in a complaint bolstered by his own statements—tape recorded by one of the women—admitting his misconduct and announcing his intent to lie about it to preserve his career. But after five years of emotionally draining pretrial motions, the three women reluctantly accepted an insurance company's offer to settle before trial for $110,000. Bates's share came to $26,000.

A state licensing board revoked Dr. X's certification as a psychologist, but two years later he was recertified. Licensed as a "professional counselor," he continued to practice for another three years, until a new complaint of sexual misconduct led the licensing board to revoke his certification again, this time permanently.

But Dr. X continued to practice. As long as he did not claim to be "licensed" or "certified," no law stood in the way of his continuing to treat patients as a marriage counselor and therapist. Another three years passed until, for the first time, Dr. X faced criminal charges. Indicted for sexually assaulting a seventeen-year-old patient, Dr. X pled guilty but still managed to escape jail. The judge sentenced him to ten years' probation, with a condition that he was "not to engage in counseling of any sort."[3] Ten years after Carolyn Bates's initial complaint and numerous victims later, Dr. X's career finally came to an end.

Bates's frustrating and painful experience has features common to many sexual encounters between therapists and their patients—the patient's vulnerability, the therapist's special access to her psychological weak points, the sense of trust that develops in a successful therapy, and the resulting impairment of the patient's ability to gauge her own needs or to refuse the therapist's sexual advances. When the patient concludes, initially or later, that the sexual contact did not "feel right," months of work building the therapeutic relationship are lost. Often the very problems that led her to seek help—depression, an inability to trust others, experiences of exploitation and abuse—are exacerbated, and her emotional progress suffers a major setback.

Concerns about exploitation and doubts about the validity of consent are especially strong when a psychiatrist has sex with a fragile patient in his care. But the problems are not limited to patients seeking mental health treatment. Similar concerns arise when a lawyer has sex with a client he represents in an emotionally wrenching divorce case, or when physicians, dentists, and other professionals become sexually involved with their patients or clients. The potential for abuse is far greater than in supervisor-subordinate liaisons at work, because the professional not only holds power over his client but also knows that she relies on his judgment and entrusts her welfare to his care. Yet patients seduced by their psychiatrists and divorce clients seduced by their lawyers generally find that the available civil remedies are meager. And criminal sanctions are typically nonexistent, except when doctors use force or take advantage of an unconscious patient.

Several states have passed statutes that begin to fill these gaps. In South Dakota it is a felony for a psychotherapist to have sex with a patient who is "emotionally dependent" on him.[4] In Arizona and Wisconsin it is a crime for a psychiatrist or psychologist to have sexual contact with any patient currently in his care.[5]

There are not many laws of this sort, and those enacted are mostly limited to mental health professionals. A few states have chosen to paint with a broader brush. In California and Idaho it is a misdemeanor for any psychotherapist or physician to have sexual contact with a patient or client, even with the patient's consent and regardless of the circumstances. The Idaho statute applies not only to psychiatrists and psychologists but also to all "medical care providers," including physicians, nurses, chiropractors, and even dentists.[6] Criminal prosecution is barred only if the patient is the doctor's spouse or if they are living together in a "domestic relationship."

Broad as they are, statutes like Idaho's still leave untouched many of the areas in which consent to sex can be tainted by a professional's power or breach of trust. The case for prohibiting fully consensual sex between a woman and her dentist, as Idaho does, is far from clear, but even Idaho makes no effort to prohibit sex between teachers and their students or between divorce attorneys and their emotionally vulnerable clients.

Another approach has been to fill the gaps by authorizing civil suits for sexual overreaching. A California statute enacted in 1994 is probably the most sweeping example. It provides a damage remedy for sexual harassment in a long list of relationships, including any association between a doctor, dentist, or psychotherapist and his patient; between lawyer and client, landlord and tenant, teacher and student, or trustee and beneficiary; between a banker, accountant, real estate broker, or appraiser and his client; or in any "relationship that is substantially similar to any of the above."[7]

The California statute's breadth of coverage is partly offset by the conditions it sets for liability. To recover damages, the man or woman who sues must prove that the defendant made unwelcome sexual advances, that they were persistent or severe, *and* that he continued pressing them after he was asked to stop. With these limits, the statute ensures that an accountant or real estate agent won't be hauled into court just for asking a new client for a date. But the limits also render the statute inapplicable to the most serious abuses, the cases in which a vulnerable patient feels *unable* to rebuff the demands of her psychologist or psychiatrist. A woman who says "yes" because, like Carolyn Bates, she is manipulated by her therapist, or is afraid he will get angry and stop treating her, can't invoke the statute because she never asked him to stop making sexual demands.

A still broader remedy was proposed in a bill that Representative Nita Lowey introduced in Congress in 1996. The bill's coverage, dwarfing that of the California statute, would extend to any relationship between a doctor, dentist, or psychotherapist and his patient; between a lawyer or accountant and his client; between a trustee and beneficiary; and even between the parties to any contract or any "persons negotiating a contract."[8] And the Lowey bill would impose sexual harassment liability not only for persistent advances, but also for any "unwelcome conduct of a sexual nature" whenever the conduct "creates an offensive environment within [the] relationship" or "unreasonably interfer[es] with the relationship."[9]

In its concern for aggressively tackling the problems of abuse, the Lowey bill would impose the vaguest of limits (no "unreasonable interfer[ence]"), constraining possibilities for intimate interaction in virtually any commercial or professional relationship. Yet even the Lowey bill might not solve the problem of the therapist or divorce lawyer who manipulates a vulnerable client, because it still requires the client to make clear that she considered the man's advances unwelcome.

The proliferation of new statutes—and proposals for still more—is no accident. Professional relationships are the setting for frequent, extremely serious abuses that existing laws largely ignore. And the rules of ethics in most professions are either too vague or too poorly enforced to offer much protection for patients and clients who are vulnerable to exploitation. Yet some of the new solutions lurch to the opposite extreme, restricting freely chosen relationships and legitimate desires for companionship without effectively addressing the abuses that most strongly demand legal control.

There are discomforts (and serious risks) whenever sexual advances intrude on a business or professional association. But these are also the settings in which people most easily meet, often more comfortably than in dating services or bars. The problem is to determine just when the potential for abuse justifies limits on sexual interaction, and to shape legal and professional regulations so that they work effectively, without destroying spontaneity and stifling an important dimension of our freedom. The difficulties that arise in professions such as law, medicine, and dentistry are in some ways distinctive. For mental health professionals, including psychiatrists, psychologists, social workers, and marriage counselors, the problems are especially acute.

Mental Health Care

Patients in psychotherapy are often emotionally vulnerable, and many have long histories of prior physical or sexual abuse. Though a patient in therapy seldom has reason to fear that her doctor will threaten her physical safety, the therapeutic relationship undermines in other ways her capacity to give authentic consent to sexual contact.

In a successful therapy, the patient must learn to lower her psychological defenses, to discuss her innermost thoughts and fears, and to place an extraordinary degree of trust in her therapist. The psychological dynamics of therapy are powerful, and the intimacy it fosters often leaves one of the parties—the patient or her doctor—with intense feelings of attraction to the other. The attraction may also be mutual. Either way, when doctor-patient relationships evolve from the professional to the sexual, serious harm to the patient usually results. For Carolyn Bates the setback was so severe that she contemplated suicide.

Dr. X eventually ran afoul of the criminal law. More often, abusive therapists escape criminal penalties and most other sanctions as well. A young man I will call Alan began experimenting with homosexual contacts when he was eleven or twelve years old. When he was fourteen, he became sexually involved with a male high school teacher. Concerned because of Alan's problems with classmates at school and his confusion about his sexual orientation, his parents sent him for counseling and treatment to Dr. Waldemar Leiding, a prominent New Mexico psychologist who had served as head of the state's Board of Psychologist Examiners.

Years later, Alan reported that when he and his doctor had developed a close relationship, Leiding began making sexual advances. Alan claimed that he was soon having sex with the therapist to whom his parents had sent him for treatment. He continued to see Leiding professionally for four years, and then, after a break of several years, he contacted Leiding for psychological counseling in 1987. He told another psychologist that he had reservations about consulting Leiding "because . . . he knew what was going to happen."[10] Nonetheless he returned to therapy with Leiding, and the sexual encounters resumed.

By the time Leiding's misconduct came to light, the statute of limitations barred prosecution for the earliest of the alleged acts, which had occurred while Alan was under sixteen, New Mexico's age of consent. But prosecutors were able to target the more recent encounters through a statute prohibiting "criminal sexual penetration," an offense requiring proof that the perpetrator used force or knew that the victim was "incapable of understanding the nature or consequences of the act."[11] Relying on the testimony of numerous expert witnesses, the state argued that the dynamic of the therapy process prevented Alan from understanding the consequences of sexual involvement with his doctor.

Leiding was convicted on nine felony counts, based on sexual contacts in 1982 (when Alan was seventeen years old) and on acts Leiding committed after treatment resumed in 1987 (when Alan was twenty-two). But a New Mexico appellate court set aside all the convictions.[12]

Like most states, New Mexico had no statute specifically prohibiting sexual contact between psychotherapists and their patients. And the court ruled that the "criminal sexual penetration" provision applied only when a victim suffered a mental impairment severe enough to prevent him from knowing the nature or implications of a sexual act. Leiding's conduct was not criminally punishable at all.

A civil suit against Leiding was settled (under terms that the parties agreed to keep confidential), and Leiding, who was by then near retirement age, voluntarily surrendered his license before any disciplinary action was brought.[13]

Therapy experiences like those of Catherine Bates and the young New Mexico man are far from rare. Every study of doctor-patient relationships confirms that sexual contact is frequent. The famous Masters and Johnson sexuality studies, conducted in the late 1960s, noted that in a "large number of reasonably documented cases," individuals with sexual problems wound up having sexual involvement with the therapist whom they had consulted for treatment. Masters and Johnson described the problem as "an overwhelming issue confronting those professionals serving as therapists in [this] field."[14]

Efforts to arrive at more precise estimates are hampered by the inherent difficulty of obtaining accurate reports about illicit behavior. For roughly twenty years, since the late 1970s, the American Psychiatric Association's code of ethics and the codes applicable to most other mental health professionals have explicitly prohibited all sexual contact between therapist and patient.[15] Yet anonymous surveys of psychiatrists and psychologists consistently find that 5–13 percent of the responding practitioners admit to sexual involvement with at least one patient who was in their care at the time.[16]

In one of the most thorough studies, University of California psychiatrist Nanette Gartrell and her colleagues found that 7 percent of male psychiatrists and 3 percent of female psychiatrists acknowledged sexual contact with at least one of their patients. A third of the offending doctors admitted involvement with more than one patient, and 13 percent reported sexual contact with three or more patients. One doctor admitted involvement with twelve of his patients![17]

These self-reports almost certainly understate the frequency of therapist-patient sexual contact. Several studies avoid the distorting effect of self-reports by asking practitioners about their knowledge of sexual misconduct by colleagues: *More than half* of practitioners respond that they have treated at least one patient who was sexually involved with a prior therapist.[18] Insurance carriers estimate that 20 percent of all therapists will become involved with at least one patient at some point in their careers.[19] Since there are roughly a million therapists and clergy involved in mental health counseling,[20] even the lowest of the frequency estimates suggests that tens of thousands of patients are exposed to potentially abusive sexual encounters with the person charged with their care.

The victims are overwhelmingly female. In one survey of nearly 1,000 patients who had been sexually involved with their therapist, 87 percent were women. Another large survey found that 94 percent of the victims were women, and among the male victims, more than half were involved with a male therapist.[21]

Some of these offending therapists are motivated by little more than the desire to satisfy their own sexual appetites. But other factors are also at work. One is a tradition, strongest among practitioners associated with the "human potential movement," of encouraging patients to drop their inhibitions and "act out" their fantasies, as a way to achieve self-knowledge and "self-actualization."[22] For a period that peaked in the late 1960s and early 1970s, encounter groups in the "est" move-ment and others like them openly encouraged experimentation with casual sex, including sex between group leaders and participants. It is probably impossible to tell whether the proponents of these ideas really believed in them or simply used them to rationalize their predatory behavior. Alan Wertheimer notes that "the sincerity with which this belief is held seems belied by the fact that the target patients are typically attractive and younger."[23] Condemnation of patient-therapist sex—now official policy of all the leading professional groups—has driven these ideas underground but probably not eradicated all traces of adherence to them.

The phenomenon of "transference" is probably a more important explanation for the frequency of sexual contact. A leading medical dictionary defines transference as the patient's "projection of feelings, thoughts and wishes onto the analyst, who has come to represent some person from the patient's past."[24] Effective therapy normally requires the therapist to create a trusting and supportive environment in which the patient can gradually reveal her most private thoughts and feelings. Feelings about sexuality are not exempt. On the contrary, sexual thoughts and fantasies provide a particularly important focal point for discussion, even when the problems that led the patient to seek help are not explicitly sexual. The patient may then begin to experience feelings for the therapist (whether of attraction or hostility) that she held, and possibly repressed, toward others close to her, especially her parents. Many contemporary methods of mental health treatment differ, of course, from the classic model of a Freudian psychoanalysis. The dynamic of transference may differ accordingly. But virtually any treatment method involves a high degree of trust, the patient's relative emotional openness, and a framework that requires her to assume that the therapist is unequivocally committed to her welfare.

In this atmosphere of trust and intimacy, it is not unusual for the patient to idolize the therapist and to develop strong feelings of sexual attraction for him. The patient may believe that she holds a "special" place in the therapist's affections and may have sexual fantasies involving him. She may even begin to flirt with him, and some patients go further, making elaborate efforts to seduce their therapists.

The therapist, of course, is supposed to understand this dynamic and keep it under control. Proper "management" of the transference is a central subject of training in most therapeutic fields and a central part of the therapist's job. He is expected to know that the patient is not really attracted to *him* and that the therapeutic process will be damaged if he permits her to act on feelings unleashed by the transference. Nonetheless, the intensity of the relationship may make it hard for the therapist to remember this, especially at times when his own private life leaves him emotionally vulnerable. The therapist may even experience countertransference, in which his patient becomes the object of his own emotional needs.

Sexual contact may begin in the office, during or after the therapy hour. Or the therapist may suggest lunch or dinner and take matters from there. Often the patient is the one to press for a meeting outside the office and to initiate or welcome sexual advances when the setting shifts. The therapist may continue to provide treatment after the relationship becomes sexual, or he may suggest that the patient begin seeing a new therapist.

In these varying conditions, sexual liaisons are not always the simple result of a therapist's predatory exploitation. In addition to those all-too-frequent situations, researchers have identified several other common patterns.[25] One is that of the insensitive, poorly trained analyst who acts on his attraction to a patient or responds to her advances, convincing himself that no harm to the patient can result. Another common situation is that of the "lovesick" therapist who becomes infatuated with a patient and initiates a sexual relationship, expecting that it will be mutual and lasting. Such relationships typically fail, and the patient typically suffers, but harmful outcomes are not inevitable. In the survey by Gartrell and her colleagues, 13 percent of the psychiatrists who admitted having sexual contact with a patient claimed that the encounter resulted in marriage or a committed relationship. (The frequency of "committed relationships" is almost certainly lower, of course, among offending therapists who chose not to respond to the Gartrell survey.)[26]

The ethics codes of all the major mental health professions ban sex between therapist and patient under any circumstances. And several states—fifteen by recent count—have made these relationships illegal, with the prospect of felony punishment for the offending therapist. Some of the statutes apply only when the sexual contact occurs during a therapy session, and others require proof that the patient was "emotionally dependent." Most prohibit any act of sexual intercourse or sexual contact, within or outside the therapy session, regardless of the patient's consent.[27]

Yet given the wide range of possible motives for both therapist and patient, the justification for severe, across-the-board prohibitions is not obvious. If the patient herself *wants* the sexual interaction, why should society foreclose that choice? We normally consider it important, indeed essential to freedom, that society leave every individual free to decide for herself whether to pursue a "risky" or "inappropriate" adult relationship.

Mental health professionals offer three reasons for the across-the-board ban on sexual contact.[28] The concerns center on the patient's unusual vulnerability to her therapist, the therapist's special responsibilities to the patient, and the likelihood of harm.

Almost invariably, the patient in therapy has sought treatment because she is hurting and needs professional help. Just as we undress for an ordinary physical examination, the mental health patient must be willing to set aside the boundaries she maintains in her personal relationships and try to speak openly about her deepest secrets and fears, all on the understanding that the therapist will never abuse her trust. This kind of openness creates unusual vulnerability, and if transference leads the patient to idolize the therapist and to begin having sexual fantasies about him, the vulnerability and distortion of ordinary judgment are heightened. Feelings analogous to transference sometimes occur in everyday relationships, especially those with teachers, mentors, or others who remind us of a parent. No one suggests that consent is flawed just because you "want a girl just like the girl that married dear old Dad." But pulls of this sort are seldom as powerful as the transference in therapy, and they do not arise in a context in which ordinary objectivity and defenses are necessarily suspended.

The therapist takes on a special responsibility to care for the patient, to make her health needs paramount, and to avoid conflicts of interest. Yet the therapist who pursues a sexual relationship, whether he is "lovesick" or simply predatory, automatically puts his own emotional needs ahead of the patient's, unless he convinces himself, against the weight of the evidence, that sexual contact is unlikely to cause her harm. At best, objective assessment and treatment become impossible if therapist and patient are sexually involved. "When sexual intimacies begin, therapy ends."[29]

Harm to the patient takes two forms. The most immediate is the impact on the treatment process. If the therapist attempts to continue providing treatment himself, the patient's ability to confide openly and the therapist's ability to offer sound clinical judgment and advice are inevitably distorted. If the therapist ends his professional role, the patient must begin treatment elsewhere, with disruption and loss of a different sort. Either way, "patients are deprived of the services they require and the therapist agreed to provide."[30]

Beyond the disruption of therapy, there are numerous risks of harm to the patient's well-being. The consequences can be serious and sometimes fatal. One study found that the impact on the patient was typically "detrimental, if not devastating"; when the sexual affairs terminated, patients experienced "rage, hurt, loneliness, and abandonment."[31]

It is difficult to know exactly how common these negative outcomes are. A few studies find that some patients were not harmed, at least in the short run, and in other studies the heavily negative outcomes may partly reflect the fact that problem cases are more likely to come to the attention of subsequent therapists and researchers. One of the better studies surveyed the effects on 559 patients who had sexual contact with their therapists. Ninety percent suffered negative consequences, including increased despondency and increased use of drugs or alcohol. In one-fourth of the cases, personal relationships deteriorated, mistrust of the opposite sex increased, and sexual relations were impaired. Eleven percent of the patients were hospitalized and one percent (6 patients) committed suicide.[32]

The largest of the studies done to date, surveying the effects on a sample of 958 sexually involved patients, found closely similar results. Ninety-five percent of the patients who had sexual contact while under treatment were harmed. Fourteen percent (134 patients) attempted suicide, and one percent (7 patients) committed suicide.[33] A careful survey of the literature concludes that "the balance of the empirical findings is heavily weighted in the direction of serious harm resulting to almost all patients sexually involved with their therapists."[34]

The high likelihood of harm to the patient provides a powerful reason for mental health experts to consider sexual contact unprofessional. In addition, sexual involvement inevitably creates a conflict of interest, because the therapist gains the personal benefit of sexual satisfaction at the likely expense of the patient. A well-enforced ban on sexual contact would also serve interests beyond those of the patient who is directly affected: it would enhance public confidence in the profession and give all patients the assurance that their therapists will respect their trust and not exploit their vulnerability.

But none of these concerns is sufficient to warrant an across-the-board criminal prohibition. Many standards of good professional conduct are designed to assure competent, loyal service to clients, but such standards are almost never backed by the criminal law; we need to have much stronger concerns to justify criminal sanctions. Similarly, conflicts of interest are seldom made illegal in themselves, and they aren't automatically unethical. Lawyers, for example, can usually represent two clients with opposing business interests, if both agree. The consent of a patient or client is usually sufficient to waive a conflict-of-interest problem.

Even the strong likelihood of harm is not decisive. Many extremely risky activities (cigarette smoking, unprotected sex with an HIV-positive partner) are not illegal. We ordinarily consider it important to let each individual decide for herself whether an intimate relationship holds sufficient promise to offset its drawbacks. Whatever may be the appropriate rule of medical ethics, legal prohibitions—and especially criminal punishments—are rarely justified when two adults consent to a sexual relationship, unless the consent is inauthentic or involuntary. And the possibility of emotional harm to the patient, even if great, is not in itself a sufficient reason to treat her consent as invalid.

Prevailing criminal laws seem to reflect these assumptions. Absent proof of force, sex between patient and therapist remains legal in more than two-thirds of the states, including Illinois, Massachusetts, New Jersey, New York, Pennsylvania, and Virginia. Despite widespread concern about the dangers of these relationships, the case for punishing the therapist remains weak unless it can be shown that the patient's consent is defective. If the patient wants a liaison and makes her choice freely, laws prohibiting sexual contact would interfere with her autonomy, not support it.

Consent in Patient-Therapist Relationships

Many advocates of an across-the-board prohibition finesse the question of the patient's desires by arguing that the therapist—like a trustee or guardian—has a "fiduciary duty" that precludes sexual interaction. The "fiduciary duty" label offers a convenient way to frame the issues, but it doesn't explain why it is justified to impose a duty, backed by severe—possibly criminal—sanctions, if both the patient and her doctor want to pursue the relationship. The fiduciary-duty argument is convincing only if there are flaws in the patient's consent or other reasons to think that sexual contact would improperly exploit the patient.[35]

The patient's right to decide for herself carries little weight, of course, when she suffers from severe mental illness. But nonhospitalized patients who seek mental health counseling are almost always considered legally competent to make decisions affecting their personal lives and their medical needs. They can give "informed consent" to their course of treatment, including the decision whether to take powerful psychotropic drugs. They are considered competent to marry, to sleep with their boyfriends, or to give valid consent to sex with a stranger they meet at a dance. But a relationship between the patient and her therapist is different. A sexual liaison between patient and therapist can arise in a variety of ways, but virtually all of them involve serious defects in the patient's consent.

The easiest cases to condemn are those in which the doctor gets the patient's consent by claiming that sexual contact will serve a useful role in therapy. Medical treatment, especially any procedure that invades the body, requires informed consent. A patient who trusts her doctor and submits to sexual contact, not out of desire but in reliance on misleading, professionally unacceptable advice, obviously has not given informed consent. In Carolyn Bates's encounters with Dr. X, the first instance of sexual contact occurred without any consent on her part, and in the subsequent episodes she apparently acquiesced because he insisted that their sexual encounters would advance her treatment. Sex under these circumstances represents a clear violation of the patient's autonomy and deserves to be treated as a serious offense.

The issues are more complicated when the doctor makes sexual advances (in or outside the office) without implying that they are a form of treatment. Nonetheless, the patient's consent, like consent to any sexual contact, is invalid if it results from coercion, decision-making incompetence, or inadequate information.[36] And a doctor who has sex with his patient, knowing she has not given valid consent, cannot claim to be respecting her autonomy. On the contrary, he commits a serious offense against her freedom of sexual choice.

Coercion is especially obvious when the doctor implies he will provide therapy only if the patient submits to his sexual demands. Since the patient has a right to receive continuing treatment without sexual conditions, she cannot refuse the advances without being made worse off than she is entitled to be. The therapist's proposal amounts to a coercive threat, a clear-cut violation of her autonomy. Some threats are even more flagrant. A California psychiatrist allegedly compelled his patient to submit to intercourse by telling her he would have her institutionalized if she did not cooperate.[37]

Coercion enters the picture in a more subtle way if the therapist makes sexual advances without threatening to terminate treatment if he is rebuffed. The patient's consent would not be coerced if she accepted the advances enthusiastically, knowing she was free to refuse. But a patient could rarely be sure that her refusal wouldn't chill the therapeutic relationship or lead the therapist to abandon her. At least when the doctor can't be sure his sexual initiative is welcome, there is a high risk that the patient's consent could be the product of fear rather than genuine desire.

The problems of potential coercion are largely absent when the therapist is confident the patient would welcome his advances. But it is usually difficult, perhaps even impossible, for the therapist to make a reliable judgment about the patient's real wishes if he is the one taking the initiative. Her desire for sexual contact can be uncertain even when she describes vivid sexual fantasies involving the therapist and makes clear her impetus to hold him, kiss him, or make love to him.

Psychologists Kenneth Pope and Jacqueline Bouhoutsos describe a case in which a patient they call Ellen discovered she was attracted to her therapist and began telling him about her feelings. The therapist was unhappy in his own current relationship, and he found Ellen beautiful and intriguing. In one session, as Ellen described sexual fantasies she'd had involving him, he put his arms around her and kissed her. Ellen, surprised and confused, tried to get away, but her thoughts became blurry, and she started to faint. The therapist, who was attracted and aroused, held her tight, pushed off her clothes, and pressed himself on her. Years later, even after intensive treatment with another therapist, Ellen still remembered the experience with terror, nausea, and shame. Pope and Bouhoutsos conclude that Ellen's sexual relationship with this therapist was "the single most destructive event in her life."[38]

The autonomy concerns are different if the patient makes the initial advance. When we are sure she encouraged the encounter, we cannot consider her consent *coerced*. But consent is still defective if it results from decision-making incompetence or seriously distorted information.

The therapy patient's ability to choose whether to initiate sexual contact is clouded in a number of obvious ways. But perfection cannot be demanded. Valid consent does not require absolute foresight, finely balanced judgment, or complete, totally accurate information. Consent to sex, like consent to most other important transactions, is normally effective unless it results from gross defects in competency or information; if the law were otherwise, beneficial interactions would be all but impossible to sustain. So flaws in the patient's decision-making ability do not by themselves show that her consent to sex should be considered invalid.

And there is no logically airtight procedure for determining when imperfections become sufficiently serious to invalidate consent. Judgments about the age at which an adolescent is sufficiently mature to consent to sex vary from eighteen to as low as fourteen. Nineteen-year-olds—often far from fully mature—are considered two years too young to drink liquor, but in all states they are considered old enough to consent to sex.[39] Conclusions about competency reflect pragmatic assessments of a wide range of factors. And to date, most states do not consider the obstacles to competent choice sufficient to render an adult patient's consent inherently defective, so that the therapist who has sex with her would be committing a serious sexual offense. Considered in isolation, none of the factors impairing the patient's decision-making capacity seems sufficiently grave to suggest incompetency to consent, regardless of circumstances. And none of these factors is altogether different from the impediments that other adults experience in their relationships, or that the patient herself experiences in interactions with other people in her life.

In combination, however, the impairments of decision-making capacity are severe. Distortions of judgment are inherent in the process of therapy. Although treatment is designed to give the patient greater insight and self-knowledge, therapy is usually structured in ways that deliberately distort her view of the therapist-patient relationship. She must relax the boundaries she maintains in her other personal interactions and place complete trust in her therapist. As the therapeutic setting permits many of her deepest feelings to emerge, transference typically leads her to "project [her] feelings, thoughts and wishes onto the analyst, who has come to represent some person from [her] past."[40] Transference gives her an inaccurate view of her feelings for her doctor, along with an inaccurate view of the basis for his interest in her. Nor can the therapist easily correct these distortions. He cannot always remind the patient that he is not her father. On the contrary, in many modes of treatment the goal is to allow those feelings to develop so that they can be understood and resolved. The therapist's job is to "manage" the transference, neither stifling it nor letting it pass from verbal expression into action.

Therapy also distorts the patient's awareness of the dangers of a sexual encounter. Few patients are likely to know what the research literature shows—that nearly all patient-therapist liaisons have un-equivocally negative outcomes for the patient. Of course, unfamiliarity with research findings can hardly be, in itself, a reason to consider a choice invalid. Ordinarily, men and women can agree to make love without first receiving the kind of detailed disclosure that must precede informed consent to a medical procedure. Neither party has a duty to provide the other with a full accounting of her bad habits or the possible downsides of a romantic involvement. But the therapist has undertaken a commitment to the patient's well-being. He has encouraged her to trust and confide in him, on the understanding that he will serve her best interests and carefully manage the feelings set loose. The therapist expressly assumes a duty, well beyond anything expected in ordinary romantic relationships, to alert his patient to the dangers of acting on the attraction that treatment is expected to arouse.

There is another reason to insist on informed consent. A sexual liaison between patient and therapist will dramatically alter the therapy process itself. Either the patient will have to start over with a new therapist, or she will have to continue treatment under conditions that radically compromise her therapist's objectivity and her own ability to discuss her emotions openly. Though the doctor may not view the sexual encounter as a form of therapy, the decision to have sexual contact is a decision to change the method of treatment. Under principles of ethics universally accepted, no therapist can permit such a drastic shift in the framework of treatment (comparable, for example, to a decision to begin treating the husband of a current patient) without first obtaining his patient's informed consent.

A formalist might insist that the absence of disclosure only invalidates the patient's consent to the new treatment framework and does not invali-date her consent *to sex*. But this is an overly technical point. The need for informed consent to the shift in treatment buttresses other concerns that separate the patient's situation from the ordinary sexual encounter, for which informed consent ordinarily is not required. The patient has a right to know the potential risks. And the therapist cannot claim protection from unrealistic or overly burdensome obligations, because he is already under a duty to provide adequate warnings and advice.

A requirement of fully informed consent would not by itself support a prohibition on all sex between patient and therapist. A patient's consent could still be valid if, before she gave it, her therapist fulfilled his duty, by warning her clearly of the damage that their liaison could do to the therapy process and to her emotional well-being. If a patient, aware of the dangers, decides that she wants to run the risks, her consent would (at least in theory) be valid.

Yet the therapist is in no position to give the information that the situation requires. A competent therapist should strenuously oppose the patient's desire to act on her attraction to him. Yet if he is attracted to her and emotionally involved, he cannot possibly give disinterested advice. If he is *not* emotionally involved, a sexual liaison would be devastating for her; any advice he gives would be seriously incomplete unless he discloses that fact. The only possibility for adequately informed consent would be for the patient to consult another therapist and discuss the problem in depth, an essentially theoretical prospect, if only because this "solution" would itself require a radical change in the structure of therapy and thus another layer of informed consent.

In sum, an affair between patient and therapist can get started in a variety of ways, and it can present a variety of distinct problems. But regardless of the particular form it takes, the liaison—in the great majority of cases—will lack at least one of the essential prerequisites for valid consent. Even when the patient initiates sexual advances, her actions will almost never result from an adequately informed decision, and the therapist will therefore violate her right to autonomous choice by engaging in sexual contact. A few exceptional patients might know just what they are doing and choose freely to initiate an affair. But working rules about competency inevitably generalize. Most states automatically consider fifteen-year-olds too immature to consent to sex, though a few might not be. In the same way, patients are best treated as incapable of giving valid, adequately informed consent to sex with their therapists, though in rare cases they might not be. The case for a complete prohibition, regardless of circumstances, should be considered clear.

Sanctions

The controversies about patient-therapist sex center not only on the question of basic standards but also on the practical question of determining the kinds of sanctions that should be invoked. Criminal law is a stringent weapon. Its use is normally appropriate when someone knowingly inflicts a serious injury on another person, and we often use criminal sanctions as well to deter conduct that creates a substantial risk of harm to others. But because criminal sanctions are severe, they normally should be confined to situations in which other remedies are insufficient. Since therapist-patient sex is already banned by ethical codes, enforced by the licensing boards of the various mental health professions, many psychiatrists and psychologists feel that more-severe sanctions are unnecessary and unfair.[41] And enactment of a penal statute could complicate efforts to pursue other remedies, because the therapist could then use his privilege against self-incrimination to avoid having to testify in other proceedings. But the codes of professional ethics, standing alone, are a wholly insufficient response to the problems of sexual abuse.

The obstacles to enforcement of the ethics codes lie mostly in small details that are seldom noticed—until a victim decides to pursue a complaint. Her first problem will be to find the board that has jurisdiction over her therapist. Often that is no simple matter, because most states divide regulatory authority among different boards for psychiatrists, psychologists, social workers, marriage counselors, and the like. If the therapist offers counseling without having a license, as almost every state permits him to do, no disciplinary body is involved, and there will be no license to revoke.[42] Not surprisingly, less than 3 percent of sexual misconduct cases are ever reported to licensing boards or other professional authorities.[43]

If the proper regulatory body is identified and a complaint is filed, the prospects for an effective sanction are slim. Some licensing boards are conscientious, and many therapists have seen their licenses revoked for sexual misconduct. But nearly all observers agree that licensing boards and ethics committees seldom pursue complaints vigorously.[44]

There are a host of reasons. Licensing boards operate with limited funds and large backlogs of cases. If the staff does investigate a case, the board, consisting of other members of the profession, often hesitates to discipline a colleague. Gender dynamics reinforce these limitations. Victims are overwhelmingly female, but licensing boards, mirroring the composition of the professions, are predominantly male. Many of the men are not predisposed to see patient-therapist sex as a grievous injury, and if they have had sexual contact with their own patients, as some might well have, they will be especially inclined to minimize the seriousness of the victim's complaint.

When the licensing board does uphold a complaint, sanctions are typically mild, often a reprimand or temporary suspension. In the rare case in which a therapist's license is revoked, he can apply to be relicensed within a short period, usually one year. And in nearly all states he can continue to practice, even after revocation, so long as he does not describe himself as "licensed" or use a term that some states protect, such as "psychologist" or "psychiatrist." With all its limitations and loopholes, the licensing system cannot come close to providing adequate deterrence or adequate redress to injured patients. Some of its defects can and should be remedied, but others are very difficult to fix. It is far from clear that a state should attempt to license and regulate every person who offers emotional counseling or spiritual advice, and it seems doubtful that such regulations could be effectively enforced.

Damage suits for malpractice provide an alternate avenue of redress.[45] Malpractice liability is clear when the doctor initiates sexual contact on the pretense that it is a suitable form of therapy.[46] Although a few courts have refused to find malpractice when a doctor does not attempt to link the sexual relationship to treatment,[47] the great majority now hold that sexual contact inevitably involves a mishandling of the transference and an unacceptable risk of harm to the patient. On this ground nearly all courts impose malpractice liability for any sexual contact with a patient currently receiving mental health treatment—whether the sex occurs in or out of the office, and whether it begins at the therapist's initiative or the patient's.[48]

Though a malpractice suit is theoretically an option in almost all states, it is frequently an empty remedy in practice. One major difficulty is that insurance carriers have had great success excluding sexual abuse from coverage under their malpractice insurance policies. When suits for therapist-patient sexual contact first began to proliferate in the 1970s, insurance companies argued that sex outside the office was not part of the therapy and therefore was not covered by their policies. They often made the same claim even when sexual contacts occurred during the therapy session. The stakes were high because sexual misconduct was, as of 1992, the largest single category of claims filed under therapist malpractice policies; sexual misconduct accounted for 56 percent of

the total amounts insurance companies paid on all mental health malpractice claims. When most courts ruled that the standard policies did
cover sexual contact—because it inevitably involves a mishandling of
the transference—the companies rewrote their policies to exclude sexual
contact explicitly. Today the typical malpractice policy either excludes
all coverage for sexual misconduct or imposes a cap, usually $25,000, on
damages for any injury related to sexual contact; the American Psychiatric Association's standard policy broadly excludes coverage for any
claim based on "undue familiarity."[49]

On its face, the absence of insurance coverage should make sexual
misconduct even riskier for the therapist, because damages must be paid
out of his own pocket. But the dynamics of litigation turn this danger
into a benefit. In the absence of insurance coverage, only a wealthy
therapist will be in a position to pay a substantial damage award
promptly—if ever. And when a substantial cash recovery is unlikely, few
lawyers are willing to file suit. In practice, the absence of insurance
coverage means that for many therapists, the risk of a damage suit is not
a realistic concern.

With administrative sanctions and civil damage remedies so often
ineffective, criminal penalties take on added importance. And the therapist's behavior is sufficiently culpable and dangerous to justify the option
of criminal prosecution. In any mental health therapy, the patient's
consent to sexual contact is likely to be the result of coercive pressure
or, at best, grossly deficient information and advice.[50] Either way, valid
consent is lacking, for reasons the therapist himself inevitably knows.
And the likelihood of severe harm to the patient is great. Intimate
contact under these circumstances represents a direct violation of the
patient's autonomy, and it deserves to be treated as a serious sexual
offense—regardless of whether patient or therapist takes the lead in
initiating the encounter. Though most states still lack criminal statutes
addressing the problem, the need to prohibit all patient-therapist sexual
contact is strong.

11

Doctors and Lawyers:
The Problem of Professional Authority

Even when a doctor is not treating a psychological problem, his patient must trust and confide in him, and she may come to depend on him for emotional support. Roberta Hoopes was experiencing numbness in her back and legs. Dr. Hammargren, a prominent Nevada neurosurgeon, diagnosed her problem as multiple sclerosis. He warned her that the disease was serious, involving the gradual deterioration of the nervous system, and he began seeing her regularly for treatment on an out-patient basis. Knowing that emotional instability was associated with her condition, he told her it was important that she try to avoid being upset because that would affect the progress of the disease. In that connection he prescribed seconal, valium, and other drugs, all potent central nervous system depressants, and he stressed that it was important she keep up the medications.

Two to three months after her initial visit, Hoopes claimed, Hammargren phoned her at home and invited her to dinner. After dinner, she said, he took her to his office, and they had sexual intercourse. Hoopes claimed that he then visited her at her home to have sex about once a month, over the next several years. She said that they never engaged in other social activities together, that their relationship was based solely on sex. Hoopes's motives for submitting to him were complex. He never threatened her, but she feared he might become angry and stop treating her if she rebuffed him. She was also enormously grateful: "He was the reason I was alive and I didn't want to upset this man."[1]

Hammargren admitted the sexual relationship but claimed that he considered Hoopes a girlfriend rather than a patient. He viewed their relationship as social and did not think it would harm her.

Years later, when Hoopes moved to Kentucky and started consulting other doctors, she was told that the drugs she was taking were unnecessary and that Hammargren's treatment had been improper. She sued him for malpractice.

Hammargren's sexual advances were a crucial part of Hoopes's claims of mistreatment. The Hippocratic oath taken by every physician flatly prohibits sexual relations between doctor and patient, and a recent American Medical Association report notes "a long-standing consensus within the medical profession that . . . sexual relations between physicians and patients are unethical."[2] Yet few American courts accept this ethical norm as an enforceable legal rule. Most hold a doctor liable for having consensual sex with a patient only when he leads her to believe that the sexual acts are a part of treatment.[3] One court expressly disregarded the broader AMA ban and said that "invocation of the Hippocratic oath as a basis of liability for professional negligence is unsupported by any authority and is without merit."[4]

In Hammargren's case, the Nevada court took a middle ground. The judges refused to presume that Hoopes was incapable of consenting, and they said that a sexual relationship between doctor and patient is permissible if it is "personal and unrelated to the parameters of treatment." But the court also held that a physician is liable for having consensual sex when the patient can show that "as a result of her illness, she was vulnerable" and that the doctor "exploited the vulnerability."[5]

The Nevada approach might be a plausible compromise, but it is far from clear what the requirements of vulnerability and exploitation really mean. The court's standard might restrict freely chosen relationships too much, or (more likely) it could protect patients too little. After the court's decision, Hoopes settled her claims out of court, under terms the parties agreed to keep confidential. Hammargren, who was serving on the State Board of Education at the time, went on to win election to the Board of Regents of the University of Nevada, and in 1994 he was elected lieutenant governor of the state.[6]

Legal safeguards remain weak even when the potential for abuse is even greater than it was for Roberta Hoopes. Exploitation and undue influence are especially serious concerns when a doctor makes sexual advances during a frightened patient's visit to his office, or when a lawyer initiates an affair with a client who desperately needs his services to fight a child custody battle or a criminal prosecution. Like psychotherapists, doctors and lawyers hold enormous power over clients who are dependent on their help. And they exercise exceptional influence because they have special claims to their clients' trust. Yet the doctor or lawyer who takes sexual advantage of a vulnerable client violates no criminal law and usually cannot even be sued for malpractice. Professional associations may frown on his behavior as unethical, but their licensing boards seldom take consistent actions in response. Harmless, entirely consensual affairs occasionally trigger harsh professional sanctions, but more often, disciplinary boards ignore or condone serious sexual abuses. The professions of law, medicine, and dentistry still lack clear standards to determine which kinds of sexual interaction should be placed off limits. And these professions, like psychotherapy, still lack an effective system of sanctions for misconduct.

Physicians and Dentists

Like the principal organizations for mental health professionals, the American Medical Association prohibits all sexual contact between a patient and her doctor. The AMA rule states that "sexual contact or a romantic relationship with a patient concurrent with the physician-patient relationship is unethical."[7] The American Dental Association has no standard specifically applicable to sexual relations, but dental licensing boards frequently suspend or revoke the licenses of dentists who become sexually involved with patients.

Some of the misconduct triggering professional discipline is egregious. A New York physician, examining a patient who sought treatment for a neck infection, told her he had to perform a pelvic examination because she might have a "tipped uterus." Instead of examining her pelvis, he subjected her to intercourse.[8] In North Carolina a doctor gave his sixteen-year-old patient a drug injection to induce unconsciousness and then had intercourse with her.[9] A Connecticut dentist used nitrous oxide to sedate his patient while he filled a cavity in a molar. He used an unusually high concentration of the gas, to the point that she lost consciousness. She awoke to find him on top of her, feeling her breasts, with his tongue in her mouth. When she struggled, he gave her more gas, and when she reawakened, he was still on top of her, again with his tongue in her mouth.[10]

Cases of this sort are clear-cut. Contact without consent—when the patient is unconscious or unaware a sex act is being performed—is assault or (in the case of intercourse) rape, both serious crimes under existing law.

But the ban on sexual contact also applies to fully consensual affairs, which appear to be common despite the AMA rule. In one survey of physicians from a variety of specialties (other than psychiatry), 9 percent admitted having sexual contact with one or more of their own patients, and 23 percent said they had patients who reported sexual contacts with another physician.[11]

The prohibition of consensual sex is supported by arguments similar to those advanced to justify the ban on sex between patients and mental health therapists. Patients consult a doctor when they are ill and need care. Often they must undress for physical examination, and they may have to provide intimate personal information in giving their medical histories. In the treatment process, they develop trust for their doctor and gratitude for his ability to heal. One expert concludes that "because feelings of trust, dependency, gratitude, and intimacy are inherent in the physician-patient relationship, patients may find it difficult to decline sexual initiatives from their physicians"; moreover, "some patients, because of their vulnerability, may interpret their physician's professional caring as personal intimacy and may even initiate sexual advances."[12]

"Consensual" physician-patient liaisons can have extremely damaging results. Some sexually involved patients report an inability to trust subsequent physicians. Many report feeling exploited or betrayed when the affair ends. Although those feelings are not unusual in the wake of any relationship that sours, doctor-patient betrayals are probably different and more severe, primarily because of the special kind of trust that the professional relationship presupposes. A Canadian task force concluded that the violation of trust is "devastating for the victim."[13]

Unfortunately, there is little solid research to show how often these encounters prove detrimental.[14] And there are other reasons to question an across-the-board ban on fully consensual affairs. The physician or dentist ordinarily has status and expertise that give him a degree of power over his patient, and she entrusts him with many important decisions concerning her health. But the doctor's role can vary enormously. Unlike the psychotherapist, the nonpsychiatric physician is not automatically involved in the intimate details of his patient's emotional life. He may see her weekly or just once a year. He may want her to discuss stresses and anxieties that could explain her physical symptoms, or he may simply examine a mole on her arm. It is far from clear that sexual involvement will always distort his judgments about her treatment. And it is far from clear that the patient's consent to sex must inevitably be coerced or misinformed.

Existing law reflects these doubts. The AMA's ethical standards, though important, are not "law"; they take effect only to the extent that courts are willing to put teeth in them. And the ethical ban on doctor-patient sex remains mostly a dead letter. Liaisons between patient and psychotherapist are criminal in fifteen states and are considered malpractice everywhere, but the legal system largely refuses to enforce the ethical rule against sex between patients and other professionals. Only two states, California and Idaho, consider it criminal for a doctor (other than a psychotherapist) to have consensual sex with an adult patient. California appears to be the only state willing to treat a doctor's unwelcome demands for sex as a basis for a sexual harassment suit.[15]

Liability for malpractice is similarly limited. Nearly all courts rule that a doctor can be sued for having consensual sex with a patient only when he tells her the sexual acts are a part of treatment. Nevada is the exception. In Roberta Hoopes's case, the Nevada court said a patient can also recover for malpractice if a doctor exploits a vulnerability that arises from her illness. This "exploitation" concept offers at best a highly uncertain opening for a damage suit, and even under Nevada's relatively flexible standard, many doctor-patient liaisons that violate the AMA rule could not be considered malpractice.

Licensing boards generally give more weight to the norms of professional ethics; a doctor's license can be suspended or revoked for sexual misconduct, and—unlike the psychotherapist—the doctor cannot legally practice without a license. In several states, boards have (with court approval) disciplined doctors for consensual encounters with their patients.

These results represent a welcome beginning, *if* the AMA rule is justified in the first place. If it sweeps too broadly, the legal enforcement effort, weak as it is, may already go too far. The situations that arise vary enormously, as do the sanctions imposed and courts' willingness to sustain them.

Mary Roe (not her real name) visited a Massachusetts dentist about twenty times over a three-year period, for teeth cleaning, fillings, and the extraction of a wisdom tooth. On one of the visits, the dentist kissed her, and on subsequent visits the two had increasingly intense sexual contacts, all while Roe was fully conscious and consenting. At various times the dentist touched her body under her clothing, undressed himself, inserted his fingers into her vagina, placed her hands on his genitals, and on one occasion attempted intercourse. Eventually Roe revealed the incidents to her husband, stopped seeing the dentist, and filed a complaint with the state's dentistry board. The board found that the dentist had not exerted psychological pressure on Roe and that they had "a mutually enjoyable sexual relationship." Nonetheless, the board suspended the dentist's license, finding that "sexual activity with a patient who has come in for treatment is . . . gross misconduct."[16]

Liaisons outside the office can trigger discipline as well. Dr. Green, a California dentist, persuaded two of his patients to undergo craniosacral therapy, a procedure involving manipulation of the head and body to relieve pain in the joints of the jaw. Over a six-month period, patient P. M. saw him once a week for treatment. The board of dental examiners found that Green performed the therapy in a "subtle and suggestive" way, making light finger movements over her face and body, and brushing her breasts and pelvic area. Green also invited P. M. to lunch and met her several times outside the office. He invited her to join him at an out-of-town meeting, and they had intercourse at the hotel where he was staying. But when he told her he would not leave his family, P. M. left the hotel, and she and Green had no further romantic involvement. In a second case, the board found, Green again stroked his patient suggestively. After one treatment session, he and the patient went to a hotel a block from his office and had intercourse. On another occasion they met for dinner, then went to a hotel and engaged in sexual acts. The board found that Green's use of "subtle and suggestive" touching to seduce his patients was an abuse of his professional position. The board placed him on probation for seven years but did not suspend his license.[17]

Dr. Perez, a Missouri gynecologist, began treating Mrs. F. for infertility. She told him she was emotionally drained because of her inability to conceive and said she did not feel "complete as a woman." Perez encouraged her to talk about her feelings and told her to call him at home when she felt depressed. The two began to talk almost daily. When Mrs. F. made office visits for artificial insemination, she often started crying, and Perez would hold her and comfort her. About six months after her initial appointment, Perez made sexual advances, and they soon began having intercourse in his private office at the hospital. On several occasions they went together to have intercourse at a hotel.

Eventually Mrs. F. became pregnant, apparently by her husband. She stopped her fertility treatments and terminated the affair. But she continued seeing Perez about other medical problems for another five years before she stopped and filed a complaint. Though Perez argued that Mrs. F. was a willing participant in their sexual encounters, the state board found that he had taken advantage of her vulnerability and abused her trust. Yet the board chose not to impose a severe penalty. It suspended his license for only two months.[18]

Dr. Gromis, a California physician, treated Ms. M. for sinus problems, ear infection, and similar ailments. After seeing him for about a year, she mentioned that she was upset about marital problems. Two months later he invited her for lunch. She talked about her distress and asked if she should see a doctor about it, but Gromis said he thought not. They had lunch again and then began meeting to have intercourse, at Gromis' house and at a motel. Ms. M. asked if she should start seeing another doctor, but Gromis said he could treat her for "anything above the waist."

A month after the affair began, Ms. M.'s husband became suspicious. She and Gromis stopped having sex but continued to see each other and talk on the phone. Within a few weeks Ms. M.'s husband confronted Gromis about the affair and filed a complaint with the state medical board. Ms. M. then ended the relationship, explaining later that "the anxiety was just more than I could control." A year later she sought psychological counseling.

The state board found Gromis guilty of unprofessional conduct and suspended his license for sixty days. But an appellate court set aside the board's decision. The court said that the rule against any sexual contact between patient and mental health therapist was justified by the greater possibility for emotional exploitation in that context. For other physicians, the court held, the mere fact of having a liaison with a patient does not make a doctor unfit to practice medicine. The court said there was no proof that Gromis abused his status to induce Ms. M.'s consent, or that he took advantage of information gained as her physician.

Although there was clear evidence that Ms. M. suffered stress and that her marital problems worsened because of the affair, the court found "no . . . evidence that it was [Gromis'] status as her doctor that led to this injury." Nor did the court think that his sexual interest had compromised his medical judgment. Though Gromis discouraged Ms. M. from seeking psychological counseling, the court held that he could be disciplined on that basis only if it were proved he gave that advice "because it was in his personal interest that her marital problems go unresolved."[19]

Cases like these suggest three distinct problems in doctor-patient liaisons. The doctor may abuse his *power*, for example by threatening to withhold drugs the patient badly needs. The doctor may abuse the patient's *trust*, for example by taking advantage of moments when her body is exposed or by exploiting emotions she reveals to aid her treatment. A *conflict of interest* may skew the doctor's medical decisions or advice. Yet problems of power, trust, or conflict of interest do not invariably arise; the context of the relationship is important.

The need for continuity of treatment is one crucial factor. When a doctor must see a patient regularly over an extended period, as Dr. Perez did in treating infertility or as Dr. Hammargren did in treating multiple sclerosis, his sexual advances, in or out of the office, carry enormous coercive pressure. The patient cannot easily switch to another physician without jeopardizing her care, and she cannot easily say no because that response may jeopardize her care as well. The pressure is especially strong if the patient's medical problem is severe or life-threatening. Like the subordinate employee who cannot easily change jobs, the patient in ongoing treatment may acquiesce out of fear rather than desire, even when no threat is stated or implied. But coercion isn't always a concern. If the patient's ailment can be treated in a single visit, without attention to a complex medical history, she can usually rebuff an unwelcome sexual advance.

Similarly, conflicts of interest vary with the circumstances. If taken literally, the AMA rule bars sexual contact with *any* current patient, including the doctor's wife. Yet physicians routinely treat their spouses for minor illnesses. Even when the problem is major, medical commentators assume that treating a spouse, though unwise, is not unethical.[20] In contrast, for a psychotherapist to treat his wife for an emotional problem would be unthinkable. When treatment and sexual intimacy coexist, conflicts of interest are by no means inevitable for the physician or dentist, as they are for the mental health professional.

Conflicts of interest are more likely to arise, and abuse of trust becomes a more serious danger, when care and treatment require emotional exposure. In asking Dr. Perez to treat her for infertility, Mrs. F. necessarily revealed some of her most private concerns, along with her deepest vulnerabilities. In contrast, there was no emotional content, beyond what the patient chose to disclose, when Ms. M. consulted Dr. Gromis for her ear infection or when Mary Roe went to her dentist for a teeth cleaning.

Even if there is no emotional interaction, physical exposure creates vulnerability—and a strong imperative to respect the patient's trust. A woman who visits her gynecologist must undress and permit him to touch her genitals. When we visit the dentist, we do not undress, but there must be no ambiguity about his intentions when he says, "Open your mouth. Stick out your tongue." The danger of blurring boundaries and confusing the clinical and personal roles justifies an unequivocal ban on sexual contact in the doctor's office.

Physical exposure and the need to respect clinical boundaries are usually not problems, however, when a doctor meets a patient for lunch or dinner and then invites her to a motel, as Dr. Gromis did. The wording of the Hippocratic oath is suggestive in this regard: "Whatever houses I may visit, I will come for the benefit of the sick, remaining free . . . of all mischief, and in particular of sexual relationships with both female and male persons."[21] Though medical commentators assume that the oath bans all physician-patient liaisons, the language seems to focus on sexual contact that occurs at the time of a visit for treatment. Yet encounters outside that context aren't necessarily free of risk. Physical vulnerability may not be a realistic concern, but implicit coercion, exploitation of confidences, emotional vulnerability, and the patient's gratitude for attention to a life-threatening ailment all may undermine her capacity to resist the doctor's advances.

With so many possibilities for a conflict of interest or defect in consent, most medical professionals seem to accept the across-the-board prohibition as justified (at least so long as it is not too vigorously enforced).[22] The clear, simple ban has obvious administrative advantages. And its supporters may be assuming that few relationships covered by the AMA ban could be truly untainted by impropriety. But that assumption is not realistic. As written, the AMA rule not only forbids sexual contact with a patient who is the doctor's spouse but also prohibits sexual contact with a patient who was a sexual partner before the doctor assumed any role as a caregiver. And consent can be free and untainted even when the professional relationship precedes the sexual one. A patient's medical problems are often minor and largely without emotional content. The rule against liaisons between individuals who meet as doctor and patient, if meant to be taken seriously, would frustrate important, entirely legitimate needs for companionship and intimacy.

The problems are compounded by ethical rules discouraging liaisons even after the doctor-patient relationship ends. The AMA bans sexual contact with a former patient whenever the doctor exploits knowledge or trust gained from the professional relationship,[23] and there is now pressure to remedy the vagueness of this ban—and expand its scope—by prohibiting all sexual encounters for a fixed period. A task force of the Ontario College of Physicians and Surgeons proposed banning sexual contact for two years after the last visit for treatment, with no social or professional contact allowed in the interim.[24] A group of American physicians led by Nanette Gartrell likewise urges enforcement of a strict two-year waiting period.[25] If adopted, these approaches will aggravate the costs of the ban applicable to current patients, because a doctor and patient who discover a genuine attraction and wish to become intimate will not be able to do so, even if the doctor ends his professional role.

Protecting Patients' Autonomy

The various legal and ethical standards governing doctor-patient relationships can fairly be described as confused. Penal statutes are drawn so narrowly that many gross abuses escape criminal punishment. Malpractice liability likewise covers only the most egregious misconduct. At the same time, the profession's ethical rules go to the opposite extreme, banning all consensual doctor-patient liaisons, regardless of circumstances.

It is probably no accident that the ethical rules are seldom taken literally and are almost never applied in the absence of aggravating factors. "Common sense" ensures that the rules will not bear too heavily on legitimate claims to privacy and sexual freedom, but overbreadth of this sort is easily mistaken for hypocrisy. The scattershot approach is a poor way to promote greater sensitivity and encourage compliance. The ethical rule needs to be made narrower, so that it more accurately identifies relationships that deserve to be placed off limits. But the formal legal prohibitions must be made much stricter, so that they provide adequate remedies for serious abuses that current law largely ignores.

Medical and dental treatments do not always involve emotional openness, and they don't inevitably require the kind of continuity that can make the patient reluctant to switch to another doctor. In addition, for some kinds of medical and dental problems, emotional involvement need not interfere with the doctor's ability to render competent service, as it does in psychotherapy. And even when a sexual liaison can affect the doctor's medical objectivity, it is not inconceivable (as it usually is in psychotherapy) that the patient could give informed consent to the doctor's having dual personal and professional roles. As a result, we cannot say that the patient's consent is inevitably defective. We cannot justify—as we can for the mental health professional—criminal punishment of all sexual encounters, regardless of consent.

Yet the scope of most existing criminal laws is far too limited. Under current law, it is a crime for a doctor to have sex with a patient when he uses force or when the patient is unaware he is committing a sexual act. Other forms of sexual abuse are typically not subject to criminal punishment at all. As a result, a doctor who obtains consent to sex by threatening to withhold care or medication usually cannot be prosecuted, even though the patient's consent is obviously coerced. A doctor who seeks sexual satisfaction in this fashion commits a clear offense against the patient's autonomy, and his conduct should be treated as a crime akin to extortion.

When a doctor obtains a patient's consent by misrepresenting that sex is part of treatment, the encounter is obviously not one the patient welcomes for emotional or erotic reasons. Existing law treats such conduct as a form of malpractice, but it cannot be prosecuted as battery or sexual assault, because courts usually say that the contact occurred with the patient's consent.[26] Yet the patient has given only *mis*informed consent, in a situation in which the doctor has a well-settled duty to give accurate information and advice. Sexual contact under the pretext of treatment represents a clear violation of the patient's autonomy; it should be treated as a serious offense.

Civil liability for malpractice is likewise unduly restricted. Under current law a doctor is normally liable for malpractice only if he has the sexual contacts "under the guise of treatment."[27] Yet sexual conduct is unquestionably unprofessional, unjustifiable, and potentially damaging to the patient in a number of other situations: sexual contacts in the office at the time of a visit for treatment; encounters outside the office when the doctor initiates advances that the patient cannot, because of the medical relationship, freely refuse; relationships that distort the doctor's judgment on decisions affecting treatment; and any situation in which the doctor uses information gained in the course of treatment to exploit the patient's emotional vulnerability. Any sexual contacts involving abuse of power, abuse of trust, or conflict of interest should subject the doctor to liability for malpractice.

Unwelcome advances, even when they are rebuffed, pose a problem for patients just as for students and employees. Yet existing sexual harassment statutes almost never extend to interactions between doctor and patient. Legal intervention is normally unnecessary when a person subjected to unwelcome advances can simply reject them and walk away. The Lowey bill, regulating sexual interaction between persons negotiating a contract, is overly broad in that respect. But many patients cannot walk away from unwelcome advances. Their medical problems may make continuity of treatment essential. And health insurance requires more and more of us to obtain treatment from a particular managed care provider. In effect, we can be tied to our doctor in much the same way we are tied to our job. Sexual harassment protection could well extend to doctor-patient relationships that cannot be terminated without tangible hardship.[28]

Although legal remedies require expansion, the rules of professional ethics need to be narrowed. As in the case of malpractice liability, professional discipline is justified whenever sexual contacts involve abuse of power, abuse of trust, or conflict of interest. And those concerns can be captured in workable rules that are not hopelessly abstract or indefinitely elastic. Sexual contacts in the office continue to deserve an unqualified ban, as do sexual initiatives that exploit information or emotions expressed in trust and sexual advances when the medical relationship inhibits the patient's ability to refuse. But standards of professional ethics, like formal rules of law, will be more plausible and better respected if they leave room for consensual relationships not tainted by a significant potential for abuse.

Lawyers

The sexually active attorneys who populate movies, television sitcoms, and popular fiction often seem to be good-natured, well-motivated romantics. Lawyers who turn up in the reported cases of real life are not always so appealing or benign.

A New Hampshire lawyer handling a divorce case knew that his client was emotionally fragile and under psychiatric care. Nonetheless, he initiated a sexual affair and then broke it off a short time later, leaving his client, who was still in love with him, doubly devastated.[29] Another New Hampshire divorce lawyer was retained by a twenty-four-year-old woman, married since she was nineteen, who had been physically abused and then abandoned by her husband. A disciplinary board found that he asked her about the men she had dated since separating from her husband. He also asked her to describe her sexual involvement with them and her reactions to the sexual contact, ostensibly to help him decide whether to file for divorce on grounds of the husband's adultery. Then, the board found, he invited her out for dinner, used a pretext to convince her to let him stay at her house overnight, and engaged in sexual acts with her there that evening.[30]

Divorce clients are especially vulnerable to the sexual appetites of their lawyers. Facing a difficult period in their lives, they are likely to be under enormous emotional stress. Often they have suffered a major blow to their self-esteem and their sense of sexual attractiveness. They also tend to be especially dependent on their lawyer for psychological reassurance and help in regaining financial independence.

Yet the client's need for affection and support does not always give the lawyer the leverage he needs to achieve sexual success. Patricia Gile retained a California lawyer to handle her divorce. At one of her first appointments to see him, Gile said, he grabbed and kissed her, but when she refused to have sex with him, he stopped working on her case and refused to return her calls. Gile charged that when she complained, he told her that if she "played the game the right way she would have the right phone number to reach him immediately." Later, she said, he told one of her friends that "when a woman client came to him, she was extremely vulnerable, so if she went to bed to get better service from him 'so be it.'"[31]

In Illinois, a woman embroiled in a wrenching divorce dispute met a prominent attorney identified in court documents under the pseudonym Richard Roe. Roe persuaded her to discharge the attorney who represented her and retain him instead. After she paid Roe a $7,500 retainer, she had few additional resources and felt she had no hope of getting anyone else to take her case if Roe proved unsatisfactory. Then, at one of her initial conferences with him, he sat beside her on his office sofa, unzipped his pants, and began pushing her head into his lap. When she resisted, he said (apparently referring to his work on her case) that "this would make it much easier." The woman complied, and in subsequent encounters Roe repeatedly made sexual demands. She continued submitting to him because she felt dependent and was afraid to risk his disapproval.[32]

But the prize for chutzpah goes to the lawyer in another Illinois divorce case. His client claimed that he not only initiated an affair with her when she was emotionally vulnerable but also billed her for phone calls in which he set up their sexual liaisons and for the time they spent together in bed.[33]

Divorce lawyers are not the only offenders. An Indiana attorney represented a woman and her husband who were defendants in a foreclosure suit. He persuaded the woman to let him take nude photographs of her, in return for reducing his fee, and he also had sex with her while the case was pending. He made similar proposals to another client who then got the police to help her secretly record his propositions. His license was suspended for a year. Ten years later, a woman retained him to represent a defendant in a burglary case. When she was unable to pay the balance on his $750 fee, she accepted his offer to reduce it by posing for him in the nude. He reduced his fee again by getting both the woman and her niece to perform oral sex for him. This time he was disbarred.[34]

Like doctors, lawyers sometimes don't even bother trying to separate their sex lives from their professional work; they make their sexual moves right in the office. In South Carolina, a Marine Corps lawyer assigned to provide legal services for military personnel had two especially vulnerable clients, one a woman seeking a divorce and the other a female Marine Corps corporal who had been accused of being homosexual. In each case, when the woman came to his office for a consultation, he attempted to stroke, fondle, and kiss her.[35] At a naval base in Georgia, a Navy lawyer went further. After his second meeting with a client to advise her about divorce and child custody problems, he invited her to a party, and later that evening they returned to the legal services building and had sexual intercourse in the military courtroom adjacent to his office.[36] An Ohio public defender visited a client held in custody, on an appointment to discuss her case, and had sex with her in a meeting room at the county jail.[37]

There are no solid data showing how frequently these kinds of abuses occur. Bar associations report a small but steady flow of complaints about sexual misconduct, roughly two or three a year in most states.[38] But in one recent year Illinois's disciplinary board received fifty complaints involving attorney-client sexual encounters.[39] And few observers think all the abuses are reported. In one study, 31 percent of attorneys said they knew another lawyer who had been sexually involved with a client.[40] Since a single case could come to the attention of several attorneys, this figure cannot tell us the percentage of attorneys who commit these acts, but it does suggest that sexual interaction with clients is by no means rare.

Like other professionals who abuse their power, these lawyers have no need to worry about existing criminal laws. A client who submits out of fear rather than desire is not the victim of a criminal offense, even when the lawyer knows that she is psychologically needy and defenseless, dependent on his services, and intimidated by his sexual demands. The lawyer may even threaten to withhold services that the client is, without question, legally entitled to have. Whether he phrases his threat obliquely or makes it explicit, he still commits no crime, because he hasn't used physical force.

Beyond criminal law, other remedies for sexual misconduct are uncertain—and limited at best. Malpractice liability and professional disciplinary sanctions are even more restricted for lawyers than for physicians, dentists, and psychotherapists.

When a client who claims sexual abuse by her attorney sues him for malpractice, she faces an uphill battle. Courts typically impose liability only in two narrow situations. The most important is when an attorney *explicitly* ties his legal services to the client's willingness to meet his sexual demands. The misconduct is very much like quid-pro-quo harassment in supervisor-subordinate relationships at work, and most courts agree in holding the attorney liable when the threat can be proved.

A malpractice suit is also an option when sexual contacts give the lawyer a conflict of interest that impairs his work. Conflicts are especially likely in divorce cases, because the lawyer-client sexual liaison may prevent reconciliation between husband and wife or affect the husband's willingness to resolve property disputes amicably. When a South Carolina woman began a sexual relationship with her lawyer while divorce proceedings were pending, her husband's attorneys used the affair to win him a divorce on grounds of fault (the wife's adultery).[41] In Illinois, a woman who had separated from her husband succumbed to her attorney's coercive pressure and began having sex with him. When her husband discovered the affair, he became so outraged that he refused to pay the attorney fees incurred by his wife. Though the woman had legal grounds to compel her husband to reimburse the fees, her lawyer didn't pursue the claim, allegedly because he feared disciplinary sanctions if the attorney-client sexual contacts were disclosed.[42]

Most courts limit malpractice liability to these situations involving a quid-pro-quo demand or a conflict of interest that affects the lawyer's work. As a result, a lawyer is usually not liable for malpractice when he manipulates a client's vulnerability, uses information imparted in confidence to aid his efforts to seduce her, or makes sexual advances in the middle of an office consultation.[43]

Another case from the Illinois divorce bar shows how far the courts will go to shelter the misconduct of their legal colleagues. On three occasions, a woman submitted to her attorney's demands for intercourse, each time because she feared he wouldn't pursue her case if she refused. After three months, she realized that sexual demands would be a constant component of his representation, and she fired him. She filed a complaint with the state's disciplinary board, but the board refused to act because she had no corroboration for her claim. She then sued for malpractice.

At an oral argument on the malpractice claim, with the woman present in court, one of the judges told her attorney that her coercion claim might be plausible if she had submitted only once. But, the judge said, since she had sex with the lawyer three times, she "must have enjoyed it."[44] The court dismissed her suit, and emphasized that a malpractice claim could not be based merely on proof that a lawyer exploited his client's vulnerability or used implicit pressure to induce her consent. Rather, the court held, malpractice liability is limited to cases of quid-pro-quo abuse or adverse legal impact. And the woman hadn't proved a quid-pro-quo demand, the court ruled, because there was no "tangible evidence" that he had linked his services to sexual compliance.[45]

Most other courts are equally strict. Though liability for quid-pro-quo misconduct exists in theory, the requirement that the lawyer make an explicit or tangible threat is stringently enforced. In a later case, Chicago lawyer Roe said that his client's compliance with his demand for oral sex "would make it much easier" for her; the court ruled that the lawyer's comment was "not sufficiently tangible."[46]

A few courts are beginning to question these strict requirements. In Illinois the appellate judges are now divided on the issues. One court limits malpractice liability to cases of quid-pro-quo abuse or adverse legal impact, but another court ruled in 1997 that an attorney could also be sued for malpractice if, in representing a client, he obtained information suggesting her vulnerability and used the information to seduce her.[47] The state's supreme court has not yet spoken to the issue.

The most important of the recent malpractice cases arose in Rhode Island. Maria Vallinoto, a Spanish citizen, married an American living in Spain and came with him to the United States, where their child was born. After a ten-year marriage, divorce proceedings were instituted. Vallinoto hired attorney Edmond DiSandro to represent her.

About three months after he was retained, DiSandro began an intimate relationship with his client. Vallinoto later testified that DiSandro had told her good lawyers usually wouldn't take a case that another lawyer had started, and she feared that if he withdrew as her counsel, she would be unable to retain another competent attorney. She also testified that DiSandro said if he stopped representing her, she would be deported and would lose custody of her child. She claimed that DiSandro's implicit threats to drop her case compelled her to submit to his sexual demands. She estimated that over the next eighteen months she had sex with DiSandro about 200 times, all without her consent. Almost half the encounters, she said, occurred in DiSandro's office during business hours.

Meanwhile DiSandro continued working on Vallinoto's legal problems. By all accounts he achieved highly successful results. Vallinoto won custody of her child, large support payments, and 60 percent of the marital assets. Not long after the divorce proceedings concluded, the sexual relationship ended. But two years later, after she had remarried, Vallinoto sued DiSandro for malpractice. She testified that she experienced shame, fear, crying spells, and nightmares as a result of DiSandro's sexual misconduct.

DiSandro vigorously denied his client's story. He said he never threatened her or told her she would be deported. He claimed that their liaison was fully consensual and had progressed to the point that they discussed marriage. The jury sided with Vallinoto. It awarded her over $200,000 in damages.[48] But the Rhode Island Supreme Court set aside the jury's award. In a 1997 decision, the court disregarded the jury's view of the evidence and concluded that Vallinoto "clearly had the ability and knowledge to discharge and leave DiSandro at any time if she was dissatisfied." The court also raised a high legal barrier to a malpractice claim, regardless of the coercive tactics employed. The court ruled that "even if . . . the legal services by DiSandro were a quid pro quo for sexual favors, Vallinoto's claim would still fail because of *the complete absence of any . . . damages that resulted to her legal position . . .* as a result of DiSandro's inappropriate sexual activities."[49]

The decision sets extremely strict limits on the attorney's liability for malpractice. The court held, in effect, that once a client's legal claims are successfully resolved, she has no basis for a malpractice complaint, even if she had to submit to hundreds of unwanted sexual encounters in order to keep her attorney working diligently on her case.[50] The court could not have made more clear its low regard for a woman's sexual autonomy. The judges understood that a client's failure to get a sufficient property settlement would be a harm deserving legal redress. But they were unable to see that submitting to sexual encounters unwillingly, because of an attorney's misuse of his professional authority, is a serious injury as well.

In the absence of criminal sanctions or liability for malpractice, control over sexually abusive attorneys rests almost exclusively with the disciplinary boards of the bar associations and state courts. In DiSandro's case, the state's disciplinary board conducted its own investigation while the jury verdict was on appeal. The board, accepting the lawyer's version over that of his client, found that the sexual relationship was consensual. But because the liaison nonetheless posed a conflict of interest, the board recommended professional discipline. Accepting the board's recommendation, the supreme court imposed "the sanction of public censure"—without any suspension of DiSandro's right to practice. The court noted that "had the client's case actually been prejudiced . . . a more serious sanction may have been appropriate."[51]

Elsewhere, professional discipline is typically tepid or inconsistent. A 1992 Georgia decision falls at the more severe end of the spectrum. A woman's divorce attorney was a man with whom she had a preexisting liaison, and their affair continued during the legal proceedings. The lawyer provided his legal services without fee, and there was no finding that he used coercion or undue influence. Nonetheless, the Georgia Supreme Court noted, a conflict of interest was inherent in the situation, and the lawyer's conduct (adultery) was illegal in Georgia. For those violations, the court suspended his license for three years, with three judges voting to disbar him permanently.[52]

Other states respond differently. A North Carolina lawyer admitted he had sex with two of his divorce clients, but the state bar ruled in 1995 that it could take no action on their complaints because the sex was consensual.[53] In Wisconsin, a public defender met with a client—recently escaped from a halfway house—who was facing revocation of her probation and incarceration on a three-year prison term. Though he knew that she was an alcoholic and that her probation barred her from consuming alcohol, he picked her up in a state-owned car and drove her to a motel, where he gave her a six-pack of beer and allowed her to drink three cans. He then undressed her and initiated sexual contacts but stopped before having intercourse. Emphasizing that he had exploited the client's vulnerability, encouraged her to violate her probation, and taken advantage of information about her alcoholism that he had learned as her attorney, the court ordered that his license to practice law be suspended—but only for six months.[54]

Medical and mental health professions sometimes deserve criticism for halfhearted enforcement of ethical standards, but these professions have adopted rules that, at least on paper, unequivocally ban sexual relationships with current patients. The legal profession, in contrast, has yet to recognize, even in theory, that lawyer-client sexual relationships are inherently improper. The codes of legal ethics in force in the various states contain vague principles that may—or may not—apply to sexual contact. They prohibit conflicts of interest, misuse of client confidences, and conduct "prejudicial to the administration of justice." But most state codes, like the American Bar Association codes used as national models, contain no rule specifically addressing the problem of lawyer-client sex. And the ABA's formal opinion on the subject, issued in 1992, went no further than pointing out that "the roles of lover and lawyer are *potentially* conflicting," that "such a relationship *may* involve unfair exploitation," and that lawyers would be "well advised to refrain" from such relationships.[55]

Only a dozen states have ethical rules addressing sexual liaisons specifically, and their rules diverge widely, reflecting important disagreements. In about half these states, the rules are narrow or ambiguous. In 1992 California, the first state to act, prohibited lawyers from demanding sex in return for legal services or using "coercion, intimidation or undue influence" to have sex with a client. Limited as the rule is, California chose to qualify it by exempting liaisons that predate the legal relationship.[56] (As written, the rule—though intended to be progressive—seems to *permit* intimidation and undue influence when the lawyer and client had a preexisting affair.) Florida and Utah now have ethical rules banning sexual conduct that "exploits" the lawyer-client relationship. New York bans all lawyer-client sex in divorce cases but does not address other types of legal matters.[57]

Half a dozen states go further, using a "bright-line" approach to prohibit *any* sexual contact between lawyer and client. Most of the rules exempt sexual liaisons that predate the legal relationship. A few of the rules exempt liaisons in "institutional representation," when the lawyer is sexually involved with a person employed by his corporate or government client—for example, when an outside lawyer who represents an insurance company is working with the company's in-house staff attorney to prepare a lawsuit, and the two then begin an affair.[58] The broadest of the bans, recently adopted by Oklahoma, prohibits any sexual relationship between lawyer and client or between a lawyer and the representative of a corporate client; the Oklahoma rule allows only one exception—when lawyer and client are married.[59] Yet the great majority of the states fall at the opposite extreme, refusing to adopt an unequivocal ban on lawyer-client sex even in divorce or other emotionally charged cases.

Some of the reasons advanced against regulation are plausible, while others only underscore the need to raise lawyers' sensitivity on this issue. Philip Corboy, a leading Chicago trial attorney, believes that "unauthorized, coerced or seduced sex may breach a moral duty." But he argues that existing ethical rules already prohibit misconduct, and he insists that "the obligation to refrain from sex is not inherent in every attorney-client contract."[60] Joseph DuCanto, one of Chicago's most prominent divorce lawyers, goes further. He argues that "neither the government nor the bar has any business legislating morality . . . Regulating sexual contact between two consenting adults constitutes an invasion of privacy." DuCanto is quoted as adding: "Lawyers are people and it is absurd to say they should just put it in mothballs. Once in a while, a client is going to walk through your door and blow your socks off."[61]

Protecting Clients' Autonomy

Like sexual encounters between doctor and patient, lawyer-client liaisons pose three distinct problems. The lawyer may abuse (or the client may fear he will abuse) his power, for example by withholding services the client needs. He may abuse the client's trust, for example by taking advantage of what he knows about the client's psychological state or finances—information she gives him in confidence to further the legal work on her case. And the liaison may pose a conflict of interest if it distorts the lawyer's judgment or gives the opposing party a weapon against his client.

Because these problems are present so often, and because it is so difficult to prove that implicit coercion or subtle exploitation actually occurred, a bright-line ban on all sexual contact has practical advantages. Resistance to this approach may simply reflect insensitivity to sexual abuse or misplaced respect for a lawyer's supposed "right" to make sexual conquests. But the bright-line approach also precludes legitimate relationships that pose virtually no danger of abuse. Problems of power, trust, or conflict of interest are inherent in many areas of law practice but almost nonexistent in others.

Vulnerability to abuse of power or trust is especially acute when a client's legal problem is emotionally charged. Emotions are at the heart of divorce cases, child custody matters, and most criminal cases. Also important are the kinds of facts the lawyer will need to know. Exposure creates vulnerability, and many legal matters require the client to fully "undress," revealing sensitive details about her psychological problems, her sex life, or her finances. Divorce and child custody cases are again the obvious examples, along with criminal defense and many matters involving trusts and wills. Tax matters, usually low on emotional content, often require extensive financial disclosure.

Vulnerability may also arise from the event that sends the client to a lawyer for help. Like some medical problems, some legal difficulties are neither urgent nor life-threatening. But when a client is confronting imprisonment, divorce, or loss of custody of a child, her need for protection is intense. Similar problems arise in other areas of practice, including compensation claims for someone who has suffered severe personal injury and probate work on behalf of bereaved relatives.

Clients are particularly vulnerable to abuse of power when they can't easily terminate the lawyer-client relationship. Legal matters are sometimes "one-shot," easily fixed difficulties. More frequently the problem takes months or years to resolve, and a client can find it costly to hire a new lawyer who will need to master the same facts and redo much of the work. An indigent criminal defendant can fire her public defender, but she will not necessarily get a lawyer more to her liking; usually her only alternative is to defend herself. A client who pays a large retainer and has few additional assets may have no hope of hiring a replacement; if she fires her lawyer, she may have to abandon her claim entirely. And the lawyer who knows his client's financial predicament will know just how tied to him and vulnerable she is. When terminating the relationship is difficult or impossible, a client will find it hard to rebuff unwelcome sexual demands, especially when she has the kind of legal problem that makes the lawyer's help essential.

"Exit" problems of a different sort arise when a lawyer makes sexual advances in his office. For doctors and dentists, the patient's physical vulnerability and the risk of blurring clinical and sexual roles justifies an absolute ban on sexual contact at the time of a visit for treatment. Unlike the medical or dental patient, the legal client is not physically exposed. And if her lawyer makes an unwelcome advance, she can slap his face and storm out of his office. But the client has come for professional help, often with a problem she desperately needs to discuss. She may be under great pressure to tolerate sexual attention, however unwelcome, in order to get her legal concerns heard. Since truly mutual sexual ardor can usually be deferred at least for a few minutes, an absolute ban on sexual contact in the office makes sense for lawyers, as it does for doctors.

An absolute ban on liaisons outside the office is harder to justify. In some areas of practice emotional content, extensive disclosure, acute needs for help, and difficulty of exit combine to leave the client extremely vulnerable to coercive pressure and emotional manipulation. Divorce, child custody, criminal defense, personal injury litigation, and probate matters are the principal examples. In these areas, the risks are high that a client's consent to a sexual advance will be inauthentic or involuntary.

Cases in which the lawyer represents an institutional client—a corporation or government agency—are at the opposite pole; virtually none of the danger signals are present. The person who deals with the lawyer on behalf of her institutional employer will want to see her company's interests well served, but her personal emotions will rarely be central to the legal work. Her financial and psychological problems usually will not be relevant. And she will not be relying on the lawyer to help her address a crisis in her own life. (If she is, she needs another lawyer, one not committed first to the interests of the institutional client.)

Even in institutional representation, the lawyer may have a kind of supervisory power over the in-house employee who deals with him on behalf of the client: he can criticize her work to her superiors. But just as often, she may have comparable power over him. If the person who is acting on behalf of the company is its forty-five-year-old vice-president, and the attorney is a twenty-eight-year-old associate in the law firm handling the company's work, there is no reason to assume that the attorney holds power over the client's representative; if anything the dangers of unwanted sexual pressure and tacit coercion could run in the opposite direction.

Ethical rules like those of Oklahoma and Minnesota, which forbid liaisons between a lawyer and the representative of a corporate client,[62] are unjustifiably broad in this respect. But these states, together with the few states that consider liaisons between the lawyer and all individual clients unethical, are the exceptions. In nearly all states, the applicable rules of criminal law, malpractice liability, and legal ethics stand at the opposite extreme, indefensibly narrow.

In the case of mental health professionals, the patient's consent to a sexual encounter is so seriously defective, in almost all cases, that the doctor should be subject to criminal punishment for a sexual offense. Criminal punishment of lawyers who have sex with their clients cannot be justified in similar terms. Because emotional content, personal disclosure, and difficulty of exit are not intrinsic to all (or even most) lawyer-client relationships, we cannot plausibly say that a client's response to a sexual advance is usually the result of fear or misinformation rather than genuine desire. Still less can we say that a client's consent is inauthentic when she herself initiates sexual contacts.

In divorce, child custody, and criminal defense matters, there are stronger reasons to consider a criminal prohibition on all sexual contact. The lawyer-client relationship in these settings is probably not, on average, as intense or as personally focused as psychotherapy is. Nonetheless, the emotional content, stressful circumstances, and difficulty of exit create high risks of coercion or manipulation. So there is some reason to view a client's consent as tainted when the lawyer has initiated the sexual advances.

A liaison initiated by the client normally does not present a danger of coercion. But there are grounds for concern about whether her consent is authentic. A divorce client is often in a fragile emotional state. Especially if she didn't initiate the marital breakup, reduced self-esteem and doubts about her sexual attractiveness can make her vulnerable to sexual attention. By itself, however, this point is not decisive. A male acquaintance does not behave admirably if he takes advantage of a recently divorced woman by insincerely showing her some temporary interest and concern, just to get her consent to sex. But we could not say that conduct of that sort makes him guilty of a criminal offense.[63] Her lawyer is in a different position. His role gives him confidential information that he is not permitted to use for personal ends. In addition, even when his client welcomes sexual interaction, she doesn't necessarily give "informed consent." A sexual relationship compromises the quality of the service she will receive, in ways that the lawyer, like the psychotherapist, is required to disclose.

But the parallels to a therapist-patient liaison are not exact. The ability of a divorce lawyer or criminal lawyer to handle his client's legal problems is only indirectly affected by a sexual relationship; the psychotherapist's ability to treat a patient who becomes his lover is shaken to its core. And if prejudice to the case is a significant risk, the lawyer can usually transfer it to a colleague without the disruption that is almost inevitable when a therapist prematurely discontinues treatment. Informed consent is necessary in the case of the lawyer-client liaison, but with proper disclosure and advice, informed consent could sometimes be given. Even in divorce and criminal matters, therefore, the potential defects in consent do not seem sufficiently severe to justify treating the attorney's conduct as a criminal offense, provided that the sexual encounters are in all other respects consensual.

Existing criminal laws are nonetheless inadequate, because they permit lawyer-client liaisons even when consent is lacking. Once a lawyer-client relationship is established, the client has a right to the lawyer's diligent professional services, with no sexual strings attached. When a lawyer gets his client to submit to sexual demands by refusing to return her phone calls or by threatening to withdraw from her case, her consent is obviously coerced. A lawyer's quid-pro-quo sexual demand, like any other form of extortion, should be treated as a serious criminal offense.

Existing limits on civil damage suits are too narrow as well. Most courts restrict malpractice liability to cases involving a quid-pro-quo demand or a conflict of interest that affects the lawyer's work. A number of other unprofessional maneuvers are sufficiently clear and sufficiently serious that they should be counted as malpractice: sexual advances in the office at the time of an appointment for legal advice; advances the lawyer initiates outside the office when the patient cannot freely refuse (for example, because she needs continuing legal service and can't easily terminate the relationship); and any situation in which the lawyer uses information acquired professionally to advance his sexual aims. Unwelcome advances could also be addressed, as in the case of doctor-patient interactions, by extending sexual harassment statutes to cover professional relationships that the client can't terminate without tangible hardship.

Damage limitations in malpractice cases likewise call for reform. Even when a quid-pro-quo demand can be proved, courts sometimes deny the injured client any redress unless the lawyer's misconduct undermined her legal claims. The fact that she had to submit to unwanted sexual encounters in order to keep her lawyer motivated is ignored. The injury to a client's sexual independence clearly deserves redress—at least as much as an injury to the monetary value of her legal claim.

Equally important is the need to tighten the prevailing rules of legal ethics. The rules in force in most states contain general norms that arguably apply to sexual encounters: no conflicts of interest, no misuse of client confidences, and no conduct prejudicial to the administration of justice. But the claim that these vague principles cover the problem is belied by the intense disagreement within the profession over whether sexual liaisons *do* involve conflicts of interest, misuse of client confidences, or prejudice to the administration of justice. To rely on nothing more than these ambiguous prescriptions is a recipe for inconsistency, unfair surprise, and pervasive underenforcement.

A bright-line prohibition (with exceptions for preexisting relationships and institutional representation) is a plausible alternative. But this approach would prohibit mutually desired liaisons arising in areas of law practice that are light-years removed from the divorce and criminal law settings that have produced shocking examples of sexual abuse. A woman may consult a real estate attorney for help on zoning issues affecting an apartment she owns. A man may ask a litigator to file suit for him in a contract dispute. An engineer may retain a lawyer to secure a patent on an invention. There is little justification for putting lawyer-client sexual relationships categorically out of bounds in situations like these.

Defenders of the bright-line approach suggest that if a romantic attraction develops, the parties would still have three choices: they could defer sexual involvement until the legal matter concludes, transfer the case to another lawyer, or take their chances and hope that if the affair sours, the disappointed party won't complain.[64] These are plausible responses to the concern that a bright-line approach is overbroad. But in most settings the permissible options would be burdensome and unrealistic. Complex legal matters seldom conclude quickly, especially when litigation is involved. Sometimes it is fair to expect romance (or sexual consummation) to wait, but not *that* long. And transfer of a complex matter to another lawyer requires time, duplication of effort, and loss of familiarity, all of which will seem an overly fastidious precaution when risks of coercion or manipulation are essentially nonexistent. As the codes of medical ethics illustrate, the risk in an overly broad ban is not just that it may chill legitimate relationships but that most practitioners will think it isn't intended literally and will assume they can disregard it.

A more narrowly tailored prohibition is preferable. An ethical rule banning all lawyer-client sexual contact is easily justified in the five areas of practice in which emotional content, personal disclosure, and difficulty of exit combine to create special risks of coercion and exploitation: a bright-line prohibition should apply to divorce, child custody, criminal defense, plaintiffs' personal injury claims, and trust, estate, and probate matters.[65]

For other areas of law practice, the existing rules of ethics remain inadequate as well. A necessary first step is for the rules to stress that sexual relations are always unethical when they involve quid-pro-quo demands, sexual contacts in the office, use of information imparted in confidence, or any other form of coercion or undue influence. A rule of that sort is a partial, imperfect remedy, but it would represent a major advance over the ambiguous, tacitly permissive standards of most existing codes. And when combined with a complete prohibition in the areas of practice in which most problems arise, this approach should help break the pattern of disrespect for sexual autonomy that now pervades judicial standards and much of the practice of law.

12

Dating:

What Counts as Consent?

How often we smile disdainfully or wince in pain when we recall the blatant "no means yes" culture that pervaded the lives of our grandparents, parents, and, for many of us, our own adolescence. A popular Mitch Miller song of the 1950s proclaims: "Your lips tell me No! No! but there's Yes! Yes! in your eyes."[1] In one of the most famous scenes from the movie *Gone with the Wind*, Rhett lifts the protesting Scarlett into his arms, and while she kicks and pummels him, he carries her up the grand central staircase to the bedroom. The camera does not follow them (in this respect, at least, times have surely changed), but we next see Scarlett, beaming and radiant, as she brushes her hair in front of her mirror the next morning. Were her protests and physical struggles all just perfunctory? Or did Scarlett get raped, only to discover that she enjoyed the experience? The film leaves viewers to draw their own conclusions.

In a liaison between supervisor and subordinate, teacher and student, or doctor and patient, the less powerful participant may consent out of fear rather than genuine desire. In encounters between acquaintances, the two participants may be peers in every sense, but sexual abuse is still a concern if the one who is bigger and stronger attempts to have intercourse before consent is given at all.

Under most existing criminal codes, the absence of consent does not by itself make intercourse illegal. Criminal penalties apply only when the sexual aggressor uses too much physical force. But respect for sexual autonomy requires a different view. Intercourse without consent should always be considered a serious offense. Valid consent is obviously lacking when a woman submits to sex because she is coerced by threats to take away her job or to withhold medical treatment she desperately needs.

In these situations the inadequacy of current law is especially clear. But even in the absence of direct interference with freedom of choice, consent is still missing if no choice was ever made.

Determining what counts as consent is fundamental to the effective protection of autonomy. Yet this question is probably the most elusive of all those that arise in unwanted sexual encounters. The problem is particularly difficult in dating situations. Two people often caress, kiss, or touch each other sexually without necessarily wanting to "go all the way." But if one of them does want to have intercourse, he may interpret his partner's actions as a signal that she is willing too. In one frequent scenario, the woman remains silent and relatively unresponsive while her date hugs and kisses her; she may even say "no." Yet the social standards reflected in *Gone with the Wind* saw no harm in treating that sort of behavior as equivalent to consent.

Throughout the 1950s and 1960s, academic discussion of the consent issue was similarly one-sided. A respected 1965 text reported as scientific fact: "Although a woman may desire sexual intercourse, it is customary for her to say, 'no, no, no' (although meaning 'yes, yes, yes') and to expect the male to be the aggressor . . . It is always difficult in rape cases to determine whether the female really meant 'no.'"[2] The *Stanford Law Review* explained in a 1966 article that the "real" meaning of "no" was obscure because "a woman may note a man's brutal nature and be attracted to him rather than repulsed. Masochistic tendencies seem to lead many women to seek men who will ill-treat them sexually . . . [Realistic determinations of consent must make] provision for [a woman's] moralistic denial of willingness, for ambivalence, or for unconscious complicity."[3]

Criticism of these attitudes has become familiar. The feminist claim that "no" means "no" is now well known, but it is far from universally accepted. Many share Camille Paglia's view that "it's ridiculous to think that saying no always means no."[4] And in our courtrooms, defendants who claim that a woman's "no" really meant yes can still get a sympathetic hearing.[5] Statutes in most states—even in the late 1990s—still do not recognize that a verbal "no" suffices to communicate unwillingness.[6] Outside feminist circles, many thoughtful academics still oppose the idea that the law should take a formal stand on this issue.[7] Yet the right to choose or refuse sexual intimacy will have little content in a world in which "no" can mean yes. Without predictable ways to decide when consent has been given, sexual autonomy will often prove an empty concept.

The problem is compounded by the notorious gender gap in sexual communication. Actions that many women consider sufficient to signal their unwillingness—for example, saying no repeatedly, moving a man's hands away, trying to get up or leave—are interpreted by many men as indicating coyness, a desire to be persuaded, or even a desire to be aggressively swept away and physically overpowered. Because men are often expected to take the initiative in sexual interaction, and because a woman who wants intercourse may refuse to say so explicitly, many men see nothing improper about continuing to press forward with physical advances in spite of a date's passivity or even direct signs of her unwillingness.

Relatively few men will interpret a woman's "no" to mean that she wants him to force himself on her immediately. More often a man will understand "no" to mean: "not yet, but don't stop." In that event, the man won't stop. But not stopping often means continuing to make physically assertive advances, pulling at the woman's clothes and even beginning attempts to penetrate her, all while she is still saying "no" and pushing him back. Necking, petting, and sexual tussling—all in good faith, as many men see it—lead right to the edge of unwanted intercourse. In one instance, a college freshman acknowledged without embarrassment that he had once used "a little bit" of force to "overpower" a woman. Because the woman wasn't crying, he assumed she wasn't really unwilling, and he concluded that she "didn't mind it after it was over."[8] The Rhett-Scarlett scenario lives on in the minds—and the actions—of many contemporary men.

When a woman finds that mild rebuffs aren't sufficient to make her wishes clear, she can cry, scream, or fight back. But even if she is emphatic, her effort to communicate may not be sufficient to bridge the gender gap. In another instance, a man made aggressive sexual advances in the apartment of a neighbor named April, a woman he had never dated. April vigorously resisted him, but he succeeded in pinning her down and penetrating her. Afterward he asked, "[Do you] usually fight so much during sex?"[9] He apparently saw no reason to think that her resistance might indicate a lack of desire for intercourse. With attitudes like these, a man accused of rape often claims he had no idea that the woman he victimized was really unwilling.

A natural way to avoid this problem would be to resolve questions of consent by focusing on what the woman herself meant. But in a criminal case, the court must decide whether the defendant was at fault. In a prosecution for robbery, for example, a defendant can't be convicted unless he *knew* that the victim didn't consent to the taking of her property.[10] Emphasis on the defendant's perspective is the traditional starting point in a criminal case, because the question to be decided is not just whether a victim has been hurt but whether the defendant deserves to suffer criminal punishment for causing the injury.

The law's emphasis on the perspective of the defendant—in a rape case, the man—has caused considerable resentment on the part of many feminists. Catharine MacKinnon, for example, argues that the law of rape is "one-sided: male-sided" because of its preference for the man's point of view. She writes: "many (maybe even most) rapes involve honest men and violated women. When reality is split—a woman is raped but not by a rapist?—the law tends to conclude that a rape *did not happen*."[11] MacKinnon is right to note that public opinion often regards a verdict of acquittal in just that way, but the public's rough way of interpreting a case outcome reflects a common misunderstanding. An acquittal in a murder case doesn't mean that the killing did not happen; it usually means only that the killing was accidental or that there is a reasonable doubt about the defendant's fault. For the same reason, when a woman was penetrated against her will, an acquittal on a rape charge may mean only that there is a reasonable doubt about whether the defendant should be punished for causing her injury.

Yet a requirement of conscious, deliberate wrongdoing, however traditional it may be for other crimes, poses a major obstacle to effective enforcement in the case of rape. The belief that many women feign reluctance or want to be sexually overpowered remains widespread among men, even if it is no longer universal. The prevalence of these attitudes renders a man's claim of mistake at once deeply disturbing and all too credible. In many acquaintance-rape situations, such attitudes all but guarantee at least a reasonable doubt about whether the man made a mistake.

For many rape reformers, the only solution to this problem is to work on changing society's understanding of what a woman's "no" means. But cultural change proceeds slowly, and porous legal standards leave many women at risk in the meantime. And porous legal standards can be, in themselves, a large obstacle to cultural change. Because, as MacKinnon notes, the public so often equates an acquittal or a refusal to prosecute with the conclusion that "a rape did not happen," legal outcomes tend to reinforce the very attitudes that critics of the culture are most concerned to change. Legal reform can play a crucial part in the effort to raise public awareness and alter social assumptions about when sexual assertiveness should be considered abusive.

For antirape activists who focus on legal doctrines, the preferred approach to the problem of the gender gap is to modify the law's concept of culpability.[12] Rather than insisting on proof that the defendant actually *knew* the woman wasn't consenting, they would permit conviction if the defendant's belief in her consent was unreasonable. In other words, the law should convict for rape not only when a man was well aware of doing something wrong but also when he was negligent. The man's culpability could be shown not only by malice or bad faith but also by carelessness or insensitivity—by his refusing to pay attention to what a woman like April was clearly signaling through her words and her behavior.

The argument for expanding liability in rape cases from deliberate wrongdoing to carelessness remains controversial. Most serious felonies, from murder to ordinary theft, require proof that the defendant knew he was causing injury or was aware of a substantial risk. Yet extreme carelessness ("criminal negligence") is sometimes accepted as a basis of criminal liability, for example in homicide prosecutions based on drunk driving or on the use of unreasonable force in self-defense.

A similar approach seems appropriate for sexual violations as well. The injury of an unwanted sexual intrusion is great, and there is a clear need to give the man some reason to pay attention to the woman's wishes.[13] Since the mid-1970s, this view has largely prevailed with the American courts; the great majority now accept a negligence standard in rape cases.[14] Negligence liability need not be unfair to defendants, as long as the law provides safeguards comparable to those it affords in negligent homicide cases: the defendant's conduct must involve a gross departure from the level of care reasonably expected, and the penalty must be substantially lower than that which applies to intentional misconduct.[15]

Unfortunately, the negligence standard does little to solve the enforcement problems that antirape reformers are concerned about. When a man claims "mistake," he may be insincere or sincere but exceptionally insensitive. More often the difficulty is that his beliefs about the woman's consent are perfectly consistent with widely held attitudes. A successful criminal prosecution therefore remains difficult even in courts that accept the reformers' recommendation to punish men who make "unreasonable" mistakes. A jury composed of committed feminists will have no trouble concluding that the victim's "no" really meant no. They will have no trouble concluding that any man who thought otherwise was unconscionably abusive. But if the jurors are women and men who hold the older view, they might well decide that the man's mistake could be considered "reasonable."

Our folklore has it that jury trial achieves commonsense results and social consensus. At least as often, in vigorously contested cases, it encourages tactical maneuvering to select sympathetic jurors and adversarial theatrics to persuade or befuddle them. Lawyers compete in deploying emotionally charged imagery, and the trial can quickly become a rollercoaster of psychological manipulation and unpredictable outcomes. The reasonableness standard produces a sound result only if the jury itself is reasonable—which is to say, "like us." If it isn't, the reasonableness standard simply invites the worst abuses of cultural stereotyping and ingrained sex bias that rape reformers have tried for so long to escape.

Because the "reasonableness" formula hides more than it clarifies, concrete reforms must move beyond that formula to specify *which* beliefs about consent count as reasonable. It seems plausible to insist that men remember to consider what "no" means, not to themselves, but to women. The still-prevalent male assumptions that "no" means yes and that women want to be physically overpowered are based partly on myth and wishful thinking. But not entirely. Sometimes women make the same assumptions themselves.

A 1988 survey of undergraduates at Texas A & M University presents an especially detailed look at this problem.[16] Over 600 women were asked whether they had ever engaged in acts of token resistance when they really wanted to have sex. Thirty-nine percent of the women reported that they sometimes said "no" even though they "had every intention to and were willing to engage in sexual intercourse." Of the sexually experienced women in the survey, 61 percent said that they had done so. Though these women were willing to engage in intercourse—eventually—they didn't necessarily want the men to disregard their "no" and force them to submit right away. Instead, many of the women wanted their dates to wait or "talk me into it." But when a woman's "no" is equivocal, it means that her date, if he reads her intention correctly, should continue to press her for sex, perhaps in a physically assertive way. In fact, some of the women said that they told their date "no" because they "want[ed] him to be more physically aggressive."

An obvious concern in this 1988 study is that the Texas A & M women may not be typical. The authors cautioned that students there showed an unusually strong tendency to view male-female relationships as adversarial and to endorse the kinds of assumptions about gender roles that were prevalent in the 1950s. But subsequent studies elsewhere report strikingly similar findings, with no regional differences.[17] A 1994 study of students at universities in Hawaii, Texas, and the Midwest found that 38 percent of the women sometimes said "no" when they meant yes.[18] In a 1995 study at Penn State, 37 percent of the women reported having said "no" when they meant yes.[19] For most women, most of the time, "no" does mean no. But sometimes it means maybe or "try harder to talk me into it." Sometimes, for some women, it means "get physical."

Because "no" doesn't always mean no, even for women, the reasonableness requirement solves very few of the problems of ambiguous sexual communication. It doesn't stop juries from acquitting men who ignore a woman's "no"—even when "no" is exactly what she meant. The reasonableness requirement doesn't stop prosecutors from deciding not to prosecute such cases, and it doesn't stop self-deluded men from continuing to act on their own view of what is reasonable. These realities underscore the need for a different approach.

Taking Responsibility

Another answer to the dilemma posed by the ambiguous "no" is for the woman to express herself more clearly. A woman who screams loudly and threatens to call the police will presumably succeed in making her desires clear to any man who has the least interest in considering them. This is the answer that the law currently gives. It puts the burden squarely on the woman to communicate her preferences clearly.

Critics of the antirape movement call this "taking responsibility."[20] They see no reason why a strong, self-respecting woman cannot make her sexual desires explicit. Naomi Wolf insists that women have "the *responsibility* [her emphasis] to be clear about [our sexual boundaries] to ourselves and to others"; she insists there is a "feminist responsibility for women to learn to speak."[21] Elizabeth Fox-Genovese urges women to "realize independence by taking responsibility for oneself, all the while knowing that some things will always be beyond control."[22] According to Katie Roiphe, rape law treats women as if they were not adults or free agents; rules to protect women who don't make their unwillingness explicit amount to a "denial of female sexual agency." Roiphe says that the woman who is uninterested should just dump a glass of milk on the jerk's head.[23]

The "take responsibility" movement has become something of a crusade, urgently and indignantly pressed by critics who seldom seem aware that prevailing law has always sided with their view that women must make their own wishes clear. And why shouldn't a woman just say what she wants?

If only it were that simple. In order to make her desires clear, the woman herself must know what they are. Those who want women to "take responsibility" insist, plausibly enough, that a woman can be expected to know her own mind. They assume that an independent, "liberated" woman will usually know what she wants in a sexual encounter. If she doesn't, she should be ready to face the risks; she shouldn't ask to be treated like a child who wants everything both ways. This argument appears to have stymied many proponents of strict rape standards, especially the many men who want to be counted as feminists on this issue. Few reformers want to push for an approach that women themselves will dismiss as demeaning or "infantilizing."

Yet the state of mind that critics of the antirape movement dismiss as "infantile"[24] is just the common adult experience of not feeling sure or not feeling ready, not just yet. A woman may not want to call in the cops, but she may not be prepared to say "yes" either. Her ambivalence may be reinforced by inexperience, peer pressure, unfamiliarity with her date, too many drinks, or a host of other factors. If she isn't sure, her efforts to say "no" will almost invariably send—and be intended to send—a mixed signal. If her date misunderstands, continues to press forward, and penetrates her before she is ready to say "yes," the result will be unwanted sex, an unsettling and seriously intrusive experience, but not (under current law) a crime.

Critics of the antirape movement would—quite literally—blame the victim in this situation. She didn't know her own mind. She didn't "take responsibility." Yet this argument conceals a puzzling assumption—that uncertainty and ambivalence should be equated with immaturity. The critics seldom spell out why it is immature to want to slow down and think. The critics don't explain why women who expect legal protection when they feel hesitant should be considered infantile, or why the more adult attitude would be to accept, with Fox-Genovese, that "some things will always be beyond control."

Those who want women to "take responsibility" see women as seeking special treatment, mainly because they implicitly take male behavior as the model for how a "grown-up" should act. And of course when it comes to sex, men ("real" men) usually know what they want. To imagine that a real man might be uncertain whether he wants to have sex makes about as much sense as asking whether a baseball batter waiting for the next pitch would be uncertain whether he wants to hit a home run. Real men want to "score."

Critics of the antirape movement have managed to label this the adult approach. They stigmatize as immature or infantile any person who wants time to think and who wants assurance that her boundaries will be protected by law while she is thinking. They seem to believe that the woman who isn't ready simply needs to say so directly. But women are usually doing just that when they say "no" or "not yet." The problem is that men often interpret these yellow or red lights as invitations to become even more insistent and physically assertive. And when they do, the law generally refuses to intervene. In practice, the law seldom affords any space within which the woman's need for time and reflection must be respected. Men may not have much need for this sort of protection when it comes to making up their minds about sex. In every other area of life, men—even adult men—don't always know their own minds. Yet no one ever disparages the rules of contract law, real property, installment sales, or informed medical consent as "infantilizing" the men whom these laws protect. A man's legal interests are never left up for grabs just because he is ambivalent or needs time for reflection.

The problems in insisting that women "take responsibility" are not confined to cases in which the woman isn't sure what she wants or when she wants it. Even when a woman is strong, independent, and perfectly sure what she wants, it may not be so easy for her to follow the simple make-it-clear approach that writers such as Fox-Genovese, Roiphe, and Wolf recommend.

Consider the situation of a woman who knows she doesn't want sex, but still has affection for her date and wants the relationship to continue. She is not going to dump a glass of milk on his head or scream for the police; she needs to find a quiet way to express both her affection and her refusal. At that point, she is sending—and intending to send—a "mixed signal." In a good relationship, experienced adults find ways to do that without being misunderstood. But it shouldn't be hard to see how the mixed signal could be misinterpreted. When it is, when the man misconstrues the refusal and presses forward, the result is rape. More precisely, the result is a violated woman and a man with a defense of reasonable mistake.

Affection for a man is not the only reason why a woman may fail to "be clear" or fail to "take responsibility." When a woman says "no" and her date continues to press forward, she may assume he is acting in good faith; if so, she will realize that she just needs to be more emphatic. But when he disregards her protests once or even twice (remember the Indiana undergraduate's "three nos" rule), she may realistically conclude that he hears her perfectly well. She may conclude that he simply isn't interested in what she is saying, that he intends to have intercourse whether she is willing or not.

A couple on their first date go out to dinner and then sit necking in the man's car. After some time of affectionate caressing and kissing, the man puts his hand on the woman's genital area and slips his hand inside her pants. She softly says "no" and pushes his hand away, but he kisses her hard on the lips and again puts his hand into her pants. She says "no" again, this time more firmly, and again pushes his hand away. The man responds by rolling on top of her and using both hands to pull down her slacks and her underpants. A pleasant evening with an attractive and seemingly sensitive man has suddenly turned sour; affection has turned to fear. The advice this woman would get from cool-headed take-responsibility advocates—just be firm, push him back, scream for help—assumes away all the psychological complexities. In this common situation, the woman "may interpret the man's persistence as an indication that he does not care if she objects and plans to have sex despite her lack of consent. She may then feel frightened by the man's persistence, and may submit against her will."[25] Once more, the result is a violated woman and a man with a defense of reasonable mistake.

The reminder that we must all take responsibility is perfectly legitimate, but it does nothing to answer the concerns about sexual overreaching. "Being clear" is a worthy goal, but in a world of mixed messages, wishful thinking, and male assumptions about what women's reluctance means, "being clear" is much easier said than done. The recommendation to scream or fight back may be good advice in some settings, but it doesn't help us decide whether we should blame the young woman, rather than her date, if she doesn't take the suggestion. Nor do the genuine ambiguities of the word "no" force us to conclude that the woman, not her date, was at fault. On the contrary, those ambiguities are the source of the problem. The "no means no" movement unfortunately invites a factual, descriptively plausible response—that "no" isn't always meant literally. But the very fact that "no" *doesn't* always mean no underscores the need to decide which meaning will be treated as controlling.

The Hidden Choice

To resolve legal disputes about consent, we must inevitably *assign* some meaning to the word "no." Whatever meaning we select, some selection is inevitable, even when cultural blinders or political rhetoric obscures the fact that a choice is being made. It is precisely because the meaning of "no" is not uniform throughout our culture that the choice is debatable. But whichever way the choice is ultimately made, we cannot pretend that law isn't choosing. Law inevitably determines the effect of a "no," in the face of ambiguity about its actual meaning.

Habitual thinking, along with the complexity of law, obscures the range of possible legal options. Two are obvious. The law could treat "no" as conclusive proof of unwillingness. Or the law could assume that a woman's intentions must be inferred from all the circumstances, regardless of the specific words she uses. As a third option, the law could treat words alone as irrelevant and look for *physical* indications of unwillingness. The last option is in effect the traditional regime requiring physical resistance. That approach still survives in some jurisdictions, but most states now follow the second approach. They treat verbal protests as relevant but not decisive in themselves.

This totality-of-the-circumstances approach is plausible enough, but it is only one of the possibilities. The important question for law is to determine whether the currently prevailing legal standard—the totality-of-the-circumstances approach—is a sensible choice or a harmful one. Whatever "no" means as a matter of the English language, the question is whether "no" should be *treated as* meaning no when we have to resolve legal disputes about consent.

Law professors Douglas Husak and George Thomas are among the few to recognize that the "no means no" slogan need not be a claim about uniform English usage. The important question, they say, is whether "no" should be taken to mean no for purposes of determining whether there was legally valid consent. Yet Husak and Thomas nonetheless opt for the totality-of-the-circumstances approach, in part because they believe that a "no means no" rule will be unfair to men.[26] In seeking greater safety for women, they argue, we should hesitate to impose an unexpected felony conviction on a man who had reason to think he was complying with the law. And the law as it now stands permits men to proceed to intercourse, even in the face of a verbal "no," provided that their belief in consent is reasonable under all the circumstances.

This criticism of the "no means no" standard makes the important point that we should not change the law retroactively and without fair warning. But this valid concern has no bearing on the problem of choosing the legal standard that will govern sexual encounters in the future. If a no-means-no rule offers the best way to sort out the ambiguities of sexual interaction, we need not tie ourselves to the standards of the past. Once the law makes clear that it is no longer permissible to proceed to intercourse in the face of a verbal "no," it will be perfectly fair to punish anyone who disregards that standard.

Husak and Thomas also suggest that a no-means-no rule will be unfair *to women,* by "making it harder for some women to get what they want." They posit the case of a woman who wants to have sex but is too reticent to say so directly:

> Suppose . . . that this woman has the misfortune to desire sex with a man who [feels obliged to interpret "no" literally]. Not wanting to be guilty of rape, he abstains from sex with this woman . . . He too feels awkward and uncomfortable about explicitly asking for sex. Someone might protest that neither adult should feel uncomfortable about expressing their desires, but that is beside the point. The point is that they do feel this way, and might resent having someone tell them how they should feel. The result is that this woman will be less successful in getting what she wants unless she changes her behavior.[27]

Their example is not entirely fanciful. In the survey of women at Texas A & M, 12 percent of the "sexually inexperienced" women in the survey reported that they had said "no" when they actually wanted to have sex. The men they were with apparently took them literally and misread their actual desires. Because the men assumed that "no means no," they held back, and the women missed getting the sexual intimacy they desired; they remained "inexperienced."[28]

The disappointment experienced by these women may not seem an especially serious concern, but even if it is, the cost it represents is misleading. When social meanings are ambiguous, any legal rule will frustrate some expectations. Some women say "no" when they mean maybe or yes, and others say "no" only when they mean it. *Any* legal rule will favor some of these women over the others. Inevitably, the law must choose sides. To know whether the totality-of-the-circumstances approach is the best solution, we need to consider *how many* women will have their actual intentions ignored under each approach. We must consider *how hard* it will be for women to make their desires understood, if they can't be sure that verbal refusals will be taken at face value. And we must consider *how severely* they will be hurt when their actual intentions are ignored.

Most women (at least 60 percent in most studies) say "no" *only* when they mean it. When the other women say "no," they also mean no—at least some of the time. Overall, a "no" is intended to mean just that, in the great majority of cases. And when the women who mean no can't rely on ordinary language to express their intentions, their only clear alternative is to scream or fight. Of greatest importance is the kind of injury that occurs if the man makes a mistake—if he assumes the woman really meant no (or yes) when she actually intended the opposite. A no-means-no standard would block a desired sexual experience for women who are too shy or inhibited to indicate their interest explicitly. But the prevailing totality-of-the-circumstances rule also defeats expectations, by allowing men to force an unwanted sexual experience on women who didn't want it—and tried to express their desires in plain language.

There shouldn't be a moment's doubt about which set of frustrated expectations is more serious or more deserving of legal protection. The common scenario is that of the man who assumes he has his date's consent, despite a verbal protest that he thinks is probably perfunctory. He must decide whether to proceed. Whatever he does, he may be making a mistake. But the injury to the woman if he proceeds to intercourse, when she doesn't want it, dwarfs the injury they both suffer if he doesn't proceed to intercourse when she does want it: "Acting on a false belief [in consent] involves immediate, serious, and irremediable harm to someone else, while refraining from acting on a true belief [in consent] would involve only a small [and often temporary] loss to anyone."29

Despite the confusion and controversy it engenders, the no-means-no claim is simply a demand for a fair allocation of risks, in an area in which misinterpretations are serious and pervasive. By requiring that verbal objections be accepted at face value, the law can provide a clear, easily manageable test for consent. And it can set a standard that will help avoid irreparable injury to women who have tried to express their preferences clearly in ordinary English. This is the very least we should expect in a sensible law governing sexual interactions that easily slide into serious abuse.

Neither "No" Nor "Yes"

A more difficult problem in sexual encounters is that when one of the participants makes physical advances, the other often says nothing.

Courts that are willing to find consent in the face of a verbal protest will inevitably find consent if the woman didn't protest or physically resist. But even for courts and juries that treat a verbal "no" as sufficient to signal unwillingness, a woman's silence is likely to be considered equivalent to consent. Only New Jersey and a handful of other states have taken the next step and insisted that consent to sex requires "affirmative and freely-given permission."[30] For most courts a refusal to infer consent when a woman lies still and utters no protest is overly fastidious and wildly unrealistic.

The assumption that silence amounts to consent makes sense in some settings. At a political convention, the presiding officer announces, "Unless I hear an objection, I assume there is unanimous consent to adjourn." Two distinct ideas are involved here. We may infer that a participant who remains silent really did consent—he was happy to adjourn. Or we may conclude that if he had reservations but chose not to express them, it is fair to treat him *as if* he consented. His consent may be actual or a justified fiction, but either way the result is the same: silence means consent.

The prevailing view, in law and in our culture, is the same for sexual encounters. If a woman is unconscious or asleep, of course, her silence can't be equated with sexual willingness; a man who penetrates her will be guilty of rape. But when the woman is *able* to say "no," the usual assumption, as at the political convention, is that the woman who remains silent must be willing; if not, she would object. Or, if she wasn't really willing, it is fair to treat her is if she were. Again, consent may be actual, or it may be an artificial but justified fiction. Either way, silence amounts to consent.

The episode on the Illinois bike path is just one of countless illustrations of this point of view. The man, six feet two inches tall and weighing 185 pounds, lifted a much smaller woman off the ground, carried her into the woods, pulled off her pants and performed several sex acts. The Illinois court, reversing the man's sexual assault conviction, said that the woman's "failure to [protest] when it was within her power to do so conveys the impression of consent."[31]

The soundness of this approach is usually accepted without question. Yet it is by no means clear that the woman in these situations does have a fair chance to protest. The Illinois woman, for example, was five feet two inches tall, weighed only 100 pounds, and was startled by a stranger in an isolated setting, with no one else in sight. Her silence might mean enthusiastic willingness, but—*at least* equally likely—it could mean she was terrified and paralyzed by fear.

In other sexual encounters, silence likewise may be explained by actual willingness or by a variety of other feelings—confusion, ambivalence, or fright. An element that routinely complicates the picture is intoxication. After a long evening of loud partying and continuous drinking and dancing, a woman, though not legally incapacitated, may be too tired and light-headed to read all the signals quickly and anticipate what her date or some other man in the room is about to do. Or she may be too drunk to express herself clearly. Yet in acquaintance-rape cases on college campuses, and in episodes involving strangers who take advantage of a woman who gets drunk in a bar, courts find that a claim of consent is plausible, under a silence-means-consent standard, because the woman was largely passive or because she failed to convey a clear aversion to sex.[32] Again, her failure to protest in these circumstances *might* mean willingness. But it could just as well mean disorientation or fear. The assumption that silence means actual willingness is clearly untenable. And the assumption that it is fair to treat her *as if* she had consented simply ignores all the situational factors that might leave her unable to think clearly, act quickly, or speak forcefully at the crucial moment.

If the prevailing silence-means-consent standard can be justified, then, its premise must be that the man who wants sex should not be obliged to clarify the inherent ambiguities of the situation. Rather, the woman who is unwilling (or just ambivalent or disoriented) should be assigned the burden of communicating her reluctance. If she doesn't, any man who wants sex with her—whether he is her date or even (as in the Illinois case) a complete stranger—is entitled to treat her silence and failure to resist physically as a sufficient sign of her consent.

The silence-means-consent assumption draws support from some antirape reformers.[33] They worry that treating passivity or ambivalence as *non*consent will "patronize" women, who should be assumed capable of asserting their own wishes. But we seldom think it "patronizing" to insist on permission, not just silence, when the interests affected are ones that men can easily recognize as important.

When a doctor asks if a patient wants a probe inserted into his rectum to check for tumors, we do not assume that the patient's silence indicates consent. The patient's willingness must be made explicit. And even then, because the doctor has a special duty of disclosure, the patient's permission is not sufficient until he considers the risks and gives "informed consent." When there is no duty of disclosure and no need for *informed* consent, many situations still require actual permission, not just silence. Suppose a real estate agent calls and says, "Unless you object now, or call me back within five minutes, I assume you agree to sell me your home for $60,000." We might object right away, but we might hesitate; we might miss the deadline or ignore it, for any of a million reasons. If we've been drinking heavily, we might not even be sure we understand what is going on. Outside the sexual context, when stakes are high, when silence can have many possible explanations, and when either party can clarify the ambiguities, we do not inevitably equate silence with consent, even if the person affected could easily object if he wished. Yet in sexual situations, the law has been willing to infer consent even when silence could indicate confusion, surprise, fear, disorientation, or intoxication just as readily as it might indicate sexual desire.

One explanation for the law's current treatment of silence is purely technical. Conviction on a charge of rape requires proof that the man's conduct was "against the will" of the woman. In other words, absence of consent is not sufficient for conviction; the prosecution must prove the *presence* of *non*consent.

To acquit, the jury need not accept the strained claim that silence and failure to resist show an actual desire for sex on the part of a heavily intoxicated woman who can scarcely speak or stand up. To justify an acquittal, courts and juries need only say that the woman's conduct left her actual desires unclear—that the prosecution failed to prove penetration *against her will*.

This insistence on proof of unwillingness—a clearly crystallized attitude of repugnance—has a certain amount of logic, within the framework of existing law. It serves not only to ensure that criminal defendants have fair warning but also to keep the criminal prohibition focused on conduct involving force. In the law's conception of rape, conduct becomes criminal only when it physically compels someone to do something abhorrent.

But once the law's concern shifts from physical force to autonomous choice, the focus of the consent inquiry must change. Clear proof of *un*willingness can no longer be essential to sustain a claim of abuse. Sexual intimacy involves a profound intrusion on the physical and emotional integrity of the individual. For such intrusions, as for property transfers or for surgery, consent cannot simply be the absence of clearly crystallized, clearly expressed opposition. For such intrusions actual permission—nothing less than positive willingness, clearly communicated—should ever count as consent.

A requirement of actual permission would not shift the burden of proof to the defendant or require doubts to be resolved against him. A defendant could be convicted only if he knew he did not have the woman's affirmative permission or if he was criminally negligent in thinking that he did. But silence, ambiguous behavior, and the absence of clearly expressed *un*willingness are evidence that affirmative consent was absent; they should no longer suggest, as they do in present law, that a defendant did nothing wrong in forging ahead to intercourse.

The ambiguities that complicate acquaintance-rape enforcement should pose far fewer problems under this approach. The significance of equivocal behavior would in effect be reversed, because equivocal behavior would reinforce prosecution claims that consent was absent, rather than serving (as under current law) to buttress defense claims that the woman had never signaled her *un*willingness. No standard can eliminate all factual uncertainty or swearing contests between witnesses. But facts that will often be quite clear—verbal protests, ambivalence, passivity, or silence—are by themselves sufficient to establish an unambiguous offense against personal autonomy and an unambiguous basis for punishment. The important point is to shift the emphasis of the consent inquiry away from concern over whether the woman explicitly communicated her opposition. The person who wants to have intercourse must be sure he has a clear indication of the other person's consent.

In the few states (New Jersey, Wisconsin, Washington) where consent means actual permission (not just the absence of protest), consent need not be in writing, of course. Permission can be communicated, these laws provide, by "actual words or conduct indicating freely given agreement to have sexual intercourse."[34] Because "body language" can still count as an expression of consent, this approach (for better or worse) doesn't eliminate *all* the uncertainties of sexual communication. A world without ambiguity in erotic interaction might be a very dull place, after all. But ambiguity is also dangerous, especially for women who justifiably want the freedom to explore intimacy and sexual contact without losing their right to stop matters short of intercourse.

To minimize the risks, Peggy Reeves Sanday, a leading expert on fraternity gang rape, proposes that nothing less than verbal permission—an explicit "yes"—should ever count as consent to intercourse.[35] The drawbacks of such a rule are evident. If body language cannot be a legally effective way to express consent, many common modes of indicating a desire for intercourse will have to change radically, or—more likely—the verbal permission requirement will simply be ignored by lovers, dating partners, and perhaps courts and juries as well.

Only unambiguous body language should suffice to signal affirmative consent, of course. Sexual petting does not in itself imply permission for intercourse, any more than does inviting a man in for coffee or permitting him to pay for dinner. A woman who engages in intense sexual foreplay should always retain the right to say "no." If she doesn't say "no," and if her silence is combined with passionate kissing, hugging, and sexual touching, it is usually sensible to infer actual willingness. Sanday's verbal-permission rule would reduce the risks of a possible misunderstanding in this situation, but at the cost of imposing a degree of formality and artificiality on human interactions in which spontaneity is especially important.

The verbal-yes rule may be worth its costs, but it seems many steps beyond the level of regulation that contemporary courts are likely to entertain. (Most courts are still willing to infer consent from passivity and silence, without any affirmative sign of consent.) And a verbal-yes rule is not mandated by a commitment to respect sexual autonomy. The central point is that sexual intimacy must be chosen freely. The first priorities are to stop insisting on proof of the woman's opposition and to stop requiring her to take actions clear enough to overcome the law's presumption that she is always interested in sex—at any time, in any place, with any person. The legal standard must move away from the demand for unambiguous evidence of her protests and insist instead that the man have affirmative indications that she *chose* to participate. So long as a person's choice is clearly expressed, by words or conduct, her right to control her sexuality is respected.

With this change of focus, criminal law should no longer have trouble reaching many of the clear-cut abuses that slip through the gaps in existing law. Men today are still free, as in the Illinois case, to take advantage of strangers they accost in isolated settings. Several men may have sex with a woman they find drunk in a bar. Or—as in the case of the lacrosse players at St. John's[36]—several men may get a woman drunk and undress her before she can resist. In cases like these, men continue to escape conviction by claiming that the woman failed to make her unwillingness clear. By requiring affirmative permission, through words or conduct, we can insist that any person who engages in intercourse show full respect for the other person's autonomy—by pausing, before he acts, to be sure that he has a clear indication of her actual consent.

13

Taking Sexual Autonomy Seriously

Of all our rights and liberties, few are as important as our right to choose freely whether and when we will become sexually intimate with another person. Yet, as far as the law is concerned, this right—the right to sexual autonomy—doesn't exist. Citizens simply do not have a legally recognized claim to protection for their freedom of sexual choice.

The law of rape suffers from well-known practical limitations. But even under the best of circumstances, its coverage is narrow. It prohibits sex with children and with unconscious adults, but in nearly all other situations it protects our sexual freedom *only* against interference by compelling physical force. No other concern that is central to the life of a free person receives such stinting protection.

A well-developed system of criminal law enforcement protects our property, our labor, our right to vote, our privacy, and our confidential information. The criminal law protects these rights against physical violence, of course. But it also does more. It makes these rights meaningful by protecting them *comprehensively*. It punishes interference by nonphysical threats, by coercive "offers," by misuse of authority, by abuse of trust, and by deception. It ensures that we retain these rights until we choose to give them to someone else; we can't simply lose them by default. And the law doesn't say, in the words of those who oppose rape reform, that people facing interference with these rights should just "take responsibility"—that they should scream, fight back physically, or "stop whining" and learn to live with the unpleasant consequences.

We know that we have to accept minor injuries and that life isn't always fair. We know that even for serious threats, self-help is sometimes the most practical remedy. But we also understand that in a civilized community, important interests can't be left to the vagaries of self-help and the rules of the jungle. We understand that vital interests must be nurtured and supported by law.

When interests in sexual autonomy are at stake, our society doesn't see matters this way. With rare exceptions, protection against physical violence is all the protection we get, as far as the criminal law is concerned. Civil remedies don't extend much farther. For all the fuss about the supposedly stringent character of sexual harassment laws, their scope remains limited. They cover only schools and workplaces, not other relationships of power and trust.

Even where they apply, sexual harassment laws don't neutralize a supervisor's coercive power. Subtle retaliation, a potent weapon, is almost always impossible to document and therefore almost always impossible to stop. A supervisor's advances are often unwanted but costly to repulse. Yet sexual harassment laws always insist that the subordinate employee resist the advances and face retaliation she'll never be able to prove; it's up to her to make clear that the advances are unwelcome. There is no burden on the supervisor to assure that his subordinate isn't responding out of fear when he presses his sexual attentions upon her. And even when a supervisor is caught making explicit threats to get sexual favors, he still isn't legally accountable for his misconduct. Only his firm is liable for damages; sometimes the supervisor keeps his job without even receiving a reprimand.

Professional regulation is similarly narrow in scope. Disciplinary boards often take misconduct seriously when it affects the outcome of the professional services a doctor, lawyer, or therapist delivers. But if the outcome is adequate, disciplinary boards and courts hearing malpractice charges are often satisfied. They often consider it irrelevant that the patient or client had to endure repugnant demands for intimacy in order to get competent service.

When a woman makes a hard choice and accepts sexual intimacy under the pressure of implicit threats or because a doctor or lawyer abused her trust, the law finds valid consent. But legal protection of autonomy is more limited yet, because the law doesn't require evidence that the woman ever made a choice at all; it treats silence and passivity as equivalent to consent. Sometimes, even today, the law finds consent in the face of a woman's explicit protests; "no" doesn't necessarily mean no. And the law doesn't unequivocally prohibit men from using force. The law only prohibits the use of *too much* force, force beyond the physical acts associated with assertive male sexuality. As a result, even when a woman is silent, reluctant, pushing a man back or saying "no," the law doesn't prohibit what it considers "normal" force—hugging, pulling, lifting a woman up, pushing her down, rolling her on her back, pulling off her clothes, and physically penetrating her body. In effect, the law permits men to assume that a woman is always willing to have sex, even with a stranger, even with substantial physical force, unless the evidence shows unambiguously that she was *un*willing.

These diverse examples of stinting, inadequate legal protection reflect a common theme—the law's refusal to recognize that sexual autonomy is *important,* an interest deserving protection in its own right. That attitude, though rarely made explicit in print, can often be found right below the surface. And in countless conversations, acquaintances (mostly but not all men) have told me that unwanted sex, unless compelled by threats of violence, is really not a big deal. "It just happens, it's over," they say.

People differ sharply, of course, in the value they place on their time or their property. Some guard their privacy jealously and with intense concern, while others are cavalier. Academics (in some fields) place notoriously little value on money. But such personal judgments are idiosyncratic; we don't assume that they justify withdrawing legal protection from those who do value their time, their money, and their privacy. And there is no reason to doubt that for the great majority—especially among women—the right to choose or refuse intimacy, and to do so freely, without coercive pressure or constraint, is among the most precious components of personal freedom.

The low value that our laws place on sexual autonomy is better explained by an entirely different concern. Autonomy is two-sided, involving both the right to *refuse* intimacy and the right to *seek* intimacy with partners who may be willing. The interest that law most often devalues or ignores is the first: the right to choose freely whether to decline a sexual encounter. Law's stinting approach to that facet of autonomy is no mere accident or oversight. It is the expression of current law's deep commitment to supporting—and above all never chilling—an interest that seems of overriding importance, especially to men: the freedom to seek sex with any potential partner who might be interested or even reluctant but persuadable, in one way or another.

Defenders of unrestrained sexual liberty sometimes speak as if this right were essential to human survival. No doubt its value can be exaggerated. But, in its place, the right to seek intimacy *is* important, extremely so. And recent efforts to prevent sexual abuse sometimes overreact, trampling unnecessarily on this important facet of freedom. There are numerous examples: the Idaho statute making it a crime for a doctor or dentist to have fully consensual sex with any patient other than his spouse, regardless of the circumstances; the Oklahoma rule that prohibits lawyers from having a fully consensual sexual relationship with any client or even with any person who acts for a corporate client (except when the other person is his spouse); the military's aggressive enforcement of antifraternization rules to block romantic relationships even when the two parties marry and when threats to military discipline are remote; the company rules that forbid all romantic liaisons between employees; the university rules that bar professors and instructors from having a sexual relationship with any student, even one from a different department.

But these examples are the exceptions. Far more common is the opposite problem—excessive obeisance to the supposed right of constant, unrestricted heterosexual exploration, and the corresponding failure to ensure meaningful freedom to *refuse* a sexual advance. Here, too, there are many examples, and in this case they typify prevailing law, not its outlying exceptions. Sexual harassment law treats a supervisor's sexual advance as presumptively welcome, unless the subordinate makes clear it isn't. Most universities permit professors to make sexual advances to students they currently teach or supervise. In almost all states, it is not a crime for a man to force sexual submission by threatening to get a woman fired from her job; or for a psychotherapist to start a sexual liaison with a troubled patient who has come to him for help; or for a doctor to get sexual favors by threatening to withhold drugs a patient needs; or for a lawyer to sit beside a shaky divorce client on the sofa in his office and get her to perform oral sex by threatening to drop her case and abandon her.

The costs of this system of unrestricted freedom fall most directly on the many individuals, mostly women, who are the target of sexual advances initiated by their superiors at work or by their teachers, doctors, dentists, psychotherapists, and lawyers. The number of women affected can only be estimated, but it is undoubtedly large—perhaps as many as a million working women per year subjected to the unwelcome advances of their job supervisors, over 200,000 women per year pressured for sex by their teachers in college, thousands or—more likely—tens of thousands of women per year having unwanted sex with their therapists and doctors. (The number of women abused by their lawyers can't be estimated, but it is almost certainly not insignificant.)

The consequences of law's refusal to protect both facets of autonomy—the right to seek intimacy and the right to refuse it—reach further still, touching flagrant physical abuse as well. A man can accost a stranger in a remote place, lift her off the ground, carry her into the woods, pull her pants down, and have sex with her. He commits no crime because the woman, paralyzed by fear, never resisted. If a man in a bar notices another patron, a complete stranger, staggering from too many drinks, he can carry her to a booth, stretch her out on the seat, tear off her clothes, and penetrate her. So long as the woman is not actually unconscious, his conduct is perfectly legal, because the woman never said "no," and he never used what the law calls "force." The force he did use is considered permissible because it is seen as a normal way for a man to show passion and engage in intercourse. The man didn't—because he didn't need to—threaten violence to compel her to submit. In each case, because sexual autonomy isn't protected in its own right, the law asks only whether the woman proved her reluctance and whether the man overcame her reluctance by too much force; the law never asks whether there is any indication that she *chose*—and chose freely—to participate.

Law has begun to move—haltingly—in a different direction. It has begun to acknowledge that extreme physical violence is not the only important concern. Court cases, statutes, and professional regulations have begun to place autonomy interests closer to center stage. But the progress remains tentative and hotly contested, constantly challenged by critics who think law already goes much too far in placing boundaries on the sexual initiatives of those who have the good fortune to be in positions of power or trust.

Women and men who value their sexual independence deserve better. The ability to set the course of one's own life—to decide where to live, what jobs to seek, what to do with one's leisure time—is the essence of freedom. And few of these decisions, if any, are more important to the shape of our lives and our opportunities for pleasure and fulfillment than the decision about whether and when to be sexually intimate with another person. When we choose freely, without coercion or constraint, we define an important part of who we want to be. We can experience fun, adventure, surprise, physical pleasure, or the deeper satisfactions of building an emotional bond and expressing our care, esteem, and love for another person. When that decision is forced on us, violently or otherwise, we must endure unwanted sex, an experience that is—at the very least—unpleasant. More often, unwanted sex proves degrading, physically painful, damaging to self-esteem, and productive of lasting psychological damage.

Violent rape at the hands of a stranger can be especially frightening, but sex coerced by an acquaintance often causes long-term injury as well. The victim of acquaintance abuse is likely to experience emotional confusion or self-blame, along with a deep sense of betrayal. And she is likely to have trouble finding support from those closest to her; her closest friend may have been the abuser himself. As a result, unwanted sex with an acquaintance tends to produce deep psychological harm, the victim may suffer a lasting inability to trust those close to her, and her emotional distress may persist as long as in the case of forcible rape by a stranger.[1]

Existing law doesn't—and can't—effectively prevent these kinds of harm, because it considers nonviolent coercion permissible. It even condones many forms of physical force. Existing law prohibits only *excessive* force. The effort to distinguish permitted from prohibited force pulls the law into a hopeless quagmire, with underenforcement the inevitable result. But this problem can't be solved by moving the line between the two kinds of force to a slightly different place. What is perhaps more surprising, and certainly more frustrating, this problem can't be solved by prohibiting *all* uses of force. That approach won't avoid the vagaries of distinguishing permitted from impermissible force, because physical activity, some of it forcible, is inherent in intercourse. And many of the other physical aspects of sexuality, though not inherent in intercourse, are expected and pleasurable, provided that there is consent.

Threats of violent injury are always intolerable forms of compulsion, but many other forms of force are not intrinsically wrongful. Getting physical—hugging, lifting a woman up, pushing her backward, removing her clothes, and physically penetrating her body—all can be unobjectionable, and even wonderful, when a woman has given her consent. The same physical movements become—or should become—acts of forcible compulsion when they occur in the absence of consent. Neither the kind of physical action nor the amount of force, as a physicist would measure it, is crucial. It is only the absence of genuine consent that turns desired physical activity into "force" in the bad sense.[2]

What decent protection of sexual autonomy requires is not a broader definition of force but a recognition that sexual intimacy must always be preceded by the affirmative, freely given permission of both parties. And criminal sanctions are normally an appropriate remedy. Criminal punishment is warranted—and is usually required by our sense of justice—when a defendant has knowingly inflicted a serious injury on another person. Any person who engages in intercourse, knowing that he does not have unambiguous permission from his partner, commits a serious sexual abuse, and he should be held guilty of a serious criminal offense. Threats of bodily harm and other acts of physical force, beyond those intrinsic to intercourse, aggravate the offense, but they shouldn't be required to justify criminal punishment if the defendant knew he was proceeding without having clear, affirmative consent.

Intercourse is also unwanted and abusive when a person gives her consent because she was coerced by threats, whether violent or nonviolent. Unwanted sex endured because of a coercive threat is likely to cause significant and possibly lasting physical or psychological harm. The person who makes the threat knows that he is attempting to induce submission to unwanted sex, and he can claim no right to do so, because a threat to violate another person's rights is always—by definition—impermissible. Just as nonviolent threats to take property amount to criminal extortion, nonviolent coercion to induce consent to unwanted intercourse should constitute a serious criminal offense.[3]

When uncoerced consent has been given, the place for criminal sanctions is far smaller. Criminal sanctions are sometimes deployed against conduct that does not knowingly inflict injury, when it creates a serious, unjustifiable risk of harm. Drunk driving is an obvious example.

But we must be sure that the conduct warrants moral condemnation, and we must be sure that severe sanctions will not bear too heavily on legitimate claims to freedom. Use of the criminal law to deter risky conduct requires confidence that the risks of harm are serious and that the restrictions on good-faith behavior are not unnecessarily severe. Laws punishing consensual sex with children are easily justified in these terms. Consensual sexual relationships between a mental health professional and a current patient warrant a similar criminal prohibition: the likelihood of harm is high, and the likelihood that the patient can give adequate "informed consent" is very low.

Similar confidence in the likelihood and degree of harm is much harder to justify in the case of other relationships between parties of unequal power. Criminal sanctions are therefore out of place in most consensual sexual relationships between supervisors and subordinates or between teachers and students, despite the undoubted dangers of these relationships. But the risks point to the need for safeguards that are less severe and more flexible than the sanctions of the criminal law. Managers and teachers who make unwanted sexual advances interfere with the right of workers and students to pursue their careers without putting their sexuality at risk. There is ample justification (and a strong practical need) for imposing personal liability for sexual harassment when people in positions of power subject their subordinates to unwanted sexual advances.

Professional regulations and rules of behavior adopted by individual firms are essential supplements to the ponderous remedies of civil damage litigation and criminal prosecution. Existing laws that make all relationships between supervisors and subordinates or between doctors and patients illegal, regardless of circumstances, foreclose many mutually desired relationships and pose a strong risk of inconsistent enforcement. Instead, professional discipline and standards in private firms should be tailored to the nuances of power and trust in particular settings. Solutions of that sort can take account of the importance of voluntary relationships, without denying all protection to women who may be at risk of exploitation and abuse. Where the effect of a ban on consensual relationships is relatively minor and temporary, as it is in the case of a rule against liaisons between professors and their current students, the prohibition carries few significant costs and can make a strong contribution to preserving the freedom to refuse an unwanted sexual relationship.

The details of various remedies can be worked out in different ways, but what should not vary is the commitment to take seriously the underlying problem. Like our rights to physical safety, to our property, our time and our labor, the right to choose—or refuse—sexual intimacy deserves the protection and support of society and its laws. Few of our other freedoms, if any, are as essential to emotional well-being and our capacity to lead a flourishing life. Sexual autonomy deserves to be protected directly and for its own sake, not with hesitation or apology, nor with irritation at victims who aren't able to help themselves. It is time to recognize sexual autonomy as an essential component of the freedoms that society properly guarantees and supports for every human being.

Model Criminal
Statute for Sexual Offenses

SECTION 201. SEXUAL ASSAULT

(a) An actor is guilty of sexual assault, a felony of the second degree, if he uses physical force to compel another person to submit to an act of sexual penetration.

(b) An actor is guilty of sexual assault, a felony of the second degree, if he commits an act of sexual penetration with another person, when he knows that the victim is less than thirteen years old.

(c) An actor is guilty of aggravated sexual assault, a felony of the first degree, if he violates subsection (a) of this section while using a weapon or if he violates subsection (a) of this section and causes serious bodily harm to the victim.

SECTION 202. SEXUAL ABUSE

(a) An actor is guilty of sexual abuse, a felony of the third degree, if he commits an act of sexual penetration with another person, when he knows that he does not have the consent of the other person.

(b) Consent, for purposes of this section, means that at the time of the act of sexual penetration there are actual words or conduct indicating affirmative, freely given permission to the act of sexual penetration.

(c) Consent is not freely given, for purposes of this section, whenever:

(1) the victim is physically helpless, mentally defective, or mentally incapacitated; or

(2) the victim is at least thirteen years old but less than sixteen years old and the actor is at least four years older than the victim; or

(3) the victim is at least sixteen years old but less than eighteen years old and the actor is a parent, foster parent, guardian, or other person with supervisory or disciplinary authority over the victim; or

(4) the victim is on probation or parole, or is detained in a hospital, prison, or other custodial institution, and the actor has supervisory or disciplinary authority over the victim; or

(5) the actor obtains the victim's consent by threatening to:

(i) inflict bodily injury on a person other than the victim or commit any other criminal offense; or

(ii) accuse anyone of a criminal offense; or

(iii) expose any secret tending to subject any person to hatred, contempt, or ridicule, or to impair the credit or business repute of any person; or

(iv) take or withhold action as an official or cause an official to take or withhold action; or

(v) violate any other right of the victim or inflict any other harm that would not benefit the actor; or

(6) the actor is engaged in providing professional treatment, assessment, or counseling of a mental or emotional illness, symptom, or condition of the victim over a period concurrent with or substantially contemporaneous with the time when the act of sexual penetration occurs; or

(7) the actor obtains the victim's consent by representing that the act of sexual penetration is for purposes of medical treatment; or

(8) the actor obtains the victim's consent by leading the victim to believe that he is a person with whom the victim has been sexually intimate, or by representing that the victim is in danger of physical injury or illness.

SECTION 203. CULPABILITY

(a) Recklessness. Whenever knowledge of a fact is required to convict an actor of violating any provision of sections 201 or 202, the requirement of knowledge can be met by proof that, at the time of his conduct, the actor was consciously aware of a substantial and unjustifiable risk that the fact in question existed.

(b) Criminal Negligence. If the actor was not consciously aware of such a risk, he can nonetheless be convicted of violating the provision in question, provided that the prosecution proves that his failure to appreciate that risk involved a gross deviation from the standard of care that a reasonable person would observe in the actor's situation. If an actor is convicted of violating Article 201 on the basis of criminal negligence, the offense shall be graded as a felony of the third degree. If an actor is convicted of violating Article 202 on the basis of criminal negligence, the offense shall be graded as a felony of the fourth degree.

Notes

1 UNCHECKED ABUSES

1. People v. Warren, 446 N.E.2d 591 (Ill. App. 1983).
2. State v. Thompson, 792 P.2d 1103 (Mont. 1990). Before the court's decision, the accused principal had resigned and allowed his teaching certificate to lapse, but he steadfastly denied the charges and subsequently recovered his license to teach. Interview with assistant district attorney Mark Murphy, June 24, 1977. For discussion of exceptions to the requirement of physical force, in Montana and other states, see Chapter 2.
3. George Fletcher, "The Metamorphosis of Larceny," 89 *Harv. L. Rev.* 469 (1976); Jerome Hall, *Theft, Law, and Society* (Indianapolis: Bobbs-Merrill, 2d ed. 1952).
4. Miss. Code Ann. §§97-3-65, 97-3-67 (offense to have intercourse with a child who is under eighteen but only when there is proof that the child is "of previously chaste character").
5. McQueen v. State, 423 So.2d 800, 803 (Miss. 1982). More recent cases emphasize the same point, e.g., State v. Schaim, 600 N.E.2d 661, 665 (Ohio 1992).
6. The data are discussed in Chapters 9–11.
7. Suppressed v. Suppressed, 565 N.E.2d 101, 106 (Ill. App. 1990).
8. Tony Parker, "Inmate Says Fear Led to Sex," *The Pantograph*, March 31, 1996, at A1.
9. In response to the reported abuses, Illinois in July 1997 enacted a law making it a felony for a prison guard to have sexual contact with a prisoner, with or without her consent. 720 Ill. Comp. Stat. §5/11-9.2 (1997). But many other states still have no statute punishing guards for having "consensual" sex with prisoners under their control. See Chapter 9.
10. Halton v. Hesson, 803 F. Supp. 1272, 1279 (M.D. Tenn. 1992).
11. *New York Times*, March 26, 1996, at A17.
12. See Peggy Reeves Sanday, *A Woman Scorned* 3–15, 28–49 (New York: Doubleday, 1996).
13. Karen Kramer, "Rule by Myth: The Social and Legal Dynamics Governing Alcohol-Related Acquaintance Rapes," 47 *Stan. L. Rev.* 115, 139 (1994).
14. See id. at 141.

285

15. Cal. Penal Code §261(3).

16. California sets its age of consent at the relatively high age of eighteen. Because Anne was twenty-four days away from her eighteenth birthday, Robert pleaded no contest to two misdemeanors: statutory rape, and providing alcohol to a minor. He was sentenced to a fine, probation, and 100 hours of community service. See Kramer, "Rule by Myth" at 143–144 & n.205. If Anne had been a month older, the episode could have ended without any criminal charges.

17. For courts taking a broader view, see Chapter 5.

18. E.g., Christina Hoff Summers, *Who Stole Feminism?* (New York: Simon & Schuster, 1994); Katie Roiphe, *The Morning After* (Boston: Little, Brown, 1993); Camille Paglia, *Sex, Art, And American Culture* 49–74 (New York: Vintage, 1992).

19. See Chapter 9. On the limited effectiveness of other civil damage remedies, see Richard A. Posner, *Sex and Reason* 81–82 (Cambridge: Harvard University Press, 1992).

20. Nichols v. Frank, 42 F.3d 503, 513 (9th Cir. 1994).

21. See, e.g., Gillian C. Mezey & Michael B. King, *Male Victims of Sexual Assault* (Oxford: Oxford University Press, 1992); Cindy Struckman-Johnson, "Male Victims of Acquaintance Rape," in Andrea Parrot & Laurie Bechhofer, eds., *Acquaintance Rape: The Hidden Crime* 192 (New York: Wiley, 1991).

22. See, e.g., C. K. Waterman, L. J. Dawson, & M. J. Bologna, "Sexual Coercion in Gay Male and Lesbian Relationships," 26 *J. Sex Research* 118 (1989).

2   DISAPPOINTING REFORMS

1. William Blackstone, 4 *Commentaries on the Laws of England* (1765) *210 (Chicago: University of Chicago Press, 1979).

2. 1 Matthew Hale, *The History of the Pleas of the Crown* 629 (S. Emlyn ed., 1778).

3. American Law Institute, *Model Penal Code and Commentaries, Part II,* Comment to §213 at 275–278 (Philadelphia, 1980) (hereafter *MPC Commentaries*).

4. United States v. Wiley, 492 F.2d 547 (D.C. Cir. 1974).

5. See id.

6. Committee on Standard Jury Instructions, *Cal. Jury Instructions—Criminal* 10.22 (St. Paul: West, 3d ed. 1970).

7. See Sanford H. Kadish & Stephen J. Schulhofer, *Criminal Law and Its Processes* 339 (Boston: Little, Brown, 6th ed. 1995).

8. Whittaker v. State, 50 Wis. 519, 520, 522 (1880) (emphasis added).

9. Brown v. State, 127 Wis. 193, 199–200 (1906).

10. State v. Cascio, 147 Neb. 1075, 1078–79 (1947).

11. Seventeen people served as reporters, associate reporters, or special consultants for the Model Penal Code project; none was a woman. Of the forty lawyers and professors who served on the institute's Criminal Law Advisory Committee, only one was a woman. See *MPC Commentaries* at v–vii.

12. Model Penal Code §213.6 (Proposed Official Draft, 1962).

13. Id. at §213.6(2).

14. Id. at §213.1(1).

15. Id. at §213.1(2).

16. *MPC Commentaries* at 301.

17. Model Penal Code §213.1(2).

18. *MPC Commentaries* at 303.

19. Id. at 279.

20. Menachem Amir, *Patterns in Forcible Rape* 130 (Chicago: University of Chicago Press, 1971).

21. E.g., Pa. Stat. §3121.

22. See Kadish & Schulhofer, *Criminal Law* at 340.

23. People v. Hughes, 343 N.Y. S.2d 240 (App. Div. 1973).

24. Amir, *Patterns* at 44.

25. Susan Griffin, "Rape: The All-American Crime," *Ramparts* 26–35 (1971); Susan Brownmiller, *Against Our Will: Men, Women, and Rape* (New York: Simon & Schuster, 1975).

26. Catharine A. MacKinnon, *Toward a Feminist Theory of the State* (Cambridge: Harvard University Press, 1989).

27. Note, "Police Discretion and the Judgment That a Crime Has Been Committed—Rape in Philadelphia," 117 *U. Pa. L. Rev.* 277 (1968).

28. United States v. Wiley, 492 F.2d 547 (D.C. Cir. 1973).

29. See William E. Nelson, "Criminality and Sexual Morality in New York, 1920–1980," 5 *Yale J.L. & Human.* 265, 302–308 (1993).

30. People v. Radunovic, 287 N.Y. S.2d 33, 35 (N.Y. 1967); People v. Croes, 34 N.E.2d 320 (N.Y. 1941).

31. Leigh Bienen, "Rape II," 3 *Women's Rts. L. Rep.* 90, 137 (1977).

32. New York's conviction rate represented less than 2 percent of the complaints. For most felonies, conviction rates during the same period ranged from 20 to 60 percent of all complaints. See Kathleen B. Brosi, "A Cross-City Comparison of Felony Case Processing" 8 (U.S. Department of Justice, April 1979).

33. Griffin, "Rape: The All-American Crime."

34. Vivian Berger, "Man's Trial, Woman's Tribulation: Rape Cases in the Courtroom," 77 *Colum. L. Rev.* 1, 14 (1977).

35. People v. Bain, 283 N.E.2d 701 (1972).

36. Jeanne C. Marsh, Alison Geist, & Nathan Caplan, *Rape and the Limits of Law Reform* 11–19 (Boston: Auburn House, 1982).

37. Leigh Bienen, "Rape III—National Developments in Rape Reform Legislation," 6 *Women's Rts. L. Rep.* 170, 171 (1980).

38. See Stephen J. Schulhofer, "The Trouble with Trials; The Trouble with Us," 105 *Yale L.J.* 825 (1995).

39. Kadish & Schulhofer, *Criminal Law* at 371, 374.

40. Linda Brookover Bourque, *Defining Rape* 110 (Durham: Duke University Press, 1989).

41. Marsh et al., *Rape and Limits of Reform* at 15.

42. Or. Rev. Stat. §§163.305–475 (Repl. 1977). See Bienen, "Rape III" at 185–189.

43. Kadish & Schulhofer, *Criminal Law* at 368.

44. Id. at 340, 339; United States v. Bonano-Torres, 29 M.J. 845, 850 (A.C.M.R. 1989) ("resistance is central to finding the element of force"); State v. Watkins, 754 S.W.2d 95 (Tenn. Crim. App. 1988); Ala. Stat. §13A-6-60(8) (1994); Idaho Stat. §18-6101(3) (1995); Ky. Stat. §510.010(2) (1996).

45. State v. Dizon, 390 P.2d 759, 764 (Hawaii 1964).

46. State v. Lima, 643 P.2d 536, 540 (Hawaii 1982) (emphasis added).

47. E.g., Mich. Comp. Laws §750.520b(1)(f).

48. Id. at §§750.520b(f), 750.520d(b).

49. Mont. Code Ann. §45-5-503.

50. Id. at §45-5-501(1).

51. State v. Thompson, 792 P.2d 1103 (Mont. 1990). In response to the *Thompson* decision, Montana broadened its statute to include in the definition of force any "threat of substantial retaliatory action." Mont. Code Ann. §45-5-501(2)(b) (1991).

52. Wash. Crim. Code §9A.44.060(1)(a); Wis. Crim. Code §940.225(3). Several states appear to extend rape or sexual assault to all nonconsensual intercourse but then define nonconsent in terms that in effect require proof of force or incapacitation. E.g., Tex. Code Ann. §§22.011(a)(1)(A), 22.011(b); Del. Code Ann., tit. 11, §§770(a)(1), 761(g)(1); N.Y. Penal Law §§130.20(1), 130.05.

53. State v. Rusk, 424 A.2d 720, 721–722, 724, 728, 733 (Md. 1981).

54. State v. Alston, 312 S.E.2d 470, 471–473, 475–476 (N.C. 1984).

55. Susan Estrich, *Real Rape* 60–65 (Cambridge: Harvard University Press, 1987).

56. Bienen, "Rape III" at 181.

57. People v. Hearn, 300 N.W.2d 396 (Mich. App. 1980).

58. Bienen, "Rape III" at 181 & n.62.

59. People v. Thompson, 324 N.W.2d 22, 23 (Mich. App. 1982).

60. Kadish & Schulhofer, *Criminal Law* at 368.

61. People v. Liberta, 474 N.E.2d 567 (N.Y. 1984); State v. Smith, 426 A.2d 38 (N.J. 1981); Warren v. State, 336 S.E. 221 (Ga. 1985).

62. Weishaupt v. Commonwealth, 315 S.E.2d 847 (Va. 1984).

63. Kizer v. Commonwealth, 321 S.E.2d 291 (Va. 1984).

64. Commonwealth v. Mlinarich, 498 A.2d 395, 400 (Pa. Super. 1985), *aff'd* by an equally divided court, 542 A.2d 1335 (Pa. 1988).

65. Wallace D. Loh, "Q: What Has Reform of Rape Legislation Wrought? A: Truth in Criminal Labelling," 37 *J. Soc. Issues* 28, 36–42 (1981). In a few jurisdictions, small studies found that victims were becoming at least somewhat more willing to report their rapes, and that the probability of conviction and imprisonment, especially for acquaintance rape, increased. In each instance, however, the improvements were very small. See Kadish & Schulhofer, *Criminal Law* at 362 n.9.

66. Cassia Spohn & Julia Horney, *Rape Law Reform: A Grassroots Revolution and Its Impact* 86, 159–160, 173 (New York: Plenum Press, 1992); see Kadish & Schulhofer, *Criminal Law* at 361–362 & n.13.

67. In one early survey of effects as perceived by criminal justice practitioners, researchers reported that prosecutors and police in Michigan said they had become more willing to investigate and to make arrests because of looser rules of evidence and the change in statutory definitions. Marsh et al., *Rape and Limits of Reform* at 41–49.

68. Cassia Spohn & Julia Horney, "The Impact of Rape Law Reform on the Processing of Simple and Aggravated Rape Cases," 86 *J. Crim. L. & Criminology* 861, 863 (1996).

69. Marsh et al., *Rape and Limits of Reform* at 107.

70. In contrast, scholars such as Vivian Berger, Susan Estrich, and Lynne Henderson have written extensively on concrete proposals for legal reform. See Berger, "Man's Trial, Woman's Tribulation"; Estrich, *Real Rape;* Lynne Henderson, "Getting to Know: Honoring Women in Law and Fact," 2 *Tex. J. Women & L.* 41 (1993).

71. The Loh study covers three years on either side of the new Washington law's effective date. The six-jurisdiction study by Spohn and Horney covers roughly six years on either side of the legal change.

72. Wash. Crim. Code §9A.44.060(1)(a); Wis. Crim. Code §940.225(3).

73. The only evaluation of the impact of this approach, the one done shortly after the Washington reform took effect, found no significant change in prosecutors' charging practices or in conviction rates. Loh, "Reform of Rape Legislation."

74. See Chapter 9.

75. U.S. Merit Systems Protection Board, *Sexual Harassment in the Federal Workplace* viii (Washington, D.C.: Government Printing Office, 1995). The stability of these incidence figures could be due, at least in part, to the possibility that some behaviors not perceived as harassment in 1980 might be reported as such today.

76. Cathy Young, "Rule of the Sexist Violence against Women Act," *Wall Street Journal,* March 23, 1994, at A15.

77. Stephanie Gutmann, "Are All Men Rapists?" *National Review,* Aug. 23, 1993, at 44.

78. 42 U.S.C. §13981(d)(2).

79. Katie Roiphe, *The Morning After* 67 (Boston: Little, Brown, 1993).

80. See Andrea Parrot, "Recommendations for College Policies and Procedures to Deal with Acquaintance Rape," in Andrea Parrot & Laurie Bechhofer, eds., *Acquaintance Rape: The Hidden Crime* 368, 369–370 (New York: Wiley, 1991); Nina Bernstein, "College Campuses Hold Court in Shadows of Mixed Loyalties," *New York Times,* May 5, 1996, at 1.

81. In 1995 roughly 8 million women were enrolled in colleges in the United States. U.S. Department of Commerce, *Statistical Abstract of the United States, 1995* (Washington, D.C.: Government Printing Office, 1995).

82. Diana E. H. Russell, *Rape in Marriage* 375–382 (Bloomington: Indiana University Press, 2d ed. 1990).

83. Va. Code §§18.2-61(B), 18.2-67.2:1 (1986).

84. Russell, *Rape in Marriage* at 375–382.

85. See Chapter 5. There is a similar but more limited retreat from the force requirement in a Montana statute enacted in 1991. Mont. Code Ann. §45-5-501(2)(b) (1991)

86. See People v. Wilson, 596 N.Y.S.2d 528 (App. Div. 1993); People v. Thompson, 551 N.Y.S.2d 332 (App. Div. 1990); People v. Kline, 494 N.W.2d 756 (Mich. App. 1992).

87. People v. Senior, 3 Cal. App. 4th 765, 775 (1992); People v. Hodges, 612 N.Y.S.2d 420 (App. Div. 1994); See also Powe v. State, 597 So.2d 721 (Ala. 1991); Caldwell v. State, 891 S.W.2d 420 (Ark. 1995); Commonwealth v. Dorman, 547 A.2d 757 (Pa. Super. 1988).

88. People v. Yeadon, 548 N.Y.S.2d 468 (App. Div. 1989).

89. People v. Howard, 555 N.Y.S.2d 376, 377 (App. Div. 1990). The Pennsylvania and Ohio decisions are similar, holding that parental authority is not always sufficient to meet the force requirement for a rape conviction. Commonwealth v. Titus, 556 A.2d 1425, 430 (Pa. Super. 1989); State v. Schaim, 600 N.E.2d 661 (Ohio 1992).

90. State v. Eskridge, 526 N.E.2d 304, 306 (Ohio 1988).

91. Ohio Rev. Code §2911(D)(2).

92. State v. Waites, 1994 Ohio App. LEXIS 3651, at *15.

3   FEAR AND DESIRE

1. Elizabeth Stanko, *Intimate Intrusions* 9 (London: Routledge, 1985).

2. Quoted in Timothy Beneke, *Men on Rape* 54 (New York: St. Martin's Press, 1982).

3. Quoted in Robin Warshaw, *I Never Called It Rape* 91 (New York: Harper & Row, 1988).

4. Quoted in Beneke, *Men on Rape* at 36.

5. Lynne N. Henderson, "Review Essay: What Makes Rape a Crime?" 3 *Berkeley Women's L.J.* 193, 221–223 (1988).

6. Quoted in Beneke, *Men on Rape* at 54.

7. Robin L. West, "Legitimating the Illegitimate: A Comment on *Beyond Rape*," 93 *Colum. L. Rev.* 1442, 1454–55 (1993).

8. Quoted in Beneke, *Men on Rape* at 60.

9. Id. at 49.

10. Margaret T. Gordon & Stephanie Riger, *The Female Fear* 10 (Urbana: University of Illinois Press, 1991).

11. Id. at 15, 16.

12. Robin L. West, "The Difference in Women's Hedonic Lives," 3 *Wis. Women's L.J.* 81, 95 (1987).

13. Id. at 106–107.

14. Stanko, *Intimate Intrusions* at 9–11.

15. Camille Paglia, *Sex, Art, and American Culture* 57, 70–71 (New York: Vintage, 1992).

16. See Carole Pateman, "Women and Consent," 8 *Political Theory* 149, 161 (1980).

17. Charlene Muehlenhard & Jennifer Schrag, "Nonviolent Sexual Coercion," in Andrea Parrot & Laurie Bechhofer, eds., *Acquaintance Rape: The Hidden Crime* 115, 119–120, 122 (New York: Wiley, 1991).

18. Catharine A. MacKinnon, *Toward a Feminist Theory of the State* 175–176 (Cambridge: Harvard University Press, 1989).

19. Id. at 177–178.

20. Id. at 174.

21. Adrienne Rich, "Compulsory Heterosexuality and Lesbian Existence," 5 *Signs* 631, 632 (1980).

22. Andrea Dworkin, *Intercourse* 124, 125–126, 137 (New York: Free Press, 1987).

23. John Stuart Mill, *The Subjection of Women*, in John Stuart Mill & Harriet Taylor Mill, *Essays on Sex Equality* 141–142 (Chicago: University of Chicago Press, ed. Alice Rossi, 1970).

24. See Martha C. Nussbaum, "Women in the Sixties," in Stephen Macedo, ed., *Reassessing the Sixties* 82, 90–96 (New York: W. W. Norton, 1997).

25. Mill, *The Subjection of Women* at 141.

26. West, "Hedonic Lives" at 123.

27. Lynne Henderson, "Getting to Know: Honoring Women in Law and Fact," 2 *Tex. J. Women & L.* 41, 56 (1993).

28. Several feminist writers, in contrast, do distinguish among coercion, "bad sex," and pleasurable sex under conditions of unequal power. E.g., West, "Hedonic Lives"; Henderson, "Getting to Know" at 57–63.

29. Katie Roiphe, *The Morning After* 67–68 (Boston: Little, Brown, 1993).

30. MacKinnon, *Feminist Theory of the State* at 175.

31. Roiphe, *The Morning After* at 62, quoting deputy public defender Susan Herman.

32. See American Law Institute, *Model Penal Code and Commentaries, Part II*, §213.1 at 279 (Philadelphia, 1980).

33. In one study most male and female students thought that men and women should be equally responsible for initiating sex. Yet only 38 percent of the women (but 70 percent of the men) actually had initiated a sexual encounter. Ilsa L. Lottes, "Nontraditional Gender Roles and the Sexual Experiences of Heterosexual College Students," 29 *Sex Roles* 645, 656 (1993).

34. Quoted in Henderson, "Getting to Know" at 55 n.76.

35. F. Scott Christopher & Michela Frandsen, "Strategies of Influence in Sex and Dating," 7 *J. Soc. & Pers. Rel.* 89 (1990); Arlette Greer & David Buss, "Tactics for Promoting Sexual Encounters," 31 *J. Sex Research* 185 (1994).

36. Timothy Perper & David L. Weis, "Proceptive and Rejective Strategies of U.S. and Canadian College Women," 232 *J. Sex Research* 455, 465–66 (1987).

37. Greer & Buss, "Tactics" at 197.

38. Quoted in Henderson, "Getting to Know" at 53.
39. Id. at 51.
40. Quoted in Gary LaFree, *Rape and Criminal Justice* 218 (Belmont, Calif.: Wadsworth, 1989).
41. Henderson, "Getting to Know" at 54.
42. Menachem Amir, *Patterns in Forcible Rape* 130 (Chicago: University of Chicago Press, 1971).
43. Robin Weiner, "Shifting the Communication Burden: A Meaningful Consent Standard in Rape," 6 *Harv. Women's L.J.* 143, 147–149 (1983).
44. Robert T. Michael et al., *Sex in America* 221 (Boston: Little, Brown, 1994) (results of national survey, conducted through the National Opinion Research Center, University of Chicago).
45. E.g., Charlene Muehlenhard & Lisa Hollabaugh, "Do Women Sometimes Say No When They Mean Yes?" 54 *J. Personality & Soc. Psychol.* 872 (1988).
46. Id. at 875–877. Unfortunately, the authors do not report *how many* women held these views.
47. Antonia Abbey, "Misperception as an Antecedent of Acquaintance Rape," in Parrot & Bechhofer, *Acquaintance Rape* at 96, 104–105.
48. Muehlenhard & Hollabaugh, "Do Women Sometimes Say No?" at 878.
49. Camille Paglia, *Vamps & Tramps* 23, 24, 47 (New York: Random House, 1994).
50. Bernie Zilbergeld, *Male Sexuality: A Guide to Sexual Fulfillment* 28 (Boston: Little, Brown, 1978).

4   THE SEARCH FOR SOLUTIONS

1. E.g., Susan Estrich, *Real Rape* 102 (Cambridge: Harvard University Press, 1987); Vivian Berger, "Not So Simple Rape," 7 *Crim. Just. Ethics* 69, 75–76 (1988).
2. An exception is the work of Donald Dripps. But Dripps too criticizes the concept of autonomy as inherently vague and incoherent. See Donald A. Dripps, "Beyond Rape: An Essay on the Difference between the Presence of Force and the Absence of Consent," 92 *Colum. L. Rev.* 1780, 1788 (1992).
3. Commonwealth v. Berkowitz, 641 A.2d 1161 (Pa. 1994).
4. Several legal scholars endorse just this approach, e.g., Dripps, "Beyond Rape."
5. See Peggy Reeves Sanday, *A Woman Scorned* (New York: Doubleday, 1996).
6. State v. Rusk, 424 A.2d 720 (Md. 1981).
7. Miranda v. Arizona, 384 U.S. 486 (1966).
8. Estrich, *Real Rape* at 41.
9. People v. Flores, 145 P.2d 318 (1944).
10. People v. Barnes, 721 P.2d 110 (Cal. 1986).
11. See Susan Estrich, "Rape," 95 *Yale L.J.* 1087, 1115 & n.75 (1986).
12. State v. Alston, 312 S.E.2d 470 (N.C. 1984). As Susan Estrich writes in her discussion of *Alston*, "Alston did not beat his victim—at least not with his fists.

He didn't have to. She had been beaten, physically and emotionally, long before." *Real Rape* at 62.

13. Estrich, for example, argues that force should be understood as "the power one need not use (at least physically)." "Rape" at 1115.

14. Goldberg v. State, 395 A.2d 1213, 1219 (Md. Ct. Spec. App. 1979).

15. Gonzales v. State, 516 P.2d 592, 593–94 (Wyo. 1973).

16. See, e.g., the several hundred words of rules and limitations in Model Penal Code §3.04(2)(b).

17. Commonwealth v. Mlinarich, 498 A.2d 395, 400 (Pa. Super. 1985), *aff'd* by an equally divided court, 542 A.2d 1335 (Pa. 1988).

18. State v. Waites, 1994 Ohio App. LEXIS 3651, at *15.

19. Mlinarich, 498 A.2d at 404 (Spaeth, J., dissenting).

5   FEMINIST CONCEPTIONS/JUDICIAL INNOVATIONS

1. Comment, "Towards a Consent Standard in the Law of Rape," 43 *U. Chi. L. Rev.* 613, 644–645 (1976).

2. Catharine A. MacKinnon, *Toward a Feminist Theory of the State* 174 (Cambridge: Harvard University Press, 1989).

3. Id. at 245.

4. Id. at 173, 175.

5. Vivian Berger, "Not So Simple Rape," 7 *Crim. Just. Ethics* 69 (1988).

6. Susan Estrich, *Real Rape* 102–103 (Cambridge: Harvard University Press, 1987).

7. See Berger, "Not So Simple Rape" at 75; Lynne N. Henderson, "Review Essay: What Makes Rape a Crime?" 3 *Berkeley Women's L.J.* 193, 228 (1988).

8. Lois Pineau, "Date Rape: A Feminist Analysis," 8 *L. & Phil.* 217, 236 (1989).

9. Id. at 239.

10. Martha Chamallas, "Consent, Equality, and the Legal Control of Sexual Conduct," 61 *So. Cal. L. Rev.* 777, 836–838 (1988).

11. Catharine Pierce Wells, "Date Rape and the Law: Another Feminist View," in Leslie Francis, ed., *Date Rape: Feminism, Philosophy, and the Law* 41, 48 (University Park: Pennsylvania State University Press, 1996).

12. See Ann Barr Snitow, "Mass Market Romance," in A. Snitow et al., eds., *Powers of Desire: The Politics of Sexuality* 245–263 (New York: Monthly Review Press, 1983).

13. Robin L. West, "The Difference in Women's Hedonic Lives," 3 *Wis. Women's L.J.* 81, 117 (1987).

14. Wells, "Date Rape and the Law" at 41, 48.

15. 18 Pa. Stat. §3121.

16. Commonwealth v. Mlinarich, 498 A.2d 395 (Pa. Super. 1985).

17. Commonwealth v. Biggs, 467 A.2d 31 (Pa. Super. 1983).

18. Commonwealth v. Rhodes, 510 A.2d 1217, 1220 (Pa. 1986).

19. Id. at 1226.

20. Id. at 1227 n.15.

21. Interview, June 23, 1997.

22. Interview, July 8, 1997. Other prosecutors agree. Interview with Monroe County District Attorney Cherie Stephens, July 8, 1997; interview with Allegheny County Assistant District Attorney Kim Clark, June 16, 1997. Proof is ordinarily insufficient, Clark stresses, if it shows only that the defendant held a position of authority over the victim; the prosecutor must ask enough questions at trial to show the jury "why there was force and why the victim was unable to resist."

23. Commonwealth v. Meadows, 553 A.2d 1006 (Pa. Super. 1989). The force was close to the traditional type in Commonwealth v. Smolko, 666 A.2d 672 (Pa. Super. 1995) (physically disabled victim abused by his nurse). Two recent cases suggest the first efforts to use *Rhodes* more expansively. A Philadelphia police officer was convicted of rape for compelling submission by telling a car-jacking suspect he would make sure she wasn't charged with the crime. *Philadelphia Inquirer,* May 28, 1997, at B3. A psychiatrist was charged with raping a former patient by allegedly arousing her fears that he would have her committed to a mental hospital. *Harrisburg Patriot,* July 21, 1997, at A3.

24. Meadows, 553 A.2d 1006 (1989).

25. There is nonetheless some ground to question the grading of the offense as a first-degree felony. In Pennsylvania, when a man avoids using force but nonetheless has intercourse without consent, he is not guilty of "rape" but only of "sexual assault," a second-degree felony with no minimum and a maximum sentence of ten years. 18 Pa. Stat. Ann. §3124.1 (1995). Meadows' five-year mandatory minimum—the same sentence that applies in a case of rape by a stranger at gunpoint—applies only when the offense is a first-degree felony involving the use of "force."

26. Meadows, 553 A.2d at 1013 (quoting the opinion of the trial judge).

27. In re M. T. S., 609 A.2d 1266 (N.J. 1992).

28. Id. at 1277.

29. The *M. T. S.* standard also permits conviction when the defendant didn't know—but should have known—that the woman had not consented. This aspect of the decision raises a concern about possible unfairness to defendants, because it permits imposition of severe first-degree felony sanctions for conduct that amounts to negligence rather than conscious wrongdoing. See Chapter 12 and Stephen J. Schulhofer, "The Gender Question in Criminal Law," 7 *Soc. Philos. & Pol.* 105, 131–135 (1990).

30. See Sanford H. Kadish & Stephen J. Schulhofer, *Criminal Law and Its Processes* 352 (Boston: Little, Brown, 6th ed. 1995). See also Miss. Code §97-3-95(1).

31. Interview, Feb. 5, 1997.

32. The New Jersey statute permits a conviction for sexual assault not only when

the actor uses physical force but also when he uses "coercion," and this term is defined to include threats of physical injury, threats to accuse someone of a crime, and other threats to cause substantial harm to someone's reputation, financial condition, or career. See N.J. Stat. §§2C:14-1(j), 2C:13-5(a). There were no allegations in the *M. T. S.* case that the defendant had attempted to use these kinds of coercion, and New Jersey prosecutors apparently have not invoked the "coercion" criterion in other cases.

33. Interview, Feb. 6, 1997.

6 THE MISSING ENTITLEMENT

1. Donald A. Dripps, "Beyond Rape: An Essay on the Difference between the Presence of Force and the Absence of Consent," 92 *Colum. L. Rev.* 1780, 1785 (1992).
2. Sanford H. Kadish & Stephen J. Schulhofer, *Criminal Law and Its Processes* 1039–88 (Boston: Little, Brown, 6th ed. 1995).
3. American Law Institute, *Model Penal Code and Commentaries, Part II* 330–332 (Philadelphia, 1980).
4. *Webster's Third New International Dictionary* 1882 (Springfield, Mass: Merriam-Webster, 1986).
5. 8 *Oxford English Dictionary* 149 (Oxford: Clarendon Press, 1961).
6. 18 Eliz. ch. 7, §4 (1576).
7. Henry Campbell Black, *Black's Law Dictionary* 1427 (St. Paul: West, 4th ed. 1951).
8. See Jerome Hall, *Theft, Law, and Society* (Indianapolis: Bobbs-Merrill, 2d ed. 1952).
9. Oliver Wendell Holmes, *The Common Law* 1 & n.a (Boston: Little, Brown, ed. Mark DeWolfe Howe, 1963).
10. See Kadish & Schulhofer, *Criminal Law* at 1048–49.
11. Lynne Henderson, "Review Essay: What Makes Rape a Crime?" 3 *Berkeley Women's L.J.* 193, 226–227 (1988).
12. Susan Estrich, *Real Rape* 103 (Cambridge: Harvard University Press, 1987).
13. The Greek Stoics, however, argued that a person with the proper mental attitude could be fully autonomous even when living under tightly constrained conditions.
14. See Martha C. Nussbaum, "Women in the Sixties," in Stephen Macedo, ed., *Reassessing the Sixties* 82, 90–96 (New York: W. W. Norton, 1997).
15. E.g., Robert Nozick, "Coercion," in Peter Laslett et al., eds., *Philosophy, Politics and Society* 101–135 (Oxford: Basil Blackwell, 1972); Nancy J. Hirschman, "Freedom, Recognition, and Obligation: A Feminist Approach to Political Theory," 83 *Am. Pol. Sci. Rev.* 1227, 1241 (1989).
16. Andrea Dworkin, *Intercourse* 137 (New York: Free Press, 1987).
17. Catharine A. MacKinnon, *Toward a Feminist Theory of the State* 174 (Cambridge: Harvard University Press, 1989).

18. See Chapters 7 and 8.
19. See Chapter 9.
20. See Chapters 10 and 11.
21. See the discussion of noncoercive but deceptive inducements in Chapter 8.
22. See Chapter 12.

7   SEXUAL COERCION

1. State v. Thompson, 792 P.2d 1103 (Mont. 1990), discussed in Chapter 1.
2. Commonwealth v. Biggs, 467 A.2d 31 (Pa. Super. 1983). An unusual statute, in Tennessee, includes extortion. See State v. McKnight, 900 S.W.2d 36, 50 (Tenn. Crim. App. 1994).
3. Ohio R.C. §2905.11(A)(4).
4. State v. Stone, 1992 WL 56778 (Ohio App. 1992).
5. See Richard A. Posner, *Sex and Reason* (Cambridge: Harvard Univerity Press, 1992); Linda Hirshman & Jane Larson, *Hard Bargains: The Politics of Heterosexuality* (Oxford: Oxford University Press, 1998) (proposing a "bargaining model" of sexuality, with "rape law as a bargaining chip"); Donald Dripps, "Beyond Rape: An Essay on the Difference between the Presence of Force and the Absence of Consent," 92 *Colum. L. Rev.* 1780 (1992) (proposing "commodity theory").
6. Martha Nussbaum, "Only Grey Matter?" 59 *U. Chi. L. Rev.* 1689 (1992); Robin L. West, "Legitimating the Illegitimate: A Comment on *Beyond Rape*," 92 *Colum. L. Rev.* 1442 (1993).
7. A property transfer could give mutual satisfaction of a sort, in the case of an altruistic charitable contribution. Sexual interactions not only can involve the altruistic sort of satisfaction; they also have the potential, not present in property transfers, for mutual satisfaction independent of altruism or any compensating quid pro quo.
8. The discussion that follows owes a large debt to the lucid analysis in Alan Wertheimer, *Coercion* (Princeton: Princeton University Press, 1987), esp. pp. 202–221.
9. Wertheimer calls this the phenomenological test. See id. at 207.
10. E.g., Robert Nozick, "Coercion," in Peter Laslett et al., eds., *Philosophy, Politics and Society* 101–135 (Oxford: Basil Blackwell, 1972).
11. See Wertheimer, *Coercion* at 202–219, for an especially clear exposition of this point.
12. State v. Rusk, 424 A.2d 720 (Md. 1981), discussed in Chapter 2.
13. See Chapter 12.
14. Tidwell v. Critz, 282 S.E.2d 104, 107 (Ga. 1981), discussed in Wertheimer, *Coercion* at 271.
15. Wertheimer, *Coercion* at 172.
16. State v. Toscano, 378 A.2d 755 (N.J. 1977) (emphasis added).

17. See Chapter 2.
18. Model Penal Code §213.1(1)(a) (Proposed Official Draft, 1962).
19. Id. at §213.1(2)(a).
20. Id. at §223.4(7).
21. "The Thomas Nomination: Excerpts from the Senate's Hearings on the Thomas Nomination," *New York Times*, Oct. 12, 1991, at A12.
22. See Susan M. Omilian & Jean P. Kamp, *Sex-Based Employment Discrimination* (Deerfield, Ill: Callaghan, 1990), §25:15 at 25–26. See Chapter 9.
23. Nichols v. Frank, 42 F.3d 503 (9th Cir. 1994).
24. Id. at 513.
25. American Law Institute, *Model Penal Code and Commentaries, Part II*, §223.4 at 223 (Philadelphia, 1980) (hereafter *MPC Commentaries*).
26. E.g., United States v. McCormick, 111 S.Ct. 1807 (1991).
27. See Stephen J. Schulhofer, "Taking Sexual Autonomy Seriously: Rape Law and Beyond," 11 *L. & Phil.* 35, 79 (1992); Carrie N. Baker, "Sexual Extortion: Criminalizing Quid Pro Quo Sexual Harassment," 13 *L. & Inequality* 213 (1994). New Jersey law has already taken this step, but rather than create an offense separate from rape for nonviolent sexual coercion, it lumps physical force together with nonviolent threats as equivalent forms of criminal sexual assault. See N.J. Stat. §§2C:14-1(j), 2C:13-5(a), discussed in Chapter 5, note 32.
28. See Chapter 9.
29. *MPC Commentaries*, §223.4 at 223.

8   SEXUAL BARGAINING

1. Lipsett v. University of Puerto Rico, 864 F.2d 881, 912 (1st Cir. 1988).
2. Under unusual circumstances, the manager's actions might be considered commercial bribery, a misdemeanor often punishable by no more than a short jail term. See United States v. Biaggi, 674 F. Supp. 86 (E.D.N.Y. 1987) (three months' maximum in New York).
3. United States v. Wright, 797 F.2d 245 (9th Cir. 1986).
4. People v. Sheridan, 186 App. Div. 211, 174 N.Y.S. 327 (1919).
5. United States v. Hyde, 448 F.2d 815, 833 (5th Cir. 1971).
6. American Law Institute, *Model Penal Code & Commentaries, Part II*, §223.4 at 208 (Philadelphia, 1980) (hereafter *MPC Commentaries*).
7. United States v. Hathaway, 534 F.2d 386, 395 (1st Cir. 1976), discussed in John T. Noonan, *Bribes* 586–587 (New York: Macmillan, 1984).
8. Model Penal Code §223.4(4) (Proposed Official Draft, 1962).
9. State v. Felton, 339 So.2d 797 (La. 1976), upheld an extortion conviction on these facts only because the unusual Louisiana statute prohibits use of threats to obtain "anything of value or any . . . advantage . . . of any description." Id. at 799.

10. Miller v. Bank of America, 418 F. Supp. 234 (N.D. Cal. 1976), *rev'd* on other grounds, 600 F.2d 211 (9th Cir. 1979).

11. See Karibian v. Columbia University, 14 F.3d 773, 776, 778 (2d Cir. 1994).

12. Dockter v. Rudolf Wolff Futures, Inc., 913 F.2d 456 (7th Cir. 1990).

13. See Susan Estrich, "Sex at Work," 43 *Stan. L. Rev.* 813, 837–838 (1991).

14. Priest v. Rotary, 634 F. Supp. 571 (N.D. Cal. 1986).

15. Broderick v. Ruder, 685 F. Supp. 1269 (D.D.C. 1988).

16. U.S. Merit Systems Protection Board, *Sexual Harassment in the Federal Workplace* 69 (Washington, D.C.: Government Printing Office, 1995) (hereafter *1995 Report*); idem, *Sexual Harassment in the Federal Workplace: Is It a Problem?* 37 (Washington, D.C.: Government Printing Office, 1981) (hereafter *1981 Report*); idem, "Sexual Harassment in the Federal Government: An Update" 16 (June 1988) (hereafter "1988 Update"). These figures include unwanted pressure from both supervisors and co-workers. Twenty-eight percent of the victims reported that a supervisor was the source of the harassment, down from 37 percent in 1980. *1995 Report* at 19.

17. *1981 Report* at 65–66. Data on expectations of penalties and rewards were not reported separately for women pressured for dates and for those pressured for sexual favors; the data cited in the text are the percentages reported for "severe sexual harassment," a category that includes both these forms of pressure, together with unwanted letters and calls. Id. at 37. Comparable data on these points are not provided in the "1988 Update" or the *1995 Report*.

18. *1995 Report* at 19.

19. See Estrich, "Sex at Work" at 813. See also Chapter 9.

20. Monge v. Beebe Rubber Co., 114 N.H. 130, 316 A.2d 549 (1974). See Martha Chamallas, "Consent, Equality, and the Legal Control of Sexual Conduct," 61 *So. Cal. L. Rev.* 777, 802–803 (1988).

21. United States v. Covino, 837 F.2d 65, 68 (2d Cir. 1988).

22. Bribery can also be committed by payoffs to private business executives who arrange special favors for certain customers, in disregard of a duty of loyalty to their firm ("commercial bribery"). See, e.g., Model Penal Code §224.8.

23. Existing law already treats the corrupt exchange of sex for official privileges as a punishable form of bribery. The law is inconsistent in this respect. Although it refuses to punish public officials for extortion when they *coercively* take sex by misusing official power, the law has long treated the *voluntary* exchange of sex for official benefits as a form of bribery. See United States v. Girard, 601 F.2d 69 (2d Cir. 1969). Recognizing sexual autonomy as an independent interest would not extend the scope of bribery law, but it would permit an appropriate response to men who exploit their power, in situations in which the exchange of sex for privileges is not only corrupt but coercive.

24. See Noonan, *Bribes* at 584–585.

25. United States v. Kenny, 462 F.2d 1205, 1211 (3d Cir. 1972), as summarized in United States v. Aguon, 851 F.2d 1158, 1165–66 (9th Cir. 1988).

26. The analysis in the text focuses on the question whether the facts are sufficient

to establish coercive extortion. When public officials are involved, some juris-dictions permit a finding of extortion based on the official's acceptance of the kickback "under color of official right," regardless of whether there was coer-cive pressure. United States v. Evans, 112 S. Ct. 1881 (1992), endorsed this theory for federal prosecutions under the Hobbs Act.

27. E.g., McNair v. State, 825 P.2d 571 (Nev. 1992).

28. Boro v. Superior Court, 210 Cal. Rptr. 122 (1985).

29. People v. Hough, 607 N.Y. S.2d 884 (Dist. Ct. 1994).

30. Boro, 210 Cal. Rptr. 122. I thank Albert Alschuler for providing additional detail about this case.

31. See *MPC Commentaries*, §213.3 at 391–392. In some states the crime was pun-ishable regardless of whether the breach was due to genuine change of heart or to deception from the outset.

32. See Mary Coombs, "Agency and Partnership: A Study of Breach of Promise Plaintiffs," 2:1 *Yale J.L. & Feminism* 11–13 (1989); M. B. W. Sinclair, "Seduction and the Myth of the Ideal Woman," 5:33 *Law and Inequality* 65–71 (1987). The tort action for seduction apparently survives in nineteen jurisdictions, but thirteen of these have not had a single reported appellate decision in the past thirty years; in the other six litigation has been sparse. See Sinclair at 59; Breece v. Jett, 556 S.W.2d 696 (Mo. Ct. App. 1977).

33. See *MPC Commentaries*, §213.1 at 329–333; §213.3 at 391–392 (four jurisdictions at one time permitted seduction charge to be based on inducements other than promise of marriage, but none made clear what kinds of deception would give rise to liability).

34. Coombs, "Agency and Partnership" at 12–13; Sinclair, "Seduction" at 83–85.

35. Coombs, "Agency and Partnership" at 13; Sinclair, "Seduction" at 90–91.

36. See Franklin v. Hill, 444 S.E.2d 778 (Ga. 1994) (holding seduction statute unconstitutional, partly on grounds of nonuse); Sinclair, "Seduction" at 59; *MPC Commentaries*, §213.3 at 391–392. Compare Model Penal Code §213.3(1)(d), preserving the offense of seduction when the actor, from the outset, does not intend to perform his promise of marriage.

37. See *MPC Commentaries*, §223.3 at 195–197.

38. United States v. Regent Office Supply, 421 F.2d 1174 (2d Cir. 1970).

39. Susan Estrich, *Real Rape* 103 (Cambridge: Harvard University Press, 1987).

40. Vivian Berger, "Not So Simple Rape," 7 *Crim. Just. Ethics* 69 (1988); Jane E. Lar-son, "Women Understand So Little, They Call My Good Nature 'Deceit,'" 93 *Colum. L. Rev.* 373 (1993); Chamallas, "Consent, Equality, and Legal Control" at 830–835. Larson recommends an especially strong civil remedy for sexual fraud, but even her far-reaching proposal stops short of suggesting criminal liability.

41. Representations are not material unless they relate to price, quality of the goods sold, or nature of the bargain. A salesman who impersonates a friend of a purchasing agent, in order to gain access and make his pitch, is not guilty of fraud. Regent Office Supply, 421 F.2d 1174 (1970).

42. Manko v. Volynsky, 1996 LEXIS 6328 (S.D.N.Y.).

43. See Robin Warshaw, *I Never Called It Rape* 65–82 (New York: Harper & Row, 1988); Andrea Parrot & Laurie Bechhofer, eds., *Acquaintance Rape: The Hidden Crime* 249–283 (New York: Wiley, 1991).

44. See Chapters 10 and 11.

45. E.g., Restatement (2d) of Torts §892B(2) (1979).

46. Neal v. Neal, 873 P.2d 877 (Idaho 1994).

47. Louis B. Schwartz, "Morals Offenses and the Model Penal Code," 63 *Colum. L. Rev.* 699, 673–674 (1963).

48. Neal, 873 P.2d at 875.

49. See Sissela Bok, *Lying: Moral Choice in Public and Private Life* 218 (New York: Vintage, 1978). Bok attributes the phrase to Coleridge. For discussion of the suspension of "reality" in sexual interaction and the importance of fantasy, see, e.g., William Simon & John H. Gagnon, "Sexual Scripts: Permanence and Change," 15:97 *Arch. Sex. Behav.* 108–109 (1986).

50. Bok, *Lying* at 129.

51. E.g., Barbara A. v. John G., 145 Cal. App. 3d 369, 193 Cal. Rptr. 422 (1983); Kathleen K. v. Robert B., 150 Cal. App. 3d 992, 198 Cal. Rptr. 273 (1984).

52. A California statute enacted in 1985 punishes the act of inducing intercourse by "false or fraudulent representation or pretense that is made with the intent to create fear." Cal. Penal Code §266c. But the provision goes on to define "fear" as "fear of unlawful physical injury or death" Id. So limited, the provision adds little or nothing to the ordinary prohibition of forcible rape.

53. State v. Lovely, 480 A.2d 847 (N.H. 1984).

54. N.H. Rev. Stat. §632-A:2, IV. At least two states have provisions that cover similar ground. A Montana statute permits a felony prosecution when an actor coerces consent to intercourse by a "threat of substantial retaliatory action." Mont. Code Ann. §45-5-501(2)(b). And a New Jersey statute permits a felony prosecution when the actor coerces consent by certain types of nonviolent threats. N.J. Stat. §§2C:14-1(j), 2C:13-5(a), discussed in Chapter 5, note 32.

55. Lovely, 480 A.2d at 850.

56. E.g., Marvin v. Marvin, 557 P.2d 106 (1976).

57. See Chapter 7.

58. See Martha C. Nussbaum, *Sex and Social Justice* (New York: Oxford University Press, in press).

59. E.g., Laurie Shrage, "Prostitution and the Case for Decriminalization," *Dissent*, Spring 1996, at 41.

9   SUPERVISORS AND TEACHERS

1. See Peter Rutter, *Sex, Power, and Boundaries: Understanding and Preventing Sexual Harassment* 85 (New York: Bantam Books, 1996).

2. Barbara A. Gutek, *Sex and the Workplace* 96 (San Francisco: Jossey-Bass, 1985).

3. Kathryn Abrams, "Gender Discriminaton and the Transformation of Workplace Norms," 42 *Vand. L. Rev.* 1183, 1205 (1989).

4. Kouri v. Liberian Services, 55 F.E.P. 124, 129 (E.D. Va. 1991); on the requirement that the complaining employee communicate unwelcomeness by her words or conduct, see Arthur Larson & Lex K. Larson, *Employment Discrimination* (New York: Matthew Bender, 2d ed. 1996), §46.03(2)(d) at 46–25.

5. Peter Rutter, *Sex in the Forbidden Zone* 22–23 (Los Angeles: Jeremy P. Tarcher, 1989).

6. See "Mocking Military Justice," *Los Angeles Times,* May 15, 1988, at V-4.

7. David S. Jonas, "Fraternization: Time for a Rational Department of Defense Standard," 135 *Mil. L. Rev.* 37, 72 (1992).

8. See Dorothy Schneider & Carl J. Schneider, *Sound Off! American Military Women Speak Out* 169–170 (New York: E. P. Dutton, 1988).

9. Hanna Rosin, "Sleeping with the Enemy," *New Republic,* June 23, 1997, at 19.

10. U.S. Merit Systems Protection Board, *Sexual Harassment in the Federal Workplace* 69 (Washington, D.C.: Government Printing Office, 1995). The report doesn't break down the frequency of harassment *by supervisors* for each type of harassment. For purposes of the calculation in text, the overall frequency of harassment by supervisors (28 percent for harassment reported by women) is assumed to apply to harassment in the form of pressure for dates. Because of ambiguities in the data, frequency figures for specific types of harassment must be considered rough estimates.

11. Id. at 19 (among federal employees who had worked outside the federal government, 56 percent said there was as much or more sexual harassment outside the federal government, 7 percent said there was less, and 36 percent said they were unable to make a comparison).

12. In 1995 there were 57.6 million women employed in the civilian labor force. U.S. Department of Commerce, *Statistical Abstract of the United States, 1996* 405 (Washington, D.C.: Government Printing Office, 1996).

13. As in the case of the figures for harassment of women, the federal reports provide no breakdown of the frequency of harassment *by supervisors* for each type of harassment. To determine the frequency of pressure to date a supervisor, I assume that the overall frequency of harassment by supervisors (14 percent of all harassment episodes reported by men; see U.S. Merit Systems Protection Board, *Sexual Harassment in the Federal Workplace: Is It a Problem?* 60 [Washington, D.C.: Government Printing Office, 1981] [hereafter *1981 Report*]) applies to harassment in the form of unwanted pressure for dates, suggesting that 0.42 percent of male workers were subjected to pressure for dates by their supervisor. Since in 1995 there were 67.3 million men employed in the civilian labor force (*Statistical Abstract of the United States 1996* at 405), the 0.42 percent frequency estimate implies that roughly 282,000 men experienced this form of harassment over a two-year period.

14. Meritor Savings Bank v. Vinson, 477 U.S. 57 (1986).

15. See Joseph Landau, "Out of Order," *New Republic,* May 5, 1997, at 9.

16. Showalter v. Allison Reed Group, 56 F.E.P. 989 (D.R.I. 1991).

17. 42 U.S.C. §2000e-2(a)(1). The principle had been recognized in federal district and appellate courts for a decade before. See, e.g., Williams v. Saxbe, 413 F. Supp. 654 (D.D.C. 1976); Barnes v. Costle, 561 F.2d 983 (D.C. Cir. 1977). See also Lin Farley, *Sexual Shakedown: The Sexual Harassment of Women on the Job* (New York: McGraw-Hill, 1978). The argument that sexual harassment can be viewed as employment discrimination against women, actionable under federal law, was most fully developed in Catharine A. MacKinnon, *Sexual Harassment of Working Women* (New Haven: Yale University Press, 1979).

18. Meritor, 477 U.S. at 65 (quoting Guidelines of the Equal Employment Opportunity Commission, 29 CFR §1604.11[a][3]).

19. Id. at 68.

20. On this and other parallels between the criminal law of rape and the law governing civil damages for sexual harassment, see Susan Estrich, "Sex at Work," 43 *Stan. L. Rev.* 813 (1991).

21. 42 U.S.C. §1983; see Larson & Larson, *Employment Discrimination*, §46.10(1) at 46–151. A prosecution in federal court, on the theory that the state official deprived the employee of her rights under color of law, seems possible in some circumstances, but federal criminal liability is uncertain even when the state official compels submission by physical force. See United States v. Lanier, 117 S.Ct. 1219 (1997).

22. E.g., Williams v. Banning, 72 F.3d 552 (7th Cir. 1995); Tomka v. Seller Corp., 66 F.3d 1295 (2d Cir. 1995); Cross v. Alabama, 49 F.3d 1490, 1504 (11th Cir. 1995); Grant v. Lone Star, 21 F.3d 649 (5th Cir. 1994); Miller v. Maxwell's Int'l, 991 F.2d 583 (9th Cir. 1993). In a few of the circuits, the issue is not yet resolved. See Rick A. Howard, "Debating Individual Liability under Title VII," 19 *Am. J. Trial Advoc.* 677, 681–683 (1996).

23. Karibian v. Columbia University, 14 F.3d 773, 778 (2d Cir. 1994).

24. Dockter v. Rudolf Wolff Futures, 913 F.2d 456 (7th Cir. 1990). *Dockter* is discussed in more detail in Chapter 8.

25. See Estrich, "Sex at Work" at 836–838. For discussion of the reasons why such "offers" are coercive, see Chapter 8.

26. E.g., Henson v. City of Dundee, 682 F.2d 897, 905 (11th Cir. 1982) (plaintiff must show "that the employer knew or should have known of the harassment in question and failed to take prompt remedial action."); see Larson & Larson, *Employment Discrimination*, §46.07(2) at 46–95.

27. Meritor, 477 U.S. at 65. In Ellison v. Brady, 924 F.2d 872, 879 (9th Cir. 1991), the court said that a hostile environment consisted of "conduct which a reasonable woman would consider sufficiently severe or pervasive to . . . create an abusive working environment." Under this approach the requirement that the employee communicate unwelcomeness by her conduct could be satisfied by the fact that the conduct would be offensive to a reasonable woman. It remains to be seen whether other courts will endorse this softening of the *Meritor* test.

28. "The correct inquiry is whether [Vinson] by her conduct indicated that the alleged sexual advances were unwelcome." Meritor, 477 U.S. at 68.

29. *1981 Report* at 65–66. Data on expectations of penalties and rewards were not reported separately for women pressured for dates and for those pressured for sexual favors; the data cited in the text are the percentages reported for "severe sexual harassment," a category that includes both these forms of pressure, together with unwanted letters and calls. Id. at 37.

30. Larson & Larson, *Employment Discrimination*, §46.10(4) at 46-161.

31. The inability in nearly all states to bring such misconduct within the scope of criminal statutes is documented in Carrie N. Baker, "Sexual Extortion: Criminalizing Quid Pro Quo Sexual Harassment," 13 *L. & Inequality* 213 (1994). Three states permit punishment of some types of nonviolent sexual harassment; only Delaware punishes quid-pro-quo harassment by supervisors in a private employment context. See id. at 244–247. In addition, a Wyoming statute, apparently the only one of its kind in the nation, makes it a crime for any person in a position of authority to obtain consent to sexual contact by abusing his power. See Wyo. Stat. §6-2-303(a)(vi).

For possible bases for a civil suit under state law in cases of nonviolent harassment, see Larson & Larson, *Employment Discrimination*, §46.10(4) at 46-163. For discussion of the inadequacies of state tort remedies, see Jane Byeff Korn, "The Fungible Woman and Other Myths of Sexual Harassment," 67 *Tul. L. Rev.* 1363, 1378–81 (1993).

32. For an overview see Anne B. Fisher, "Getting Comfortable with Couples in the Workplace," 130:7 *Fortune* 138 (1994); Mary Loftus, "Frisky Business: Romance in the Workplace," *Psychology Today,* March 1995, at 34.

33. N.Y. Labor Code, §201-d(1)(b).

34. See Dean J. Schaner, "Romance in the Workplace: Should Employers Act as Chaperons?" 20 *Employee Rel. L.J.* 47, 60, 70 n.25 (1994).

35. See Ruth Shalit, "Sexual Healing," *New Republic,* Oct. 27, 1997, at 17, 19.

36. Id.

37. Shaner, "Romance in the Workplace" at 66. In accord, see the views of Robert Ford, quoted in Loftus, "Frisky Business" at 34.

38. Quoted in Loftus, "Frisky Business" at 34.

39. Id.

40. Susan Estrich puts forward, perhaps tentatively, the argument that "there is no such thing as truly 'welcome' sex between a male boss and a female employee who needs her job." "Sex at Work" at 831. But she concludes that "one need not adopt [this] radical approach" if unwelcomeness is dropped as a separate element of a sexual harassment claim. She also suggests that "if there is [truly consensual sex between a boss and a female subordinate], then the women who welcome it will not be bringing lawsuits in any event." That practical reminder does not eliminate the concerns, however. Since the subordinate can sue her firm, she might choose to do so, even if she held no grudge against her lover.

And intimate relationships are seldom static; the parties to a consensual liaison may find themselves bitterly at odds a month or a year later. (Even when the attraction leads to marriage, the relationship will end, about half the time, in divorce.) When an affair ends unhappily, we should not let one party sue over sexual contacts she permitted initially, unless we have grounds for concern that the liaison was not consensual at the outset.

41. E.g., Model Penal Code §250.4; Cal. Penal Code §646.9 (Supp. 1994).
42. See, e.g., Elizabeth Grauerholz & Richard T. Serpe, "Initiations and Responses: The Dynamics of Sexual Interaction," 12 *Sex Roles* 1041 (1985).
43. Kouri v. Liberian Services, 55 F.E.P. 124, 129 (E.D. Va. 1991).
44. Susan Estrich advocates a more stringent approach, in which quid-pro-quo harassment would be presumed whenever a male supervisor initiates a sexual advance; courts would "place on the man an affirmative burden of production, if not also of persuasion, to make clear that no threat was intended in his request." "Sex at Work" at 835.
45. United States v. March, 32 M.J. 740, 741 (A.C.M.R. 1991).
46. Interview with Lt. Col. William A. Stranko, assistant to the General Counsel of the Army, July 28, 1997. In the Army, both officers and enlisted soldiers express a "general sense of confusion regarding the circumstances that constitute fraternization." 1 U.S. Department of the Army, "Senior Review Panel Report on Sexual Harassment," July 1997, at 67.
47. United States v. Boyett, 42 M.J. 150 (C.M.A. 1995); United States v. Reister, 44 M.J. 409 (C.M.R. 1996); United States v. Van Steenwyk, 21 M.J. 795 (N.M.C.M.R. 1985).
48. Art. 134, Uniform Code of Military Justice, 10 U.S.C. §934.
49. See Jonas, "Fraternization."
50. See Schneider & Schneider, *Sound Off!* at 169–170; "Mocking Military Justice," *Los Angeles Times,* May 15, 1988, at V-4.
51. Department of the Army, "Sexual Harassment" at 56–68.
52. Alexander v. Yale University, 459 F. Supp. 1, 3 (D. Conn. 1977).
53. Lipsett v. University of Puerto Rico, 864 F.2d 881 (1st Cir. 1988).
54. Korf v. Ball State University, 726 F.2d 1222 (7th Cir. 1984).
55. Parks v. Wilson, 872 F. Supp. 1467 (D.S.C. 1995).
56. Bolon v. Rolla Public Schools, 917 F. Supp. 1423 (E.D. Mo. 1996).
57. P. L. v. Aubert, 545 N.W.2d 666, 667–668 (Minn. 1996).
58. In P. L.'s case, the teacher was not criminally prosecuted, but her teaching license was suspended for a minimum of five years, and P. L.'s suit against her was settled out of court. Interview with Katherine Flom (attorney for P. L.), Aug. 6, 1997.
59. Smith v. Metropolitan School District of Perry Township, No. IP 93 707 C, U.S. District Court, S.D. Ind., opinion dated Aug. 2, 1995; interview with Shannon Robinson, attorney for the school district, June 17, 1997.
60. The studies cited in text are summarized in Linda J. Rubin & Sherry B. Borgers,

"Sexual Harassment in Universities during the 1980s," 23 *Sex Roles* 397, 404–405 (1990). See also Louise F. Fitzgerald et al., "The Incidence and Dimensions of Sexual Harassment in Academia and the Workplace," 32 *J. Voc. Behav.* 152 (1988).

61. U.S. Department of Commerce, *Statistical Abstract of the United States, 1996* (Washington, D.C.: Government Printing Office, 1996), table 240 at 158 (8.2 million women in college in 1994).

62. A few courts have raised an even higher barrier to liability, ruling that the school district cannot be held responsible unless an administrator has actual knowledge of the teacher's misconduct. E.g., Doe v. Lago Vista Independent School Dist., 106 F.3d 1223 (5th Cir. 1997). The Supreme Court has agreed to resolve the issue. Doe, *cert. granted*, 118 S.Ct. 595 (1997).

63. Lipsett, 864 F.2d 881; Nelson v. Temple University, 920 F. Supp. 633, 655 (E.D. Pa. 1996).

64. Teachers in public schools can be sued for misconduct under 42 U.S.C. §1983, but their actions must be sufficiently "outrageous" to deprive the student of a constitutionally protected right. Quid-pro-quo harassment may qualify, but indirect sexual pressure and unwelcome advances probably do not.

65. The summary that follows is based on policies collected in M. Cynara Stites, "University Consensual Relationship Policies," in Michele A. Paludi, ed., *Sexual Harassment on College Campuses* 153 (Albany: SUNY Press, 1996); Jerome Stokes & D. Frank Vinik, "Consensual Sexual Relations between Faculty and Students in Higher Education," 96 *Educ. L. Rptr.* 899 (1995); Sherry Young, "Getting to Yes: The Case against Banning Consensual Relationships in Higher Education," 4 *Am. U. J. Gender & L.* 269, 271 (1996); Bruno Leone, ed., *Rape on Campus* 89 (San Diego: Greenhaven, 1995). Information on the University of Chicago Law School was provided by Assistant Dean Holly Davis, interview, June 18, 1996.

66. Stites, "University Policies" at 163.

67. "Student-Professor Sexual Relations: A Forum Discussion," in Leone, *Rape on Campus* at 94.

68. Id.

69. Jane Gallop, *Feminist Accused of Sexual Harassment* 11 (Durham: Duke University Press, 1997).

70. "Student-Professor Sexual Relations" at 90.

71. Quoted by Stites, "University Policies" at 166.

72. Id. at 160.

73. Stokes & Vinik, "Relations between Faculty and Students" at 899.

74. Laural S. Jin, "Statutory Rape Laws: The Need for Change" (1997), paper on file, DiAngelo Law Library, University of Chicago.

75. Stokes & Vinik, "Relations between Faculty and Students" at 899.

76. See note 41, above.

77. Stites, "University Policies" at 169.

78. Such a claim could be made, however, if the professor creates an expectation that students must "offer" themselves in order to be treated fairly. The situation would be comparable to that of the New Jersey political machine discussed in Chapter 8.

79. Naragon v. Wharton, 737 F.2d 1403, 1405 (5th Cir. 1984).

80. Stites, "University Policies" at 158.

81. U.S. Dept. of Justice, Bureau of Justice Statistics, "Prisoners in America 1996" (1997); Stan C. Proband, "Rapid Increase in Woman Prisoners," *Overcrowded Times,* April 1997, at 4.

82. U.S. Dept. of Justice, Bureau of Justice Statistics, "Prison and Jail Inmates at Midyear 1996" 4, 6 (Jan. 1997).

83. Women Prisoners of D.C. Dept. of Corrections v. District of Columbia, 877 F. Supp. 634, 640 (D.D.C. 1994), *rev'd* on other grounds, 93 F.3d 910 (D.C. Cir. 1996).

84. See Human Rights Watch Women's Rights Project, *All too Familiar: Sexual Abuse of Women in U.S. State Prisons* 1117–18 (New York, 1996) (hereafter HRW). See also Neal v. Director, D.C. Dept. of Corrections, 1996 WL 293525 (D.D.C.) at *1 (reporting court's finding that the department "engaged in a pattern or practice of retaliation against employees who challenged or complained of sexual harassment").

85. Women Prisoners, 93 F.3d 910.

86. Prison Litigation Reform Act of 1996, P.L. 104-134, 18 U.S.C. §3626. Human Rights Watch found that the department began responding more effectively to sexual abuse complaints after the 1994 court decree, but that allegations of sexual misconduct persisted. See HRW at 124–125.

87. Id. For similar findings, see Agnes L. Baro, "Spheres of Consent: An Analysis of the Sexual Abuse and Sexual Exploitation of Women Incarcerated in the State of Hawaii," 8 *Women & Crim. Just.* 61 (1997); "Cruel and Unusual: A Special Report on Women and the Prison System," *Women's Review of Books,* July 1997, at 3–25.

88. HRW at 77.

89. See id. at 38–43. Illinois enacted a prohibition in July 1997. See Ill. Comp. Stat. §5/11-9.2 (St. Paul: West, 1997).

90. Stephen Andrews, "The Criminalization of Sexual Relations between Guards and Inmates" (1997), paper on file, DiAngelo Law Library, University of Chicago, p. 5.

91. Colo. Rev. Stat. 18-3-403 (1986 & Supp. 1995). See Andrews, "Guards and Inmates" at 5–6. The language of the statutes in Texas and Wyoming is slightly different, but both have the effect, like Colorado's statute, of making some guard-inmate sexual relationships permissible.

92. Andrews, "Guards and Inmates" at 6–7.

93. Id.

94. *New York Times,* April 23, 1996, at A12.

95. In a 1997 case, the federal government charged Joe McManus, a guard at a federal detention facility in Oklahoma, with having sex with an inmate. Although such conduct is a federal offense regardless of whether the inmate consents, McManus denied the inmate's claim that he threatened her with transfer to a disciplinary unit and said that the sex was voluntary. John Parker, "Federal Guard Freed while Sex Charge Is Pending," *Daily Oklahoman*, March 26, 1997, at 14.

96. *New York Times*, April 23, 1996, at A12.

97. See HRW at 13–16. For examples of prosecutors' reluctance to bring charges, even after laws were amended to eliminate inmate consent as a defense, see Baro, "Spheres of Consent" at 71–78.

98. HRW at 338.

10   PSYCHIATRISTS AND PSYCHOLOGISTS

1. Carolyn M. Bates & Annette M. Brodsky, *Sex in the Therapy Hour: A Case of Professional Incest* (New York: Guilford Press, 1989).

2. Id. at 35.

3. Id. at 114.

4. S.D. Codified Laws §22-22-29.

5. Ariz. Stat. §13–1418; Wis. Stat. Ann. §940.22.

6. Idaho Code §18-919; Cal. Bus. & Prof. Code §729.

7. Cal. Civ. Code §51.9.

8. H.R. 3646, 104th Cong., 2d sess., §2(b)(3) (1996).

9. Id. at §2(b)(2).

10. State v. Leiding, 812 P.2d 797, 805 (N.M. App. 1991).

11. N.M. Stat. Ann. §30-9-10(A) (1984).

12. Leiding, 812 P.2d 797.

13. Interview with Michael E. Virgil, attorney for Leiding, June 18, 1997.

14. William Masters & Virginia Johnson, *Human Sexual Inadequacy* 389, 391 (Boston: Little, Brown, 1970).

15. See, e.g., Susan Baur, *The Intimate Hour: Love and Sex in Psychotherapy* 84 (Boston: Houghton Mifflin, 1997) (citing 1973 code of the American Psychiatric Association, 1977 code of the American Psychological Association, and similar codes of other groups of mental health professionals); Kenneth S. Pope & Jacqueline C. Bouhoutsos, *Sexual Intimacy between Therapists and Patients* 31 (New York: Praeger, 1986) (citing in addition the 1980 code of the National Association of Social Workers and the 1982 Code of the American Association for Marriage and Family Therapy).

16. Baur, *Intimate Hour* at 90; Nanette Gartrell et al., "Psychiatrist-Patient Sexual Contact: Results of a National Survey, I: Prevalence," 143 *Am. J. Psychiatry* 1126 (1986).

17. Gartrell et al., "Psychiatrist-Patient Sexual Contact" at 1126, 1128.

18. E.g., id. at 1126; see also Baur, *Intimate Hour* at 152.

19. Pope & Bouhoutsos, *Sexual Intimacy* at 28.

20. Baur, *Intimate Hour* at 92.

21. Kenneth S. Pope & Valerie A. Vetter, "Prior Therapist Sexual Involvement among Patients Seen by Psychologists," 28 *Psychotherapy* 429, 433 (1991); Jacqueline Bouhoutsos et al., "Sexual Intimacy between Psychotherapists and Patients," 14 *Prof. Psychol.* 185, 188 (1983).

22. See Baur, *Intimate Hour* at 73–76; Pope & Bouhoutsos, *Sexual Intimacy* at 27.

23. Alan Wertheimer, *Exploitation* 167 (Princeton: Princeton University Press, 1996).

24. *Stedman's Medical Dictionary* 1473 (5th Lawyers ed., 1982), quoted in Wertheimer, *Exploitation* at 165.

25. See Baur, *Intimate Hour* at 119–129; Stewart Twemlow & Glen Gabbard, "The Lovesick Therapist," in Gabbard, ed., *Sexual Exploitation in Professional Relationships* 74 (Washington, D.C.: American Psychiatric Press, 1989).

26. Gartrell et al., "Psychiatrist-Patient Sexual Contact" at 1128. The 13 percent figure is probably inflated by a double bias. The information comes from therapists who had violated professional norms and therefore had an obvious incentive to exaggerate the positive ("committed") character of the ensuing relationship; in addition, therapists involved in sexual contacts that proved genuine and lasting were presumably more likely than other violators to respond to the survey in the first place.

27. Katherine C. Haspel et al., "Legislative Intervention regarding Therapist Sexual Misconduct," 28 *Prof. Psychol.* 63 (1997).

28. Pope & Bouhoutsos, *Sexual Intimacy* at 22–25.

29. Id. at 25.

30. Id.

31. Id. at 60.

32. Bouhoutsos et al., "Sexual Intimacy" at 190.

33. Pope & Vetter, "Prior Therapist Sexual Involvement" at 431. In the absence of a controlled experiment, one cannot be sure that these harms were *caused* by the sexual contact. But in one small study, the only one to compare patients who had sexual contact with those who had not, the former group had more serious psychological symptoms after treatment than the latter, though the two groups had not differed prior to treatment. Shirley Feldman-Summers & Gwendolyn Jones, "Psychological Impacts of Sexual Contact between Therapists or Other Health Care Practitioners and Their Clients," 52 *J. Consulting & Clinical Psychol.* 1054, 1058 (1984).

34. Pope & Bouhoutsos, *Sexual Intimacy* at 63. See also Baur, *Intimate Hour* at 151–156. The studies have overwhelmingly concentrated on female patients; the few small samples of sexually involved male patients hint that harm to men may be less frequent or less severe.

35. See Wertheimer, *Exploitation* at 184–185.

36. A rigorous analysis of the elements of valid consent, on which I draw heavily, appears in id. at 172–188. Wertheimer notes the importance of informed

consent but emphasizes it less than I do here. He suggests that the patient's consent might, even if competent and informed, still be disregarded because (like Ulysses) she has previously bound herself not to have sex and voluntarily surrendered her right to change her mind. Id. at 185–186 & n.80. But this approach is somewhat artificial to the extent that the patient is not really permitted to choose, at the outset of therapy, between precommitting herself or keeping her options open.

37. Waters v. Bourhis, 709 P.2d 469, 471 (Cal. 1985).

38. See Pope & Bouhoutsos, *Sexual Intimacy* at 8–11.

39. Laural S. Jin, "Statutory Rape Laws: The Need for Change" (1997), paper on file, DiAngelo Law Library, University of Chicago.

40. *Stedman's Medical Dictionary* 1473, quoted in Wertheimer, *Exploitation* at 165.

41. E.g., Patricia Illingworth, "Patient-Therapist Sex: Criminalization and Its Discontents," 11 *J. Contemp. Health L. & Policy* 389 (1995); cf. Baur, *Intimate Hour* at 168–169, 188–189.

42. Steven B. Bisbing, Linda M. Jorgenson, & Pamela K. Sutherland, *Sexual Abuse by Professionals: A Legal Guide* 407 (Charlottesville, Va.: Michie, 1995).

43. J. Parsons & J. Wincze, "A Survey of Client-Therapist Involvement in Rhode Island," 26 *Prof. Psychol.* 171 (1995).

44. Pope & Bouhoutsos, *Sexual Intimacy* at 160; Note, "Sexual Abuse by Psychotherapists," 17 *Am. J.L. & Med.* 289, 293–299 (1991).

45. For analysis of other possible civil causes of action, see Linda Jorgenson et al., "The Furor over Psychotherapist-Patient Sexual Contact," 32 *Wm. & Mary L. Rev.* 645, 684–713 (1991).

46. Roy v. Hartogs, 381 N.Y. S.2d 587 (App. Div. 1976).

47. Atienza v. Taub, 239 Cal. Rptr. 454 (Cal. App. 1987).

48. Zipkin v. Freeman, 436 S.W.2d 753 (Mo. 1968); Simmons v. United States, 805 F.2d 1363 (9th Cir. 1986). Some states assure the same result by statute. E.g., Ill. Stat. Ann., ch. 740 §140/1 (1996).

49. Bisbing et al., *Sexual Abuse by Professionals* at 910–913. Courts generally uphold the validity of these exclusions and caps. E.g., American Home Assurance Co. v. Stone, 61 F.3d 1321 (7th Cir. 1995).

50. S.D. Code §22-22-27(4) defines the situations to which the ban on consensual sex applies as those involving "the professional treatment, assessment or counseling of a mental or emotional illness, symptom or condition."

11   DOCTORS AND LAWYERS

1. Hoopes v. Hammargren, 725 P.2d 238, 240 (1986).

2. Council on Ethical and Judicial Affairs, "Sexual Misconduct in the Practice of Medicine," 266 *JAMA* 2741 (1991).

3. Odegard v. Finne, 500 N.W.2d 140, 143 (Minn. App. 1993); Jennings v. Friedman, 875 F.2d 864, 1989 U.S. App. LEXIS 7352 (6th Cir.).

4. Atenzia v. Taub, 194 Cal. App. 3d 388, 394 n.3 (1987).

5. Hoopes, 725 P.2d at 243 .

6. Interviews with Frederic Berkley, attorney for Hoopes, and Daniel Polsenberg, attorney for Hammargren, June 17, 1997. See also Mary Hynes, "The Long Road to Recovery," *Las Vegas Review-Journal,* April 13, 1997, at B1.

7. Council on Ethical and Judicial Affairs, "Sexual Misconduct" at 2745.

8. Abruzzi v. Board of Regents, 422 N.Y. S.2d 168 (App. Div. 1979).

9. Kincheloe, 157 S.E.2d 833 (N.C. 1967).

10. Sciola v. Shernow, 577 A.2d 1081 (Conn. App. 1990).

11. Nanette K. Gartrell et al., "Physician-Patient Sexual Contact," 157 *Western J. Med.* 139 (1992).

12. Id. at 142.

13. Quoted in id.

14. One study found that patients involved with a physician suffered harm to the same extent as patients involved with a mental health therapist, but the sample was too small to be more than suggestive. Shirley Feldman-Summers & Gwendolyn Jones, "Psychological Impacts of Sexual Contact between Therapists or Other Health Care Practitioners and Their Clients," 52 *J. Consulting & Clinical Psychol.* 1054 (1984).

   Most physicians surveyed express the opinion that sexual contact is "always harmful." Gartrell et al., "Physician-Patient Sexual Contact" at 142.

15. See Cal. Civil Code §51.9; Cal. Bus. & Prof. Code §729; Idaho Code §18-919. In several states, sexual contact is considered criminal when the doctor tells the patient that the contact is a necessary part of treatment. E.g., Mich. Stat. §520b(1)(f)(iv). In Wyoming, a doctor who has consensual sex with a patient might be subject to prosecution under Wyo. Code §6-2-303(a)(vi), which makes it an offense for anyone to use a "position of authority" to cause another person to submit to sex.

16. Roe v. Federal Ins. Co., 587 N.E.2d 214, 216 (Mass. 1992).

17. Green v. Board of Dental Examiners, 47 Cal. App. 4th 786, 791 (Ct. App. 1992).

18. Perez v. Board of Registration, 803 S.W.2d 160 (Mo. App. 1991).

19. Gromis v. Medical Board, 10 Cal. Rptr. 2d 452, 455, 458–459 (Ct. App. 1992). A California statute enacted the following year makes any sexual relationship with a patient (other than the doctor's spouse) a sufficient basis for disciplinary action, without need for the specific findings that the court required in *Gromis.* Cal. Bus. & Prof. Code §726 (1993). But that court's requirements remain typical of judicial approaches in other jurisdictions.

20. Gartrell et al., "Physician-Patient Sexual Contact" at 143.

21. Id. at 139.

22. One recent medical commentary is unique in acknowledging that the AMA position fails to accommodate "deeply held beliefs that intimate relations should be protected from intrusion by society." Paul S. Appelbaum et al.,

"Sexual Relationships between Physicians and Patients," 154 *Arch. Internal Med.* 2561 (1994); yet even these authors ultimately favor a per se ban on relationships between doctors and current patients.

23. Council on Ethical and Judicial Affairs, "Sexual Misconduct" at 2745.

24. See id.

25. Gartrell et al., "Physician-Patient Sexual Contact" at 157. A more cautious proposal suggests a waiting period of three to six months. Appelbaum, "Sexual Relationships."

26. Coopersmith v. Gold, 568 N.Y. S.2d 250 (App. Div. 1991).

27. Jennings, 1989 U.S. App. LEXIS at *3.

28. Cf. Cal. Civ. Code §51.9(a)(3).

29. Drucker's Case, 577 A.2d 1198 (N.H. 1990).

30. Bourdon's Case, 565 A.2d 1052 (N.H. 1989).

31. McDaniel v. Gile, 281 Cal. Rptr. 242 (Cal. App. 1991).

32. Doe v. Roe, 289 Ill. App. 3d 116 (1997); John S. Elson, presentation to Ill. S.Ct., Jan. 22, 1996.

33. In re Kantar, 581 N.E.2d 6 (Ill. App. 1991).

34. Matter of Wood, 489 N.E.2d 1189 (Ind. 1989); 358 N.E.2d 128 (Ind. 1976).

35. Matter of Bellino, 417 S.E.2d 535 (S.C. 1992).

36. Matter of Manson, 676 N.E.2d 347 (Ind. 1997).

37. Disciplinary Counsel v. Booher, 663 N.E.2d 522 (Ohio 1996).

38. Linda Jorgenson & Pamela Sutherland, "Fiduciary Theory Applied to Personal Dealings: Attorney-Client Sexual Contact," 45 *Ark. L. Rev.* 459, 463–466 (1992).

39. In re Kantar, 581 N.E.2d at 12 n.2.

40. J. Bernard et al., "Dangerous Liaisons," *ABAJ*, Aug. 1992, at 82.

41. Matter of McDow, 291 S.C. 468 (1987).

42. Doe, 1997 Ill. App. LEXIS at 321.

43. Id.

44. John C. Elson, Statement to Ill. S.Ct. Rules Comm., Dec. 27, 1995.

45. Suppressed v. Suppressed, 565 N.E.2d 101, 105 (Ill. App. 1990).

46. See Elson, Statement, Dec. 27, 1995. The judge's dismissal of the complaint was reversed on other grounds (including proof of adverse legal impact), Doe, 289 Ill. App. 3d at 130–131, but the appellate court did not question the trial judge's ruling on the quid-pro-quo issue.

47. Id.; see also King v. Landry, 686 N.E.2d 33, 40 (Ill. App. 1997).

48. A. L. Presser, "Lawyer Liable for Coerced Sex," *ABAJ*, Feb. 1993, at 24–25; Vallinoto v. DiSandro, 688 A.2d 830 (R.I. 1997).

49. DiSandro, 688 A.2d at 835–836; accord, Suppressed, 565 N.E.2d at 106.

50. Other tort theories are similarly unhelpful. In *DiSandro*, the court dismissed the client's claim for intentional infliction of emotional distress, on the ground that the client must prove some "physical symptomatology resulting from the alleged improper conduct," including proof by medical experts that any physical

ailments were caused by the lawyer's conduct and "were not simply the aftermath of her recently concluded tumultuous marriage." 688 A.2d at 838.

51. Matter of DiSandro, 680 A.2d 73, 75 (R.I. 1996).
52. Matter of Lewis, 415 S.E.2d 173 (Ga. 1992).
53. State Bar v. Sharpe, cited in "States Move to Regulate Attorney/Client Sex," 95 *Lawyers Weekly USA* 1141 (Dec. 4, 1995).
54. Matter of Ridgeway, 462 N.W.2d 671 (Wis. 1990).
55. ABA Formal Op. No. 92-364, July 6, 1992 (emphasis added).
56. Cal. Bus. & Prof. Code §6109.9(b)(1996).
57. Utah Rules of Prof. Cond., R. 8.4 (1997); "States Move to Regulate."
58. "States Move to Regulate."
59. Okla. Op. No. 308 (Dec. 9, 1994); *ABA/BNA Lawyer's Manual on Professional Conduct* §1001:7001 (Chicago: American Bar Association, 1984) (Supp. 1994).
60. "At Issue: Attorney Discipline," *ABAJ,* Jan. 1992, at 34, 35.
61. Quoted in Bill Ibelle, "Should Attorney/Client Sex Be Banned," 95 *Lawyers Weekly USA* 1140 (Dec. 4, 1995).
62. Okla. Op. No. 308; Minn. R. Prof. Conduct §1.8(k)(2)(1996).
63. On the possibility of criminal or civil liability for using deceptive stratagems to obtain consent, see Chapter 8.
64. See Elson, Statement, Dec. 27, 1995.
65. An exception for preexisting relationships could be appropriate for most of these areas, but the conflict-of-interest problem would normally make sexual contacts improper in divorce and child custody cases, even when the liaison predates the legal relationship.

12   DATING

1. Cliff Friend, "There's Yes! Yes! in Your Eyes," in Mitch Miller, ed., *Sing Along with Mitch: The Mitch Miller Family Songfest, A Treasury of Funtime Favorites* 67 (New York: B. Geis Associates, 1961); quoted in William E. Nelson, "Criminality and Sexual Morality in New York, 1920–1980," 5 *Yale J.L. & Human.* 265, 310 (1993).
2. Ralph Slovenko, "A Panoramic View," in Slovenko, ed., *Sexual Behavior and the Law* 5, 51 (Springfield, Ill.: Charles S. Thomas, 1965).
3. Note, "The Resistance Standard in Rape Legislation," 18 *Stan. L. Rev.* 680, 682 (1966).
4. Camille Paglia, *Sex, Art, and American Culture* 58 (New York: Vintage, 1992).
5. Compare Comm. v. Sherry, 437 N.E.2d 224 (Mass. 1982), rejecting that view.
6. See Chapter 2.
7. E.g., Douglas Husak & George Thomas, "Date Rape, Social Convention, and Reasonable Mistakes," 11 *L. & Philos.* 95, 110–125 (1992).
8. See Chapter 3.
9. See Chapter 3.

10. See Sanford H. Kadish & Stephen J. Schulhofer, eds., *Criminal Law and Its Processes* 329–330 (Boston: Little, Brown, 6th ed. 1995). Recklessness (requiring *conscious* awareness of the risk of harm) is sufficient for many criminal offenses, but not for robbery and theft.

11. Catharine MacKinnon, "Feminism, Marxism, Method, and the State," 8 *Signs* 635, 653–654 (1983).

12. Lynne Henderson, "Getting to Know: Honoring Women in Law and Fact," 2 *Tex. J. Women & L.* 41, 72 (1993).

13. See Susan Estrich, *Real Rape* 97–98 (Cambridge: Harvard University Press, 1987).

14. See Kadish & Schulhofer, *Criminal Law* at 326–328.

15. Problems of fairness in using a negligence standard are discussed in Stephen J. Schulhofer, "The Gender Question in Criminal Law," 7 *Soc. Phil. & Policy* 105, 132–133 (1990).

16. Charlene Muehlenhard & Lisa Hollabaugh, "Do Women Sometimes Say No When They Mean Yes?" 54 *J. Personality & Soc. Psychol.* 872 (1988).

17. Susan Sprecher et al., "Token Resistance to Sexual Intercourse and Consent to Unwanted Sexual Intercourse," 31 *J. Sex. Res.* 125, 129 (1994); Charlene Muehlenhard & Marcia McCoy, "Double Standard/Double Bind," 15 *Psychol. of Women Q.* 447 (1991) (37 percent at University of Kansas); Lucia O'Sullivan & Elizabeth Allgeier, "Disassembling a Stereotype," 24 *J. Applied Soc. Psychol.* 1035 (1994) (only 25 percent at Bowling Green State University in Ohio, but the survey covered a shorter time frame, one year instead of the usual two).

18. Sprecher et al., "Token Resistance" at 129.

19. R. Lance Shotland & Barbara Hunter, "Women's 'Token Resistant' and Compliant Behaviors Are Related to Uncertain Sexual Intentions and Rape," 21 *Pers. & Soc. Psychol. Bull.* 226, 229 (1995).

20. Katie Roiphe, *The Morning After* xiv (Boston: Little, Brown, 1994).

21. Naomi Wolf, *Fire with Fire* 192–193 (New York: Fawcett Columbine, 1994).

22. Elizabeth Fox-Genovese, *Feminism Is Not the Story of My Life* 164 (New York: Doubleday, 1995).

23. Roiphe, *The Morning After* at 84, 101.

24. Camille Paglia, *Vamps & Tramps* 24 (New York: Random House, 1994).

25. Robin Weiner, "Shifting the Communication Burden: A Meaningful Consent Standard in Rape," 6 *Harv. Women's L.J.* 143, 147–149 (1983).

26. Husak & Thomas, "Date Rape and Reasonable Mistakes" at 125.

27. Id. at 114.

28. Muehlenhard & Hollabaugh, "Do Women Sometimes Say No?" at 874.

29. E. M. Curley, "Excusing Rape," 5 *Philos. & Pub. Affairs* 325, 346 (1976).

30. In re M. T. S., 609 A.2d 1266 (1992); Wis. Crim. Code §940.225(4).

31. People v. Warren, 446 N.E.2d 591 (Ill. App. 1983), discussed in Chapter 1.

32. See, e.g., *New York Times*, March 26, 1996, at A17; Karen Kramer, "Rule by Myth: The Social and Legal Dynamics Governing Alcohol-Related Acquaintance Rapes," 47 *Stan. L. Rev.* 115, 139 (1994), discussed in Chapter 1.

33. Vivian Berger, "Not So Simple Rape," 7 *Crim. Just. Ethics* 69, 75–76 (1988).
34. Wash. Rev. Code §9A.44.010(6).
35. Peggy Reeves Sanday, *A Woman Scorned* 284 (New York: Doubleday, 1996).
36. Id. at 3–15, discussed in Chapter 1.

13   TAKING SEXUAL AUTONOMY SERIOUSLY

1. Andrea Parrot & Laurie Bechhofer, eds., *Acquaintance Rape: The Hidden Crime* 249–283 (New York: Wiley, 1991). See also Robin Warshaw, *I Never Called It Rape* 65–82 (New York: Harper & Row, 1988).
2. The *M. T. S.* case adopts a similar framework, though the court was obliged to graft its analysis onto a statute drafted in entirely different terms. See Chapter 5.
3. For the specific language necessary to put these prohibitions in statutory form, see the Model Criminal Statute that follows this chapter.

Index